Selling War in a Media Age

The Alan B. Larkin Series on the American Presidency

UNIVERSITY PRESS OF FLORIDA

Florida A&M University, Tallahassee
Florida Atlantic University, Boca Raton
Florida Gulf Coast University, Ft. Myers
Florida International University, Miami
Florida State University, Tallahassee
New College of Florida, Sarasota
University of Central Florida, Orlando
University of Florida, Gainesville
University of North Florida, Jacksonville
University of South Florida, Tampa
University of West Florida, Pensacola

SELLING WAR

IN A
MEDIA AGE

The Presidency and Public Opinion in the American Century

Edited by Kenneth Osgood and Andrew K. Frank

Afterword by David Halberstam

University Press of Florida

Gainesville · Tallahassee · Tampa · Boca Raton

Pensacola · Orlando · Miami · Jacksonville · Ft. Myers · Sarasota

15 14 13 12 11 10   6 5 4 3 2 1

Library of Congress Cataloging-in-Publication Data
Selling war in a media age: the presidency and public opinion in the American
century/edited by Kenneth Osgood and Andrew K. Frank;
afterword by David Halberstam.
p. cm.—(Alan B. Larkin series on the American presidency)
Includes bibliographical references.
ISBN 978-0-8130-3466-9 (alk. paper)
1. Presidents—United States—History—20th century. 2. Presidents—United
States—Public opinion—History—20th century. 3. Rhetoric—Political
aspects—United States—History—20th century. 4. Public opinion—United
States—History—20th century. 5. Mass media and war—United States—
History—20th century. 6. Politics and war—United States—History—20th
century. 7. Communication in politics—United States—History—20th
century. 8. Political leadership—United States—History—20th century.
9. United States—History, Military—20th century.
I. Osgood, Kenneth Alan, 1971– II. Frank, Andrew, 1970–
E743.S4327 2010
306.209739-dc22   2010001918

The University Press of Florida is the scholarly publishing agency for the State
University System of Florida, comprising Florida A&M University, Florida
Atlantic University, Florida Gulf Coast University, Florida International Uni-
versity, Florida State University, New College of Florida, University of Central
Florida, University of Florida, University of North Florida, University of South
Florida, and University of West Florida.

University Press of Florida
15 Northwest 15th Street
Gainesville, FL 32611-2079
http://www.upf.com

In Memory of Alan B. Larkin (1922–2002)

CONTENTS

PREFACE

History represents a conversation with the past, one that is often inspired by the problems of the present. So it should come as no surprise to discover that the presidency of George W. Bush prompted historians to take a hard look at how modern American presidents have "sold" episodes of war and international conflict to the public. After all, the Bush administration was both brazen and open about its campaign to sell the Iraq War in 2003, publicly describing its efforts to garner support for the invasion as a "product launch."[1] A 2008 memoir by former Bush press secretary Scott McClellan provoked a media frenzy merely for confirming what many observers had suspected all along: that the administration had deliberately manipulated public opinion to secure its support for the invasion of Iraq. In a chapter titled "Selling the War," McClellan revealed how Bush and his advisors created "enormous momentum for war" through a "carefully orchestrated campaign" of political propaganda. Shading the truth and manipulating the press, the Bush administration "managed the crisis [with Iraq] in a way that almost guaranteed that the use of force would become the only feasible option."[2]

George W. Bush may have drawn attention to the ways in which a president sells a war, but the essays in this volume reveal that he was hardly the first to do so. Throughout U.S. history, America's chief executives have worked to shape public opinion on issues of war and peace, efforts that have become more systematic in the past century. The communication and information revolutions of the twentieth century made influencing mass public opinion a prominent feature of presidential leadership—so much so, in fact, that political science and communication scholars have characterized the modern presidency as "the rhetorical presidency"—in which public persuasion is the president's primary task.[3] As President Bush confessed to a group of schoolchildren in an unscripted remark in 2005, "See, in my line of work you got to keep repeating things over and over and over again for the truth to sink in, to kind of catapult the propaganda."[4]

Although the American public often considers propaganda to be the work of enemies or despots, the contributors to this book illuminate how the central goal of propaganda—influencing public opinion—has shaped how American presidents have approached the most momentous duty of their office: waging war. From garnering support for a war not yet launched, to waging a "cold war" with no shots being fired, to maintaining support for an unpopular engagement, presidents have worked to shape and manipulate the public's perceptions of international conflicts involving their country. Many of these essays analyze the ways in which American presidents—from William McKinley to George W. Bush—sought to influence how the media covered, and the public perceived, major wars and undeclared conflicts involving U.S. forces. Some of the essays focus predominantly on how the American people responded to these efforts, stressing the limits to the president's ability to sustain public support for protracted military engagement abroad.

Several of the essays pertain to the Cold War, even though it was not, strictly speaking, a war. As the preeminent conflict of the twentieth century, one that spawned numerous wars and conflicts around the globe, the Cold War was often perceived as a war by government officials and the public alike. Moreover, from the earliest days of the conflict until the collapse of the Soviet Union, U.S. presidents and their advisors worked to "sell" the Cold War to the American public with sustained rhetorical and propaganda campaigns that exerted a profound impact on both domestic and foreign affairs.

As a whole, the essays in this volume suggest that presidents have experienced mixed success in their campaigns of salesmanship, often producing unfortunate unintended consequences. Short-term successes created long-term problems and complications. Many presidents, as Scott McClellan noted of George W. Bush, "confused the propaganda campaign with the high level of candor and honesty so fundamentally needed to build and then sustain public support during a time of war."[5] Not infrequently, as a result, Americans became cynical, doubtful, or outright hostile to the country's wars and to the presidents who sold them. Occasionally, the very efforts to sell a war backfired and produced not patriotic fervor but skepticism and disillusionment. Indeed, it seems generations of Americans learned and re-learned what the Greek dramatist Aeschylus observed over 2,000 years ago: "In war, truth is the first casualty."

Selling War in a Media Age: The Presidency and Public Opinion in the American Century is the inaugural volume of the University Press of Florida's Alan B. Larkin Series on the American Presidency. The series promises to explore issues of contemporary and historical importance through the research and wisdom of eminent scholars. We hope that the books in this series will engage both public and academic audiences and invigorate our conversations about the history of the presidency.

The essays published here are revised versions of papers originally presented in February 2007 at the first annual Alan B. Larkin Symposium on the American Presidency. Hosted by the History Department at Florida Atlantic University, the symposium and the series that shares its name are testaments to the generosity and vision of the Larkin family. Named in memory of Alan B. Larkin—a devotee of American history with a passion for presidential history—the symposium and the series seek to become authoritative forums for debating the history of the presidency and its impact on American life. The desire of the Larkin family to leave a lasting contribution to academia is a remarkable testament to Alan's love of learning. Students of the presidency, at FAU and beyond, owe a tremendous debt to the Larkin family for making such a meaningful contribution to history.

The editors would also like to thank Florida Atlantic University, the University Press of Florida, and the following people for their assistance: Meredith Morris-Babb, Michael Bocco, Eli Bortz, Sallie Brown, Polly Burks, Steven Casey, Rachelle Durand, Jeffrey A. Engel, Steven Engle, Eric Hanne, Dawn Hutchins, Nicole Jacobsen, Patricia Kollander, Anna Lawrence, Elaine Otto, Mark Rose, Stacia Smith, Heather Turci, Derrick White, and the amazing scholars who contributed essays to this volume. We owe special thanks to Zella Linn for her hard work coordinating the Larkin Symposium.

We also would like to acknowledge David Halberstam, a remarkable journalist, historian, and social critic, who delivered one of his last public addresses at the symposium—a "worm's-eye view," as he called it, of his being on the wrong side of a presidential campaign to sell a war in Vietnam. We are grateful to his family for permitting us to publish his remarks.

We dedicate the volume to the memory of Alan B. Larkin, who shared our belief in the power and importance of history.

Kenneth Osgood
Andrew K. Frank

Notes

1. On the relationship between product marketing and the selling of the Iraq War, see especially Sheldon Rampton and John Stauber, *Weapons of Mass Deception: The Uses of Propaganda in Bush's War on Iraq* (New York: Jeremy P. Tarcher/Penguin, 2003).

2. Scott McClellan, *What Happened: Inside the Bush White House and Washington's Culture of Deception* (New York: Public Affairs, 2008), 143, 125.

3. Scholarship on the "rhetorical presidency" abounds. For an introduction, see Jeffrey K. Tulis, *The Rhetorical Presidency* (Princeton: Princeton University Press, 1987).

4. White House Press Release, "President Participates in Social Security Conversation in New York," 24 May 2005, <http://www.whitehouse.gov/news/releases/2005/05/20050524–3.html>.

5. McClellan, *What Happened*, 312.

INTRODUCTION

HAIL TO THE SALESMAN IN CHIEF

Domestic Politics, Foreign Policy, and the Presidency

Andrew L. Johns

> The people can always be brought to the bidding of the leaders. That is easy. All you have to do is tell them they are being attacked, and denounce the peacemakers for lack of patriotism and exposing the country to danger. It works the same in any country.
>
> Hermann Göring

In September 2002, White House chief of staff Andrew H. Card Jr. initiated a multifaceted campaign designed to help move the country toward support of military action against Iraq. Card told reporters that the George W. Bush administration "was following a meticulously planned strategy to persuade the public, the Congress, and the allies of the need to confront the threat from Saddam Hussein." Although the public relations program to shape opinion had been crafted during the summer, the Bush administration decided to wait until after the Labor Day weekend to implement the plan because, as Card suggested, "From a marketing point of view . . . you don't introduce new products in August."[1] Card's comments might seem more appropriate for a CEO of a Fortune 500 company than for the leader of a global superpower. Yet America's chief executives have long recognized the accuracy and necessity of that aspect of the presidency. In addition to being commander in chief, the president of the United States is also the country's salesman in chief.

This role should not be a surprise to anyone familiar with the dynamics of the American political system, the presidency, and U.S. history.[2] Policy communication between the White House and the American people, which encompasses both explaining a policy agenda and persuading the public to support it—"comprises an integral part of modern American presidential leadership" and has become a "necessary component of governance."[3] The relevance of this aspect of the presidency is most apparent when dealing with questions of war and diplomacy. The eminent historian of U.S. foreign relations Walter LaFeber has argued that "conducting a successful foreign policy for the United States requires a dual approach: constructing a strategy that is workable abroad, and developing a political explanation that creates and maintains sufficient consensus at home."[4] Presidential historian Robert Dallek made a similar observation: "Foreign policy commitments have required presidential initiative to educate and sell the country on topics of less immediate moment to people's daily lives."[5] The reason? Because Americans have traditionally paid less attention to foreign affairs than domestic issues, and thus their significance must be explained and justified.

The contributors to *Selling War in a Media Age: The Presidency and Public Opinion in the American Century* focus on the nexus of foreign policy and domestic political considerations, demonstrating how presidents since William McKinley framed their policies in an effort to gain or increase public acceptance and support during times of war. They do so using a variety of conceptual and theoretical approaches, including the expansion of technology and the media; the growing sophistication and omnipresence of propaganda and polling; and the evolution of the state. In addition, the case studies examine issues such as the relationship between presidential popularity and success, how institutional memory affects the way administrations craft their sales pitches to the American people, and—most strikingly—the costs associated with presidential efforts to sell war. More broadly, the essays reflect an effort to grapple with the nature and limitations of presidential power; the role of the media in U.S. political life; the relationship between public opinion and U.S. international engagement; and the ways in which war affects politics, and vice versa, in the American context.

Scholars generally agree that the modern presidency can be traced (at least in its embryonic form) to William McKinley's tenure in the White House. Moreover, the rise of the United States to world power status coincides with the evolution and expansion of presidential power and responsibility. Given these facts, along with the revolutionary advances in communications, media, and technology during the twentieth century, this volume focuses chronologically on the "media age" and the American century when examining the phenomenon of selling war. In addition, it should be noted that the focus of the volume goes beyond war per se. Along with analyzing the Spanish-American War, World War I, and World War II (all officially declared conflicts in the manner prescribed by the Constitution), the authors consider how U.S. presidents marketed their policies during the Cold War, the Korean "police action," combat authorized by congressional resolution, and military-related policies such as the Soviet-American arms race and the Strategic Defense Initiative—in other words, wars and elements of war by other means.

Perhaps the most significant theme that emerges in the essays is the recognition that the justification for a war is crucial to influencing and moving public opinion. Whether fighting to make the world safe for democracy, maintain the freedom of a people threatened by communism, or ensuring that a rogue dictator does not have access to weapons of mass destruction, presidents must justify their decision to the American people to take the country to war. The domestic political imperatives that Alexis de Tocqueville identified two centuries ago—and which observers continue to recognize as fundamental to understanding the making and implementation of American foreign relations—are both unique to the United States and incontrovertibly linked to the making and implementation of foreign policy, and they require the president and his advisors to frame their policies in recognizable and digestible ways to the American public as an accelerant to acceptance.[6]

A plethora of rhetorical devices exist to facilitate public understanding of the importance of a given presidential policy, which then (ideally) leads to support for that policy. Linking a war's importance to core national values and as intrinsic to national security is perhaps the most effective tool; after all, it is difficult to oppose a policy designed and marketed to keep America safe.[7] Another common trope consists of speaking in broad idealistic terms, using the ideological language of American exceptionalism, freedom, and democracy, and framing any conflict in stark "good vs. evil" discourse. Recent history is replete with examples of this black-and-white dichotomy, with the rhetoric employed during the forty-year U.S.-Soviet confrontation in the Cold War being only the most obvious.[8] One strategy that has proven quite useful (if not accurate) is using the memory of past events to shape contemporary understanding and acceptance of the issues at stake with a particular policy as well as inculcating public support. Presidents "simplify and reduce stories to conventional symbols for easy assimilation by audiences," utilizing metaphors and historical analogies to sell a policy by making it more identifiable and emotionally powerful. Warranted or not, invoking a comparison between Saddam Hussein and Adolph Hitler evokes a palpable sense of dread and an immediately recognizable frame of reference.[9]

The essays explore a wide array of such strategies. For example, Kenneth Osgood and Paul Boyer point out that Dwight Eisenhower and Ronald Reagan attempted to market their foreign policies using the rhetoric of peace. Osgood contends that the Eisenhower administration incorporated a psychological warfare strategy that used the language of peace to sell the Cold War and convince the world that the Soviet "peace offensive" was nothing more than propaganda and *maskirovka* originating from the Kremlin. Eisenhower maneuvered his policy and rhetoric so that he met expectations at home and abroad for progress toward peace while avoiding any conciliation in actual policy. Similarly, Boyer suggests that Reagan's Strategic Defense Initiative proposal provides a classic example of a president shoring up support for his military policies by stressing the reassuring themes of peace and security. By suggesting that nuclear weapons could be rendered powerless through technology, Reagan played on American fears to manipulate public opinion in his favor.

These examples demonstrate the reality that presidents must choose how to frame their arguments, making calculations based on the vagaries of the situation, their reading of public opinion, the resources they are willing to expend, and their sense of which combination of strategy and tactics resonates most strongly with their target audiences. Would it be better, for instance, to argue that the administration is fighting to spread democracy and freedom in the Middle East or to protect U.S. access to oil in the region? Regardless of the strategies employed by an administration, selling war requires carefully crafted public relations campaigns to implement the plan and to bolster support for the administration's agenda. Discrete steps for educating and persuading the public, maintaining public approval in the short- and long-term, and measuring public sentiment must be in place. To be sure, the challenges and obstacles to success are daunting. Yet for U.S. presidents, these efforts simply are not optional; indeed, they stand as pivotal determinants of a leader's effectiveness and, potentially, longevity in office. Moving the public "provides one of the clearest tests of presidential leadership," and to be successful, presidents must do as Theodore Roosevelt did: "I simply made up my mind what they [the American people] ought to think, and then did my best to get them to think it."[10]

Beyond the goal of seeking support for U.S. military activity or international engagement, presidents also sell war in order to ensure their own electoral or political success.[11] George Kennan, the venerable diplomat and foreign policy commentator, identified the "domestic self-consciousness of the American statesmen." According to Kennan, American politicians, when considering matters of foreign policy (including war), tend "to be more concerned for the domestic political effects of what he is saying or doing than about their actual effects on our relations with other countries."[12] It should be noted that presidents and their advisors rarely admit that they make decisions or calculations on this basis, especially in the documentary record. Nevertheless, American history in the twentieth century is replete with examples of public relations campaigns being tied directly into policy proposals, both in the planning and implementation phases.

Lyndon Johnson's preparations for the escalation of the Vietnam conflict are a perfect case study. At numerous points during 1964 and 1965, the administration focused on creating a public justification of its proposed actions through public informational and domestic political steps designed to elicit support for an expansion of the U.S. commitment in Southeast Asia.[13] Chester Pach's essay focuses specifically on the Johnson administration's efforts in this regard during the Progress Campaign in 1967. This program, launched as a public relations offensive designed specifically to establish that the United States was achieving its goals in Vietnam, was a direct response to criticism from the media that had begun to erode public support for the war and the administration. As Pach's title suggests, LBJ recognized the need to "get a better story to the American people." War and politics, then, are inextricably linked.

Indeed, one of the most recognizable aphorisms in military and political history is the Prussian military theorist Carl von Clausewitz's assertion that war is a continuation of politics by other means.[14] While undoubtedly accurate in the volatile nineteenth-century European context from which Clausewitz emerged, it takes on a new meaning when considered from a contemporary American perspective. For the United States to be involved in a war necessitates a political foundation; U.S. presidents—particularly in the twentieth and twenty-first centuries—face significant constraints that authoritarian leaders did not need to take into account when making such decisions. European nations fought the Hundred Years' War and the Thirty Years' War; the American public has increasingly grown accustomed to overwhelming victories that last a mere 100 days and that employ 30-second televised cruise missile attacks. The relatively brief attention span of the public in the United States virtually requires quick, decisive, and nearly bloodless conflicts. If military action drags on and American soldiers come home in body bags in large numbers, maintaining public support has often been problematic.

In the American context, therefore, war poses a crucial test of presidential leadership. It requires the nation's chief executive to enlist the nation in support of a policy that demands the expenditure of American blood and treasure. Dallek recognized this as well, asking rhetorically, "Would the sacrifices required in World Wars I and II have been conceivable without presidential attention to building public support for them prior to 1917 and Pearl Harbor?"[15] Emily Rosenberg and Mark Stoler, in their respective essays, discuss how Woodrow Wilson and Franklin Delano Roosevelt dealt with these issues in their chapters on World War I and World War II, respectively. Rosenberg considers how the Wilson administration created a new political art form—selling war through a combination of persuasion and coercion—to mobilize a hesitant American public in support of "the war to end all wars." She also examines how this effort sparked a debate— which continues to the present day—regarding the relationship between the manipulation of public opinion and the health of the democracy. Stoler argues that FDR succeeded brilliantly in selling a series of different wars and policies to the American people during World War II, but that the price for his success was extraordinarily high and contributed to the abuses of presidential power that followed during the Cold War.

The focus of this book notwithstanding, the idea of selling war is by no means exclusive to the modern presidency. The words and deeds of the nineteenth-century presidents resonate with parallels during the "media age" and set precedents for their successors, although the rhetorical presidency was neither as systematic nor as sustained before the twentieth century as it would become after the Spanish-American War. Indeed, the selling of war—or any U.S. foreign policy initiative—to the American public predates the American century. Even before the advent of the "yellow journalism" of William Randolph Hearst; the creation of the Committee for Public Information during World War I; the proliferation and omnipresence of television, the Internet, and the blogosphere; and sophisticated spin and public relations campaigns that are described by the authors in this volume, presidents utilized the means available to them in order to manufacture or bolster public support for their agenda. In fact, propaganda as a tool of foreign relations—for both external and internal consumption—predates the United States by centuries.[16] Political leaders have always intuited the importance of dealing with public opinion, both in terms of reacting to it and shaping it. Franklin Delano Roosevelt, one of the most effective communicators to sit in the Oval Office, understood this well. "All of our great Presidents," he asserted, "were *leaders* of thought at times when certain historic ideas in the life of the nation had to be clarified."[17]

Some scholars have posited a stark disjuncture between the modern presidency and its antecedents when considering the question of rhetoric and public opinion. In *The Rhetorical Presidency*, Jeffrey Tulis argues that prior to the twentieth century, presidents lacked the mechanisms and institutional precedents to effectively move public opinion.[18] Moreover, they rarely spoke on their own behalf to avoid the perception of "unseemly ambition and demagoguery." Once in office, nineteenth-century chief executives "rarely if ever went public to mobilize public opinion in the manner we have come to expect of presidents."[19] While Washington and his immediate successors considered oratory and persuasion to be important elements of democratic politics, they did not believe that it was the president's job to engage in such conduct. Indeed, the founders designed the presidency to be insulated from public opinion, fearing that popular passions could become a crucible for tyranny.[20]

Thus maintaining a low profile was integral to the public images of the early presidents, who were "expected to be above the political fray and not to engage too blatantly in the world of partisan politics." For a president to do so, as political communications scholar Mary Stuckey has written, "would have been equivalent to demagoguery; rabble-rousing was not among the virtues . . . ascribed to a successful president." The founders were "profoundly suspicious" of popular leadership as a means of soliciting support; they saw the president as being apolitical, "not as a leader who would mobilize governing coalitions but as an executive who would rise like a patriot king above party."[21] Yet it is telling that the Federalists did recognize that appeals to public opinion by the president "might be good if it were a means to a good end, such as preservation of a decent nation or successful prosecution of a just war."[22] This attitude suggests two conclusions: first, a president possessed a greater freedom to act publicly if he could successfully define a conflict as "just" and, second, political expediency apparently forgave a multitude of sins, even for the founders.

Furthermore, while chief executives during the country's first century may have demonstrated a disinclination to cater directly to public sentiment as a matter of tradition or expectation, they rarely missed an opportunity to engage in such politicking and salesmanship using other methods. Most notably, as political scientist Mel Laracey has argued, newspapers were a partisan tool in early American politics and performed many of the functions of "going public" in comparison to the broader media of the twentieth century. The *Federalist Gazette of the United States*, for example, was established in April 1789 by Alexander Hamilton and other prominent Federalists to provide a "reliable political organ" for the Washington administration. It quickly became the source from which Federalist supporters took their political cues. From the very beginning of the republic until the eve of the Civil War, presidents relied on these partisan papers to "reach the public with information on national affairs and administration policy" and to "present the administration's position" on policy issues.[23] Clearly, appealing to public opinion for support was not an exclusively twentieth-century phenomenon, even if it did occur within distinct and restrictive eighteenth- and nineteenth-century parameters.

The limitations on influencing domestic sentiment placed on the presidency by the expectations of the founders waned with the growth in territory and population, particularly during the Jacksonian period. In order to reach a broad and diverse population, politicians had to rely heavily on technology—the extensive partisan press being the most effective—to obtain support for their policies and politics. Presidents were still expected to be above the fray; according to Stuckey, for a president to speak on matters that did not "relate directly to his administrative function was for a president to speak inappropriately and risk his legitimacy."[24] Direct presidential communications during this period were primarily written and directed at other elites rather than the public. Infrequent speeches by the chief executive were reserved for loftier and more idealistic purposes. Nevertheless, the president's voice was heard through the press and through political surrogates, and the president's evolving role as party leader made that traditional stipulation less realistic in any event. Newspapers grew in significance from the mid-1820s until the 1850s, when the rise of independent papers and the professionalization of journalism reduced the effectiveness of official partisan journals. In addition, party officials communicated directly with the public on behalf of the president and mobilized support through rallies and other political events.

James K. Polk stands as a prime example of how nineteenth-century presidents used the methods and tools available to them to promote their policies and influence public opinion. According to Jeffrey Tulis, Polk gave surprisingly few speeches during the Mexican-American War—a time when one would expect the president to solicit public support for the conflict. He "judiciously avoided popular appeals because they contradicted the 'custom' of the period" and would have involved a "sacrifice [of] his dignity to beg in person for support."[25] This perspective did not, however, preclude him from trying to influence public opinion in his favor. Polk's written message to Congress requesting a declaration of war against Mexico, while factually flawed, was politically potent. When asked by doubting Whigs for evidence of the alleged Mexican attack on U.S. forces that provoked the request, Polk and his supporters responded that, although the documents were at the printer's and not available, Congress should trust the president. Congress responded by voting overwhelmingly (174 to 14 in the House, 40 to 2 in the Senate) for war.

Polk also used his own newspaper, the *Washington Union* (acquired in 1845 through a transfer of $50,000 in U.S. Treasury funds to a bank in a small town in Pennsylvania), to push for the annexation of Texas. Later, Polk used the *Union* to frame and spin the progress of the Mexican War. What is striking about Polk's involvement with the paper is that he was so closely engaged with the daily operations of the *Union*, not only exercising direct editorial control over its content but also going so far as to write anonymous articles that appeared in the paper trumpeting his policies and attempting to shape opinion about his administration.[26] Presidents may have been re-stricted by tradition from speaking extensively about their policies or on their own behalf, but they utilized any other means at their disposal to ac-complish the same ends.

The reticence to use the presidency in pursuit of partisan goals or to ap-peal directly to public opinion continued to diminish during the Civil War as Abraham Lincoln tried desperately to hold the fragile country together while prosecuting a divisive war of unprecedented proportions. Lincoln expressed a reluctance to overuse this strategy, however, believing that he "needed to choose his public moments and words carefully to protect his position." As he framed the issue, "It is at all times proper that misunder-standing between the public and the public servant should be avoided; and this is far more important now than in times of peace and tranquility."[27] Lincoln said, "Public sentiment is everything. With public sentiment noth-ing can fail, without it nothing can succeed." Nevertheless, he used reporters to convey messages to the public and helped to establish the presidency as "the locus of national identity."[28] According to Tulis, Lincoln's most specific policy pronouncements as president were "those in which he justifies war activity after the fact. The most important of these are his defenses of sus-pension of *habeas corpus* and of martial law."[29] As president, Lincoln acted cautiously within the contemporary expectations of the office as a political strategy, but took advantage of every opportunity to communicate with the public.

Lincoln's successors possessed neither the political acumen nor the resources requisite to build on his relationship with the American public. It would not be until the McKinley administration and the Spanish-American War that the ability to sell war and foreign policy became a veritable prerequisite for the presidency. In the first chapter of the book, George Herring addresses not only the Spanish-American War, for which McKinley needed simply to sustain the widespread popular support that already existed for the conflict in the wake of the explosion of the USS *Maine* and other perceived Spanish provocations, but also the more daunting task of persuading the American public to support the annexation of the Philippines. The president quickly grasped the growing importance of public opinion and developed new means to influence it in his favor. Herring concludes that McKinley's actions created not only new standards in presidential rhetoric that would prove instructive to his successors in the Oval Office, but also set precedents that foreshadowed the problems and risks inherent in manipulating public opinion.

As the nation moved into the twentieth century, the advent of technology, the evolution in the role and scope of the federal government, and the increasing sophistication of propaganda and public relations techniques would fundamentally alter the relationship between the Oval Office and domestic political opinion. As a result, the public dimension of the presidency has expanded exponentially since McKinley pioneered new techniques to garner public support and Theodore Roosevelt used the White House as his "bully pulpit" to further his political agenda. Consequently, as political scientist Bruce Miroff notes, "One of the most distinctive features of the modern presidency is its constant cultivation of popular support," as the president "not only responds to popular demands and passions but also actively reaches out to shape them."[30]

One of the realities of post–World War II U.S. foreign relations is that selling "war" takes on an entirely new meaning. During the Cold War, the "new world order," and the current "war on terror," administrations have had to market foreign policies and military activities that fall well outside the conventional rubric of "war." Undeclared conflicts, military interventions, and policy decisions in a hostile international environment have expanded the fronts on which presidents must actively engage the public to solicit support for its policies. In his chapter on the Cold War, Robert Schulzinger argues that as the conflict became the centerpiece of U.S. foreign policy, presidents from Truman to Nixon felt compelled to seek popular support and utilized a variety of rhetorical strategies to justify U.S. positions in international affairs. But like the other authors in the book, Schulzinger points to the significant costs associated with Cold War presidential rhetoric. As the British social critic Bertrand Russell commented in 1950, "There is no nonsense so arrant that it cannot be made the creed of the vast majority by adequate governmental action." There is a fine line between influencing and manipulating public opinion, and the evidence presented in the essays that follow strongly suggests that presidential efforts to achieve the former result in the undemocratic tendencies of the latter.

Moreover, the American public is only one of the three fronts on which presidents must attempt to mold opinion. As a growing body of scholarship demonstrates, public diplomacy—which encompasses a wide range of diplomatic activities, including propaganda, cultural exchange, and explaining common interests since nations act in their self-interest—aims at convincing both allies and adversaries of the credibility and worth of American policies.[31] In addition, chief executives must negotiate with Congress in order to gain support, although Ronald Reagan and other media savvy presidents have made an art form of appealing directly to the public in an effort to put pressure on the "meddlesome committee of 535" and force congressional compliance with their agendas. These are not mutually exclusive "publics." Indeed, it is abundantly clear that each exerts influence over the others, which underscores the difficult paths that presidents must navigate to obtain and preserve support from each of their constituencies. In the book's concluding chapter, Lloyd Gardner explains how the United States navigated these multiple audiences when dealing with the issue of Saddam Hussein over the course of two decades and two wars. Gardner focuses on White House and Pentagon efforts in both Bush administrations to manipulate opinion at home and abroad in the effort to demonize Hussein; identify Iraq as a threat to world peace (not to mention world oil supplies); and sell the American people, Congress, and international community on the need to take military action to deal decisively with the invasion of Kuwait in 1990 and Hussein's possession of weapons of mass destruction in the wake of the tragic events of September 11, 2001.[32]

The success or failure of a president's efforts to sell war—or really any policy—depends not only on the sophistication of the message but also the public's predisposition regarding the conflict. As Marilyn Young contends in her essay on the consistently unpopular Korean conflict, once the public loses faith in the administration or comes to believe that there is no credible threat or that victory has become unlikely, presidents are faced with the dilemma of either extricating the country from the conflict to salvage public support or continuing to prosecute an unpopular war and suffer the political consequences. Indeed, as Harry Truman, Lyndon Johnson, and George W. Bush have discovered to their chagrin, the difficulty of sustaining a national consensus for long-term expenditures of American lives and expanding defense budgets can wreak havoc on not only presidential popularity but also their broader policy agendas. In an effort to preempt such problems, presidents have had to "assure that a clear understanding and commitment preceded involvement in drawn-out warfare." The most successful wartime presidents "have been those who systematically built a consensus in the Congress, the press, and the country before taking up arms."[33] Of course, preparation is no guarantee that the public will remain steadfastly behind the administration, as the current conflict in Iraq clearly attests.

Moreover, the American public should be deeply troubled by the manipulations of fact, manufacturing of evidence, and distortions of the truth that have occurred as presidents have attempted to sell their policies. Truth may be the first casualty of war, and there are certainly times when national security factors into a president's decision-making process. Yet it is striking how cavalier the nation's chief executives have been with the truth in times of conflict during the media age. This is not only a moral objection; history has demonstrated that building consensus on subterfuge or a lack of candor can undermine the very policy for which the president desperately needs public support. Presidents need to act not only in the best interests of the country but also in full compliance with their constitutional responsibilities. To do otherwise in pursuit of personal or partisan aggrandizement violates the public trust and undermines confidence in the institution of the presidency and the nation.

The philosopher William James observed that the challenge of politics in peacetime is to find a moral equivalent of war. That perspective helps to explain LBJ's "war on poverty" and Reagan's "war on drugs."[34] As the essays that follow demonstrate, however, simply having a war or international crisis does not make the politics of war any easier. Presidents have had varying degrees of success in selling war, and they recognize that doing so poses tremendous challenges in the media age. The presidency provides a major propaganda advantage in shaping public opinion, yet the proliferation of media allows an administration's political opponents to sell alternative viewpoints almost as effectively and efficiently. "Going public," as political scientist Samuel Kernell has argued, has become the norm, but it is not a harbinger of success.[35]

Notes

1. *New York Times*, 7 September 2002. According to Frank Rich, Card created the White House Iraq Group to "market a war in Iraq." See Rich, *The Greatest Story Ever Sold: The Decline and Fall of Truth from 9/11 to Katrina* (New York: Penguin, 2006), 189. For a detailed examination of the evolution of the campaign to sell the U.S. public on the need to confront Iraq, see Sue Lockett John, David Domke, Kevin Coe, and Erica S. Graham, "Going Public, Crisis after Crisis: The Bush Administration and the Press from September 11 to Saddam," *Rhetoric & Public Affairs* 10, no. 2 (2007): 195–220.

2. There is a significant literature on how presidents utilize rhetoric, propaganda, and the media to further their policies, both foreign and domestic. See, for example, Steven Casey, *Selling the Korean War: Propaganda, Politics, and Public Opinion, 1950–1953* (New York: Oxford University Press, 2008); Samuel Kernell, *Going Public: New Strategies of Presidential Leadership*, 3rd ed. (Washington, D.C.: Congressional Quarterly Press, 1997); Jeffrey K. Tulis, *The Rhetorical Presidency* (Princeton: Princeton University Press, 1987); Richard J. Ellis, ed., *Speaking to the People: The Rhetorical Presidency in Historical Perspective* (Amherst: University of Massachusetts Press, 1998); Stephen Skowronek, *The Politics Presidents Make: Leadership from John Adams to George Bush* (Cambridge, Mass.: Belknap Press, 1993); Jon Western, *Selling Intervention and War: The Presidency, the Media, and the American Public* (Baltimore: Johns Hopkins University Press, 2005); Richard E. Neustadt, *Presidential Power and the Modern Presidents: The Politics of Leadership from Roosevelt to Reagan*, rev. ed. (New York: Free Press, 1990); Kathleen Hall Jamieson, *Eloquence in an Electronic Age: The Transformation of Political Speechmaking* (New York: Oxford University Press, 1988); Amos Kiewe, ed., *The Modern Presidency and Crisis Rhetoric* (Westport, Conn.: Praeger, 1994); Chris Tudda, *The Truth Is Our Weapon: The Rhetorical Diplomacy of Dwight D. Eisenhower and John Foster Dulles* (Baton Rouge: Louisiana State University Press, 2006); and Kenneth Osgood, *Total Cold War: Eisenhower's Secret Propaganda Battle at Home and Abroad* (Lawrence: University Press of Kansas, 2006).

3. Meena Bose, "Words as Signals: Drafting Cold War Rhetoric in the Eisenhower and Kennedy Administrations," *Congress & the Presidency* 25, no. 1 (Spring 1998): 23.

4. Walter LaFeber, "Johnson, Vietnam, and Tocqueville," in Warren I. Cohen and Nancy Bernkopf Tucker, eds., *Lyndon Johnson Confronts the World: American Foreign Policy, 1963–1968* (New York: Cambridge University Press, 1994), 31. In this vein, Jarol Manheim discusses how leaders craft public discourse with the goal of creating, controlling, distributing, and using mediated messages as a political resource in *All of the People, All of the Time* (Armonk, N.Y.: M. E. Sharpe, 1991).

5. Robert Dallek, *Hail to the Chief: The Making and Unmaking of American Presidents* (New York: Hyperion, 1996), 87.

6. Tocqueville, the French historian and political commentator who famously toured the United States in the 1820s and 1830s, argued that democracies like the United States tend to have "confused or erroneous ideas on external affairs and decide questions of foreign policy on purely domestic considerations." See Alexis de Tocqueville, *Democracy in America*, 2 vols. (New York: Vintage, 1990), 1:232–36. There is a vast literature on the relationship between domestic politics, public opinion, and foreign policy in the United States. Representative scholarship includes Eugene R. Wittkopf and James M. McCormick, eds., *The Domestic Sources of American Foreign Policy: Insights and Evidence*, 4th ed. (Lanham, Md.: Rowman and Littlefield, 2004); Melvin Small, *Democracy and Diplomacy: The Impact of Domestic Politics on U.S. Foreign Policy, 1789-1994* (Baltimore: Johns Hopkins University Press, 1996); Andrew L. Johns, *Vietnam's Second Front: Domestic Politics, the Republican Party, and the War* (Lexington: University Press of Kentucky, 2010); and Douglas C. Foyle, *Counting the Public In: Presidents, Public Opinion, and Foreign Policy* (New York: Columbia University Press, 1999).

7. For a penetrating discussion of the relationship between core values and national security, see Melvyn P. Leffler, "National Security," in Michael J. Hogan and Thomas G. Paterson, eds., *Explaining the History of American Foreign Relations*, 2nd ed. (New York: Cambridge University Press, 2004), 123–36. This strategy also helps to explain the names of the National Defense Highway Act at the height of the Cold War and the Patriot Act after the events of September 11, 2001.

8. John et al., "Going Public, Crisis after Crisis," 200.

9. Bruce Miroff, "The Presidency and the Public: Leadership as Spectacle," in Michael Nelson, ed., *The Presidency and the Political System*, 4th ed. (Washington, D.C.: Congressional Quarterly Press, 1995), 276. On the utility, accuracy, and effectiveness of historical analogies for policymakers, see Richard E. Neustadt and Ernest R. May, *Thinking in Time: The Uses of History for Decision Makers* (New York: Free Press, 1986). See also Frank Costigliola, "Reading for Meaning: Theory, Language, and Metaphor," and Robert D. Schulzinger, "Memory and Understanding U.S. Foreign Relations," in Hogan and Paterson, eds., *Explaining the History of American Foreign Relations*, 279–303 and 336–52.

10. Quoted in George C. Edwards III and Stephen J. Wayne, *Presidential Leadership: Politics and Policy Making*, 3rd ed. (New York: St. Martin's Press, 1994), 90.

11. Douglas Kellner makes this argument stridently in, "Bushspeak and the Politics of Lying: Presidential Rhetoric in the 'War on Terror,'" *Presidential Studies Quarterly* 37, no. 4 (December 2007): 622–45.

12. George F. Kennan, *American Diplomacy*, expanded ed. (Chicago: University of Chicago Press, 1984), 176.

13. The *Foreign Relations of the United States* volumes covering this period contain multiple instances of these considerations in the administration's internal deliberations. See, for example, National Security Memorandum 308, 22 June 1964, *Foreign Relations of the United States, 1964-1968*, vol. I: Vietnam 1964 (Washington, D.C.: Government Printing Office, 1992), 523. For an analytical overview of this period, see

Fredrik Logevall, *Choosing War: The Lost Chance for Peace and the Escalation of War in Vietnam* (Berkeley: University of California Press, 1999). Obviously, Vietnam is not a unique case; this phenomenon can be found throughout the twentieth century during military conflicts and with other foreign policy decisions. See, for example, Osgood, *Total Cold War*, on the Eisenhower administration, and Steven Casey, "Selling NSC-68: The Truman Administration, Public Opinion, and the Politics of Mobilization, 1950–51," *Diplomatic History* 29, no. 4 (September 2005): 655–90.

14. In his seminal work, *On War*, Clausewitz wrote, "We see, therefore, that War is not merely a political act, but also a real political instrument, a continuation of political commerce, a carrying out of the same by other means. . . . for the political view is the object, War is the means, and the means must always include the object in our conception." See Carl von Clausewitz, *On War*, ed. Anatol Rapoport (New York: Penguin Books, 1968), 119.

15. Dallek, *Hail to the Chief*, 109. Even FDR struggled to fully convince the American public of the need to enter into another European conflict. Nicholas John Cull explores the British effort to affect and mobilize U.S. public opinion in favor of intervention in *Selling War: The British Propaganda Campaign Against American "Neutrality" in World War II* (New York: Oxford University Press, 1995).

16. During the Crusades, for example, Richard I of England plucked the eyes from his prisoners and returned them to Saladin in an effort to mold the image that Richard's enemies had of him. For an overview on how propaganda has been employed in support of foreign policy goals, see Oliver Thomson, *Easily Led: A History of Propaganda* (Gloucestershire: Sutton, 1999).

17. Quoted in Edwards and Wayne, *Presidential Leadership*, 90.

18. Tulis's thesis has been challenged by several authors, including Richard J. Ellis and Alexis Walker, who argue that mid-nineteenth-century presidents faced competing expectations—the constraints stemming from the founders' vision of a president above party versus the demands that stemmed from the president's evolving role as party leader. See Ellis and Walker, "Policy Speech in the Nineteenth-Century Rhetorical Presidency: The Case of Zachary Taylor's 1849 Tour," *Presidential Studies Quarterly* 37, no. 2 (June 2007): 248–69.

19. Richard J. Ellis, introduction to *Speaking to the People*, 1.

20. On this point, see David K. Nichols, "A Marriage Made in Philadelphia: The Constitution and the Rhetorical Presidency," in Ellis, ed., *Speaking to the People*, 16–34.

21. Mary E. Stuckey, *The President as Interpreter-in-Chief* (Chatham, N.J.: Chatham House, 1991), 15–16; and Jack N. Rakove, *Original Meanings: Politics and Ideas in the Making of the Constitution* (New York: Knopf, 1996), 268. Nearly all references by the founders to "popular leaders" are pejorative. See Tulis, *The Rhetorical Presidency*, 27. A prime example appears in Federalist #1, written by Alexander Hamilton, which warns against the threat of demagogues: "those men who have overturned the liberties of republics, the greatest number have begun their career by paying an obsequious court to the people; commencing demagogues, and ending tyrants." See Alexander Hamilton,

John Jay, and James Madison, *The Federalist: A Collection of Essays, Written in Favor of the Constitution of the United States, as Agreed Upon by the Federal Convention, September 17, 1787*, ed. by Michael Loyd Chadwick (Springfield, Va.: Global Affairs, 1987), 3.

22. Tulis, *The Rhetorical Presidency*, 30.

23. Mel Laracey, "The Presidential Newspaper: The Forgotten Way of Going Public," in Ellis, ed., *Speaking to the People*, 67, 69. Thomas Jefferson, James Madison, and Henry Lee responded with the founding of the *National Gazette* in October 1791 to counter Federalist propaganda and mobilize Republicans across the country. Laracey gives an example of Jefferson's use of the *National Intelligencer* to prop up the administration's embargo against Britain.

24. Stuckey, *The President as Interpreter-in-Chief*, 17.

25. Tulis, *The Rhetorical Presidency*, 63, 76.

26. Laracey, "The Presidential Newspaper," 77–78. When dealing with criticism from General Zachary Taylor (the commander of U.S. forces in Mexico) of his plans for war with Mexico, for example, Polk instructed his secretary of war to write an article "vindicating the government" and have it published in the *Union*. He also frequently instructed the paper's editor to run regular attacks on a recalcitrant Congress.

27. Quoted in Laracey, "The Presidential Newspaper," 84.

28. Quoted in Edwards and Wayne, *Presidential Leadership*, 89; and Stuckey, *The President as Interpreter-in-Chief*, 19.

29. Tulis, *The Rhetorical Presidency*, 83. Robert Dallek suggests that Lincoln's strategy in dealing with the South in 1861 "was brilliantly devised to give Lincoln the moral and political upper hand in any possible war. . . . the onus of the war would fall upon the South and create a northern consensus to meet the Confederate challenge. . . . In one stroke he had declared his determination to preserve the Union and the future of constitutional rule, shown himself to be a resourceful pragmatist capable of formulating a workable policy to meet an unprecedented crisis, and assured himself of broad support for the most demanding commitment a president can ask of his people." See Dallek, *Hail to the Chief*, 110–11.

30. Miroff, "The Presidency and the Public," 273.

31. For scholarship on public diplomacy, see, for example, Richard T. Arndt, *The First Resort of Kings: American Cultural Diplomacy in the Twentieth Century* (Washington, D.C.: Potomac Books, 2005); Penny Von Eschen, *Satchmo Blows Up the World: Jazz Ambassadors Play the Cold War* (Cambridge: Harvard University Press, 2004); Robert Dallek, *The American Style of Foreign Policy: Cultural Politics and Foreign Affairs* (New York: Oxford University Press, 1983); Gifford D. Malone, *Political Advocacy and Cultural Communication: Organizing the Nation's Public Diplomacy* (Lanham, Md.: University Press of America, 1988); Jarol B. Manheim, *Strategic Public Diplomacy and American Foreign Policy: The Evolution of Influence* (New York: Oxford University Press, 1994); Gregg Wolper, "Wilsonian Public Diplomacy: The Committee on Public Information in Spain," *Diplomatic History* 17, no. 1 (Winter 1993): 17–34; Wilson P. Dizard, *Inventing Public Diplomacy: The Story of the U.S. Information Agency* (Boulder: Lynne

Rienner, 2004); Jessica Gienow-Hecht, *Transmission Impossible: American Journalism as Cultural Diplomacy in Postwar Germany* (Baton Rouge: Louisiana State University Press, 1999); Walter L. Hixson, *Parting the Curtain: Propaganda, Culture, and the Cold War, 1945–1961* (New York: St. Martin's Press, 1998); Nancy Snow, *Propaganda, Inc.: Selling America's Culture to the World* (New York: Seven Stories Press, 1998); Hans N. Tuch, *Communicating with the World: U.S. Public Diplomacy Overseas* (New York: St. Martin's Press, 1990); and Osgood, *Total Cold War*.

32. Harvard political scientist Robert Putnam suggests that a good way to get a clearer picture of the interaction between competing forces in government and international relations is to consider the chief of government as playing two games simultaneously—international and domestic—and understand that he does not dare to lose either one. In this "two-level game theory," the leader has to construct "win sets"—conceivable agreements useful to himself and the nation—and get them to overlap with the win sets of the people with whom he is negotiating. If necessary, the leader must manipulate his win sets to overlap with those of his negotiating adversary. For a full explanation of the theory, see Robert D. Putnam, "Diplomacy and Domestic Politics: The Logic of Two-Level Games," in Peter B. Evans, Harold K. Jacobson, and Robert D. Putnam, eds., *Double-Edged Diplomacy: International Bargaining and Domestic Politics* (Berkeley: University of California Press, 1993), 431–68.

33. Dallek, *Hail to the Chief*, 109.

34. On the infusion of war and militarization into American culture in the twentieth century, see Michael Sherry, *In the Shadow of War: The United States since the 1930s* (New Haven: Yale University Press, 1995). Fred Anderson and Andrew Cayton argue that war has been a central feature of the nation's development since its founding in *The Dominion of War: Empire and Liberty in North America, 1500–2000* (New York: Penguin Books, 2005).

35. Kernell, *Going Public*. The expansion of media "has linked public approval more closely to the exercise of presidential power." See Edwards and Wayne, *Presidential Leadership*, 10–11.

1

IMPERIAL TUTOR

William McKinley, the War of 1898, and the New Empire, 1898–1902

George C. Herring

In December 1898, former Union army major and now president of the United States William McKinley mounted a bold foray into South Carolina, Alabama, and Georgia, the heart of the former Confederacy. The president's ostensible purpose was to further the spirit of national reconciliation bolstered by the recent victory over Spain. But with the Senate soon to vote on the treaty ending that war, he also used the trip to sell the fruits of victory: the acquisition of the Philippine Islands. At every stop, McKinley hailed the valor of Confederate war dead; he wore a badge of gray and on occasion jumped to his feet and waved his hat when "Dixie" was played. While repeatedly playing on the theme of national unity, he moved seamlessly into homilies on imperial responsibility. "If following the clear precepts of duty, territory falls to us, and the welfare of an alien people requires our guidance and protection," he asked in Savannah, "who will shrink from that responsibility, grave though it may be?"[1] McKinley's southern trip was nothing short of triumphal. His speech to the Georgia legislature in Atlanta won such thunderous applause that, according to legend, the dome of the state capitol trembled. The fact that he made the trip suggests the importance he attached to mobilizing public support for the new empire. The methods he used tell a great deal about how he carried out his new role as imperial tutor to the nation.[2]

This essay will examine President McKinley's selling of the War of 1898, the overseas empire that resulted from that war, and the so-called Philippine Insurrection that followed. It focuses squarely on the White House. It will look at the importance McKinley and his advisors attached to public opinion and the ways they evaluated and sought to manipulate it. It will analyze their successes and failures. It will show how their actions created important precedents in the selling of war and thus marked the birth of the modern presidency.

By today's standards, the U.S. government's promotion of the war with Spain in 1898 was neither systematic, sophisticated, nor sustained. The methods used to assess and manipulate public opinion seem primitive, amateurish, even quaint. Such appearances can be misleading. William McKinley was among the first U.S. politicians to recognize the growing importance of public opinion in turn-of-the-century foreign policy. He studied it carefully and took it into account in shaping policies. He paid special attention to the press as both a reflection of public attitudes and a means of influencing them and he pioneered new ways of shaping what and how journalists wrote. He went far beyond his predecessors in seeking to educate the public on important foreign policy issues. McKinley faced unique challenges. His task in the spring of 1898 was to tamp down, without quelling, popular enthusiasm for war and, once war had come, to sustain support for an immensely popular conflict, a task at which he succeeded mainly because the war lasted a mere 100 days and ended in unqualified victory. Yet he barely managed to secure the votes to ratify the treaty providing for annexation of the Philippines, and he struggled to defend the difficult war that followed. Neither he nor his fellow advocates of empire created a solid base of support for the acquisition of additional territory. This said, McKinley is a major figure. Now generally recognized as the first modern chief executive, he established a foundation for the so-called imperial presidency of the twentieth century. He developed public backing for the concept of the United States as a world power. The McKinley administration thus provides a benchmark against which to evaluate the government's changing role in the selling of war in the American Century.

Presidents, Public Opinion, and Policy

Before looking at the War of 1898 and the new empire, it is useful to offer some generalizations about public opinion in that era: what it consisted of, how it was shaped, and how politicians sought to interpret and manipulate it. Obviously, given the lack of polling data and other scientific instruments, it is difficult to draw firm conclusions. Ernest May has speculated that the voting public of the 1890s consisted of less than 20 percent of the total population, or about 13 to 15 million males, mostly white, over 21 years of age. That group, in turn, was composed of a large number of farmers and smaller numbers of business and professional men and skilled and unskilled workers. Within this voting public, May identifies a smaller foreign policy public of 1 to 3 million people, roughly 10 to 20 percent of the larger public, who took a close interest in foreign policy issues. This group was made up largely of college and high school graduates located mainly in urban areas where daily newspapers presenting foreign news were readily accessible.[3]

May also identifies a group of opinion leaders in communities across the nation who shaped public attitudes on key issues like imperialism and served as conduits of opinion to political leaders. These people generally had a wide knowledge of world events. Some had traveled abroad, spoke foreign languages, or even had diplomatic experience. Many had friends abroad and were kept informed about important events worldwide, especially in Great Britain and Western Europe. They were the people the press quoted and whose views politicians sought. They might be businessmen, clergy, educators, or what we now call public intellectuals. The list included such people as Thomas Jefferson Coolidge and Charles W. Eliot of Boston, journalists Whitelaw Reid, William Randolph Hearst, and Joseph Pulitzer of New York, business leader Marshall Field, historian Hermann von Holst of Chicago, lawyer Albert Beveridge, writer Lew Wallace, and industrialist Mark Hanna of Indianapolis.[4]

The rationale for overseas expansion that took shape in the 1890s emanated as much from these opinion makers as from the political leadership. To be sure, in the 1860s and 1870s, Secretary of State William Henry Seward laid out a vision for an American commercial empire in the Caribbean, the Gulf of Mexico, and the Pacific, pushing for the establishment of naval bases, the construction of a canal across the Central American isthmus, and even for the acquisition of Cuba, Puerto Rico, and Haiti. He eyed the purchase of Greenland and Iceland and in the Pacific acquisition of Hawaii and the Fiji Islands. Outside of the purchase of Alaska, Seward's expansionist dreams ran afoul a national absorption in domestic issues and rabidly partisan politics. "How sadly domestic disturbances of ours demobilize the national ambition," he lamented in 1868.[5] In the 1880s, Secretary of State James G. Blaine revived Seward's dreams, sketching a blueprint for empire that included U.S. preeminence in the Western Hemisphere, commercial domination of the Pacific, an American-owned canal, and even acquisition of Hawaii, Cuba, and Puerto Rico. Like Seward, his accomplishments were limited, but his vision endured, and he served as a mentor to individuals like John Hay and William McKinley, who became architects of the new empire of the 1890s.[6]

By that tumultuous decade, the vision of these two post–Civil War expansionists was fleshed out by opinion leaders into a full-fledged rationale for overseas empire. In the mid-1890s, imperialists such as Henry Cabot Lodge, Theodore Roosevelt, Rear Admiral Alfred Thayer Mahan, clergyman Josiah Strong, and others through their speeches, writings, and other forms of advocacy had developed various arguments for the expansion of U.S. influence and even the acquisition of colonies. According to the "glut thesis," popular at the time, the United States needed foreign markets to absorb the surplus of industrial and agricultural products blamed for the economic instability of the era. Some Americans feared that the late nineteenth-century worldwide scramble for colonies might threaten U.S. commercial and political interests and insisted that the nation must enter the competition out of self-interest. Still others argued that the United States as a rising world power must assume responsibility for maintaining world order even if that entailed acquiring overseas colonies. The United States as one of the world's civilized nations must take up the burden of uplifting less fortunate people in less developed areas. These ideas had probably not infected the body politic by the mid-1890s, but they did find their way into the Republican Party's platform in 1896. Indeed, the Democrats tried to make the election a referendum on imperialism, but McKinley's lopsided victory over Democrat William Jennings Bryan turned far more on domestic issues than on foreign policy.[7]

The late nineteenth century also brought the beginnings of mass public interest in foreign affairs. The communications revolution resulting from rapid transportation, the telegraph, and the telephone made more information more accessible to more people far more quickly. Higher literacy rates along with the emergence of periodicals and newspapers with mass circulation created a wider readership. Newspapers and magazines sent correspondents abroad to report newsworthy events, and larger numbers of Americans followed them avidly. The mass public in the 1890s was especially volatile because of economic distress, social dislocation, and the stresses caused by industrialization, responding to minor crises with Italy and Chile with marked bellicosity. It became a matter of increasing concern to those elites long accustomed to managing affairs of state with no public interference.[8]

McKinley's Gilded Age predecessors had not vigorously exercised their power to influence the public. Some believed it was not their job to do so. Their mandate was to follow rather than to lead and direct public opinion.

Others believed the public was sufficiently docile and trusting that "they will cheerfully follow wherever you may jointly lead," as a friend wrote President Ulysses S. Grant's secretary of state in 1873. Presidents of this era were not overly concerned by public opinion and did not develop methods for evaluating and influencing it. They did not oversee in any systematic way the release of information for maximum public impact. They did little to cultivate writers from the major newspapers. They began to keep scrapbooks of newspaper clippings as one means of judging public attitudes, but never really decided how to use them. The Gilded Age White House relied on occasional public statements to inform the public. It reacted to problems as they arose. Because most foreign policy decisions did not necessitate popular backing, the president and his advisors did not think of public opinion as a major factor in its shaping.[9]

McKinley initiated major changes. Historians have long ago demolished the traditional image of McKinley as a spineless president driven to action by an aroused public. He is now generally viewed as one of the nation's more effective chief executives.[10] As a congressman and governor of Ohio, he had developed exceptional political skills, and he honed them further in the presidency. A plain, down-home man of simple tastes, he was what would now be called a "people person." Accessible, kindly, and a good listener, his greatest political asset was his understanding of people and his ability to deal with them. He had an extraordinary memory for names and faces. He was, in Henry Adams's words, a "marvelous manager of men."[11] He was also an early master of what political scientist Fred Greenstein has labeled the "hidden-hand" presidential style, exerting strong leadership without appearing to do so.[12] He "had a way of handling men," his secretary of war, Elihu Root, observed, "so that they thought his ideas were their own."[13] He moved quietly and unobtrusively toward his goals. His studied ambiguity concealed his intentions. He skillfully neutralized opposition and closely directed the political battle while seeming to remain above it.

In shaping policy and making decisions, McKinley paid close attention to public opinion. One friend said of him that "his faith in the public intelligence and conscience was supreme. He believed that people knew more than any man. He never tried to lead but studied so constantly public opinion that he became almost infallible in its interpretation."[14] He carefully read the White House mail, scanned as many as a dozen newspapers daily, and examined scrapbooks of press clippings from across the nation. He used public receptions as sounding boards, asking his visitors what people in their areas thought about the issues of the day. He consulted with people from all walks of life. He believed himself a good judge of what the public was thinking.[15] Like most politicians, he also had a knack of hearing what he wanted to hear.

From the time he took office, McKinley was especially sensitive to the care and feeding of the press. As a member of the House of Representatives he had come to appreciate the importance of newspapers in politics and the need for good relations with journalists. The press itself was changing at this time from an organ of political parties to large, independent, mass circulation dailies dependent on advertising, in need of news to draw readers, and therefore less reliable and predictable as far as politicians were concerned. Sensing the changes, McKinley cultivated friends among Washington reporters. He met privately with journalists and invited them to attend Christmas and New Year's functions at the White House. His top aides, Joseph Addison Porter and George Cortelyou, developed additional means to influence news coverage. In a hallway on the second floor of the White House they set up a table and chairs where reporters could do their work and question visitors. Porter became an early equivalent of the modern press secretary, meeting daily at noon and 4 P.M. with journalists, briefing them on major developments, and conducting question-and-answer sessions with them. Cortelyou drafted press releases, compiled "Current Comment," the daily scrapbooks of press clippings from hundreds of papers across the country, and handled public relations for the president's trips. McKinley expanded the White House clerical staff from six to eighty assistants. A reserved individual who did not seek the limelight, the president did not inspire especially good copy himself, and he shunned photographs. But he was far more accessible than his predecessors. The measures he pioneered made the White House the center for news in ways it had not been before.[16]

McKinley, Public Opinion, and the Cuban Crisis

The Cuban crisis of 1897–98 provided a stern test for McKinley's management of public opinion. Cuba's rebellion against Spanish rule dragged into its third year with no end in sight, vast destruction inflicted on the island and its people, and mounting concern in the United States. The bloody and stalemated civil war threatened substantial U.S. economic interests in Cuba. It became for Americans an object of humanitarian and emotional concern. Many sympathized with the Cuban rebellion, sometimes portraying it as an extension of their own. The sensationalist yellow press of William Randolph Hearst and Joseph Pulitzer, at this time engaged in a fierce circulation war, distorted news to their own ends, highlighted Spanish atrocities, and screamed for U.S. intervention. Such sentiments resounded in Congress, which called for the United States to recognize the Cuban rebels and even intervene to stop the war. Advocates of war noisily appealed to Americans' patriotic duty to end Spanish tyranny, eliminate an outpost of European imperialism from the Western Hemisphere, and secure freedom for the noble Cubans.

McKinley first publicly addressed the Cuban issue in his annual message of December 1897. Seeking to dampen popular and Congressional ardor for intervention without undermining support for a hard line against Spain, he counseled in deliberately ambiguous language a policy of watchful waiting. The president condemned as "extermination" Spanish general Valeriano Weyler's policy of herding Cubans into concentration camps. He categorically rejected annexation of Cuba—for years the object of U.S. expansionists—and also refused recognition of Cuban independence. While urging that negotiations be given a "reasonable chance," he insisted that the United States must have an outcome to its liking and hinted at intervention should negotiations fail. He assured the Congress that he would keep a close watch and bring about an "honorable and enduring" peace. His message appeared to have the desired effect at home. Editorial opinion, one of the most commonly used measures of public attitudes, strongly supported the president's cautious approach.[17]

A series of dramatic events in early 1898 threatened McKinley's measured response to the Cuban crisis. In late 1897, Spain had promised reforms leading toward Cuban autonomy, but colonial authorities in Cuba rejected Madrid's proposals, and in January pro-Spanish groups in Havana, backed by the army, rioted against giving Cubans greater control over their own affairs. On February 9, a letter from the Spanish minister in Washington, Dupuy de Lome, to friends in Cuba was leaked to the press. De Lome's unflattering comments about McKinley inflamed an already agitated American public. But what drew special attention in the White House were the minister's cynical comments suggesting that the Spanish government had never intended to abide by its commitments to the United States. Less than a week later, the battleship U.S.S. Maine, sent to Cuba to show the flag and protect U.S. interests, exploded and sank in Havana harbor, killing 260 officers and men.

The Maine provoked fervent popular outrage in the United States. Patriotic hysteria gripped the nation. "Remember the Maine, to Hell with Spain" became a popular rallying cry. Numerous images were cast to commemorate the sinking of the U.S. battleship. The sensationalist yellow press called for war. Demonstrations erupted in major cities and on college campuses. Theater audiences cheered, wept, and stamped their feet when the national anthem was played.[18] In the 1890s, sheet music was an important means of addressing popular issues. Within weeks of the sinking of the *Maine*, more than sixty song titles were published, eulogizing the noble sailors and calling for a unified nation to avenge this grievous affront to national honor and free Cuba from Spanish tyranny.[19]

McKinley handled this entirely new and explosive situation with the utmost care. He did not share the popular zeal for war. "I have been through one war," he told a visitor. "I have seen the dead piled up, and I do not want to see another."[20] In any event, he recognized that the nation was not prepared to fight even a second-rate power. Hence he sought to keep the war spirit alive without further inflaming it and to use it to pressure Spain into concessions that might yet avert conflict. He made clear to nervous legislators that he would not be stampeded. "I don't propose to be swept off my feet by the catastrophe," he emphatically informed one senator. The nation would not go to war until it was ready.[21] Characteristically, he let others take the lead. The secretary of the navy informed the press that the disaster was probably an accident. There was "no cause for alarm." The secretary of state urged friendly newspapers to highlight examples of antiwar sentiment in the nation. McKinley appointed a board of inquiry to determine the cause of the *Maine* explosion while administration spokespersons urged withholding judgment until its work was done. For the most part, the president pursued a strategy of silence, remaining in the background, fearing that anything he said might further agitate public opinion.[22] His one public speech was at the University of Pennsylvania on George Washington's birthday. Praising the first president's steady hand in times of crisis, he added an elliptical—but unmistakable—reference to the *Maine*: "Such judgment, my fellow citizens, is the best safeguard in the calm of tranquil events, and rises superior and triumphal above the storm of woe and peril."[23]

While continuing to negotiate with Spain, McKinley worked carefully behind the scenes to manage public opinion. To ensure that the press got reliable information, the administration released copies of cables from Havana. By expanding the amount of information available to journalists, it maintained some control over what the press reported. For the first time, the White House authorized regular releases of information and issued more frequent, written statements, making the job easier for Washington correspondents and enabling the administration to get to the public the information it wanted them to have. The administration made the press more dependent on it for information. It favored the wire services, which would reach a broad national audience by giving them information first and providing special interviews. It used the Washington press corps as an "instrument of indirect persuasion."[24]

The White House paid special attention to the work of the naval board of inquiry. It kept the board in the public eye by issuing periodic statements and by having cabinet members make statements. Following a cabinet meeting on March 1, for example, the secretary of the navy expressed doubt that Spain had been responsible for the explosion. While the board was deliberating, the president met regularly with members of Congress of both parties. The board's report was handled with especial care. By concluding that the *Maine* had been sunk by an external explosion it appeared to confirm Spanish responsibility, but it stopped well short of assigning blame. When the report leaked out despite elaborate secrecy, the administration quickly released it with its own spin, doing nothing to inflame the anger it would naturally incite but making clear that war could be prevented only if Spain effectively dealt with the issues that had caused the ship to be sent to Havana in the first place. McKinley stressed to Congress that "no evidence has been obtainable fixing the responsibility for the destruction of the *Maine* upon any person or persons." Pending Spain's response to U.S. representations, "deliberate consideration is invoked."[25]

To get ready for a war that seemed increasingly likely, the president in early March asked Congress for $50 million for national defense and urged its appropriation without debate to avoid giving the warmongers a platform. His purpose was not to agitate the public but rather to indicate that essential precautionary steps were being taken and to further pressure Spain. McKinley and his advisors could not have been reassured to hear that in response to the message "a hundred Fourth of July's had been let loose in the House [of Representatives]."[26]

At least in terms of managing public opinion, McKinley's subtle measures for the short term achieved their desired purpose. The yellow press continued to scream for war, but the administration publicly paid little attention. Top officials privately joked about this "product of degenerate minds." McKinley claimed not to read the sensationalist newspapers. Clippings in the bulging "Current Comment" scrapbooks indicated broad support for his firm but restrained diplomacy. Ninety percent of the letters to the White House, Cortelyou estimated, approved war only as a "necessity and for the upholding of national honor." Whitelaw Reid of the *New York Tribune* toured the nation at the president's behest and reported that the "more intelligent classes" endorsed his policies. Religious leaders and members of Congress similarly confided that "a quiet but influential class" agreed that war should be a last resort.[27]

But public relations could not solve the president's basic problem. Despite increased U.S. pressure, Spain offered no more than token concessions, rejecting the president's essential if vaguely worded insistence upon independence for Cuba. By early April, clamor for war was mounting. U.S. business leaders, many of whom had opposed war, increasingly endorsed it as a means to eliminate the uncertainty they believed was holding back economic recovery. Members of Congress introduced resolutions authorizing McKinley to compel Spain to comply with U.S. demands and demanding recognition of Cuban independence. "By ___ ! Don't your president know where the war-making power is lodged?" one agitated senator roared upon bursting into the assistant secretary of state's office. "Well tell him, by ____! That if he doesn't do something Congress will exercise the power and declare war in spite of him!"[28] Nervous White House aides and party leaders steeled themselves for a veto and counted votes to make sure that Congress could not override it.

Never enthusiastic for war, McKinley increasingly concluded that it was inevitable. He was close to giving in on April 6, but he used the glimmer of hope provided by a new cable from Havana to delay once again, on this occasion insisting that more time was needed to get U.S. citizens out of Cuba. In a rare display of anger, he hotly informed a delegation of legislators that he would not go to Congress as long as there was a "single American life in danger in Cuba."[29] When he finally acquiesced on April 11, he sent to Congress a curious and notably ambiguous message seeking an extraordinary grant of power. He did not request a declaration of war. Rather, he asked Congress to empower him to end the war in Cuba, establish a stable government there, and employ U.S. military forces to attain those ends. "Even at this moment of greatest crisis for his administration," Lewis Gould has written, "McKinley was broadening the scope of presidential power."[30] Although war hawks were furious, the message generated broad support. After days of heated debate and frantic parliamentary maneuvering, Congress on April 19 gave McKinley the authority he sought while attaching the Teller Amendment, which he opposed, disavowing any U.S. intention to annex Cuba. When the president signed the resolution, Spain broke diplomatic relations. The United States in turn imposed a blockade of Cuba, Spain declared war, and on April 25, McKinley asked Congress to declare that a state of war existed. It was not a simple case of an excited public and a nervous Congress pushing a reluctant president into an unwanted war, as is often alleged. McKinley had done an exceptional job of parrying public pressures for weeks. Rather, his inability to extract essential concessions from Spain, combined with rising public and congressional pressures, left him no choice but war.[31]

The Splendid Little War

It was not necessary to "sell" the war with Spain. Many Americans bought into this war, often with great enthusiasm and long before the president did. The war became a rallying point for a nation suffering from the birth pangs of modernization. It helped seal the reunification of North and South. The nation excitedly set out to free Cuba from Spanish tyranny. Huge numbers of young—and old—men eagerly volunteered for military service—indeed, far more than could be absorbed by an antiquated military bureaucracy. Prominent citizens offered cash, services, and their property to the cause; for example, Helen Gould provided $100,000 and her yacht. The war represented a last gasp of nineteenth-century voluntarism and military amateurism in the face of a military establishment just beginning to professionalize. "Patriotism was not merely aroused," one soldier recalled, "it was in conflagration."[32]

The McKinley administration's central wartime task was to sustain the strong public support that already existed. From the outset, the president took firm control of the war, using modern technology to exert direct personal authority over its various components. He created a War Room on the second floor of the White House complete with maps to chart the movement of ships and troops and the course of military operations. He installed fifteen telephone lines to connect him to the various departments of government and Congress, and twenty telegraph lines to link him to military forces in Cuba, the Caribbean, and later the Pacific.[33] The president was alert to the public relations aspects of the war. He sought to identify himself with and exploit Admiral George Dewey's crushing of the Spanish fleet at Manila Bay on May 1 by issuing a formal proclamation of victory in a special message to Congress. He publicly ordered Gen. Nelson A. Miles to take Havana, making clear his role as commander in chief and his determination to wage the war decisively.[34]

The administration used various means to influence the reporting of the war. Porter continued to brief the journalists daily, and the White House issued periodic press releases. The correspondents' work space was moved closer to the president's office, making it easier to get news releases to them and also giving officials greater control over the information they received by making sure it came from official sources and not from conversations with visitors.[35] The government took firm action to prevent leaks in Washington. Secretary of the Navy John D. Long forbade naval personnel to converse with the press on any official subject. The information the department wanted the newspapers to receive—generally innocuous—was posted on bulletin boards in Navy headquarters. The War Department followed similar procedures and also declared all its records "strictly confidential" and to be discussed with no one.[36] By limiting the news available elsewhere, the White House heightened its control over war information and increased the importance of the news it dispensed.

To meet urgent military needs—and better manage public opinion— the administration also imposed censorship. Such action was essential, of course, to keep from the enemy vital information about naval operations and troop movements. The journalists of this era were reckless adventurers, notorious for their feats of derring-do. As the yellow press had demonstrated, they could also be irresponsible, manufacturing news where none existed, exaggerating and distorting the facts. Having played a role in the onset of war, the newspapers naturally lusted to report it. Some 200 to 300 journalists were assigned to cover the action. The major newspapers maintained a "fleet" of boats as large in numbers as the squadron the U.S. Navy sent to Cuba. It was necessary under these circumstances to restrict vital information. Censorship, of course, also had the advantage of helping to conceal government screw-ups.

Even before the war began, the government seized the telegraph offices at Key West, Florida, a major staging area for naval operations in the Caribbean. Authorities subsequently instituted censorship at Tampa, a point of debarkation for military operations, and in New York City. They also threatened reporters with loss of their credentials if they broke the rules, producing a form of indirect censorship in which journalists held back or sugar-coated stories for fear of reprisals. The institution of censorship plus the very limited number of cables and the large number of reporters undoubtedly made it difficult for journalists to do their work. The Associated Press generally endorsed the system on grounds that it was necessary to "sustain the general government in the conduct of the war" by avoiding the publication of "any information likely to give aid to the enemy or to embarrass the government." But many correspondents and newspapers loudly protested.

The *New York Herald* called that city's censor the "autocrat of all the great news of the world . . . the censor of censors."[37] Journalistic protests aside, the system helped safeguard ship and troop movements. It also enabled the administration to control the flow of information, permitting it to highlight victories in the Philippines, for example, while playing down mobilization snarls that delayed the beginning of military operations in Cuba.

As applied in the War of 1898, however, the government's censorship was far from crippling. Enterprising correspondents found ways to get around it. Once U.S. troops were in Cuba, for example, they evaded censorship at Santiago by using cables on Jamaica and Haiti. Censorship did not prevent and may indeed have encouraged the continued fabrication of stories. The tight control of information regarding the departure of U.S. forces from Tampa for the invasion of Cuba, for example, did not stop the *New York Journal* from reporting inaccurate numbers of troops, landings that did not take place, and battles that never occurred. As Thomas C. Leonard has observed, moreover, much of the news Americans received about the war came from local correspondents writing for local audiences. Many state units mobilized for war were accompanied by journalists from state newspapers. Smaller local newspapers enlisted soldiers to send them stories and reported information gleaned from letters home. Such letters were not subjected to censorship, and although soldiers were not supposed to write for publication, the rule was not enforced. Readers of state and local newspapers thus got full accounts of military mismanagement, racial tensions, desertions and drunken sprees, and the horrors of battle. "Never in the twentieth century," Leonard concludes, "would the press be so free of the military spokesperson, the photo opportunity, the press release, and the controlled interview with troops. Plain talk from citizens who saw war up close reached the American people."[38]

McKinley did not launch any sort of public relations campaign to boost popular support for the war. There was no tradition for such activities, and in any event they seemed unnecessary. Remarkably, during the entire 100 days, he made only one major statement, that on July 6, a brief "Address to the People for Thanksgiving and Prayer," hailing naval victories at Manila Bay and Santiago, Cuba, and the army's taking of Santiago. The address included a typically florid nineteenth-century proclamation of thanksgiving to "Almighty God, who in his inscrutable ways . . . has watched over our cause and brought nearer the success of the right and the attainment of a just and honorable peace." The president contented himself with recommending war heroes for medals and expressing thanks to the generals and admirals for their victories.[39]

U.S. management of the ground war was near scandalous. Since the 1880s, Congress had given the Navy attention and funds. It was ready for battle and acquitted itself splendidly in victories over decrepit Spanish fleets in the Philippines and Cuba. Mobilization of land forces was another story entirely. The army had been left to languish since the Civil War. A sclerotic military bureaucracy could not begin to handle the flood of volunteers and recruits that rushed to arms. The army lacked uniforms and equipment. Training was haphazard at best. Mobilization at Tampa, the major port of debarkation, brought nightmarish tangles.

Had the war not ended so quickly and decisively, McKinley could have faced major problems with domestic support. The public mood shifted from exhilaration at the prospect of war to frustration at the delays and foul-ups and eventually anger at the government's manifest ineptitude. Major problems also developed in Cuba after the troops had landed, especially the horrendous scourge of disease that took far more lives than Spanish bullets. In early August, Col. Theodore Roosevelt and other soldiers signed a round robin letter published in the press pointing to the problems and demanding that the troops be brought home.[40] McKinley escaped serious problems mainly through timely victories and the early end of the war. Congress was away from Washington for the summer, sparing him the inevitable carping that would have accompanied its presence. Dewey's brilliant victory at Manila in early May evoked huge celebrations across the nation. As frustration and anxiety began to develop, Sampson's July 3 victory at Santiago brought relief and more celebrations. Spain agreed to an armistice on August 12, just as complaints surfaced about the condition of troops in Cuba. Only belatedly did the public learn the full story of the bungling that could have brought disaster and the horrific conditions in Cuba. These problems led to a national scandal eventually placed at the door of Secretary of War Russell Alger.[41]

Selling the New Empire

The greatest challenge for McKinley was to secure public support for the results of the war with Spain: acquisition of the new empire. By virtue of the Teller Amendment, of course, Cuba was to get its freedom. This happened in 1901, although the island's "independence" was tightly circumscribed by the Platt Amendment. The administration made Puerto Rico into an un-incorporated dependency without much fanfare or public discussion. The most contentious issue was the Philippines, which, beyond talk about a possible naval base, had seldom been included on lists of possible acquisitions by advocates of colonies. Exactly when the president decided to take the islands remains unclear, probably sometime in the summer of 1898. Keeping his mouth shut and his options open, he moved stealthily toward annexation. Shortly after Dewey's victory, he sent troops to the Philippines to take possession for the United States. He insisted that the islands be included in discussions regarding the armistice, despite strong protests from Spain and Filipinos seeking independence. He refused to submit to his cabinet a proposal that the United States take only a naval base for fear, he told an advisor, it might carry.[42] He stacked the peace commission with expansionists and insisted that disposition of the Philippines be left in their hands. While taking these tangible steps to prepare the ground for annexation, he remained publicly silent, not risking any misstep that might provoke opposition or set off a premature debate.

McKinley mounted a public campaign for retention in October 1898. Often depicted as that time when the public persuaded the president to annex the Philippines, his fall speaking tour of the Midwest was in fact designed to solidify public backing for a goal he had already committed himself to. In typically hidden-hand fashion, he used the trip to make it appear that the public had sold him on what he was trying to convince them to support. During the so-called "front-porch campaign" of 1896, McKinley had scarcely left his Canton, Ohio, home. It was also unusual in these years for a president to intervene in off-year congressional elections. The 1898 tour was thus extraordinary in terms of tradition and McKinley's modus operandi, making clear the importance he attached to it. The itinerary perfectly suited his purposes. In contrast to the South and Northeast, where he might have encountered strong opposition, the Midwest was friendly territory. Those states had overwhelmingly voted for him in 1896 and could be expected to receive him warmly. The speaking tour was designed to shore up support for Republican candidates in the upcoming congressional elections, strengthen the hands of the commissioners negotiating with Spain in Paris, and build popular backing for annexation of the Philippines.[43]

Administration officials orchestrated the trip with great care. Major speeches were scheduled for public expositions in Omaha and Chicago, guaranteeing large crowds, but the White House also arranged for a special train that would permit whistle stop speeches several times a day at various points between Ohio and the Dakotas—in all McKinley spoke fifty-six times in ten days. The president's aides took great pains with the details of the trip, especially its public relations aspects. Reporters were invited aboard the train and given advance copies of the speeches. At each stop, a stenographer recorded McKinley's words and passed the transcript on to reporters. The speeches were also disseminated to the wire services and major newspapers, indicating the national importance given a regional tour. A person was assigned to "measure" and record the response of the audience to presidential statements. As a wartime commander in chief, McKinley had significantly expanded presidential power. He reveled in his new role. His postwar public appearances were managed with considerable fanfare, and he was treated with almost regal deference. "Th'proceedin's was opened with a prayer that Providence might r-remain under th' protection iv th' administration," humorist Finley Peter Dunne's fictional character Mr. Dooley quipped after one such occasion.[44]

In tone and theme, the tour was vintage McKinley. Taken together, the speeches formed a paean to American exceptionalism. The president told his audiences exactly what they wanted to hear, and they responded with near adoration. He hailed the return of prosperity, the patriotism displayed in the recent war, and the heroic feats of U.S. sailors and soldiers. In virtually every speech, he emphasized that the unity manifested in war must carry over to the making of peace. Reflecting the president's caution, he neither mentioned the Philippines nor advocated the acquisition of additional territory. His early statements obscured where he stood on the issue. In Iowa, he seemed to equivocate, insisting that the United States must "preserve carefully" its "cherished institutions," but proceeding to affirm that "we do not want to shirk a single responsibility that has been put on us by the results of the war."[45] In Omaha on October 12, he inched closer to a commitment. He spoke of America's "manifest destiny," a term historically identified with expansion. He insisted that although the United States had not sought war with Spain, it could not avoid the obligations deriving from that war. Typically, he asked the audience to tell him what he had already decided to do. "Shall we deny to ourselves what the rest of the world so fully and justly accords us?" he would ask, and the crowd would respond emphatically, "No."[46]

Returning east from Omaha, McKinley repeatedly played on the themes of duty, destiny, and the nation's responsibility in carrying out its new world role by bringing to less fortunate peoples the blessings of Anglo-Saxon civilization. "Territory sometimes comes to us when we go to war in a holy cause," he stated, "and whenever it does the banner of liberty will float over it and bring, I trust, blessings and benefits to all the people."[47] In Abraham Lincoln's Springfield, Illinois, he affirmed that "having gone to war for humanity's sake, we must accept no settlement that will not take into account the interests of humanity." "My countrymen, the currents of destiny flow through the hearts of the people," he added in Chicago. "Who will check them, then; who will direct them, who will stop them?" In Columbus, Ohio, where he had served as governor, the last major stop on his itinerary, he elaborated the same theme. Pointedly noting that he did not know what future territory the United States might include, he closed by proclaiming to exuberant cheers and applause that "we must take up and perform and as free, strong, brave people accept the trust which civilization puts upon us."[48]

Although it is impossible to measure precisely, the tour appears to have achieved what McKinley sought. Dewey's smashing victory had sparked popular interest in islands many Americans could not have located on a map. Some citizens found exhilarating the idea of their country's flag flying on faraway lands. Businessmen were enticed by the prospect of markets, missionaries by new souls to save. According to one survey, roughly 40 percent of the nation's newspapers endorsed expansion; 25 percent opposed. Leading Republicans voiced strong support.[49] The speaking tour appeared to solidify such backing and check possible Republican losses in the election. The stenographer recorded at various stops the enthusiastic responses to McKinley's perorations: "strong applause," "great applause," "prolonged applause," and "applause and cheers."[50] The "continuous ovation" the president received on the return trip from Omaha cheered the party faithful and muted criticism of mismanagement of the war.[51] Secretary of State John Hay informed the president that his tour had been "splendidly successful." The "Current Comment" scrapbooks and White House mail confirmed that appraisal. McKinley sought to use these results to influence the commissioners in Paris, advising them that the "well-considered opinion of the majority would be that duty requires we should take all the archipelago."[52] The election results were not unequivocal—the Republicans lost nineteen seats in the House. But they still held a majority of twenty-two. More important, although they expected losses in the Senate, which would have to approve the treaty, they actually added six seats. "You have pulled us through with your strength," Hay flattered the president.[53]

Signing of the Treaty of Paris on December 10, providing for U.S. annexation of the Philippines, opened the next stage in the great debate. The administration's hand would have been stronger had McKinley chosen to wait until a new Congress convened in December 1899. But he refused to delay. Rather, he plunged ahead in what was certain to be a tough battle. Democratic senator George Vest of Missouri had already introduced a resolution holding acquisition of the islands unconstitutional. Opposition to annexation was likely to grow once the issue was out in the open and the Senate faced ratification.

Striking the first blow, McKinley launched his southern swing in mid-December. He had no reason to expect there the sort of welcome he had received in the Midwest. That region was solidly Democratic; the wounds of the Civil War were not entirely healed. Many southern leaders adamantly opposed overseas expansion. Some claimed the islands would be a strategic liability; others argued that by intervening in that remote area, thus violating its own Monroe Doctrine, the United States would invite European intrusion in the Western Hemisphere. Still edgy from Reconstruction, southerners warned that the dangerous expansion of executive power inherent in overseas expansion might be turned against them. They insisted that imperialism and republicanism were not compatible. They worried about economic competition. But the major issue was race. Virginia senator John W. Daniel claimed that the Philippines was inhabited by a "mess of Asian pottage" and hence unsuitable for the Union. Others warned that the admission of more people unfit to govern themselves would threaten the nation's traditional values.[54]

McKinley's venture into potentially hostile territory succeeded smashingly. The main stop was in Atlanta, where he attended a gigantic Peace Jubilee. But as in the Midwest, side trips were arranged to ten other cities and towns in three former Confederate states. As with the midwestern tour, the southern trek was skillfully handled. McKinley went to great lengths to seal the sectional reconciliation promoted by the war with Spain. He repeatedly celebrated the glory of reunion. With the treaty now signed, he abandoned the subtlety of the midwestern tour to openly advocate acquisition of the Philippines on grounds of destiny and moral obligation.[55] As before, he used questions to prompt the answers he sought. Hailing the U.S. flag now flying over two hemispheres as the "symbol of liberty and law, of peace and progress," he asked his listeners, "Who will withdraw it from the people over whom it floats in protective folds? Who will haul it down? Answer me ye men of the South, who is there in Dixie who will haul it down?"—a statement that set off "tremendous applause." The United States was duty bound, he insisted, to help those people it had liberated. Having destroyed their government, it must give them a "better one." "Should we proclaim to the world our inability to give kind government to oppressed peoples?" he queried, and his listeners shouted "No." "Shall we now, when the victory won in war is written in the treaty of peace, and the civilized world applauds and waits in expectation, turn timidly away from the duties imposed upon the country by its own great deeds?"[56] Southerners, like midwesterners, applauded and cheered. As Woodrow Wilson would learn, popular acclaim did not necessarily translate into Senate votes. A tough fight lay ahead. But the wildly enthusiastic response in the South boosted McKinley's spirits and provided an edge as the debate over empire began.[57]

The administration pulled out all the stops in the treaty fight. McKinley personally directed the campaign for ratification, much as he had run the war. He had appointed senators and Democrats to the peace commission, a shrewd move that helped ensure approval of its handiwork. The White House urged state legislatures to endorse the treaty, thereby putting pressure on senators that helped sway at least one key vote. Administration supporters urged approval on the pragmatic grounds that it was necessary to end the war. They also emphasized that rejection would embarrass the president and the nation before the world. Republican senator George Hoar of Maine, a major opponent of the treaty, claimed that the administration was "moving Heaven and earth, to say nothing of other places, to detach individual Senators from the opposition." Still two votes short of two-thirds in early February 1899, with hours to go before the vote, the president won over two senators, one with assurances of patronage in his home state, the other with promises to endorse his resolution stating that the United States would not annex the Philippines as part of the United States. The treaty received one vote more than needed. "There are few better examples, before the time of Franklin D. Roosevelt, of the exercise of presidential power in foreign affairs than McKinley's successful effort to obtain Senate approval for the Peace of Paris," Lewis Gould has concluded.[58]

The president also benefited from some extraordinary good fortune. Perhaps influenced by the triumphal southern tour, the titular head of the opposition party and leading foe of imperialism, William Jennings Bryan, urged Democratic senators to vote for a treaty he did not like in order to end the war. His party must not put itself in the position of obstructing peace. With curious logic and singular lack of foresight, Bryan also insisted that the Philippines could be dealt with later: the election of 1900 could be a referendum on imperialism. Bryan's politically naive stance may not have decided any votes, but it further divided an already fragmented opposition during the heat of the debate. Ironically, by exchanging fire with U.S. troops on February 4, two days before the Senate voted, those Filipinos who opposed American rule may also have contributed to the vote that doomed the last fleeting chance of their independence. What McKinley called "the unexpected" created a crisis atmosphere that may have led some senators to rally around the president. "How foolish these people are," the president privately exulted. "This means the ratification of the treaty; the people will understand now, the people will insist upon its ratification."[59]

The Philippine-American War

What seemed a boon in early February 1899 would become a lingering burden. The incident near Manila sparked a brutal war that would last for more than three years, take thousands of American and many more Filipino lives, and provoke bitter anti-imperialist opposition at home. In seeking to consolidate control over the new empire and defend it against domestic critics, McKinley and his successor, Theodore Roosevelt, became more imperial, branding their Filipino foes as little better than ungrateful savages, accusing their domestic critics of treason, defending censorship, and soft-pedaling charges of atrocities.

The outbreak of war in the Philippines spurred growing anti-imperialist agitation in the United States. Opposition had developed late in the war against Spain and increased sharply with McKinley's decision to acquire the Philippines, resulting in November 1898 in formation of the Anti-Imperialist League. Claiming a nationwide membership of 30,000, the League was centered in the Northeast, but it was active in other regions and had national headquarters in Chicago. It included such luminaries as inventor, businessman, and professional agitator Edward Atkinson, industrialist Andrew Carnegie, author Mark Twain, and soldier, diplomat, and journalist Carl Schurz. An uneasy collection of dissident Republicans and Bryan Democrats, the anti-imperialists saw the Philippine war as fulfillment of their predictions of the evils of imperialism. They shared their foes' convictions about Anglo-Saxon superiority, but believed, as Moorefield Storey put it, that annexation of regions "unfit to govern themselves would govern us." Imperialist policies would require a large standing army and navy, violate the Constitution, destroy American democracy, undermine the nation's "unique position as a leader in the progress of civilization," and reduce it to just another of those "grasping and selfish nations of the present day."[60] As the war in the Philippines heated up, the anti-imperialists charged the

United States with "laying waste the country with fire and sword, burning villages and slaughtering the inhabitants because they will not submit to our rule."[61] Twain warned of a "quagmire from which each fresh step renders the difficulty of extraction immensely greater."[62]

Alarmed by the growing dissent, McKinley vigorously defended his policies. At first, he countered his critics by emphasizing the unreadiness of Filipinos for independence and the good the United States was doing in the islands. In February 1899, shortly after ratification of the Treaty of Paris, he ventured to Boston, the center of anti-imperialist agitation, where he spoke to nearly 4,000 people in Mechanics Hall. Standing beneath huge portraits of Washington, Lincoln, and himself, festooned with red, white, and blue bunting and captioned "Liberators," he abandoned the Socratic approach, offering a full justification of his policies in a speech devoted exclusively to the Philippines. The islands had been entrusted to America by providence, he averred, a trust from which "we will not flinch." The United States must annex them to fulfill this obligation. It could not leave their people in anarchy. Those people in turn must understand that "their welfare is our welfare, but that neither their aspirations nor ours can be realized until our authority is acknowledged and unquestioned." It was no time for the "liberator to submit important questions concerning liberty and self-government to the liberated while they are engaged in shooting down the rescuers." He admitted that the shedding of every drop of Filipino or American blood brought "anguish" to his heart, but vowed that under U.S. direction the Philippines would become a "land of plenty and possibilities." Future generations of Filipinos would "bless the American republic because it had emancipated their fatherland, and set them in the pathway of the world's best civilization." Later, during a swing through the northern states, he reiterated these themes, damning the insurgents for resisting U.S. benevolence at the cost of their own peoples' lives. The rebellion might delay but it would not thwart America's "blessed mission of liberty and humanity."[63]

As the war continued and opposition at home grew, McKinley's response grew sharper, evoking rhetoric that sounds eerily familiar today. Speaking in Pittsburgh in August 1899 in celebration of the return of the Tenth Pennsylvania Regiment from the Philippines, he praised the troops for remaining until replacements had arrived. They "did not stack their arms. They did not run away. They were not serving the insurgents in the Philippines or their sympathizers at home." He denounced the leaders of the rebellion and their pitiable followers and defended U.S. refusal to engage in "useless parley." He dismissed the anti-imperialists as "few in numbers" and "unpatriotic."[64]

In New York, he condemned the rebels as ungrateful savages who reciprocated U.S. "kindness" with a Mauser and their "cruel leaders" who "sacrificed their own people" for the gratification of their own "ambitious designs." In a fall 1899 western tour extending from Illinois into North and South Dakota and back to Ohio, this gentle and usually genial man increasingly wrapped himself in the flag. Over twelve days, he gave more than seventy-five speeches, many of them before groups of soldiers, most of them offering a spirited defense of the war to wildly enthusiastic audiences. He reveled in and played on the intense patriotism of that era and linked it to overseas expansion. The United States had not sought additional territory, he repeated over and over. It had been "put in our lap" as the result of a providential victory in war. To pick up and leave would mean turmoil and civil war. The nation must fulfill its God-given duty by bringing civilization to peoples who were not ready for self-government. McKinley downplayed the insurrection as "some trouble in the Philippines." He dismissed the rebels as few in number, mainly from one tribe, and led by men pursuing their own selfish ambitions. He would not trade peace for independence, as the rebels proposed. The insurgency would be "put down and the authority of the United States will be made supreme." He praised U.S. troops for their restraint in the face of provocation and danger. He dismissed the anti-imperialists as "orators without occupation." Speaking in Minnesota, territory acquired through the Louisiana Purchase, he reminded his listeners that short-sighted Americans had also opposed that windfall and had been proven wrong many times over. He compared his domestic foes to Civil War Copperheads, whose dissent encouraged the enemy to fight on and thereby cost American lives. Above all, he insisted on the nobility of the nation's mission. "Wherever we have raised our flag, we have raised it not for conquest . . . not for national gain, but for civilization and humanity. And let those lower it who will!" he would conclude to resounding cheers. To some extent his attacks were partisan and aimed at Democrats in the year before a presidential election. But his larger purpose was to whip up popular support for the Philippine War in the face of domestic opposition he feared might bring pressures for U.S. withdrawal.[65]

While seeking to fend off the anti-imperialists, the administration also grappled with problems of censorship. Following Carl Schurz's appeal to "press on without ceasing," gadfly Edward Atkinson set out to prove how the imposition of rule on other peoples threatened basic freedoms at home. He sought from the government addresses of 500–600 U.S. soldiers in the Philippines to mail them pamphlets whose titles—"The Hell of War and Its

Penalties," "The Cost of a National Crime"—left no mistake about their tone and intent. When ignored by the War Department, he mailed the materials to U.S. military officials in the Philippines. Angered by what they considered sedition, some officials urged prosecuting Atkinson. The postmaster general ordered authorities in San Francisco to seize the materials from the Manila mail pouches. Delighting in his notoriety, Atkinson vigorously protested the government's suppression of free speech. The affair generated great publicity, leading to the distribution of an additional 130,000 pamphlets. Content with what he had accomplished, Atkinson did nothing more. To avoid further problems, the government did not prosecute him, apparently agreeing with a Boston newspaper that the septuagenarian was "too old for punishment and not young enough for reformation."[66]

A potentially much more difficult issue arose in the summer of 1899 when war correspondents issued a round robin letter protesting censorship in the Philippines. The problem resulted partly from the inherent tension between press and military in time of war and also from the way the American commander, Gen. Ewell Otis, conducted his business. A good officer but cautious by nature and blithely ignorant of the people he was fighting, Otis tightly controlled the one cable out of Manila. While he issued platitudinous statements that all was well and that no more troops were needed, journalists got a very different story from junior officers in the field. The round robin accused Otis of suppressing critical information not from military necessity but for fear of undermining support at home. It charged him with holding back casualty reports and branded his rosy statements lies. The protest naturally gained attention in the United States and provoked heated attacks on U.S. policies. Although censorship was applied by the military in Manila, the administration itself came under fire. The issue brought together newspapers of different political persuasions, threatening to arouse further opposition to the war and undercut McKinley's massaging of the press.[67]

The president handled this possibly damaging issue with great care. Refusing to abandon or even modify military censorship and leaving responsibility firmly in Otis's hands, he gently admonished the general that "all consideration within limits of good of the service should be shown."[68] By making clear that Otis was responsible, he removed himself from the picture. By soon after easing out Secretary of War Alger, McKinley appeared to lay some of the responsibility at his door and to address the issue by relieving him. The problem of censorship never came up again, in part because military conditions in the Philippines gradually improved and also because Otis's successors handled the correspondents somewhat more adeptly.[69]

Remarkably, given the controversy of 1899, the Philippine war was not a major issue in the 1900 presidential campaign. Improvement in the military situation and the first steps toward establishing a civilian government narrowed the opposition's target. True to his 1899 position, Democratic nominee Bryan sought to make imperialism the "paramount" issue. Again, however, he played into McKinley's hands, this time by calling for the establishment of a stable government in the Philippines (how it was to be achieved he did not say), then for granting independence with promises of U.S. "protection from outside interference."[70] In accepting the Republican nomination, McKinley dismissed as "scuttle" policies Bryan's call for what amounted to a protectorate and Senator Hoar's proposal for a pledge of eventual independence. The choice was between "duty and desertion," he affirmed in his acceptance letter to the Republican national convention. "We must be supreme and our supremacy must be acknowledged."[71]

In the first stages of the campaign, Bryan and the Democrats continued to attack U.S. imperialism, but they hesitated to criticize the war for fear of being labeled Copperheads. Believing it improper for an incumbent president to campaign for his own reelection, McKinley returned home to Canton, conducting the nation's business by telephone. War hero and vice presidential nominee Theodore Roosevelt campaigned in his customary, frenetic style, hailing the return of prosperity but also dismissing the Filipino insurgents as "Chinese half-breeds" and the anti-imperialists as their dupes, and defending with characteristic hyperbole "the most righteous foreign war that has been waged within the memory of the present generation." In the crucial last month before the election, Bryan all but dropped the issue, shifting to the domestic reform that was closest to his heart. Ultimately, prosperity trumped lingering concerns about a distant war that touched few Americans directly. The Republicans had the advantage of numbers and money; Democrats had the burden of Bryan's fixation on free silver. McKinley won a solid victory, if not exactly a landslide, increasing his popular and electoral margin from 1896. He made only brief mention of the Philippines in his December 1899 annual message to Congress and in his March 1900 inaugural address, and he said nothing in the September 1901 speech in Buffalo immediately preceding his assassination.[72]

The last gasp of the anti-imperialists and public controversy over the Philippine War came with a brief summer 1902 uproar over charges of atroc-

ities committed by U.S. soldiers against insurgents and the civilian population. The U.S. command did not, with several notable exceptions, authorize
or condone atrocities, although some orders gave the soldiers enormous
latitude. Officers and men tended to excuse those that occurred by blaming the harsh climate, the peculiarly brutal nature of jungle warfare, and
the savagery of an uncivilized enemy. Atrocities occurred from the beginning of the war and increased dramatically after the insurgents shifted to
guerrilla warfare. Under Gen. Arthur MacArthur and his successors, the
United States took the war to the enemy in often brutal style. MacArthur
implemented in some areas a concentration policy not unlike those which
Weyler had used in Cuba. Americans burned villages suspected of harbor-
ing insurgents, sometimes with civilians in the houses. The command denied prisoner of war status to captured guerrillas. U.S. troops used torture,
including, of course, the infamous water cure, to extract information from
captives. The longer the war went on, the more ferocious it became. In late
1901 mopping up campaigns in Batangas province and especially on Samar,
Americans employed particularly brutal methods to wipe out resistance.
Gen. Jacob "Hell Roaring" Smith allegedly ordered his troops to turn Samar
into a "howling wilderness." Reports of these campaigns drew attention from
anti-imperialists and were picked up by the press. In January 1902, Senator
Hoar demanded that Congress investigate the conduct of the war.[73]

By this time, McKinley had fallen to an assassin's bullet, and Roosevelt
treated the revelations of atrocities as a public relations issue rather than a
moral failing that demanded attention. TR had no use for the anti-imperialists. He dismissed Democratic criticism as partisan. He believed harsh
measures were essential to deal with "savages." He excused, if he did not
openly endorse, the methods used. His administration mounted a full-scale
counteroffensive to defuse the charges. Lodge chaired the Senate investigation and conducted it in a way to minimize political fallout. Even then, it
exposed major examples of military misconduct. Secretary of War Elihu
Root converted an internal War Department investigation into a whitewash.
The administration insisted that any misdeeds that had occurred were cases
of individual wrongdoing. Smith and several other handy scapegoats were
prosecuted. Publicly, the president minimized the atrocities: "few indeed
have been the instances in which war has been waged by a civilized power
against semi-civilized or barbarous forces where there has been so little
wrong doing by the victors as in the Philippine Islands."[74] In a ringing Memorial Day speech at Arlington Cemetery, while claiming that he was not
defending wrongdoers, he insisted that "every guilty act committed by one

of our troops" was matched by a "hundred acts of far greater atrocity by the enemy." Those "walking delicately" in the "soft places of the earth" had no right to criticize. Taking a potshot at his Democratic foes, he charged that the lynching of African Americans in the southern United States was far worse for victim and perpetrator than atrocities committed by U.S. soldiers in the Philippines.[75]

The administration's public relations blitz stilled the outcry. To be sure, some intellectuals and diehard anti-imperialists continued to protest, but they were faint voices in a very large wilderness. The government seems to have persuaded the nation that the instances of misconduct were few and isolated and had been effectively addressed. Interest groups such as business, labor, and the clergy did not latch on to the issue. The majority of Americans, strongly patriotic, believed their country was a force for good and was carrying out a noble mission against difficult obstacles. They thrilled to the heroic exploits of U.S. soldiers and the dramatic capture of rebel leader Emilio Aguinaldo and ignored charges of misbehavior. The press's interest in the issue proved fleeting. Fortunately for the government, the news of atrocities came late in the war. Roosevelt's July 4, 1902, announcement that the Philippines Insurrection was officially over, although premature by several years and countless lives, silenced further criticism and removed the issue from the political agenda. The conflict receded from the nation's collective memory, remaining its forgotten war until Vietnam in the 1960s evoked renewed interest and historical parallels.[76]

In leading the United States into a new century and more active involvement in the world, William McKinley initiated the process of educating Americans to the role of a great power. The United States did not go on to acquire additional colonies. While McKinley had repeatedly and earnestly proclaimed that the burden of empire provided the nation with an opportunity to do good in the world, many Americans, including some ardent expansionists such as Theodore Roosevelt, came to see the costs of formal empire as greater than the benefits. Under Roosevelt, however, the United States by other means established hegemony in the Western Hemisphere. As the century progressed, it employed its power on a much broader scale and intervened forcibly in many areas around the world in ways that would have been unthinkable in the nineteenth century.

Such a new world role required new techniques to gain and maintain public support, and McKinley also pioneered in this regard. As president, he quickly grasped the growing importance of public opinion, and he and his advisors developed new means to assess and sway it. Certain that the press was crucial to understanding—and influencing—what the public thought, the McKinley administration lavished attention on journalists and devised new methods to control not only what they reported but also how they wrote. Most important, the press came to rely on the White House for information in ways it had not in the past. During the War of 1898, McKinley faced the unusual situation of sustaining public support for a wildly popular war. His experience suggests the ephemeral nature of such support, and he could have faced serious problems had the war persisted much longer. In selling the fruits of war, McKinley assumed a much more proactive role. His speaking tours were quite without precedent. Other presidents had made the so-called swing around the circle, but he covered much more ground and used the carefully staged speaking appearances as imperial tutorials. In defending the Philippine War, his rhetoric as well as his actions set new standards. By dehumanizing his enemies and equating dissent at home with lack of patriotism, he established unfortunate precedents that would be employed time and again by his successors to defend dubious ventures. Crude as they may seem, McKinley's assessment of the importance of public opinion and the means he developed for selling war and empire pointed toward the more clever and carefully orchestrated campaigns of the American Century.

Notes

1. December 17, 1898, *Speeches and Addresses of William McKinley from March 1, 1897 to May 30, 1900* (New York: Doubleday & McClure, 1900), 174.

2. The term "imperial tutor" is from Lewis L. Gould, *The Presidency of William McKinley* (Lawrence: University Press of Kansas, 1980), 121.

3. Ernest R. May, *American Imperialism: A Speculative Essay* (New York: Atheneum, 1968), 17–42.

4. Ibid., 45–94.

5. Albert Castel, *The Presidency of Andrew Johnson* (Lawrence: Regents Press of Kansas, 1979), 205.

6. Edward P. Crapol, *James G. Blaine: Architect of Empire* (Wilmington, Del.: Scholarly Resources, 2000), 137–42.

7. May, *American Imperialism,* 165–86.

8. Kenneth Osgood, *Total Cold War: Eisenhower's Secret Propaganda Battle at Home and Abroad* (Lawrence: University Press of Kansas, 2006), 17–18.

9. Robert C. Hilderbrand, *Power and the People: Executive Management of Public Opinion in Foreign Affairs, 1897–1921* (Chapel Hill: University of North Carolina Press, 1981), 98–99.

10. Joseph A. Fry, "William McKinley and the Besmirching and Redemption of a Historical Reputation," *Diplomatic History* 3 (1979): 77–97, and Lewis L. Gould, "Chocolate Éclair or Mandarin Manipulator: William McKinley, the Spanish-American War, and the Philippines: A Review Essay," *Ohio History* 94 (1985): 182–87.

11. H. Wayne Morgan, *William McKinley and His America* (Syracuse, N.Y.: Syracuse University Press, 1963), 478.

12. Fred I. Greenstein, *The Hidden-Hand Presidency: Eisenhower as Leader* (New York: Basic Books, 1982).

13. Hilderbrand, *Power and the People,* 18.

14. Gerald F. Linderman, *The Mirror of War: American Society and the Spanish-American War* (Ann Arbor: University of Michigan Press, 1974), 18.

15. Hilderbrand, *Power and the People,* 12.

16. Ibid., 10–12; Stephen Ponder, "The President Makes News: William McKinley and the First Presidential Press Corps, 1897–1901," *Presidential Studies Quarterly* 24 (1994): 823–32.

17. First Annual Message, December 6, 1897, in *A Compilation of the Messages and Papers of the Presidents,* ed. James D. Richardson (New York: Bureau of National Literature, 1916), 14: 6263; Hilderbrand, *Power and the People,* 15–16

18. Ernest R. May, *Imperial Democracy: The Emergence of America as a World Power* (New York: Harcourt, Brace and World, 1961), 133–47.

19. Jill DeTemple, "Singing the *Maine:* The Popular Image of Cuba in Sheet Music of the Spanish-American War," *Historian* 63 (2001): 715–29.

20. Morgan, *McKinley,* 362.

21. Margaret Leech, *In the Days of McKinley* (New York: Harper, 1959), 167–68.

22. Hilderbrand, *Power and the People,* 18; May, *American Imperialism,* 40.

23. February 22, 1898, *Speeches and Addresses,* 67–78. The quotation is from p. 77.

24. Hilderbrand, *Power and the People,* 19.

25. Ibid., 19–20; message to Congress, March 28, 1898, in *Messages and Papers,* 14: 6280.

26. Hilderbrand, *Power and the People,* 21.

27. Ibid., 21–28.

28. Morgan, *McKinley,* 370.

29. Charles S. Olcott, *The Life of William McKinley,* 2 vols. (Boston: Houghton Mifflin, 1916), 2: 26–29.

30. Gould, *McKinley,* 86. The April 11 message is in *Messages and Papers,* 14: 6281–92.

31. Gould, *McKinley,* 87–90. Yet old myths die hard. In a May 6, 2007, *New York Times* op-ed piece, Geoffrey Perret repeated the old canard that McKinley had been forced into war by an aroused public.

32. Morgan, *McKinley,* 382.

33. Gould, *McKinley,* 91–93.

34. Hilderbrand, *Power and the People,* 30–31.

35. Ibid., 31; Ponder, "The President Makes News," 828.

36. Charles Henry Brown, *The Correspondents' War* (New York: Scribner, 1967), 227.

37. Charles Henry Brown, "Press Censorship in the Spanish-American War," *Journalism Quarterly* 42 (1965): 589.

38. Thomas C. Leonard, "The Uncensored War," *Culturefront* 7 (1998): 62.

39. The July 6 "address" is in American Presidency Project, <http://www.presidency.ucsb.edu/ws/print.php?pid+72487.>

40. Gould, *McKinley*, 119–20.

41. A balanced treatment of mobilization may be found in Graham Cosmas, *An Army for Empire: The United States Army in the Spanish-American War* (Columbia: University of Missouri Press, 1971).

42. Hilderbrand, *Power and the People*, 35.

43. Ibid., 38; Morgan, *McKinley*, 407.

44. Morgan, *McKinley*, 324.

45. October 11, 1898, *Speeches and Addresses*, 90–91.

46. October 12, 1898, *Speeches and Addresses*, 105; Hilderbrand, *Power and the People*, 39.

47. October 13, 1898, *Speeches and Addresses*, 114.

48. Hilderbrand, *Power and the People*, 39–40; Morgan, *McKinley*, 136; October 15, 1898, *Speeches and Addresses*, 128; October 21, 1898, ibid., 153.

49. Gould, *McKinley*, 116.

50. Warren Zimmermann, *First Great Triumph: How Five Americans Made Their Country a World Power* (New York: Farrar, Straus and Giroux, 2002), 319–20.

51. Gould, *McKinley*, 137.

52. Hilderbrand, *Power and the People*, 41.

53. Gould, *McKinley*, 137.

54. Joseph A. Fry, *Dixie Looks Abroad: The South and U.S. Foreign Relations, 1789–1973* (Baton Rouge: Louisiana State University Press, 2002), 128–30.

55. The southern speeches are in *Speeches and Addresses*, 156–84.

56. Ibid., 164.

57. Leech, *In the Days of McKinley*, 348–49; Gould, *McKinley*, 143.

58. Gould, *McKinley*, 150.

59. Ibid., 146.

60. Zimmermann, *First Great Triumph*, 340.

61. Gould, *McKinley*, 187; Frank Freidel, "Dissent in the Spanish-American War and the Philippine Insurrection," *Proceedings of the Massachusetts Historical Society* 81 (1969): 167–84.

62. *American Conservative*, December 15, 2003, 15.

63. Hilderbrand, *Power and the People*, 45; Leech, *In the Days of McKinley*, 361–63. The Boston speech was on February 16, 1899, and is in *Speeches and Addresses*, 185–93.

64. Leech, *In the Days of McKinley*, 408–9. The August 28, 1899, speech is in *Speeches and Addresses*, 185–93.

65. Hilderbrand, *Power and the People,* 46–47. The quotations are from *Speeches and Addresses,* 256, 329, 237, 304–5.

66. Robert Beisner, *Twelve against Empire: The Anti-Imperialists, 1898–1900* (New York: McGraw-Hill, 1968), 99–100; Gould, *McKinley,* 182–83.

67. Brian McAllister Linn, *The Philippine War, 1899–1902* (Lawrence: University Press of Kansas, 2000), 132–36; Hilderbrand, *Power and the People.*

68. Gould, *McKinley,* 183.

69. Hilderbrand, *Power and the People,* 49.

70. Gould, *McKinley,* 220.

71. Ibid., 226.

72. Zimmermann, *First Great Triumph,* 400; Richard E. Welch, *Response to Imperialism: The United States and the Philippine-American War, 1899–1902* (Chapel Hill: University of North Carolina Press, 1979), 67–71. These references are in *Messages and Papers,* 15: 6441, 6469.

73. Welch, *Response to Imperialism,* 133–36.

74. Zimmermann, *First Great Triumph,* 412–13.

75. Lewis L. Gould, *The Presidency of Theodore Roosevelt* (Lawrence: University Press of Kansas, 1991), 57; Welch, *Response to Imperialism,* 145.

76. Welch, *Response to Imperialism,* 147–49; Richard E. Welch Jr., "American Atrocities in the Philippines: The Indictment and the Response," *Pacific Historical Review* 43 (1974): 233–53.

2

WAR AND THE HEALTH
OF THE STATE

The U.S. Government and the Communications Revolution during World War I

Emily S. Rosenberg

Randolph Bourne, who composed some of the most famous dissents against U.S. participation in World War I, famously suggested that "war is the health of the state." In penning his antiwar essays, he stood in opposition to his father, a congregational minister who begged him not to disgrace the family name, to his teacher at Columbia, John Dewey, and to many of his radical friends who echoed Dewey's support of the war. In monthly articles for *Seven Arts*, Bourne excoriated political and intellectual elites for deluding themselves that this "well-bred war" would promote liberty and democracy around the world. The financial backer of *Seven Arts* soon shut down the magazine because of its outspoken antiwar politics, and governmental surveillance agencies shadowed Bourne until he died at age thirty-two during the great influenza epidemic in 1918.

The fragment of Bourne's writing that contained the passage "war is the health of the state" came from a manuscript left unfinished at his death. With these words, Bourne warned about how war's "irresistible forces for uniformity" coerce and intimidate minority opinions, forcing them into line with state-sponsored social norms and ideologies. By invoking both "drastic penalties" and "a subtle process of persuasion," Bourne wrote, war promotes a "collective community" that galvanizes and imparts purpose to nations and their citizens. He feared that development of this "herd sense," as he called it, imperiled creativity, freedom, and democratic values.[1] Bourne's warnings provided only one of many World War I era analyses that grappled with questions about a future in which war, nationalism, and new media techniques intertwined.

This essay examines how the wartime presidency of Woodrow Wilson—soothed by faith in progressive history, a divinely inspired national destiny, and a positive government—helped transform methods of governance and establish precedents for dealing with perceived national emergencies during the rest of the twentieth century and beyond. Specifically, the Wilson administration embraced processes (1) to use the techniques of mass advertising to shape governmentally controlled messages, (2) to censor information, and (3) to establish surveillance over domestic dissent. The wartime bureaucracies in charge of political persuasion, censorship, and surveillance tapped new technologies in communications and employed older ones in innovative ways in order to constitute and represent both a conforming nation and its opposing enemies. "Selling war"—through a combination of persuasion and coercion—became a new political art form during the wartime presidency of Woodrow Wilson.

The Wilson administration's efforts to mobilize minds for war, however, also touched off considerable domestic soul-searching over how the marriage of nationalism to "mass culture" might affect democracy. Randolph Bourne's wartime writings were only part of a broader and diverse body of social commentary about the possible consequences of the manipulation of public opinion. Both the marketing of war and the debates it stimulated would continue to shape American life in the decades to come.

Techniques of Political Persuasion

"If a censor is to be appointed, I want to be it," wrote forty-one-year-old George Creel to Secretary of Navy Josephus Daniels three weeks before the United States entered the war. Creel had owned and edited a small weekly newspaper in the Midwest, written muckraking-style articles for leading magazines, and served as the Democratic National Committee's publicity director. Outgoing, self-confident, and zealous, he claimed to have once supported himself by selling jokes for one dollar apiece. Energized by Wilson's vision of reforming the world through war, Creel would get his chance to place his skills for publicity and controlling information into the service of victory. He advocated an affirmative emphasis on selling a grand crusade rather than a more negative emphasis on overt censorship.[2]

Before April 1917, the government had no office that oversaw the connection between information and state policy. After the United States entered the war, Wilson quickly adapted the general pattern of European states and established new controls. These took two interrelated forms: pressure to promote self-censorship by encouraging "voluntary" adherence to governmental messages, and overt regulation of content accompanied by the surveillance and prosecution of dissenters. A "Committee on Public Information" (CPI) assumed the first role; the Post Office and the Justice Department generally took on the second.

The president appointed George Creel to head the CPI and financed the undertaking directly from his own discretionary war budget, thus shielding the CPI, at least partially, from congressional critics. Many reform-minded intellectuals, journalists, and advertising people rushed to assist Creel. They imagined that wartime mobilization could stimulate a forward-looking agenda that would emphasize efficiency, expertise, cohesion, and general social improvement. President Wilson's idealistic rhetoric, in such pronouncements as his "Fourteen Points," in addition to his credentials as a scholar and as a "progressive" reformer, inspired many to hope that war would become the crucible for a more open and democratic world.

The CPI threw itself into selling the war, and its efforts became a model for the emerging profession of public relations. It not only wielded informal tools that encouraged media self-censorship but also devised a wide variety of other ways to shape messages to governmental purpose. Creel tailored specific persuasive techniques to both older print and newer image-based media.[3]

Claiming that the American press was too disorganized for an official censorship system on the British model, Creel urged editors to act as their own censors and clear questionable material with his office. For those who did not cooperate, Creel could ask the Post Office or the Justice Department to take legal action, or he could ask the War Trade Board to cut off a print publication's supply of newspaper. "Victory rests upon unity and confidence," Creel warned in a twenty-page "Preliminary Statement to the Press of the United States." "The term *traitor* is not too harsh in application to the publisher, editor, or writer who wields this power without full and even solemn recognition of responsibilities."[4]

Not depending solely on editors, however, Creel's staff wrote press releases (an average of ten a day), newspaper stories (estimated at 20,000 columns per week), and an *Official Bulletin,* which went free to newspapers and Post Office bulletin boards. The CPI also issued hundreds of booklets and leaflets, some with runs of over five million. Many of these offered published versions of President Wilson's speeches, which were resonant with inspiring rhetoric. Others detailed U.S. idealistic war aims and contrasted them with alleged German atrocities. Specialized divisions targeted specific audiences. For example, a Division of Women's War Work produced articles and news stories for women's publications and organizations; a Division of Work with the Foreign Born provided material in various languages for immigrant presses and groups. A Bureau of Cartoons tried to muster "the nation's cartoon power" to support the CPI's various campaign messages. This barrage of government-produced information sought to keep official messages dominant in newsrooms and public spaces.[5]

Creel appointed Guy Stanton Ford, a professor of European history at the University of Minnesota, as director of the Division of Civic and Educational Cooperation. Under Ford, scholars undertook "histories" designed to educate Americans about their own progressive civilization and about the evils and lies of "Prussianism." Many wrote alarmingly of German plots against U.S. neutrality. These materials framed the war as one pitting democracy and peace against autocracy and imperial expansionism. Perhaps the most notable use of historians during the war involved the so-called Sisson documents. A former CPI agent in Petrograd, Edgar Sisson, had submitted to Washington a group of letters that seemed to unmask Lenin and Trotsky as paid German agents. Although reports into the U.S. State Department from England and elsewhere suggested that the letters were forgeries designed to inflame public opinion against both Germany and the new Bolshevik regime, the CPI obtained an endorsement from eminent historians, such as J. Franklin Jameson, and issued these documents as genuine. These Sisson documents helped provide a rationale for Wilson's dispatch of U.S. troops to the Soviet Union to aid the anticommunist factions in the civil war that followed the Bolshevik revolution. Newspaper editors who cast doubt on the authenticity of the Sisson documents, according to Creel, rendered service to the enemy and "struck a blow at America more powerful than could possibly have been dealt by German hands."[6]

A cadre of volunteers called "Four Minute Men," numbering 40,000 by September 1918, served the CPI's speakers' bureau. These volunteers presented stirring pro-war talks in movie theaters during the four-minute gaps in which projectionists changed reels. The short speeches (with gestures and speaking style carefully coached) reprised specific themes, each designed to reinforce whatever particular topic was simultaneously appearing in the Committee's editorials or booklets. As with the other campaigns, the speeches maximized the arts of persuasion by dissemination through local people and reliance on stirring visions of American exceptionalism mixed with lurid details of alleged "Hun" barbarity and lies. In an age before radio broadcasting had yet entered Americans' living rooms, the network of "Four Minute Men" could help establish a unified national message with consistent and repetitive themes. Creel estimated that a million speeches, reaching millions of Americans, were made during the program's year and a half of existence.[7]

Posters, advertisements, and motion pictures represented newer techniques of visual media, and Creel dove enthusiastically into shaping images to serve state policy. Creel's staff and other units of government rallied artists and illustrators to donate their skills in designing hundreds of war posters and display ads. Moreover, the CPI established fairly direct control over the content of Hollywood motion pictures, which were shown to 10 to 12 million people in more than 12,000 theaters around the country. Hollywood executives, eager to prove their service to the war effort and always under threat that the government could withhold scarce supplies of petroleum-based film, voluntarily enlisted in the CPI's program to stoke war enthusiasm. Creel's committee read, censored, and molded scripts, and Hollywood eagerly cooperated in bringing to the screen gripping confrontations between evil and good. The CPI also directly produced documentary films, short features at first, then longer dramas such as *Pershing's Crusaders* (1918), which depicted Germany's aggression and America's military and home-front responses.

This overview of the CPI's myriad forms of persuasion, however, understates the genuine communications revolution that the Creel committee both reflected and accelerated. The age of mass advertising was dawning, and *How We Advertised America* (the title of Creel's own book about the CPI effort) provided a sketch book for how to mold new campaigns of persuasion within a highly diverse nation. Creel's interconnected sales efforts rested upon what now seem to be classic propaganda themes that sought to interpellate "American" subjects into the national family by presenting the enemy as an opposing "other." Memorable images might appeal across the lines of ethnicity, class, and region to construct a more unified American identity for a mobile, fractured, and immigrant nation with little common heritage or even language. A generation of people engaged in public relations and advertising would look back to the CPI's work as a model of how to deploy both organizational expertise and psychological appeals.

The CPI's use of imagery related to national defense work, to gender, and to German beasts helps illuminate how government messages during World War I structured identities and identifications. Early poster and ad campaigns emphasized military recruitment, military maneuvers, and supposedly united home-front support. The CPI's film division drew heavily on Signal Corps images, taken in the United States and in France, to produce documentaries such as *Ready for the Fight* (showing artillery and cavalry), *Soldiers of the Sea* (on the Marine Corps), and *Fire and Gas* (a display of an Engineer Regiment). Other films, targeting particular groups where war support might be thin, emphasized national unity: *Labor's Part in Democracy's War*, *Woman's Part in the War*, *Our Colored Fighters*, and *Men Who Are Doing Things*.[8] One Liberty Loan poster entitled "Americans All" showed a beautiful Lady Liberty with a list of about fifteen very ethnically diverse names that were serving her. As immigrant soldiers served the nation, the poster implied, Americanization became assured.

The war poster creators prominently featured women as mothers, Red Cross nurses, and YWCA canteen workers. (The YWCA ran food and other services for U.S. troops.) Sometimes the posters conflated these women's roles. One of the most memorable images, by Alonzo Earl Foringer, for example, depicted a large Red Cross nurse holding a wounded soldier. The *pieta*-style scene presented the caption "The Greatest Mother in the World." The feminization of home and health worked in a dual way, suggesting that women served to support the troops, while the troops also served to protect the domestic realm of women. By positioning women as both the guarantors and the beneficiaries of victory, official representations of the conflict aimed to encourage women's support for the war and men's willingness to serve.[9]

The images of self-confident mobilization and of supportive women continued as staples of war posters and ads throughout the war, but by 1918 the campaigns became more rousing and graphic, emphasizing German atrocities. Pictures of large, hideous animalistic brutes, representing German soldiers, suggested pillage and the endangerment of women and children. The famous Ellsworth Young poster "Remember Belgium" depicted in dramatic silhouette, backlit by flames, a German soldier leading a young maiden to a fearsome fate. A widely used Liberty Bond poster by Henry Patrick Raleigh featured the words "HALT THE HUN" above a rendering of a tall U.S. soldier pushing away a German soldier who was brandishing a bayonet at a cowering woman and child. A series of "Kaiser" movies, such as *The Kaiser: The Beast of Berlin*, featured confrontations between German villains—generally drinking, looting, and raping—and innocent young women and children. Such films proved to be successful box-office attractions. The formula of innocence (usually represented through women and children) meeting beasts often produced a standard ending—rescue by brave American men.[10]

D. W. Griffith's famous movie *Hearts of the World* probably attracted the most viewers—and certainly the most critical acclaim—of any other World War I film. The British War Office had hired Griffith, the world's leading director, to make a pro-Allied film, and he employed the basic structure that he had previously used in *Birth of a Nation*—brutes threaten womanhood and then are vanquished. *Hearts of the World* presents a love story set against scenes of trench warfare, guns, tanks, and hand-to-hand combat in France. It ends with the victorious arrival of troops. (It came into theaters just before the Armistice, however, so it had little direct propaganda value.)[11]

The power of the "Hun" images rested on the contrast they suggested with the life and values of the United States: absolute German evil provided an implied or explicit mirror for absolute American goodness. One poster text read, "Because your mind is clean, because you have been surrounded from childhood by an atmosphere of uprightness, and decency, and kindliness . . . you have listened, with a doubting shrug, to the tales of German atrocities." But "the worst half has never been told in this clean land of ours, has never been told because unprintable." Speeches by the Four Minute Men also carried out this theme, as did CPI pamphlets. *Why America Fights Germany,* for example, featured a tale of Germany's surprise invasion of peaceful New York City and New Jersey, after which leading citizens are lined up and shot, town forests are burned, and "robbery, murder, and outrage run riot."[12]

How well did the CPI's techniques to sell the war succeed? Studies of Creel's peripatetic campaigns have tended to take the former newspaperman at his word and assume that his efforts must have had significant impact. And, without a doubt, Creel's methods influenced future studies of marketing and propaganda. It would be difficult, however, to test the hypothesis of CPI success, and there may be some evidence on the other side. Jeanette Keith, for example, examines the tremendous amount of draft resistance in the South and suggests that parts of the country may have been well outside the reach of Creel's web of official messages. Rural people, especially, may also have harbored scarcely recorded suspicions of local pro-war elites and failed to see the war as advancing any issue with which they could identify. Elizabeth McKillen and others have, likewise, shown significant antiwar sentiment in ethnic organizations and in some labor locals. Moreover, the reports of military intelligence and the congressional criticism of Creel's methods suggest that plenty of opposition to Mr. Wilson's war and its methods remained visible and vocal.[13] Moreover, if the propaganda had been wholly successful, the widespread surveillance carried on during the war might have been less pervasive.

Censorship and Surveillance

General John J. Pershing reportedly promised to "smash the German line in France, if you will smash the damnable Hun propaganda at home." Pershing and the country's military intelligence branch asserted (as would later influential studies of World War I propaganda) that the domestic front in this "modern" war constituted, as never before, an integral part of military strategy.[14]

As with the World War I informational campaigns, new bureaucracies, technologies, and techniques combined to create more energetic forms of domestic censorship and surveillance. Such coercion comprised not the opposite of persuasion but its complement.[15]

U.S. officials worried about the loyalty of America's large German and Irish immigrant populations. Not only might antiwar ethnics be open to recruitment by enemy agents, they feared, but such agents might themselves be able to hide almost invisibly in workplaces where espionage and sabotage could be carried out. Moreover, anarchist and socialist movements had grown in numbers, particularly within labor organizations, and these groups often opposed the war, regarding it as a manifestation of elite control and capitalist injustice.

Fearing domestic opposition to the war, the Wilson administration quickly asserted a federal power that judicial precedents already supported: authority over materials that could be delivered through the Post Office. The Postmaster General assumed broad jurisdiction to remove antiwar materials from the mail. Moreover, a Censorship Board (on which Creel also served) began coordinating the Post Office's effort with those of various other censoring agencies in the War and Navy departments and in the War Trade Board. Because almost any kind of written communication designed for a mass national audience traveled to intended receivers through the Post Office system, the ability to censor mailed materials provided a major weapon of informational control. Government, in effect, took control of the revolutions of mass printing and mass mailing.[16]

The Wilson administration also marshaled other tools of censorship. The Selective Service Act, which Wilson signed in May 1917, required men between the ages of twenty-one and thirty to register for the draft and made it illegal to interfere with registration or to aid draft resisters. Anarchists Alexander Berkman and Emma Goldman, to name only the most celebrated targets, were arrested and brought to trial within a few months after passage of the act for their anti-conscription speeches.[17] In addition, the government took over the country's wireless telegraph, telephone, and cable systems to prevent enemy use of these vital communication links. The U.S. Navy seized all commercial wireless stations and ordered all amateur radio operators to dismantle their equipment.[18]

A new military intelligence code and cipher unit, MI-8, began to develop forms of secret messages and to decipher intercepted communications. Governmental officials read and censored thousands of telegrams, the secrecy of which had supposedly been guaranteed in the Radio Act of 1912. This effort, although shut down briefly at the end of the war, reemerged in 1919, when the State and War departments reconstituted a secret eavesdropping and code-breaking agency, called "Black Chamber," and assigned it to work on the prompt deciphering of Japan's, Britain's, and Germany's diplomatic codes. Headed by Major Herbert Yardley, this cipher bureau was a forerunner of the later National Security Agency.[19]

The Espionage Act, which Congress enacted shortly after America's declaration of war, also strengthened censorship powers. The law made it a crime to steal government secrets to aid the enemy, required fingerprinting and registration of resident aliens from enemy nations, and prohibited statements that interfered with military recruitment and operations or promoted the success of the nation's enemies. Attorney General Thomas Gregory's agents vigorously spied on and arrested dissenters. Some federal judges, however, did not always convict those whom governmental officials believed should be silenced or jailed, and agents of the Justice Department and military intelligence called for broader powers.[20]

The staff of military intelligence, in 1918, secretly compiled what it regarded as a comprehensive study of antiwar propaganda that necessitated stronger legal action. It detailed three classes of threat: a German spy system that used churches, newspapers, film, and informal networks to distribute antiwar propaganda; "co-operating agencies" including religious antiwar messages, conscientious objectors, philanthropic "slackers," labor organizations, and anarchists; and "propaganda by dissension," which included any stirring of discontent among "Negroes" and "friendly aliens." According to the report, the potential of more rapid and widespread communications magnified all of these threats:

> Everybody reads and writes, and the postal service is of vast propor-
> tions. The telephone, telegraph, and cable systems bring the remotest
> ears within access of the whispers of gossip. The newspapers go into
> every home and make the whole world one neighborhood. By their
> generous use of the wire-service, long articles may be made to appear
> simultaneously at almost every breakfast table in the land. . . . We are
> all neighbors, and at the mercy of one another's tongues.[21]

The report concluded that the government's inability to stop antiwar rumors and lies pointed to the urgent *military* need for new legislation. It is "an absolute fact that any diminution [whatsoever] of the maximum power and enthusiasm of a nation at war has a direct and perilous military effect."[22] Antiwar speech might, for example, encourage evasion of the draft and directly impair the Army. By defining speech as action in this way, the report argued that the Espionage Act did not sufficiently cover the problem of antiwar utterances.

In May 1918, Congress amended the Espionage Act by adding more explicit categories of illegal speech. This amendment (popularly called the Sedition Act) forbade "disloyal, profane, scurrilous, or abusive language" about the U.S. government, Constitution, flag, or armed services or language that might promote the enemy cause.[23]

Using this broad formulation, the Wilson administration focused on antiwar critics of various persuasions and ultimately prosecuted around 2,000 people, approximately 10 percent of whom were women. Socialist Party leaders, such as Charles Schenck (the party's general secretary), Eugene Debs (its presidential nominee in five elections between 1900 and 1920), and popular speaker Kate Richards O'Hare were convicted for antiwar statements. Police rounded up more than 150 leaders and members of the antiwar radical labor organization, the Industrial Workers of the World (IWW). The FBI interviewed or arrested a wide array of pacifists, German and Irish Americans, and others accused of disloyal speech. In landmark cases, the Supreme Court approved the Espionage Act and the sedition amendment, ruling that antiwar speech did not constitute constitutionally protected expression but, in Justice Oliver Wendell Holmes's words, represented a "clear and present danger" to the nation. To further strengthen protections against antiwar expressions, an Immigration Act of 1918 allowed deportation of resident aliens who identified with anarchist or revolutionary groups.[24]

Several entities carried out surveillance. The Justice Department expanded its Federal Bureau of Investigation (FBI); the Office of Naval Intelligence increased by almost 3,000 reservists and volunteers; and the Military Intelligence Division (MID) increased from 3 employees in 1916 to 1,441 in 1918. These arms of government surveillance received significant support from the private sector. Indeed, it was the semiprivate American Protective League (APL) that emerged as perhaps the most important surveillance entity. A businessmen's organization formed in March 1917, the APL's members volunteered to assist Justice Department agents by reporting what they considered to be disloyal activities or speech. The APL, which quickly spread to encompass perhaps several hundred thousand people throughout the country, grew ever bolder in their actions until they constituted a national vigilante force that spied, censored, burglarized, and sometimes even assaulted dissenters of various kinds. The APL's "slacker raids" against draft evaders in 1918 illustrated its extralegal power—and the Justice Department's implicit authorization of its activities.[25]

The censorship and surveillance practices put in place during the war held lasting significance. First, many of these practices did not end with hostilities against Germany. Because surveillance and apprehension of threats had focused on radical organizations, fear of Bolshevism and the wave of labor strikes in the immediate postwar era increased pressure on dissenters. The "Red Scare"—the wave of hysteria, raids, and deportations that followed the war—further entrenched and enlarged the surveillance bureaucracies such as the FBI and MID.[26] Second, under the pressure of the war, governmental officials saw international and domestic threats as virtually synonymous and treated them in similar ways—that is, as dangers that required executive-branch emergency authority to censor, conduct surveillance, and undertake deportations. The need to "sell war" to America's very diverse population, in short, expanded executive branch power, provided precedents for secret agencies, and worked to erase distinctions between "at home" and "overseas."

Democracy, Nationalism, and the "Mass"

World War I constituted a significant moment in the communications revolution. Various forms of mass media—posters and advertising displays, newspapers and magazines, news wire services, telegraph and telephone networks (bringing new forms of code making and breaking), radio technologies, and motion pictures—seemed critical to the war effort. Moreover, sophisticated understandings about how to shape strategies of persuasion and coercion forged a new art of information management, nurtured within state bureaucracies.

These new forms and practices raised issues about how military efforts and the mobilization of nationalism fit with ideals and practices of democracy. After the war, historian Brett Gary claims, the ramifications of techniques of mass persuasion caught widespread attention as both "a problem for democratic theory" and "a problem for national security."[27] Most commentators believed that the CPI had exerted a great impact, and they either heralded it or blamed it for being able to whip up the spirit of "100% Americanism" that pervaded wartime and postwar American culture. The Wilson administration's methods for selling war thus provided a basis both for the growth of advertising techniques and for a range of critical writing about what came to be called "mass" media and "mass" culture.

Many post-WWI commentators saw what they called "propaganda" as a modern, twentieth-century problem related to technologies of mass distribution and the new capacities for mobilizing and manipulating the irrational impulses that many people were coming to claim governed human behavior. The war therefore stimulated observations about the effects of "mass" persuasion on the future of democracy—observations that helped solidify divisions within modern American liberalism over, in Gary's words, "the relationship among public capacity, expert responsibility, and democratic theory in an age of propaganda." Propaganda provided new and potentially powerful means to exercise leadership in a democracy. It also provided innovative and possibly potent means to deceive and mislead.[28]

Randolph Bourne, of course, had viewed emerging trends with apprehension about how war would cultivate the "herd sense" and stifle individuality and dissent. Many other intellectuals took similar concerns in different directions. Surveying a few of the postwar commentators will provide examples of some of the post–Creel Committee commentary.

Walter Lippmann, who had himself probably wanted the job that Creel gained, warned even before the war that stirring fear and hatred as a method of recruiting and mobilizing an army might eventually imperil democratic values. During the war he served as a captain in U.S. Army Intelligence in Europe, where he bitterly denounced what he perceived as the CPI's incompetence. He then joined others in Wilson's famed "Inquiry," a secret group of experts convened to prepare detailed studies for possible use in devising the postwar settlements at the Versailles peace conference. After the war Lippmann formulated one of the most influential works on the problem of "public opinion" in an age of manipulation. "The symbol," he wrote, is "an instrument by which a few can fatten on many, deflect criticism, and seduce men."[29]

Articulating a pessimistic view of public irrationality, Lippmann promoted the idea that experts needed to run affairs of governance and to insulate themselves from the influences of the unreliable herd. Technocrats and experts, not some easily manipulated and volatile "public," needed to provide the core decisionmaking for successful governance. Democracy must not, he wrote, "burden every citizen with expert opinions on all questions, but push that burden away from him towards the responsible administrator." For Lippmann and others, the war had exposed the dangerous possibility that democracy could easily degenerate into irrational mob rule. His critique bore some similarity to Bourne's fear of the "herd," but whereas Bourne emphasized the threat to individuality and dissent, Lippmann worried more about preserving the ordered liberty that he believed could come only from enlightened and elite-run policies.[30]

Harold Lasswell, a young assistant professor of political science at the University of Chicago, shared the view that the "mass" would be volatile and irrational. In his 1927 classic, *Propaganda*, however, Lasswell explicitly welcomed political persuasion as a new technique by which experts could gain broad consent for their presumably enlightened views and policies. Arguing that propaganda had become an inescapable component of modern war, Lasswell investigated its "conditions and methods" during the Great War in order to set forth more general theories. He wrote that "such matchless skill as Wilson showed in propaganda has never been equaled in the history of the world." Where both Bourne and Lippmann (in different ways) had warned pessimistically of the "herd sense" to which war appealed, Lasswell saw advantages: "Monarchy and class privilege have gone the way of all flesh, and the idolatry of the individual passes for the official religion of democracy. It is an atomized world. . . . The new antidote to willfulness is propaganda. If the mass will be free of chains of iron, it must accept its chains of silver. If it will not love, honour, and obey, it must not expect to escape seduction." Propaganda, it seemed, would provide the seduction that would hold democracies together and allow great leaders the cohesive power that could make the modern world work rather than dissolve into individualistic chaos.[31]

Those who stressed public incompetence and elite management of opinion, however, came under challenge from those who considered such logic to be undemocratic and who continued to hold out the possibility of competent public opinion. John Dewey, for example, had joined those social justice progressives who came to support President Wilson's war. He argued that Wilson might be able to use the war to usher in an era of peace and social progress. At the end of the war, however, Dewey published a warning that wartime repression had gone too far and was being used to serve the anti-labor agenda of business interests. To Dewey and those who shared his perspective, propaganda threatened democracy only if its methods remained secreted in a ruling elite. Education could help people guard against deceptions and manipulations. Individuality and rationality could still trump mass irrationality. Although "scientific" experts provided essential services to government, they should see themselves not as manipulators of mass opinion but as providers to the public of accurate information to combat manipulation.[32]

People associated with the new profession of advertising expressed few qualms about the new era of the "mass." One of the founders of modern American advertising, Edward L. Bernays, who had served the CPI in Latin America during the war, wrote an influential 1928 study called *Propaganda*. With some of the message but less of the subtlety of Lasswell's work, Bernays's book saw modern advertising as a tool to forge a bright future. He praised how modern public relations experts might allow the "leadership class" to steer democracies toward the desirable ends of patriotism, unity, and achievement.[33]

Bruce Barton, another pioneer of advertising technique, provided a particularly revealing example of the interactions between war, peace, and persuasion—and of the confidence, even hubris, displayed by the heralds of the new ad age. During the war, the devout Barton, son of a pastor, designed advertisements and posters to enlist public contributions for the YWCA's support for military troops.[34] After this formative experience, he built a successful ad agency that advised many political and business clients, and he became famous for his best-selling 1925 book, *The Man Who Nobody Knows*, which presented Jesus Christ as a consummate salesman. In the 1930s, as threats of another global war loomed in Asia and Europe, Barton saw advertising as the key that could now convince people to stay out of any future struggle and embrace peace. In an article entitled "Let's Advertise This Hell!" published in the May 1932 issue of *American Magazine*, Barton proposed that Congress appropriate 5 percent of the U.S. budget for armaments, about $48 million a year, to fund an advertising campaign to discredit war and popularize peace.

A group called Peaceways joined with Barton in 1933 to design and launch a now little-known advertising campaign against war. Board members or endorsers of the new group included Norman Thomas, Franz Boas, Reinhold Niebuhr, Rabbi Jonah Wise, and Max Winkler. Using arresting images and short messages, carried without charge in a number of magazines, the Peaceways campaign drew from, and fed, the disillusionment that most Americans now expressed about their country's participation in World War I.

Barton's ads for Peaceways repudiated the very war he had earlier glorified. One, for example, showed long rows of marching soldiers labeled "these are the dead"; the text invited the reader to watch them parade, "ten in a row, two seconds apart . . . for 1 day . . . for 10 days . . . for 20 days . . . for 40 days . . . FOR 46 DAYS . . . THESE ARE THE SOLDIERS DEAD IN THE WAR." Another ad showed a bed-ridden, dying boy with his grieving parents; the message stated that "A hospital would save his life . . . but he will have to die. . . . You see, we spent our money in the war. It was a very expensive war. It cost the nations of the world almost a billion dollars every four days. THE ANNUAL BUDGET OF ALL OUR HOSPITALS BLOWN UP, IN POWDER AND SHOT EVERY 96 HOURS!" A third ad displayed a horrendous scene of battle with the caption "THE FIELD OF *DIS*HONOR."[35]

The Peaceways efforts, of course, hardly kept the United States out of World War II, and after Pearl Harbor, Barton volunteered to sell the war he had, a few years earlier, created ads to avoid. Working as advertising chairman for war bond drives in World War II, he was one of many who provided a bridge of technical know-how that extended between Wilson's and Roosevelt's wars.[36]

To Barton, it seemed, democracy and Christianity could be advanced, not undermined, by good marketing. Selling the right policy, as he defined it, always seemed to be the right thing, and he expressed little discomfort over any complications about what might be seen as right at any given time. For him, as for Bernays and many other advertising professionals, the arts of persuasion, the creation of an audience, the preservation of democracy, and support for war or peace—all melded comfortably together. Mobilization of opinion, itself, seemed to be the objective that challenged and fascinated.

Bourne, Lippmann, Lasswell, Dewey, Bernays, and Barton represent a spectrum of views about the meaning of the new "mass" communications age that became visible in Wilson's war effort. Their various perspectives about how the manipulation of public opinion might undermine, challenge, or serve to support democratic governance helped sketch the parameters of ongoing debates over the implications of advertising and "mass" culture. Although such robust theorizing would be reinvigorated and reshaped by the Nazi Party's cultural manipulations during the late 1930s and 1940s, intense engagement with the role of "propaganda" dates from the Wilson administration.

Woodrow Wilson's effort to sell war contributed to many of the practices and structures that would become a part of the twentieth-century American state. In one sense, these wartime departures emerged from the traditions of that complex, and almost indefinable, movement called "progressivism." These included faith in expertise; belief that enlarging government power could enlarge the sphere of public good; interest in "Americanizing" a disparate immigrant population around common ideals; and conviction that American power in the world, unlike that of other states, could be benign and disinterested.

To Wilson and his supporters, new wartime techniques of persuasion and coercion offered the opportunity to galvanize the nation behind such lofty, "progressive" goals. Wilson's presidency coincided with and helped consolidate three long-term trends that were already altering the relationship between war and society: the rise of an increasingly powerful, bureaucratic state; the growing sophistication of the new profession of advertising; and the revolution in technologies of mass communication. The Wilson administration experimented with new techniques and instituted new bureaucracies designed to conduct political persuasion, censorship, and surveillance.

Just as World War I brought forth new ways in which the state tried to sell its programs, however, it also prompted diverse responses to the possible effects on democracy of the mass marketing of state-sponsored ideologies. Writings by Bourne, Lippmann, Lasswell, Dewey, Bernays, and Barton suggest the range of views. The presidency of Woodrow Wilson during World War I thus helped form the structures for a new public relations state, and it also encouraged various discursive traditions that both defended and critiqued this new politics of professionalized popular manipulation.

Notes

1. See "The State," in Randolph Bourne, *The Radical Will: Selected Writings, 1911–1918*, selection and introduction by Olaf Hansen, preface by Christopher Lasch (New York: Urizen Books, 1977), 355–95. Leslie J. Vaughan, *Randolph Bourne and the Politics of Cultural Radicalism* (Lawrence: University of Kansas Press, 1997), 113, points out that Bourne's analysis, less systematically, anticipated the state theories of Gramsci.

See also Christine Stansell, *American Moderns: Bohemian New York and the Creation of a New Century* (New York: Metropolitan Books, 2000), 328–33.

2. Stewart Halsey Ross, *Propaganda for War: How the United States Was Conditioned to Fight the Great War of 1914–1918* (Jefferson, N.C.: McFarland, 1996), 218–26 [quote, 218].

3. On the CPI generally, see Ross, *Propaganda for War*; James R. Mock and Cedric Larson, *Words That Won the War: The Story of the Committee on Public Information, 1917–1919* (Princeton, N.J.: Princeton University Press, 1939); George Creel, *How We Advertised America: The First Telling of the Amazing Story of the Committee on Public Information That Carried the Gospel of Americanism to Every Corner of the Globe* (New York: Harper and Brothers, 1920); and Stephen Vaughn, *Holding Fast the Inner Lines: Democracy, Nationalism, and the Committee on Public Information* (Chapel Hill: University of North Carolina Press, 1980).

4. Quoted in Ross, *Propaganda for War*, 226–27.

5. Mock and Larson, *Words That Won the War*, 77–112; Ross, *Propaganda for War*, 229–39; Vaughn, *Holding Fast the Inner Lines*, 30–35.

6. George T. Blakey, *Historians on the Homefront: American Propagandists for the Great War* (Lexington: University Press of Kentucky, 1970); Vaughn, *Holding Fast the Inner Lines*, 39–60; Creel to Editor of *New York Evening Post*, September 30, 1918, quoted in Ross, *Propaganda for War*, 141–42. A list of wartime publications is in Creel, *How We Advertised America*, 455–59.

7. Creel, *How We Advertised America*, 84–98; Ross, *Propaganda for War*, 245–48; Vaughn, *Holding Fast the Inner Lines*, 116–40.

8. United States Committee on Public Information, *The Creel Report: Complete Report of the Chairman of the Committee on Public Information, 1917:1918:1919* (New York: Da Capo Press reprint, 1972), 47–49.

9. Susan Zeiger, "She Didn't Raise Her Boy to Be a Slacker: Motherhood, Conscription, and the Culture of the First World War," *Feminist Studies* 2 (1996): 7–39. Posters mentioned in this essay may be located at "American Posters of World War One," Georgetown University library, <http://www.library.georgetown.edu/dept/speccoll/amposter.htm>, and "World War I Poster Collection," Tutt Library, Colorado College, <http://www.coloradocollege.edu/Library/SpecialCollections/HistoricalCollections/WWI/WWIGuide.html>. On the Division of Women's War Work, see Creel, *How We Advertised America*, 212–21.

10. Ross, *Propaganda for War*, 261–66; Michael T. Isenberg, *War on Film: The American Cinema and World War I, 1914–1941* (East Brunswick, N.J.: Associated University Presses, 1981).

11. Leslie Midkiff Debauche, *Reel Patriotism: The Movies and World War I* (Madison: University of Wisconsin Press, 1997); Ruth Vasey, *The World According to Hollywood, 1918–1939* (Madison: University of Wisconsin Press, 1997).

12. Ross, *Propaganda for War*, 239–50 [quotes, 250 and 239].

13. Harold D. Lasswell, *Propaganda Technique in the World War* (New York: Al-

fred A. Knopf, 1927), 45, provides examples of senators who charged that Creel was "smeared all over with treason," a "candle-snuffer," and a "gangrened egotist afflicted with an ingrowing conceit." Creel used his account of his war service to get back at his congressional "enemies," writing, "The heavens may fall, the earth be consumed, but the right of a Congressman to lie and defame remains inviolate." Creel, *How We Advertised America*, 52.

14. Military Intelligence Branch, General Staff, *Propaganda in Its Military and Legal Aspects* (Washington, D.C.: Government Printing Office, 1918), 181 [quote].

15. On surveillance during World War I, see especially Harry N. Scheiber, *The Wilson Administration and Civil Liberties, 1917–1921* (Ithaca: Cornell University Press, 1960); William Preston Jr., *Aliens and Dissenters: Federal Suppression of Radicals, 1903–1933* (New York: Harper and Row, 1963); Paul L. Murphy, *World War I and the Origin of Civil Liberties in the United States* (New York: W. W. Norton, 1979); Geoffrey R. Stone, *Perilous Times: Free Speech in Wartime from the Sedition Act of 1798 to the War on Terrorism* (New York: W. W. Norton, 2004), 135–233; Athan G. Theoharis, *The FBI and American Democracy: A Brief Critical History* (Lawrence: University of Kansas Press, 2004), 21–28; Paul Starr, *The Creation of the Media: Political Origins of Modern Communications* (New York: Basic Books, 2004), 274–94.

16. Murphy, *World War I and the Origin of Civil Liberties*, 81, 97–103.

17. Stone, *Perilous Times*, 143–44.

18. Starr, *The Creation of the Media*, 222–30; Susan J. Douglas, *Inventing American Broadcasting, 1899–1922* (Baltimore: Johns Hopkins University Press, 1987), 281, 297.

19. Herbert O. Yardley, *The American Black Chamber* (London: Faber, 1931); Wayne G. Barker, ed., *The History of Codes and Ciphers in the United States during World War I* (Laguna Hills, Calif.: Aegean Park Press, 1978). Broader studies include James Bamford, "Big Brother Is Listening," *Atlantic Monthly* (April 2006): 69; G. J. A. O'Toole, *Honorable Treachery: A History of U.S. Intelligence, Espionage, and Covert Action from the American Revolution to the CIA* (New York: Atlantic Monthly Press, 1991), 271–310; and Christopher Andrew, *For the President's Eyes Only: Secret Intelligence and the American Presidency from Washington to Bush* (New York: HarperCollins, 1995), 52–62.

20. Murphy, *World War I and the Origin of Civil Liberties*, 76–83.

21. Military Intelligence Branch, 124.

22. Ibid.

23. Norman L. Rosenberg, *Protecting the Best Men: An Interpretive History of the Law of Libel* (Chapel Hill: University of North Carolina Press, 1990), 211; David Rabban, *Free Speech in Its Forgotten Years, 1870–1920* (New York: Cambridge University Press, 1997).

24. Stone, *Perilous Times*, 184–203. In *Disloyal Mothers and Scurrilous Citizens: Women and Subversion during World War I* (Bloomington: Indiana University Press, 1999), Kathleen Kennedy examines how trials of women became arenas for defining, and also contesting, women's obligations to the wartime state.

25. Andrew, *For the President's Eyes Only,* 53; Murphy, *World War I and the Origin of Civil Liberties,* 123–32; David M. Kennedy, *Over Here: The First World War and American Society* (New York: Oxford University Press, 1980), 82.

26. Theodore Kornweibel Jr., *Seeing Red: Federal Campaigns against Black Militancy, 1919–1925* (Bloomington: Indiana University Press, 1998); Preston, *Aliens and Dissenters,* 208–37.

27. For this discussion I am indebted to Brett Gary, *The Nervous Liberals: Propaganda Anxieties from World War I to the Cold War* (New York: Columbia University Press, 1999), and J. Michael Sproule, *Propaganda and Democracy: The American Experience of Media and Mass Persuasion* (Cambridge: Cambridge University Press, 1997), 1–97.

28. Gary, *The Nervous Liberals* 2–3 [quote], 53.

29. Walter Lippmann, *Public Opinion* (New York: Macmillan, 1922), 236.

30. Lippmann, *Public Opinion,* 399; Ronald Steel, *Walter Lippmann and the American Century* (Boston: Little, Brown, 1980); Gary, *The Nervous Liberals,* 29–34. W. Trotter, *Instincts of the Herd in Peace and War* (New York: Macmillan, 1920) presents a classic distrust of the mass.

31. Lasswell, *Propaganda Technique,* 217, 222 [quotes]; Gary, *The Nervous Liberals,* 59–62.

32. Gary, *The Nervous Liberals,* 34; John Dewey, *The Public and Its Problems* (New York: Henry Holt, 1927); John Dewey, "The Cult of Irrationality," *New Republic,* November 9, 1918, 34–35.

33. Edward L. Bernays, *Propaganda* (New York: Liveright, 1928); Gary, *The Nervous Liberals,* 82–84.

34. Barton's materials (including war posters) as publicity director for the United War Work Campaign are in boxes 144 and 158, Bruce Barton Papers (BBP), University of Wisconsin Historical Society, Madison. For background, see Richard M. Fried, *The Man Everybody Knew: Bruce Barton and the Making of Modern America* (Chicago: Dee, 2005).

35. Correspondence, pamphlets, and posters for the Peaceways campaign are in folder "World Peaceways," box 73, BBP.

36. Information on Barton's World War II campaigns is in folder "U.S. Treasury," box 70, BBP.

3

SELLING DIFFERENT KINDS OF WAR

Franklin D. Roosevelt and American Public Opinion during World War II

Mark A. Stoler

On the evening of November 8, 1942, Katherine Marshall sat in Washington's Griffith Stadium watching a football game without her husband, Army Chief of Staff General George C. Marshall, who had told her he could not be out of touch with his office. In the middle of one play, a voice from the loudspeaker explained why: "Stop the game! Important announcement!" yelled the announcer. "The President of the United States of America announces the successful landing on the African coast of an American Expeditionary Force. This is our Second Front." In her memoirs Mrs. Marshall described the extraordinary reaction of the 25,000 people in the stadium to this announcement of the launching of Operation TORCH, the Anglo-American invasion of French North Africa:

> Like the waves of the ocean, the cheers of the people rose and fell, then rose again in a long-sustained emotional cry. The football players turned somersaults and handsprings down the center of the field; the crowd simply went wild, for this was the heartening news America, agonized by one defeat after another, had been waiting to hear. We had struck back.[1]

Had General Marshall been able to attend the game that evening and hear the announcement, his reaction would have been quite different. For him this operation represented a stinging personal defeat and anything but the "Second Front" for which he had strongly pressed earlier in the year. Indeed, he saw the North African invasion as actually postponing that Second Front, perhaps indefinitely, and with it hopes of victory in the war. Furthermore, this postponement had been forced upon Marshall and his colleagues on the newly created Joint Chiefs of Staff (JCS) by a president who had rejected their advice and insisted upon Operation TORCH not for military reasons but for political ones that included the desire to obtain the very impact on public opinion that Mrs. Marshall witnessed that evening.

Franklin D. Roosevelt's overwhelming concern with public opinion in the years preceding Pearl Harbor is well known and thoroughly researched. Indeed, it has produced a rich secondary literature, though hardly a consensus. Historical debate has raged for more than sixty years now regarding the extent to which Roosevelt led, manipulated, or merely followed public opinion regarding participation in World War II.[2] Less scholarly attention has been given to Roosevelt's concern with public opinion once the United States officially entered the war. Yet the relatively few studies that have been done show conclusively that his concern with public opinion continued after Pearl Harbor and that it deeply affected both his wartime strategic decisions and his postwar plans, though again there is disagreement as to exactly how and why.[3]

Throughout his presidency, Roosevelt paid close attention to the new public opinion polls that had begun to appear during the interwar years. He was also a master at influencing those polls and public opinion in general—most notably through his highly effective use of the new medium of radio that beamed his "fireside chats" as well as his congressional addresses and other speeches to millions of American homes. His other major means of influencing the public included the extensive use of private organizations and individuals who shared his views, his informal and highly entertaining press conferences,[4] and some early efforts at propaganda. After U.S. entry into the war Roosevelt also possessed a propaganda bureau in the Office of War Information as well as censorship powers.[5] Yet at no time could he be considered the master of public opinion, able to manipulate it at will. To the contrary, it deeply constrained and influenced him at the same time that he heavily influenced it, thereby creating a complex web of interactions that this essay will attempt to analyze. In the process of doing so, it will emphasize the fact that Roosevelt was intensely concerned not simply with "selling war" to the American people from 1939 to 1945 but also with selling particular kinds of war at different times.

At first FDR focused on persuading a doubting public and Congress to agree to sell war supplies to the nations at war with the Axis powers. By early 1941 he had expanded his goal to obtaining agreement to "lend" such supplies without demanding immediate payment and, by the fall, to waging an undeclared naval war in the Atlantic so as to ensure that those supplies reached their destinations. After Pearl Harbor, the goal shifted to "selling" a global coalition war and a Europe-first strategy, along with postwar internationalism, to a public focused on the Pacific and unilateral behavior. This was far from an easy task, later mythology about wartime public unity to the contrary, and it deeply affected both the military strategies Roosevelt supported and his public statements about the postwar world.

One reason Roosevelt monitored public opinion on these matters so carefully is that he feared it, primarily as a result of his experiences during and after World War I. In 1919–20 he had watched Woodrow Wilson's public support evaporate during the fight over the League of Nations and Treaty of Versailles, leading not only to Senate rejection of that treaty and of U.S. membership in the League but also to his own defeat as the Democratic vice presidential nominee in the 1920 election. "It is a terrible thing," he would later state in obvious reference to these experiences, "to look over your shoulder when you are trying to lead—and to find no one there."[6] He would consistently act in such ways as to make sure that "terrible thing" did not happen to him.

He would do so indirectly and without clear statements regarding his plans—an approach that makes reaching a definitive historical assessment extremely difficult. Roosevelt was a notoriously secretive man who wrote no memoirs and who left little direct evidence regarding his specific intentions. Indeed, he often prohibited note-taking during his meetings with key advisors, and on at least one occasion he "blew up" when his military chiefs brought a recording secretary to a meeting with him, warning that poor individual to "put that thing up" when he took out a notepad. He also vetoed publication of the minutes of the 1919 Paris Peace Conference with the revealing comment that those minutes should never have been kept in the first place, and he explicitly requested on at least one occasion a doctoring of the official record regarding strategic proposals made to him by the JCS so as to mislead future historians.[7] As one of his biographers has aptly concluded in reference to a "recurring and maddening dream" of watching FDR steal cards from a deck and place them up his sleeve, "it's safe to say . . . all of Franklin Roosevelt's cards were never on the table."[8] Given such behavior, historians are virtually forced into a series of inferences regarding Roosevelt's intentions based primarily upon his actions and the few comments to his advisors that actually revealed rather than obfuscated his thought patterns.[9]

Selling Material Aid to the Allies

From 1939 through early 1941 Roosevelt focused on selling the idea of providing material aid to the nations opposing Nazi Germany. At first this involved obtaining agreement to sell American arms and munitions to any belligerent willing to pay for them. That was no easy task given the fact that Americans saw such sales as having led them into the First World War and they were intent upon avoiding entry into a second such conflict. To make matters worse, such sales soon proved inadequate. Roosevelt consequently offered more direct aid via executive agreement in September 1940, and in December he pressed the public and Congress to allow him to provide Great Britain with war material free of charge. Congress with strong public support agreed in March 1941, thereby making the United States an unofficial belligerent in the war.

These presidential initiatives from 1939 through 1941 constituted a dramatic departure from Roosevelt's earlier behavior. Throughout his first six years as president, from 1933 to 1938, he had been primarily concerned with influencing public opinion in regard to his domestic New Deal program to combat the Great Depression, not foreign affairs. Consequently he seldom addressed international relations in his public statements. The major exception, his famous 1937 speech suggesting a "Quarantine" of aggressor nations, was apparently intended merely as a "trial balloon" and had no follow-up whatsoever.[10] Indeed, in that year as well as in the previous two years, he signed Neutrality Acts designed to keep the United States out of any war that might erupt overseas, even though he opposed many of the provisions in these bills. He did so because he did not want to alienate pro–New Deal but isolationist sentiment within the Congress. In a 1936 speech in Chautauqua, New York, he sounded like an isolationist himself when he asserted, "I hate war," that in any new war Americans would "face the choice of profits [which he labeled "fool's gold"] or peace," and that they should choose the latter.[11] If anything, the courting of such isolationist sentiment became even more important after the congressional revolt against his 1937 "court packing" proposal.

The following year witnessed the last major burst of New Deal legislation, however, and the beginnings of a shift in presidential focus to foreign affairs as Europe lurched toward war. But within this shift Roosevelt moved very cautiously and always in line with what the public opinion polls revealed and what he concluded the public would accept. When those polls in late 1938 showed majority support for the Munich Conference (59 percent) but belief by a much greater majority (90 percent) that Hitler had lied and would soon grab more territory, for example, the president initiated a major rearmament program but justified it in terms of maintaining a strong defense that would deter aggressors and thus enable the United States to stay out of any war that erupted. In line with such reasoning he focused on a major expansion of U.S. air and naval forces, which the public viewed as defensive in nature and thus acceptable, rather than ground forces that were viewed as more aggressive as well as more of a threat to American lives. "American mothers don't want their sons to be soldiers," Roosevelt would later quip, though they "don't seem to mind their sons becoming sailors."[12] Revealingly, he also tried to make the material results of this rearmament available to Britain and France by encouraging the latter to place aircraft orders and by asking in early 1939 for repeal of the U.S. arms embargo. But his intervention in the ensuing congressional debate was late, halfhearted, and inept, and he lost by two votes in the House of Representatives and by one vote in Senate committee.

Roosevelt had greater success after the European war actually began in September, as Congress in the following month agreed to his second request for repeal of the arms embargo during the special session that he had called to obtain that repeal. In doing so it was clearly following a public that overwhelmingly favored Britain and France over Nazi Germany while continuing its desire to stay out of the war (Roosevelt pointedly stated in a September 3 Fireside Chat that he would issue a neutrality proclamation but could not ask the nation to remain neutral in thought as well, as Wilson had done in 1914).[13] Sale of war material to Britain and France on a "cash and carry" basis, rather than placing U.S. ships and citizens in danger, clearly reflected such public desires, as well as the general belief that London and Paris would not need anything beyond such arms purchases to defeat Germany.

Hitler's stunning military victories in Western Europe during the spring of 1940, culminating in French defeat and surrender in June, quickly ended such beliefs. Deeply fearful of Nazi Germany, and impressed by British courage during the ensuing Battle of Britain as reported from London by Edward R. Murrow on the radio and by numerous journalists in their published articles, Americans now overwhelmingly favored aiding the British. Indeed, an extraordinary 80 percent of those polled favored such aid. Equally significant, by the early fall nearly 60 percent considered such aid more important than staying out of the war—a figure nearly double what it had been in May.[14]

Roosevelt's statements during this period both reflected and influenced this dramatic shift in public opinion. On June 10 in Charlottesville, Virginia, for example, he denounced isolationism as well as Germany and Italy while pledging "the material resources of this nation" to Great Britain. Simultaneously, however, he remained well aware of the fact that an even larger percentage of those polled than the 80 percent favoring aid to England (more than 90 percent) opposed any U.S. declaration of war on Germany.[15] Working within this context, and indeed strengthening it, Roosevelt moved to provide aid to Britain but justified it as part of a major effort both to strengthen U.S. defenses and to keep the United States officially out of the war. While Congress agreed to massive and unprecedented defense expenditures as well as the institution of the first peacetime draft in U.S. history, Roosevelt echoed the arguments of those favoring aid to England, most notably the recently established Committee to Defend America by Aiding the Allies. London, he asserted, now constituted America's first line of defense against Hitler, and helping the British to stay in the war via the sale of scarce war material thus kept the conflict away from American shores. To prevent such sales from becoming a partisan political issue, Roosevelt also appointed to his cabinet during the summer of 1940 two distinguished Republicans who favored aid to England—former secretary of war and state Henry L. Stimson and former vice presidential nominee Frank Knox—as his secretaries of war and navy, respectively. In September, after much prodding from new British prime minister Winston Churchill, he responded to desperate pleas for naval assistance with an executive agreement to provide London with fifty overage warships in exchange for ninety-nine-year leases on eight British bases in the Western Hemisphere, a move he and Chief of Naval Operations Admiral Harold R. Stark justified as a net strategic gain for the United States and one that 70 percent of the public approved, even though it ended any semblance of American neutrality in the conflict.[16]

These moves proved inadequate in light of both the German U-boat offensive in the Atlantic and Britain's looming inability to pay for American war supplies. Churchill made these facts perfectly clear to Roosevelt soon after FDR's reelection to an unprecedented third term in November 1940.[17] In response, the president dramatically proposed in December that Congress remove "that silly, foolish old dollar sign" by agreeing to lend or lease war material to Britain, arguing once again that this would actually keep war away from America's shores by maintaining Britain as the first line of U.S. defense, and that in this crisis the United States should become the "arsenal of democracy." In his annual message to Congress less than two weeks later, he in effect sketched out a broad set of ideological U.S. war aims, despite America's official neutrality, by calling for the creation of a new world order based upon four freedoms—freedom of speech and of worship, freedom from want and from fear—as attainable "in our own time and generation" and as "the very antithesis of the so-called new order of tyranny which the dictators seek to impose with the crash of a bomb."[18]

Anti-interventionists were furious over what they considered the president's duplicity. They argued that Lend-Lease would actually lead the United States into war rather than keep it out. After fierce debate, however, Congress in March agreed to a Lend-Lease bill by votes of 60–31 in the Senate and 317–71 in the House, with an appropriation of $7 billion and presidential authority to lend or lease war material to any nation whose defense he deemed essential to U.S. security. It thereby made the United States an unofficial belligerent in the war and ally of Britain. Public support for such aid as more important than staying out of the conflict now topped 60 and approached 70 percent. Nevertheless, the percentage of those favoring entry into the war remained under 10 percent.[19]

Under Roosevelt's leadership, the American people had thus moved during the years 1939–41 from rigid neutrality to open support of Great Britain as the nation's first line of defense. Yet they remained doggedly opposed to entering the war. Indeed, their agreement to aid Britain was based on the belief that such aid could keep them out of the war—even though it clearly risked exactly what they wished to avoid.

Selling a Limited Naval War

Whether Roosevelt shared such conflicting sentiments with the public or merely realized he had to work within and/or manipulate them remains uncertain. His actions during the remaining months of 1941 tend to support the latter interpretation, though far from completely.

Roosevelt's major problem during this period focused on how to get Lend-Lease supplies to their destination in the face of the German U-boat threat. His moves to address this problem resulted in a shooting war with the Germans by the fall of 1941, albeit one that remained undeclared and limited to naval conflict in the Atlantic Ocean.

Using his powers as commander in chief, Roosevelt first sanctioned secret Anglo-American military staff conversations in late 1940 and early 1941 to determine a combined military strategy for the two nations should the United States officially enter the war. Then in April he unilaterally extended the hemispheric security zone enunciated two years earlier in the Pan-American Declaration of Panama, within which European military activity would not be allowed, from 300 to over 1,000 miles—all the way to 25 degrees west longitude. He also ordered the occupation of Greenland, established naval and air patrols to enforce the expanded security zone, and ordered the U.S. Navy to trail German U-boats within it and report their positions to the British. In May he declared a state of unlimited national emergency in response to the breakout of the German battleship *Bismarck* into the Atlantic and major German offensives against the British in the Balkans, Mediterranean, and North Africa as well as the Atlantic. In June he welcomed the Soviet Union as an ally and promised aid after Hitler invaded that country, and in July he extended the hemispheric security zone all the way to Iceland by ordering U.S. occupation of the island—a "creative geography" as Warren Kimball has quipped, "that only Popes had tried before."[20]

Then in August Roosevelt met with Churchill off the coast of Newfoundland, and together they issued the Atlantic Charter as a statement of joint Anglo-American war aims. According to Churchill, FDR also indicated privately his intention "to wage war but not declare it" and to "force an 'incident' . . . which would justify him in opening hostilities."[21] In the following month he did just that by using a confrontation in the Atlantic between the U.S. destroyer *Greer* and a German U-boat to order the navy both to "shoot on sight" whenever a U-boat was spotted and to escort all merchant ships as far as Iceland. Although he painted the incident as an unprovoked German attack on the *Greer,* he conveniently failed to mention in his public statements that the U.S. warship had been trailing the U-boat and radioing its position back to British naval and air forces that had responded by attacking it.[22]

Interestingly, the percentage of Americans favoring formal U.S. entry into the war increased substantially during this period, topping 10 percent for the first time in April and then doubling by August and September. Whether this increase precipitated the above-mentioned presidential actions or resulted from them remains an open and perhaps unanswerable question. Britain's King George VI provided perhaps the most provocative and truthful answer when he informed FDR in June that he had been "struck by the way you have led public opinion by allowing it to get ahead of you."[23]

Nevertheless, the House in August agreed by only one vote (203–202) to extend the term of service for those drafted in 1940. Moreover, public support for formal U.S. entry into the war still stood at less than 25 percent in October, when Roosevelt asked for an end to what he labeled the "crippling provisions" of the Neutrality Acts so that U.S. merchant ships could be armed and allowed to carry Lend-Lease supplies to Britain. After bitter debate and U-boat attacks on two U.S. destroyers, one of which (the *Reuben James*) was sunk on October 31 with the loss of 115 American lives, Congress agreed to repeal the Neutrality legislation, albeit by the close votes of 212–194 in the House and 50–37 in the Senate. The United States was now engaged in an undeclared naval war in the Atlantic that included the transport of Lend-Lease supplies by armed U.S. as well as British merchant vessels, their protection by U.S. warships, and combat between these ships and German U-boats. In effect, the United States had entered World War II with everything except troops and an official declaration.

Those were huge exceptions, however, and ones that Roosevelt insisted on maintaining. Indeed, Churchill had come to Newfoundland in August to obtain U.S. entry into the war and had left the conference convinced he had failed, despite the supposed private pledge to "wage war but not declare it."[24] Furthermore, Roosevelt rejected army calls in the September "Victory Program" for the creation of a huge force of 8.5 million men in 215 divisions to be used against Germany in Central Europe, despite the fact that his military advisors had been consistently warning him over the past year that Germany could not be defeated without such full-scale U.S. participation.[25] Indeed, the Victory Program had been created in response to a far more limited presidential request for an estimate of the *production* requirements needed to defeat America's potential enemies,[26] and Roosevelt was far from pleased with the fact that the armed forces had gone far beyond this to estimate manpower requirements and overseas deployments. In a lengthy and "very frank" discussion of the estimate with Secretary of War Stimson on September 25, the president specifically made clear his displeasure over the army's assumption in this regard "that we must invade and crush Germany," an assumption he feared would elicit "a very bad reaction" from the public. Instead, he continued to focus on the naval conflict in the Atlantic and with it the possibility of sending small expeditionary forces to islands in the Atlantic and/or French West Africa—moves he could justify as defensive efforts to preclude German takeover of such areas as "launch pads" for attacks on the Western Hemisphere and that the public would therefore support.[27]

Whether Roosevelt *ever* accepted before Pearl Harbor the army's argument that such limited moves could not result in German defeat, and if so when he did so, remain open questions upon which historians continue to disagree.[28] So is the related but broader question of whether he could have ever obtained a formal declaration of war from Congress or indeed whether he even desired one. His behavior throughout 1941 reveals a general movement toward that outcome, but also a continued fear of losing public support. It also reveals a continued belief that material and naval aid to Germany's foes would be sufficient.

In this regard, the closest historical parallel to the undeclared naval war that developed in the Atlantic during the fall of 1941 was the undeclared naval "Quasi War" with France of 1798–1800, not the full-scale U.S. participation of 1917–18 or 1942–45. While some scholars maintain that Roosevelt held back primarily due to his fear that public opinion would not tolerate full belligerency, it is equally if not more likely that FDR, a former assistant secretary of the navy who followed Admiral Alfred Thayer Mahan and his sea power theories, believed that naval warfare to ensure the delivery of Lend-Lease supplies to Britain (and by November to Russia as well) would be sufficient. One way or the other, if Roosevelt was indeed trying to "sell war" to the American people in 1941, it was a limited war in the Atlantic far removed from the unlimited global conflict for total victory in which the United States would engage from 1942 to 1945—and from the looming conflict with Japan that he and his military advisors sought to avoid in light of the threat posed by Nazi Germany. Their failure to do so led not only to Pearl Harbor but also to a new set of serious problems with public opinion.

Selling a Global Coalition War and Europe-First Strategy

Contrary to what appears obvious in hindsight, selling an unlimited global war to the American people after Pearl Harbor was far from easy. In this regard we have been somewhat misled by the "Good War" and "Greatest Generation" mythology and have incorrectly assumed that an aroused and unified public was ready after December 7 to follow Roosevelt's lead and fight to total victory around the globe, no matter what the cost or the time involved.[29] Reality was far more complex and problematic. Indeed, despite statements to the contrary both at the time and later, what is usually (and incorrectly) labeled as "isolationism" was far from dead,[30] and after Pearl Harbor Roosevelt and his advisors remained deeply worried that it might reemerge in new forms. Related to this was a fear that the public would neither understand nor accept the need for a long global war fought in conjunction with allies and according to previously agreed-upon strategic priorities.

Obtaining and maintaining public unity for such a long coalition war and strategy remained a top worry and priority for Roosevelt throughout the remainder of his life and one that heavily influenced his strategic decisions and postwar plans as well as his public statements.

In the days and weeks immediately following Pearl Harbor, Roosevelt faced the first and in some ways the most serious problem in this regard. He and his military advisers had agreed long before the Japanese attack that in the event of official U.S. entry into a global war against the Axis powers, the United States would join with Britain to focus on defeating Germany first while maintaining a defensive position in the Pacific. Indeed, the previously mentioned secret military staff conversations of January–March 1941 had resulted in a formal Anglo-American agreement on this matter, known as ABC-1.[31] But on December 7 the United States was attacked by Japan, not by Germany. The administration publicly asserted in the ensuing days that Tokyo had acted at the instigation of Hitler, who had actually masterminded the attack as part of his global strategy. Roosevelt himself emphasized such an interpretation and the ensuing need for a global coalition-oriented response during his December 9 Fireside Chat. Such efforts and Hitler's December 11 declaration of war against the United States resolved the immediate problem and resulted in the near-unanimous public and congressional support for a declaration of war against Germany as well as Japan that Roosevelt clearly desired.[32]

Such unity did not extend to global strategy, however. To the contrary, Roosevelt still faced a Congress and public intent on immediate and unilateral revenge against Japan rather than combined action against the more powerful and dangerous Germany. Indeed, many Americans (30 percent in January) appeared willing to consider a negotiated compromise peace with Berlin in order to focus on the hated Japanese. Such desires were only reinforced by the series of humiliating defeats that followed in the Pacific.[33] Rather than being his "back door to war," as some of his early critics claimed and contemporary conspiracy theorists continue to assert,[34] Pearl Harbor created for Roosevelt enormous and what appeared to be nearly insoluble political-strategic dilemmas.

In light of these dilemmas as well as his previously expressed interest in the area, Roosevelt thus approved a British plan for a combined Anglo-American invasion of French Northwest Africa in 1942, Operation GYMNAST. As proposed to him by Churchill during the January–February ARCADIA Conference in Washington, that invasion would be launched in conjunction with a renewed British offensive against General Erwin Rommel's German and Italian forces in the Libyan desert so as to obtain Allied control of the entire North Africa littoral. By March, however, continued U.S. and British military setbacks in the Pacific, Southeast Asia, Libya, the Mediterranean, and the Atlantic had forced the indefinite postponement of the operation. At that very moment, army planners were proposing an end to the global dispersion of U.S. forces and their immediate concentration in the United Kingdom for a cross-Channel assault, the so-called "Second Front" that the hard-pressed Soviet Union under Josef Stalin had been demanding from its allies for months. Simultaneously, Roosevelt found himself not only under increasing pressure by a public still intent on revenge against Japan and an end to the string of American defeats in the Pacific, but also under increasing attacks by political opponents, many former isolationists (now labeled "divisionists") who questioned his strategic priorities as well as his competency as a commander in chief in light of those defeats and who favored a negotiated settlement with Germany. Some even called for General Douglas MacArthur to be recalled to Washington in order to, in effect, run the war effort instead of Roosevelt. The president was also deeply worried by a related public ignorance about the war and a troubling public mood scholars have described as a mixture of complacency, passivity, indifference, and/or defeatism, all of which he feared could lead to a revival of isolationism as well as divide the public and negatively affect morale, productivity, and the entire war effort.[35]

In this situation Roosevelt grasped onto the army plan for a cross-Channel assault as a way to raise public morale and awareness, refocus its attention on the European theater, and silence his critics. It would also enable him to respond positively to Stalin's demands for such an operation and hopefully to talk the Soviet leader out of his additional demand for postwar territorial agreements with the British regarding Eastern Europe. Such agreements, FDR feared, would alienate American public opinion much as the "secret treaties" had done after World War I, thereby threatening public support for the Allied war effort and endangering his postwar plans.

By early April Roosevelt had therefore agreed to the army plan to concentrate all available forces in the United Kingdom for a huge cross-Channel assault in the spring of 1943 or a much smaller operation in the fall of 1942 with whatever forces were by then available. The British at first concurred, if only to preclude an American turn toward the Pacific. In June, however, they raised serious objections to any 1942 operation on the grounds that it would fail disastrously, while Churchill pressed instead for a revival of the old GYMNAST plan to invade French Northwest Africa.[36]

Both the British and the American chiefs of staffs concluded at a second Anglo-American summit conference in Washington during June that offensive operations should be undertaken in the European theater during 1942 only "in case of necessity" or "an exceptionally favorable opportunity," in which case crossing the Channel, invading Norway, or recapturing the Channel islands were all preferable to North Africa. Roosevelt and Churchill disagreed vehemently, however, asserting that it was "essential" for their two nations to "be prepared to act offensively in 1942" within the European theater and emphasizing a return to GYMNAST in this regard if a successful cross-Channel attack in 1942 looked "improbable."[37] When Churchill argued in the following month that this was indeed the case and proposed a revival of GYMNAST as the "true second front" for 1942, Roosevelt concurred over the vehement objections of his chiefs of staff. Indeed, he angrily overruled their objections and alternative proposals that focused on the Pacific, signing his messages in this matter "commander in chief" for emphasis and forcing them to fly to London and agree to the North African operation, now renamed TORCH.[38] His reasoning was overwhelmingly political: a successful European operation in 1942 was essential to reassure the Soviets, refocus public opinion on the primacy of the war against Germany, highlight the importance of acting in conjunction with allies, squelch continuing attacks on his military leadership, and counter the "separate peace" sentiment propagated by his isolationist enemies—whom he sarcastically described in early October as wanting to win the war only "(a) if at the same time Russia is defeated, (b) at the same time, England is defeated, (c) at the same time, Roosevelt is defeated."[39]

Marshall and his JCS colleagues thus concluded in mid-July that Roosevelt and "apparently our political system would require major operations this year in Africa." The army chief was even blunter after the war, asserting that one of the most important lessons he had learned during the conflict was that a democracy required a successful offensive every year. "We failed to see that the leader in a democracy has to keep the people entertained," he sardonically told his biographer in 1956. "That may sound like the wrong word but it conveys the thought. . . . People demand action"[40]

Roosevelt clearly would have preferred TORCH to be launched before the midterm congressional elections of 1942, pleading with Marshall on one occasion to "please make it happen before Election Day" while holding up his hands in prayer.[41] He did not press the point when informed that this was not possible, however, for he had bigger political goals in mind than a few congressional seats: the full mobilization of public opinion for a total war effort and the manipulation of that opinion to support the Europe-first coalition strategy that he considered essential to victory in that effort. As Steven Casey noted, "Instead of merely reacting to opinion, FDR was hoping to shape it. His aim was to employ American troops against the Wehrmacht as a method of finally eradicating the lingering problems of apathy, defeatism, and weak support for a 'Germany-first' strategy, and North Africa was the only feasible area for such action in 1942."[42]

Nevertheless, neither Roosevelt nor the Joint Chiefs totally ignored the Pacific at this time. Indeed, they could not do so, either militarily or politically. Something had to be done to halt the Japanese advance beyond the naval victory at Midway in May, especially in the Southwest Pacific Theater where they were threatening to cut lines of communication to Australia. And as in the years 1939–41, public opinion could not be totally ignored. Pressure for action in the Pacific had to be mollified to some extent.

In the same month that Roosevelt forced the Joint Chiefs to agree to TORCH, those chiefs thus ordered the initiation of operations against the Japanese in the southern Solomon Islands. Launched in August, these operations turned into a massive six-month campaign on and around the island of Guadalcanal. That campaign did succeed in mollifying public pressure for Pacific action, but it forced Roosevelt as well as the Joint Chiefs to support major reinforcements in October at the expense of the European theater,[43] even as final preparations were being made for the early November invasion of French North Africa—which also turned into an extensive six-month campaign. Both campaigns would eventually prove successful, but events in the Pacific would result in a major modification of American strategy: while "Germany-first" remained the official strategy, 1942 ended with more U.S. forces deployed in the Pacific and Far East than in the European theater.[44]

Altering that pattern, and convincing the public to accept such an alteration in favor of Europe, continued to inform Roosevelt's strategic decisions. TORCH had successfully addressed many of his concerns about public opinion, but continued public support for his policies nevertheless required continued military action.[45] At the January Casablanca Conference he consequently agreed with Churchill to continue in the Mediterranean via an invasion of Sicily so as to have some European land offensive in mid-1943 and to an expanded Anglo-American air campaign against German cities—despite the fact that to date this offensive had been militarily ineffective—at least partially so as to show both Stalin and the American people some direct action against Germany. Furthermore, at the end of the Casablanca Conference he acted to squelch once and for all talk of a negotiated peace with Germany, as well as criticism of his willingness during and after TORCH to work with such Vichy French collaborators as Admiral Jean Darlan and Marcel Peyrouton,[46] by publicly enunciating during a press conference Unconditional Surrender of the Axis Powers as official Allied policy. Actually this policy was far from new. Indeed, it had long been the unstated policy of all members of the Grand Alliance and one of their most important lowest common denominators. All that was new was its public enunciation at this time, an enunciation dictated by Roosevelt's desire once again to influence public opinion as well as to reassure the Soviets in light of the probable lack of a cross-Channel attack in 1943.

In the spring and summer of 1943, Roosevelt began once again to support calls by the JCS for that cross-Channel attack instead of additional Mediterranean operations, albeit now in 1944 and in conjunction with expanded offensives against the Japanese in the Central as well as the Southwest Pacific Theaters. Such multiple offensives were now possible due to the massive expansion of American war production—provided Mediterranean offensives were limited. Once again Roosevelt was heavily influenced in his choice of strategic priorities by the need to provide the Soviets with what they demanded militarily to stay in the war and by the need to keep public opinion focused on Europe yet mollified regarding Japan by some activity in the Pacific. In 1943, however, each desire had a different emphasis than it had had the previous year. Whereas the Soviet focus in 1942 had been on crossing the Channel so as to relieve the pressure on the hard-pressed Red Armies and thereby enable the Russians to survive the German onslaught, the focus in 1943 was on preventing a possible Russo-German peace by providing Stalin with the operation he demanded to stay in the war—and simultaneously land enough troops in Europe to prevent him from dominating the entire continent if he did stay in the war.[47] Similarly, the focus on public opinion shifted from the 1942 emphasis on *any* European operation (even against the Vichy French instead of the Germans) so as to raise morale and shift attention away from the Pacific, to a focus in 1943 on the only operation deemed capable of obtaining quick and decisive victory against Germany.

The desire for such quick and decisive victory was political as well as military. The Joint Chiefs and their planners strongly believed that continuation of British strategy in the Mediterranean would lead to a long and indecisive war that neither the public nor the Soviets would tolerate. While the latter might very well respond with a separate peace, the former would return to their preoccupation with the Pacific, both of which would preclude the possibility of victory over the much more dangerous German enemy. As

Stimson informed Churchill in July, the American people viewed the Italians "as a joke as fighters; that only by an intellectual effort had they been convinced that Germany was their most dangerous enemy and should be disposed of before Japan; that the enemy whom the American people really hated, if they hated anyone, was Japan which had dealt them a foul blow." Indeed, the public had accepted Germany-first only with the caveat that the European war end quickly as well as decisively so that they could refocus on Japan. Only cross-Channel operations, Stimson argued, could provide that quick and decisive victory.[48] War weariness was a related worry. Democracies were historically notorious for their inability to remain unified and focused for a long war, and a potential breakdown in public unity remained a constant concern of the JCS and their planners as well as the president. Particularly telling in regard to both concerns was Marshall's postwar comment that in the European war he was always concerned with four issues: casualties, duration, expense, and the Pacific and that "We had to go ahead brutally fast" in Europe because "We could not indulge in a Seven Years' War. A king can perhaps do that, but you cannot have such a protracted struggle in a democracy in the face of mounting casualties. I thought that the only place to achieve such a positive and rapid military decision was in the Lowlands of Northwestern Europe. Speed was essential."[49]

The American desire for quick and decisive victory in Europe was thus political as well as military, and it led to an insistence that Mediterranean operations be dramatically limited in 1943 so as to be able to cross the Channel in force in 1944. Pressed first by a united front between Roosevelt and his military advisors on this matter in the spring and summer of 1943, and then at year's end by a united front between Roosevelt and Stalin, Churchill was forced to agree at the November Big Three summit conference in Teheran. By that time, however, Roosevelt was also seriously concerned about public opinion on postwar issues and was therefore "selling" the war in some very specific directions on this topic.

Selling Postwar Internationalism in Wartime

Although Roosevelt had at first mobilized public support for war in the very idealistic terms of the Four Freedoms and Atlantic Charter, his own vision of the postwar world ran in a more realistic direction. Having experienced two German bids for world supremacy, he feared a third if the Grand Alliance fell apart after victory. Roosevelt therefore spoke as early as May 1942 of the victors acting in concert as four global "policemen" after the war in order to preclude such a possibility and to maintain world order.[50] But would the American people support such internationalism after the war, or would they revert to some form of isolationism and/or ineffective unilateralism as they had after World War I? Throughout the war Roosevelt continued to fear the latter.

During this time, however, leading internationalists and their organizations had succeeded in convincing the American people that their refusal to join the League of Nations after World War I had been a tragic mistake and had helped precipitate this second world war. That war, they and the public came to believe, provided a "second chance" to correct their previous error by forming and joining this time a new postwar collective security organization. By July 1942, 59 percent favored entry into a new League; by early 1943 the percentage had risen to 72.[51]

Having experienced the failure of the first collective security organization during the 1930s, Roosevelt had little faith in the ability of any new one to do better. Indeed, in August 1941 he had deleted mention of such an organization from Churchill's draft of the Atlantic Charter, asserting that he preferred an Anglo-American police force. "The time had come," he commented, "to be realistic."[52] But he soon recognized that promotion of such a body with U.S. membership could bury isolationism and unilateralism permanently and commit the United States to a major postwar international role. Consequently he fused his power-oriented concept of the "Four Policemen" with a postwar international security organization. Far from accidentally, that organization took the official name of the World War II Grand Alliance— the United Nations—with the Allies maintaining their dominance and preserving peace through the Security Council. During the summer and fall of 1944, Allied representatives meeting at Dumbarton Oaks in Washington hammered out the basic structure of this new organization.[53]

But concerted Allied action in the postwar era, Roosevelt recognized, would require extensive wartime compromises with those allies—including agreement to certain Soviet as well as British policies that the American people would find repugnant. Particularly notable in this regard were British insistence on maintaining their overseas empire and Stalin's continued insistence on re-creating one in Eastern Europe via both retention of the territories he had obtained through the 1939 Nazi-Soviet Pact and postwar control of the nations on his expanded western border. The American people, Roosevelt feared, would respond to such power politics and imperialism by reverting to isolationism and unilateralism as they had after World

War I, thereby splitting the Grand Alliance and enabling Germany to revive and make yet another bid for world domination.

To preclude such a possibility, Roosevelt hid many of his diplomatic compromises with his allies while continuing to speak in idealistic terms that would appeal to the public. So did high officials within his administration. Most notable and notorious in this regard were the absurd comments of Secretary of State Cordell Hull after the 1943 Moscow Foreign Ministers' Conference, during which the Soviets agreed to future cooperation within the framework of a new League of Nations. Convinced that such agreement laid the basis for a new and successful Wilsonian world order, Hull informed Congress: "There will no longer be need for spheres of influence, for alliances, for balance of power, or any of the other special arrangements through which, in the unhappy past, the nations strove to safeguard their security or to promote their interests."[54] While Hull was uttering these words, Roosevelt and Churchill were privately agreeing at the Teheran Conference to a westward shift in Polish boundaries so as to provide Stalin with the portion of Eastern Poland that he had taken in 1939 and now demanded to keep along with his other 1939 territorial acquisitions—to which they also agreed: the three Baltic states of Estonia, Latvia, and Lithuania, and the Rumanian provinces of Bessarabia and Bucovina.

Throughout the remainder of the war, Roosevelt continued to speak in idealistic and universalistic terms about the postwar world while privately practicing power politics. He acquiesced in West European retention of their overseas empires and Soviet control of Poland and the rest of Eastern Europe—both in order to keep the Grand Alliance together and because he realized that he did not have the power to prevent any of this. Occasionally he verbalized that reality. In 1943, for example, he told Francis Cardinal Spellman that Russia would "predominate" in postwar Europe in general and in Eastern Europe in particular, and that while the results might be brutal, the United States and Britain "cannot fight the Russians." In that same year he bluntly asked the Polish ambassador, "Do you expect us and Great Britain to declare war on Joe Stalin if they can cross your previous frontier? Even if we wanted to, Russia can still field an army twice our combined strength, and we would just have no say in the matter at all."[55] Usually, however, FDR kept such hard facts to himself for fear of the public reaction. Better, he probably thought, to get the American people committed to internationalism via membership in a new collective security organization no matter what wartime and postwar realities needed to be hidden from them in order to do so.

Such logic led Roosevelt and his advisors to keep secret not only Soviet territorial demands but also Soviet demands at the Dumbarton Oaks Conference for an absolute veto in the Security Council and for sixteen seats in the General Assembly—one for each Soviet "republic"—as the price for their membership in the organization. "My God," said Roosevelt when he heard of the latter demand, directing Undersecretary of State Edward R. Stettinius to warn the Soviets "privately and personally and immediately" that this could never be accepted and that it "might ruin the chance of getting an international organization accepted in this country." Stettinius was so concerned that he took extraordinary precautions to keep the Soviet demand secret, even from other members of the U.S. delegation, pressing for its removal from the official minutes and referring to the topic in his own notes and memoranda as the "X Matter."[56]

Roosevelt's policies in this regard reached their logical conclusion at the February Yalta Conference. There he in effect traded Soviet postwar control of Poland that he knew he could not prevent for Soviet concessions on General Assembly votes and the Security Council veto, as well as Soviet agreement to a combined Allied occupation of Germany and participation in the war against Japan for territorial concessions in the Far East. The public, however, remained ignorant of the contents of these agreements and compromises. Indeed, as Eric Alterman has accurately concluded, in his speech to Congress after the conference, Roosevelt flatly lied about the accords—from his general statement (similar to Hull's in 1943) that they spelled "the end of the system of unilateral action and exclusive alliances and spheres of influences and balance of power," to his specific comments about the Polish, German, and UN agreements.[57]

Whether such dissembling could have been maintained had Roosevelt lived is an unanswerable question. What is clear is that the Yalta Accords themselves began to break down with the Soviets even before his April death, and that public faith in them collapsed as soon as their specific components became known—so much so that "Yalta" quickly became a major issue in U.S. domestic politics, virtually a dirty word in the English language, and a symbol of naïve and craven appeasement by Roosevelt.[58] It remains so to this very day. In reality, however, it was nothing of the sort.

The Consequences of Selling War

Roosevelt thus tried to "sell" a series of very different wars and U.S. policies to the American people throughout World War II. Overall he succeeded brilliantly. Whether by following, by leading, or as King George noted, by leading while appearing to follow, he successfully sold the idea of aid to the Allies—first in the form of sale of war material, then in the form of Lend-Lease, and finally in the form of an undeclared naval war to deliver that aid. After Pearl Harbor he successfully sold the Germany-first strategy, even though it was Japan rather than Germany that had attacked the United States and aroused strong public emotions, and along with it a combined global war effort with allies that stood in sharp contrast to the unilateralism that had previously marked U.S. foreign and military policies. He also "sold" the American people on a new internationalist role in the world within the framework of membership in a new collective security organization, and in retrospect he buried isolationism and unilateralism for at least the next fifty years in favor of internationalism and multilateralism. Perhaps most important, and most difficult, he mobilized public opinion for a huge global and total war effort, and he kept that opinion largely unified throughout the entire conflict. Only the failure of his successors to do so in their own wars in Korea, Vietnam, and Iraq has made clear in hindsight how difficult this was—and how important.

The price for these successes was steep, however. Whether Roosevelt led or followed public opinion from 1939 to 1941, and whether or not he ever desired full U.S. entry into the war, he never really gave Congress and the public the opportunity to debate his measures on those grounds. Instead, he justified those measures as designed to keep the United States out of war, and he implemented many of them by executive decree rather than congressional vote. As Richard W. Steele has aptly concluded, "From the president's perspective, the issue of war and peace was too important a subject for debate."[59] Furthermore, he clearly and deceitfully manipulated public opinion in September 1941 with the *Greer* episode, which led to the undeclared naval war with Germany. He thereby established precedents for the abuse of presidential powers as commander in chief that others have followed with disastrous results, most notably Lyndon Johnson in the 1964 Tonkin Gulf episode off the coast of Vietnam—an episode that bears a striking and eerie similarity to the *Greer* episode. As Senator J. William Fulbright pointedly noted in this regard, "FDR's deviousness in a good cause made it much easier for [LBJ] to practice the same type of deviousness in a bad cause."[60]

Roosevelt's insistence with Churchill on the North African invasion also had a high price. It delayed cross-Channel operations for two years and thereby increased Soviet suspicions enormously—of the United States as well as Britain. As Stalin bitterly noted the night before the cross-Channel assault finally was launched in June 1944, "Churchill is the kind who, if you don't watch him, will slip a kopeck out of your coat pocket. . . . Roosevelt is not like that. He dips in his hand only for bigger coins."[61]

The highest price of all resulted from FDR's duplicity with the public regarding the shape of the postwar world. Rather than attempting to educate the American people about the unavoidable wartime and postwar continuation of *realpolitik* within international affairs in general and the Grand Alliance in particular, he continued to mouth Wilsonian rhetoric for fear that telling the truth would simply lead to another U.S. withdrawal similar to the one that had taken place in 1919–20 and thus to yet another world war. It was a completely understandable fear given U.S. history, especially the history through which Roosevelt himself had lived. But it set the stage for severe disillusionment and public hysteria during the ensuing Cold War.

It also set the stage for a consistent misuse and abuse of analogies to the World War II years by every president since Roosevelt in their efforts to win public support for their own policies and for continued public myopia regarding the rest of the world. From the 1947 Truman Doctrine that in effect announced the opening of the Cold War, through the Bush Doctrine and invasions of Afghanistan and Iraq as part of the so-called War against Terror fifty-five years later, presidents have consistently sought to equate their overseas adversaries with Adolf Hitler and domestic opponents of their policies with 1930s appeasers and isolationists. In the process they have not only ignored more appropriate historical analogies that might not support their policies but also fostered a series of myths about American behavior during the 1930s and the World War II years—most notably myths about isolationism before Pearl Harbor and exceptional public unity afterwards. They have also tended, at least in their public utterances if not in their actual behavior, to reinforce the public's naïve and incorrect notions about the nature of relations between nations.

Whether Roosevelt could have successfully countered these notions and educated the public to the realities of international affairs we will never know. Given his extraordinary popularity as well as his knowledge and media savvy, however, one can only look back with the desperate wish that he had at least tried.

Notes

1. Katherine Tupper Marshall, *Together: Annals of an Army Wife* (New York: Tupper and Love, 1946), 129–30.

2. For an annotated sample of the rich literature available, see Robert L. Beisner, ed., *American Foreign Relations since 1600: A Guide to the Literature* (Santa Barbara, Calif.: ABC-CLIO, 2003), 1: 856–67. For a historiographical assessment, see Justus D. Doenecke, "U.S. Policy and the European War, 1939–1941," in *Paths to Power: The Historiography of American Foreign Relations to 1941*, ed. Michael J. Hogan (New York: Cambridge University Press, 2000), 224–67.

3. See Beisner, *American Foreign Relations*, 1037–40.

4. See Russell D. Buhite and David W. Levy, eds., *FDR's Fireside Chats* (Norman: University of Oklahoma Press, 1992); Samuel I. Rosenman, *Public Papers and Addresses of Franklin D. Roosevelt*, 13 vols. (New York: Random House, 1938–50); and *The Complete Presidential Press Conferences of Franklin D. Roosevelt* (New York: Da Capo Press, 1972).

5. See Allan M. Winkler, *The Politics of Propaganda: The Office of War Information, 1942–1945* (New Haven: Yale University Press, 1978). For Roosevelt's early interest in propaganda and precursors to the Office of War Information, see Richard W. Steele, "Preparing the Public for War: Efforts to Establish a National Propaganda Agency, 1940–41," *American Historical Review* 75 (1970): 1640–53; "The Great Debate: Roosevelt, the Media, and the Coming of the War, 1940–1941," *Journal of American History* 71 (1984): 69–92; "The Pulse of the People: Franklin D. Roosevelt and the Gauging of American Public Opinion," *Journal of Contemporary History* 9 (1974): 195–216; and *Propaganda in an Open Society: The Roosevelt Administration and the Media, 1933–1941* (Westport, Conn.: Greenwood Press, 1985). For censorship see Michael S. Sweeney, *Secrets of Victory: The Office of Censorship and the American Press and Radio in World War II* (Chapel Hill: University of North Carolina Press, 2001).

6. Justus D. Doenecke and John E. Wilz, *From Isolation to War, 1931–1941* (Wheeling, Ill.: Harlan Davidson, 2003), 75–76.

7. Larry I. Bland, ed., *George C. Marshall: Interviews and Reminiscences for Forrest C. Pogue* (Lexington, Va.: George C. Marshall Research Foundation, 1991), 623; James MacGregor Burns, *Roosevelt: The Soldier of Freedom* (New York: Harcourt Brace Jovanovich, 1970), 427–28; and memo, Marshall to King, July 15, 1942, Record Group (RG 165), Records of the War Department General and Special Staffs, WDCSA 381 War Plans, folder 1, National Archives, College Park, Md., reproduced in Larry I. Bland, ed., *The Papers of George Catlett Marshall* (Baltimore: Johns Hopkins University Press, 1991), 3: 276.

8. Geoffrey C. Ward, "On Writing about FDR," *American Heritage* 23 (1991): 119.

9. For excellent examples of what can be done in this regard, see Waldo Heinrichs, *Threshold of War: Franklin D. Roosevelt and American Entry into World War II* (New York: Oxford University Press, 1988), and Warren F. Kimball, *The Juggler: Franklin Roosevelt as Wartime Statesman* (Princeton, N.J.: Princeton University Press, 1991).

10. U.S. Department of State, *Foreign Relations of the United States: Japan, 1931–1941* (Washington, D.C.: Government Printing Office, 1943) 1: 379–83 (hereafter cited as FRUS with subtitle or year and volume); Dorothy Borg, "Notes on Roosevelt's Quarantine Speech," *Political Science Quarterly* 72 (1957): 405–33.

11. Edgar B. Nixon, ed., *Franklin D. Roosevelt and Foreign Affairs: January 1933–January 1937* (Cambridge: Harvard University Press, 1969), 3: 377–84. Robert A. Divine argues in his *Roosevelt and World War II* (Baltimore: Johns Hopkins University Press, 1969), 1–23, that such statements accurately reflected Roosevelt's isolationist views at that time. Robert Dallek disagrees in *Franklin D. Roosevelt and American Foreign Policy, 1932–1945* (New York: Oxford University Press, 1979), 3–168. For FDR's views of Europe, see John L. Harper, *American Visions of Europe: Franklin D. Roosevelt, George F. Kennan, and Dean G. Acheson* (New York: Cambridge University Press, 1994).

12. Robert Murphy, *Diplomat among Warriors* (Garden City, N.Y.: Doubleday, 1964), 69.

13. Buhite and Levy, *FDR's Fireside Chats*, 148–51.

14. See Hadley Cantril and Research Associates in the Office of Public Opinion Research, Princeton University, *Gauging Public Opinion* (Princeton, N.J.: Princeton University Press, 1944; Port Washington, N.Y.: Kennikat Press, 1972), 222. For the role of British propaganda in creating favorable public sentiment, see Nicholas John Cull, *Selling War: The British Propaganda Campaign against American "Neutrality" in World War II* (New York: Oxford University Press, 1995).

15. Cantril, *Gauging Public Opinion*, 222; Mark Lincoln Chadwin, *The Warhawks: American Interventionists before Pearl Harbor* (New York: Norton, 1970), 30–31; Rosenman, *Public Papers of Roosevelt*, 9: 259–64.

16. See Chadwin, *The Warhawks*, 74–108, for the important role played by the informal Century Group in proposing and winning support for this executive agreement.

17. Warren F. Kimball, ed., *Churchill & Roosevelt: The Complete Correspondence* (Princeton, N.J.: Princeton University Press, 1984), 1: 87–111.

18. Roosevelt Lend-Lease comments from December 17, 1941, press conference and December 29, 1941, radio address, in *Complete Presidential Press Conferences*, vols. 15–16: 353–55; and State Department *Bulletin* 4 (1941): 3–8. For the Four Freedoms, see Rosenman, *Public Papers of Roosevelt*, 9: 663–78.

19. See Warren F. Kimball, *The Most Unsordid Act: Lend-Lease, 1939–1941* (Baltimore: Johns Hopkins University Press, 1969); and *Forged in War: Roosevelt, Churchill, and the Second World War* (New York: William Morrow, 1997), 72–75; Cantril, *Gauging Public Opinion*, 222.

20. Warren F. Kimball, "Franklin Roosevelt: Dr. Win-the-War," in *Commanders in Chief*, ed. Joseph Dawson (Lawrence: University Press of Kansas, 1993), 95–96.

21. Dallek, *Roosevelt and American Foreign Policy*, 285. On the Atlantic Conference and Charter, see Theodore A. Wilson, *The First Summit: Roosevelt and Churchill at Placentia Bay, 1941*, rev. ed. (Lawrence: University Press of Kansas, 1991).

22. See Thomas A. Bailey and Paul B. Ryan, *Hitler vs. Roosevelt: The Undeclared Naval War* (New York: Free Press, 1979), 169–87.

23. Gloria J. Barron, *Leadership in Crisis: FDR and the Path to Intervention* (Port Washington, N.Y.: Kennikat Press, 1973), 72.

24. David Reynolds, *Creation of the Anglo-American Alliance, 1937–1941: A Study in*

Competitive Co-operation (Chapel Hill: University of North Carolina Press, 1981), 214–16, and *From Munich to Pearl Harbor: Roosevelt's America and the Origins of the Second World War* (Chicago: Ivan R. Dee, 2001), 148–49; Kimball, *Forged in War*, 102–103.

25. See Mark A. Stoler, *Allies and Adversaries: The Joint Chiefs of Staff, the Grand Alliance, and U.S. Strategy in World War II* (Chapel Hill: University of North Carolina Press, 2000), 29–58.

26. Roosevelt to Stimson and Knox, July 9, 1941, Franklin D. Roosevelt Papers, PSF, boxes 28 and 40, Stimson and Knox folders, Franklin D. Roosevelt Library, Hyde Park, N.Y. (hereafter cited as FDRL), reproduced in Steven T. Ross, ed., *American War Plans, 1919–1945* (New York: Garland, 1992), 5: 146–47.

27. Henry L. Stimson Diary, September 25, October 6 and 7, 1941, Stimson Papers, Yale University Library, New Haven. For evidence that Hitler had just such plans, see Gerhard Weinberg, *A World at Arms: A Global History of World War II* (New York: Cambridge University Press, 1994), 86–87, 175–78, 182, 238–46, and 250–63; and Norman Goda, *Tomorrow the World: Hitler, Northwest Africa, and the Path toward America* (College Station: Texas A&M University Press, 1998). Dated September 11, 1941, the Victory Program is in JB 355, serial 707, RG 225, National Archives; it is reproduced in its entirety and with relevant correspondence in Ross, *American War Plans*, 5: 143–298.

28. While some historians conclude that he accepted the inevitability of fully entering the war sometime in 1941, I join those who believe Roosevelt at no time before Pearl Harbor agreed with the army point of view regarding the need to send a large land force onto the European continent.

29. Studs Terkel, *The Good War: An Oral History of World War II* (New York: Pantheon, 1984), and Tom Brokaw, *The Greatest Generation* (New York: Random House, 1998).

30. I join those who find the term *isolationism* so limited in its application as to be misleading, and I prefer *unilateralism* as a general descriptive term and *anti-interventionism* as a specific one regarding the European war.

31. The key documents in this regard consist of the November 1940 "Plan Dog" memorandum and the April 1941 revised RAINBOW 5 Plan as well as ABC-1. All three are available in the National Archives and/or the Roosevelt Library, and all three are reproduced in Ross, *American War Plans*, 4: 3–66, 225–74, and 5: 3–43. See also Stoler, *Allies and Adversaries*, 29–40.

32. Buhite and Levy, *FDR's Fireside Chats*, 198–205; Dallek, *Roosevelt and American Foreign Policy*, 312. On administration efforts to paint Pearl Harbor as German-inspired and public agreement with this interpretation, see Richard F. Hill, *Hitler Attacks Pearl Harbor: Why the United States Declared War on Germany* (Boulder: Lynne Rienner, 2003).

33. See Richard W. Steele, "American Popular Opinion and the War against Germany: The Issue of Negotiated Peace, 1942," *Journal of American History* 65 (1978): 704–23; and Steven Casey, *Cautious Crusade: Franklin D. Roosevelt, Public Opinion,*

and the War against Nazi Germany (New York: Oxford University Press, 2001), 48–56.

34. The expression comes from Charles C. Tansill, *Back Door to War* (Chicago: Regnery, 1952). The latest version is Robert B. Stinnet, *Day of Deceit: The Truth about FDR and Pearl Harbor* (New York: Free Press, 2000).

35. Richard W. Steele, *The First Offensive, 1942: Roosevelt, Marshall, and the Making of American Strategy* (Bloomington: Indiana University Press, 1973), 81–93, and "American Popular Opinion," 704–23; Casey, *Cautious Crusade*, 48–56.

36. Steele, *The First Offensive*, 100–149; Mark A. Stoler, *The Politics of the Second Front: American Military Planning and Diplomacy in Coalition Warfare, 1941–1943* (Westport, Conn.: Greenwood Press, 1977), 36–53.

37. *FRUS: The Conferences at Washington, 1941–1942, and Casablanca, 1943*, 422–43, 434–35, 465–69, and 478–79; Arthur Bryant, *The Turn of the Tide: A History of the War Years Based on the Diaries of Lord Alanbrooke, Chief of the Imperial General Staff* (Garden City, N.Y.: Doubleday, 1957), 324–27.

38. Kimball, *Churchill & Roosevelt*, 1: 520; Roosevelt to Marshall, July 13–14, 1942, Roosevelt Papers, Map Room file, box 7-A, folder 2, FDRL; Stoler, *Allies and Adversaries*, 79–87.

39. As quoted in Casey, *Cautious Crusade*, 77. See also 56–79 and 90–91. When asked in June/July 1942 who should make the final decision on military plans, only 21 percent said Roosevelt and Churchill while 64 percent said military leaders. Somewhat paradoxically, given the information cited by Casey and Steele, other polls at this time showed public support for a 1942 invasion of Europe. See Hadley Cantril, ed., *Public Opinion, 1935–1946* (Princeton, N.J.: Princeton University Press, 1951), 1064.

40. Memo, Wedemeyer to Handy, July 14, 1942, RG 165, OPD Exec. 5, Item 1, Tab 10, National Archives, quoted in Bland, *Marshall Papers*, 3: 275–76; Bland, *Marshall Interviews*, 622.

41. Bland, *Marshall Interviews*, 593, 599.

42. Casey, *Cautious Crusade*, 93.

43. Roosevelt to JCS, October 24, 1942, Henry H. Arnold Papers, box 3, Misc. Corres., August–December 1942 folder, Library of Congress, Washington, D.C.

44. Richard M. Leighton and Robert W. Coakley, *Global Logistics and Strategy, 1940–1943, in United States Army in World War II: The War Department* (Washington, D.C.: Government Printing Office, 1955), 662.

45. Steele, "American Popular Opinion," 722, notes that public support for a negotiated peace with German generals never disappeared completely. Indeed, it reached its wartime polling high of 38 percent as late as the spring of 1944!

46. Casey, *Cautious Crusade*, 109–29, emphasizes the importance of public reaction to the Peyrouton appointment as opposed to the more famous Darlan deal.

47. Stoler, *Politics of the Second Front*, 85–91, 102–6, 116–23.

48. Henry L. Stimson and McGeorge Bundy, *On Active Service in Peace and War* (New York: Harper and Brothers, 1947), 429–30.

49. "Interview with General George C. Marshall" by Dr. Sidney T. Matthews et al.,

July 25, 1949, George C. Marshall Research Library, Lexington, Va., microfilm reel 322. Whether Marshall meant that a democracy would not fight for seven years, or that it would cease to be a democracy after seven years of war, remains an unanswered and interesting question in light of these comments.

50. FRUS, 1942, 3: 573–74. See also Kimball, *The Juggler,* 83–105.

51. Robert A. Divine, *Second Chance: The Triumph of Internationalism in America during World War II* (New York: Atheneum, 1971), 68–69, 85.

52. Ibid., 43–44.

53. See Townsend Hoopes and Douglas Brinkley, *FDR and the Creation of the UN* (New Haven: Yale University Press, 1997); and Robert C. Hilderbrand, *Dumbarton Oaks: The Origins of the United Nations and the Search for Postwar Security* (Chapel Hill: University of North Carolina Press, 1990).

54. Cordell Hull, *The Memoirs of Cordell Hull* (New York: Macmillan, 1948), 2: 1313–15.

55. Robert I. Gannon, *The Cardinal Spellman Story* (Garden City, N.Y.: Doubleday, 1962), 222–24; Lloyd C. Gardner, *Spheres of Influence: The Great Powers Partition Europe, from Munich to Yalta* (Chicago: Ivan R. Dee, 1993), 208–9.

56. Hilderbrand, *Dumbarton Oaks*, 96–97.

57. Eric Alterman, *When Presidents Lie: A History of Official Deception and Its Consequences* (New York: Penguin, 2004), 23–41.

58. See Athan G. Theoharis, *The Yalta Myths: An Issue in U.S. Politics, 1945–1955* (Columbia: University of Missouri Press, 1970).

59. Steele, "The Great Debate," 92.

60. Alterman, *When Presidents Lie,* 17.

61. Milovan Djilas, *Conversations with Stalin,* trans. Michael B. Petrovich (New York: Harcourt, Brace, and World, 1962), 73, 81.

4

CEMENTING AND DISSOLVING CONSENSUS

Presidential Rhetoric during the Cold War, 1947–1969

Robert D. Schulzinger

The war in Vietnam was not going as well as President Lyndon B. Johnson and his top defense advisors hoped at the end of 1965. During the year, Johnson ordered 150,000 U.S. ground troops into the fight, but the North Vietnamese and the National Liberation Front remained undefeated. Congress and the public were growing impatient, and Johnson's ambitious program of domestic reform, the Great Society, had slowed. The president hoped to recapture the public's enthusiasm for his agenda with his 1966 State of the Union address. As his team of speechwriters worked on the text, they had trouble drafting a message that would maintain the optimism of the days following LBJ's landslide election of 1964. Six of them worked throughout the night of January 11–12 until they sent a draft to the president's bedroom at 4:00 A.M. Johnson did not like it. He considered it a grocery list of domestic programs whereas he wanted a thematic summary of the nation's role in the world. At 7:15 A.M., he summoned the writers into his bedroom and ordered them to cut the speech by a third. They hacked away at the language until 90 minutes before he delivered it in the House of Representatives. Still, it was poorly received, and 1966 turned into a bad year for Johnson.[1]

The frantic rewriting of the address, the enormous hopes placed upon it, and the crashing sense that it had failed to move public opinion provide a glimpse of the importance presidents and their principal advisors gave to a president's most watched speeches. During the first two decades of the Cold War, Presidents Harry S Truman, Dwight D. Eisenhower, John F. Kennedy, Lyndon B. Johnson, and Richard M. Nixon spoke regularly to the American people about the contest with the Soviet Union and communism. Most of their speeches were televised; a few early in the period were carried only on the radio. They explained the reasons the United States confronted the Soviet Union and the outcome the public could expect.

This paper examines what these presidents said publicly about the nature of the Cold War. It follows a lengthy tradition of examining the language, imagery, and metaphor of public statements by leaders about a nation's adversary. Harold Lasswell, one of the pioneers of public opinion research, published a highly influential study, *Propaganda Technique in the World War*, in 1927. Observing how officials during World War I decried "the insolence and depravity of the enemy," Lasswell identified a "cult of satanism" in which the enemy is demonized and war is justified on ethical grounds.[2] More recently, the historian Frank Costigliola has observed that analysis of the words, figures of speech, and metaphors of political leaders leads to comprehension of what they wanted to accomplish. He writes that "by evaluating the word choices of historical actors in describing their perceived reality, historians can learn something about the assumptions and agendas of those actors."[3]

The ways in which presidents addressed the public and the world offers a window into their modes of persuasion and the ways in which they framed public discussion of the Cold War.[4] They deployed various rhetorical strategies to justify U.S. positions in international affairs. They appealed to the lessons of recent history, the religious traditions of the American people, and international opinion. They portrayed the United States as responding to Soviet aggression in ways that served the interests of the United States and the world at large. They analyzed Soviet communist ideology and society. Some of their remarks may sound simplistic to the twenty-first-century ear, but they were no less sophisticated than what was found in the works of hundreds of social scientists who studied and wrote about events in the Soviet Union. Presidents declared that the Soviet Union bore the responsibility for threatening the peace and security of the world. They predicted that the struggle would be long and would require patience. Ultimately the United States would prevail because of the superiority of its social system, its wealth, its military power, its friendship with other nations, and its advocacy of universally shared values. These rhetorical devices remained staples of presidential rhetorical from 1947 until 1962.

Presidential appeals often achieved their goals of solidifying public support for a tough stance in the Cold War, but sometimes they carried significant costs. The Cold War intensified in part because of the rhetoric. As Truman, Eisenhower, and Kennedy assailed the Soviet Union, their confrontational rhetoric provoked Soviet leaders into taking more belligerent stances. Assertive language sometimes raised fears in Europe, the place where a shooting war between the nuclear superpowers was most apt to break out.

Presidential rhetoric that demonized the Soviet Union and its economic and political system and glorified the motives and actions of the United States fit the mood of the first decade of the Cold War. Americans were surprised that the victory over Germany, Italy, and Japan had not created a peaceful and harmonious world. People were anxious. Communism was perceived as a grave threat internationally and domestically. Until 1957, American culture was highly conformist, with dissent considered at least misguided and often dangerous and treasonous. Americans were highly religious, and their religious observance had a distinctly anticommunist cast.[5] The public therefore responded well to presidential rhetoric that stressed Soviet responsibility for the breakdown of relations between the superpowers, the defects of the Soviet system, and the political, economic, moral, and religious virtues of the United States.

Presidents changed their tone in the aftermath of the Cuban missile crisis. Popular insistence that the United States and the Soviet Union lessen the danger of nuclear war impelled Kennedy, Johnson, and Nixon to adjust the ways in which they spoke about the Cold War. While they continued to refer to conflicts in which they asserted that the Soviet Union was in the wrong, they also explained common interests between the two countries. Most notable was the mutual need to avoid the outbreak of a catastrophic nuclear war.

Growing public unhappiness with the war in Vietnam also dissolved much of the earlier consensus over American policy in the Cold War. More and more Americans became distressed by the physical, financial, and moral burdens of the Vietnam War. Their opposition to Vietnam led to broader skepticism about U.S. policies in the Cold War. Learning that the United States had sponsored undemocratic, authoritarian, or brutal governments weakened popular confidence that the United States had acted in the Cold War to promote liberty and oppose tyranny. This increased popular skepticism about the benevolence and altruism of the United States forced presidents to alter the ways they justified U.S. foreign policy.

Truman and the Early Cold War

From 1947 to 1953, Harry Truman spoke regularly about the nature of the conflict between the United States and the Soviet Union. He sought to rally a public that was surprised that victory in the war had not brought a lasting peace and that was afraid of Soviet-style communism. He set many of the themes of presidential rhetoric for the next two decades in his speech to Congress on March 12, 1947, in which he requested military aid to Greece and Turkey. He appealed to the lessons of recent history and drew explicit connections between the successful war against Germany and Japan and the present competition with communist-inspired revolutionaries in Greece. This universal effort to allow nations to flourish without outside coercion, he said, "was a fundamental issue in the war with Germany and Japan." Truman said that his plan for providing military aid to Greece and Turkey supplemented the work of the United Nations. He explained, "We shall not realize [the UN's] objectives, however, unless we are willing to help free peoples to maintain their free institutions and their national integrity against aggressive movements that seek to impose upon them totalitarian regimes."

The idea of totalitarianism was a familiar image to Americans two years after the end of WWII.[6] Truman explained that "totalitarian regimes imposed upon free peoples, by direct or indirect aggression, undermine the foundations of international peace and hence the security of the United States." Truman then provided a capsule history of events in Europe in the nearly two years since VE Day. "The peoples of a number of countries of the world have recently had totalitarian regimes forced upon them against their will," he said. He characterized the conflict as a universal one between freedom and tyranny. "At the present moment in world history nearly every nation must choose between alternative ways of life. . . . One way of life is based upon the will of the majority, and is distinguished by free institutions, representative government, free elections, guarantees of individual liberty, freedom of speech and religion, and freedom from political oppression."[7]

By mid-1947 the contest between the United States and the Soviet Union had a name, the Cold War, and Truman regularly referred to the nature of the competition with the Soviet Union. In his State of the Union address of January 7, 1948, Truman reminded his listeners that "twice within our generation, world wars have taught us that we cannot isolate ourselves from the rest of the world." He presented previous conflicts and the current confrontation with the Soviet Union as a long process of understanding that threats to what he characterized as "freedom" in other countries represented threats at home.

Truman also analyzed the social structure of the Soviet Union. He described it as a "way of life based upon the will of a minority forcibly imposed upon the majority. It relies upon terror and oppression." He then laid out the global role that the United States would play in words that came to be known as the Truman Doctrine. "I believe that it must be the policy of the United States to support free peoples who are resisting attempted subjugation by armed minorities or by outside pressures."[8]

After the Cold War intensified in 1948 and 1949, Truman added other themes designed to reassure his listeners that the United States would prevail. He spoke increasingly of the "strength" of the United States. In his State of the Union address of January 4, 1950, he said, "The greatest danger has receded. . . . Today, the free peoples of the world have new vigor and new hope for the cause of peace." Truman's emphasis on power suggested that the United States had the means of confronting the Soviet Union and would eventually be successful against it. "Our national production has risen from about $50 billion, in terms of today's prices, to the staggering figure of $255 billion a year." This enormous power carried global responsibility. He asserted that "other nations look to us for a wise exercise of our economic and military strength, and for vigorous support of the ideals of representative government and a free society."[9]

Six months later, the Korean War began, and by the time Truman delivered his next State of the Union message on January 8, 1951, the United States had encountered serious difficulties in Asia. Truman presented some of the fullest explanations of U.S. Cold War coupled with stinging denunciations of the Soviet Union and communism. He identified communism as posing "a total threat" and "a common danger." He linked the fate of the United States to that of "all free nations" that are "in peril." Truman said that the Soviet Union advanced a type of imperialism that was "even more ambitious, more crafty, and more menacing" than that of the Russian czars. For all of the adversary's cunning, however, Truman assured his listeners that the United States and the rest of the Free World had the advantage. "We have skilled and vigorous peoples, great industrial strength. . . . And above all, we cherish liberty. . . . These ideals are the driving force of human progress." He said that Europe's religious tradition linked it to the United States and the Western powers as an advantage over communists. Europe was the homeland of "religious beliefs . . . which are now threatened by the tide of atheistic communism."[10]

Truman's popularity declined as the situation in Korea deteriorated, and it plunged to a miniscule 24 percent after he dismissed General Douglas MacArthur as commander of U.S. and United Nations forces in Korea.[11] The president tried to rally popular support in a radio address on April 11,

1951. He portrayed the Korean War as designed to prevent the outbreak of a larger war. He spoke of the Soviets' "monstrous conspiracy to stamp out freedom all over the world. If they were to succeed, the United States would be numbered among their principal victims." Once more, Truman referred to the lessons learned from the failure to block Germany's and Japan's aggression in the 1930s. "If history has taught us anything, it is that aggression anywhere in the world is a threat to the peace everywhere in the world." He said that the United States joined other potential victims of aggression. "If the free countries had acted together to crush the aggression of the dictators, and if they had acted in the beginning when the aggression was small—there probably would have been no World War II."[12] The fighting in Korea took its toll on Truman's standing with the public over the next two years. In November 1952, voters elected Republican Dwight D. Eisenhower over Truman's choice, Democrat Adlai E. Stevenson.

Truman delivered two speeches to the nation in January 1953 in which he outlined the history and the future of the Cold War. In his State of the Union address on January 7, he said, "The world is divided, not through our fault or failure, but by Soviet design. They, not we, began the Cold War." He saw the Soviet-controlled areas as "a world that bleeds its population white to build huge military forces; a world in which the police are everywhere and their authority unlimited; a world where terror and slavery are deliberately administered both as instruments of government and as means of production; a world where all effective social power is the state's monopoly—yet the state itself is the creature of the communist tyrants." Truman introduced a new danger: atomic war that could destroy civilization itself now that the Soviet Union as well as the United States possessed atomic weapons. The existence of these weapons was another reason that Soviet communist ideology was obsolete. He addressed Josef Stalin directly. "You claim belief in Lenin's prophecy that one stage in the development of communist society would be war between your world and ours. But Lenin was a pre-atomic man, who viewed society and history with pre-atomic eyes. Something profound has happened since he wrote. War has changed its shape and its dimension. It cannot now be a 'stage' in the development of anything save ruin for your regime and your homeland."[13]

On January 15, 1953, five days before he left office, Truman delivered a farewell address. "I suppose that history will remember my term in office as the years when the 'Cold War' began to overshadow our lives," he reflected. The phrase "I suppose" set a chatty and informal tone, suggesting that the Cold War had not been sought by him or the American public. He explained why patience was warranted and victory likely. He said that "when history says that my term of office saw the beginning of the Cold War, it will also say that in those eight years we have set the course that can win it." He contrasted the timidity of the democracies in the face of aggression in the 1930s with the firmness of the Cold War years. "Think about those years of weakness and indecision," he urged his listeners, "and [about] World War II which was their evil result. Then think about the speed and courage and decisiveness with which we have moved against the communist threat since World War II." He said that the danger posed by atomic war required patience for a long competition rather than a preemptive nuclear strike against the Soviet Union. "Now, once in a while," he recalled, "I get a letter from some impatient person asking, why don't we get it over with? Why don't we issue an ultimatum, make all-out war, drop the atomic bomb?" The answer, he said, was "quite simple: We are not made that way. We are a moral people. . . . We cannot, of our own free will, violate the very principles that we are striving to defend. . . . Starting a war is no way to make peace."

So if patience were required for a long conflict, how would it end? He said the defects of the Soviet system—its brutality, its tyranny, and its hostility to religion—would eventually cause it to collapse. "There is a fatal flaw in their society. Theirs is a godless system, a system of slavery; there is no freedom in it, no consent." He spoke confidently that "in the long run the strength of our free society, and our ideals, will prevail over a system that has respect for neither God nor man."[14]

Eisenhower Continues and Contains the Cold War

In his eight years as president, Eisenhower continued to stress the flaws in the Soviet system, its "godlessness," and the peaceful and generous intentions and acts of the United States. Barely two weeks after taking office, Eisenhower decried "the calculated pressures of aggressive communism." In his State of the Union address on February 2, 1953, he promised a foreign policy that would recognize "that no single country, even one so powerful as ours, can alone defend the liberty of all nations threatened by Communist aggression." He repeatedly coupled observations about American "strength" with its "wisdom" to devise "a steady course to be followed between an assertion of strength that is truculent and a confession of helplessness that is cowardly."[15]

Vast changes in international affairs and a reduction in tensions in the Cold War occurred in 1953. Josef Stalin died in March, and an armistice ended the Korean War in July. In his January 7, 1954, State of the Union address, Eisenhower explained that the United States had gained the upper hand against the Soviet Union. A threat to "American freedom" remained "so long as the world Communist conspiracy exists." He promised that the United States would respond to this threat by fostering military alliances in Europe, cooperating with governments in the Western Hemisphere, and strengthening the United Nations." He placed the burden of promoting peace on the shoulders of the new Soviet leaders. The United States would work for peace, he said, "but no government can place peace in the hearts of foreign rulers. It is our duty then to ourselves and to freedom itself to remain strong in all those ways—spiritual, economic, military— that will give us maximum safety against the possibility of aggressive action by others."[16]

Eisenhower called on Americans to understand "the true nature of the struggle now taking place in the world." He used some of the most explicitly biblical imagery of any president during the period. "Either man is the creature whom the Psalmist described as 'a little lower than the angels,' crowned with glory and honor, holding 'dominion over the works' of his Creator; or man is a soulless, animated machine to be enslaved, used and consumed by the state for its own glorification." Eisenhower also highlighted the dangers posed by the Soviet Union's military. "The massive military machines and ambitions of the Soviet-Communist bloc still create uneasiness in the world," he told Congress on January 6, 1955. Unlike the American military, whose intentions he asserted were defensive and peaceful, the Soviet Union's "power, combined with the proclaimed intentions of the Communist leaders to communize the world, is the threat confronting us today."

In 1954, the United States adopted a military strategy of employing massive retaliatory power on the Soviet Union to counter what it considered to be Soviet aggression anywhere in the world. Eisenhower justified deterrence this way: "To protect our nations and our peoples from the catastrophe of a nuclear holocaust, free nations must maintain countervailing military power. . . . If Communist rulers understand that America's response to aggression will be swift and decisive—that never shall we buy peace at the expense of honor or faith—they will be powerfully deterred from launching a military venture engulfing their own peoples and many others in disaster."[17]

Beginning in the mid-1950s, Eisenhower referred more and more to the American desire for peace. He continued to demonize the Soviet Union.[18] Yet even as he berated Soviet ideology and behavior publicly, Eisenhower realized that his public attacks on the Soviet Union created tension with America's European NATO allies. In Great Britain, the Federal Republic of Germany, and France, sizeable portions of the public thought that the United States endangered peace.

He portrayed the Soviet Union as a continuing threat, but also as a subtle adversary, as likely to confront the United States and what he called, interchangeably, "free peoples" or "the free world" economically or politically as militarily. He asserted that "Communist tactics against the free nations have shifted in emphasis from reliance on violence . . . to reliance on division, enticement and duplicity." These new tactics posed "a dangerous though less obvious threat."[19]

Eisenhower also stressed that the Soviet Union led a threatening empire. He identified America's interests and safety with those of the free world or free peoples. In 1958, after the Soviet Union had launched Sputnik, the first satellite to orbit the Earth, and American public opinion became sharply pessimistic about the United States' position in the world, Eisenhower offered reassurance. He sought simultaneously to clarify the nature of the Soviet threat and to convince the public that the United States was in the right and would prevail. He said that "the threat to our safety, and to the hope of a peaceful world, can be simply stated. It is communist imperialism." "Soviet spokesmen," he said, "from the beginning, have publicly and frequently declared their aim to expand their power, one way or another, throughout the world." This threat was especially dire because of Soviet totalitarianism in which "every human activity is pressed into service as a weapon of expansion."

Eisenhower recognized the public's yearning for an end to war, so he placed the onus for the ongoing struggle on the Soviets, who were, "in short, waging total Cold War." His use of a variation on the phrase "total war" continued Truman's pattern of linking the current confrontation with the Soviets to the total war against Germany and Japan during World War II. The United States, he said, did not choose to wage the Cold War; consequently, "the only answer to a regime that wages total Cold War is to wage total peace." Lest the public weary of the struggle and feel that the United States was isolated, he reminded them that the United States had true allies while "the Soviet Union has surrounded itself with captive and sullen nations." The United States had another significant advantage: its high international standing. "The world thinks of us as a country which is strong, but which will never start a war."[20]

In Eisenhower's last years in office, he spoke more about achieving peace than about waging war. In his January 9, 1959, State of the Union speech he said that "we seek only a just peace for all, with aggressive designs against no one." For the first time he acknowledged that the consequences of nuclear war were so great that other nations could legitimately worry that the United States was not doing everything it could to avoid one. He acknowledged that "there is uneasiness in the world because of a belief on the part of peoples that through arrogance, miscalculation or fear of attack, catastrophic war could be launched." All the while he blamed the communist states for keeping tensions high and declining to join in a genuine effort to halt the race in nuclear arms. "We have learned the bitter lesson," he said "that international agreements, historically considered by us as sacred, are regarded in Communist doctrine and in practice to be mere scraps of paper."[21]

Détente with the Soviet Union seemed to be a real possibility at the beginning of 1960, and Eisenhower noted in his State of the Union address on January 7 that "recent Soviet deportment and pronouncements suggest the possible opening of a somewhat less strained period in the relationships between the Soviet Union and the Free World. If these pronouncements be genuine, there is brighter hope of diminishing the intensity of past rivalry." He promised to "strive to break the calamitous cycle of frustrations and crises which, if unchecked, could spiral into nuclear disaster; the ultimate insanity."[22]

Eisenhower experienced a series of disappointments in 1960, his last year in office. The expectations for better relations with the Soviet Union fostered by Soviet Communist Party General Secretary Nikita Khrushchev's visit to the United States in September 1959 were dashed. A four-party summit meeting among the leaders of the United States, the Soviet Union, the United Kingdom, and France scheduled for May was canceled by Khrushchev after Eisenhower refused to apologize for U-2 flights over Soviet territory. Things got worse in the fall of 1960. Khrushchev used some of the harshest language of the Cold War in a speech denouncing the United States at the UN General Assembly meeting. Senator John F. Kennedy, the Democratic Party's presidential candidate, criticized Eisenhower for letting the initiative pass to the Soviet Union and its allies in the worldwide Cold War. Kennedy won the election over Vice President Richard M. Nixon at least in part because the public believed that he would wage the Cold War more assertively than Eisenhower had done in his second term.

So Eisenhower was in a reflective mood when he delivered his final speeches as president in January 1961. Like Truman before him, Eisenhower surveyed the previous eight years of U.S. foreign policy. He characterized the continuing goal as "peace, liberty, and well-being." He asserted that "the aspirations of all peoples are one—peace with justice in freedom." He contrasted the benevolent intentions of the United States with the bellicosity of the Soviet Union. "While *we* [italics added] have worked to advance national aspirations for freedom, a divisive force has been at work to divert that aspiration into dangerous channels. The Communist movement throughout the world exploits the natural striving of all to be free and attempts to subjugate men rather than free them."[23]

Eisenhower continued in this almost somber fashion in his televised farewell to the American people on January 17. He consciously contrasted his careful management of international affairs, in which he strove to maintain peace, with what he thought was the incoming Kennedy administration's impetuousness. He said that "our basic purposes have been to keep the peace; to foster progress in human achievement, and to enhance liberty, dignity and integrity among people and among nations." He regretted that "the danger" Soviet ideology "poses promises to be of indefinite duration." Because the Cold War was likely to last a long time, Eisenhower warned against seeking quick victories. He urged "not so much the emotional and transitory sacrifices of crisis, but rather those which enable us to carry forward steadily, surely, and without complaint the burdens of a prolonged and complex struggle—with liberty the stake." He warned that in meeting crises "there is a recurring temptation to feel that some spectacular and costly action could become the miraculous solution to all current difficulties."

He said, "Together we must learn how to compose differences, not with arms, but with intellect and decent purpose." He added, "I wish I could say tonight that a lasting peace is in sight." But war remained a danger. "Happily, I can say that war has been avoided. Steady progress toward our ultimate goal has been made. But, so much remains to be done." Eisenhower concluded his farewell in the overtly devout style he had adopted early in his presidency. "You and I—my fellow citizens—need to be strong in our faith that all nations, under God, will reach the goal of peace with justice." He offered "America's prayerful and continuing aspiration: We pray that peoples of all faiths, all races, all nations, may have their great human needs satisfied; that those now denied opportunity shall come to enjoy it to the full; that all who yearn for freedom may experience its spiritual blessings . . . and that, in the goodness of time, all peoples will come to live together in a peace guaranteed by the binding force of mutual respect and love."[24]

Kennedy from Ardent Cold Warrior to Advocate of Détente

Kennedy adopted a much more militant stance in the Cold War in his first year in office. He presented many of the themes of his foreign policy in his Inaugural address on January 20. In a direct criticism of Eisenhower's apparently languid conduct of the Cold War, Kennedy said this new generation was "unwilling to witness or permit the slow undoing of those human rights to which this nation has always been committed, and to which we are committed today at home and around the world."

He employed the metaphors of strength versus weakness: the former would preserve the precarious nuclear balance of terror that had avoided war, while the latter invited war. "We dare not tempt" the Soviets "with weakness," he asserted. He continued Eisenhower's emphasis on arms control. He wanted both the United States and the Soviet Union to "formulate serious and precise proposals for the inspection and control of arms—and bring the absolute power to destroy other nations under the absolute control of all nations."

Kennedy called on his fellow citizens to bear "the burden of a long twilight struggle, year in and year out." This phrase, "a long twilight struggle" became a shorthand phrase for the long Cold War. Toward the end of his Inaugural speech, Kennedy referred once again to the importance of generations in defining significant human activity. "In the long history of the world, only a few generations have been granted the role of defending freedom in its hour of maximum danger." He doubted "that any of us would exchange places with any other people or any other generation." He challenged his "fellow citizens of the world: ask not what America will do for you, but what together we can do for the freedom of man." Once more Kennedy identified the interests of the United States with those of the rest of the world.[25]

Kennedy asserted that crises mattered much more than Eisenhower had suggested. He told Congress on January 30, 1961, "Each day the crises multiply. Each day their solution grows more difficult. Each day we draw nearer the hour of maximum danger, as weapons spread and hostile forces grow stronger." He surveyed the world and found that "in each of the principal areas of crisis—the tide of events has been running out and time has not been our friend." He decried "the relentless pressures of the Chinese Communists," which menaced "the security of the entire area." Close to home "in Latin America, Communist agents seeking to exploit that region's peaceful revolution of hope have established a base on Cuba, only 90 miles from our shores."

The Cold War competition with the Soviet Union and the People's Republic of China remained "the first great obstacle" to world peace and security. He insisted that "we must never be lulled into believing that either power has yielded its ambitions for world domination—ambitions which they forcefully restated only a short time ago." He defined his administration's aim as convincing the communist powers "that aggression and subversion will not be profitable routes to pursue." He contrasted Freedom (capitalized) with Communism and invited "open and peaceful competition—for prestige, for markets, for scientific achievement, even for men's minds." He predicted the eventual success of the American side in the Cold War. "If Freedom and Communism were to compete for man's allegiance in a world at peace, I would look to the future with ever increasing confidence."[26]

Like his predecessors, Kennedy sought to persuade the public to endorse his foreign policies by analyzing and deploring the Soviet Union's beliefs, sensitivities, and behavior. "Since the close of the Second World War, a global civil war has divided and tormented mankind," he said in 1962. What distinguished the United States from its communist adversaries, he said, was "our belief that the state is the servant of the citizen and not his master." He contrasted the American willingness to allow other nations to "choose forms and ways that we would not choose for ourselves.... We can welcome diversity—the Communists cannot." The Soviets were doomed to fail in the demands for conformity, since "the way of the past shows clearly that freedom, not coercion, is the wave of the future."[27]

Kennedy wanted to show progress at the beginning of 1963. He also recognized the extraordinary fear which had gripped people globally when the world approached the brink of nuclear war during the Cuban missile crisis of October 1962. He asserted that his policies had reversed the worrisome trends of the Cold War where "communism ... [was] closing in on a sluggish America and a free world in disarray." In his 1963 State of the Union address, he surveyed developments in the Cold War from Europe to Asia to Africa to the Western Hemisphere and proclaimed, "Steady progress has been made in building a world of order." He noted proudly (and, of course, ironically) that "the spear point of aggression has been blunted in Viet-Nam."

Kennedy once more turned social scientist and political philosopher to explain why the United States was in the ascendancy. "We have reaffirmed the scientific and military superiority of freedom" with the successes of the

American space program and the military buildup of the past two years. In contrast to the American successes, the unity of the communist world had been disrupted by the split between the Soviet Union and China. He advised caution in assessing this division because "the Soviet-Chinese disagreement is over means, not ends. A dispute over how best to bury the free world is no grounds for Western rejoicing."

Still, he reasoned that the split revealed something fundamentally wrong with communism as a philosophy of life and government. "Nevertheless, while a strain is not a fracture, it is clear that the forces of diversity are at work inside the Communist camp, despite all the iron disciplines of regimentation and all the iron dogmatisms of ideology. Marx is proven wrong once again: for it is the closed Communist societies, not the free and open societies which carry within themselves the seeds of internal disintegration." Communism's disarray resulted from "the historical force of nationalism— and the yearning of all men to be free." In addition, "the gross inefficiency of their economies" made the Soviet Union and China unattractive models of development." A closed society, he said "is not open to ideas of progress— and a police state finds that it cannot command the grain to grow."[28]

In June, however, Kennedy moved sharply away from such anticommunist rhetoric. His policy toward the Soviet Union since the missile crisis had stressed the need to avoid nuclear war. He spoke forcefully about the desire and necessity for peace which united the American and Russian people. He told the graduates at American University that "no government or social system is so evil that its people must be considered as lacking in virtue." Americans and Russians both abhorred war, he said. "We are both devoting massive sums of money to weapons that could be better devoted to combating ignorance, poverty, and disease. We are both caught up in a vicious and dangerous cycle in which suspicion on one side breeds suspicion on the other, and new weapons beget counter-weapons."[29]

Johnson, Nixon, and the Unraveling of the Cold War Consensus

Kennedy was murdered in November 1963. Among the many unknowns of history is how he would have continued to conduct U.S. foreign relations had he lived and been reelected. Would the tentative détente he commenced with the Soviet Union in the months after the Cuban missile crisis have flourished? Would he have escalated the American military role in Vietnam as his successor, Lyndon B. Johnson, did? Or would he have disengaged from that war? Foreign affairs experts and the public at large have speculated about these questions for over forty years. No definitive answer is ever possible, although the weight of the evidence and scholarly opinion now suggests that Kennedy actively sought to reduce Cold War tensions and preferred not to escalate in Vietnam.[30]

What is known, however, is that Johnson believed he was continuing Kennedy's policies during his first eighteen months as president. After his election to the presidency in 1964, Johnson surveyed the last four years of American foreign policy and proclaimed that "the United States has re-emerged into the fullness of its self-confidence and purpose." He recalled Kennedy's 1960 campaign slogan that he would "get America moving again," and he announced that "no longer are we called upon to get America moving. We are moving. No longer do we doubt our strength or resolution. We are strong and we have proven our resolve." He followed the Cold War presidential practice of asserting that the United States had the initiative. "We know," he said, "that history is ours to make. And if there is great danger, there is now also the excitement of great expectations." Johnson offered an olive branch to the Soviet Union. He invited the Soviet leadership to visit the United States and address the public on television. But in Asia, he said, "communism wears a more aggressive face. We see that in Viet-Nam."

As the war deepened for the United States, Johnson justified the American participation in the fight as fulfilling the commitments made to the South Vietnamese by Eisenhower, Kennedy, and himself. He also said that "our own security is tied to the peace of Asia." In January 1965 he likened the fight in Vietnam to World War II and Korea, saying "twice in one generation we have had to fight against aggression in the Far East. To ignore aggression now would only increase the danger of a much larger war."[31] A year later, in his January 12, 1966, State of the Union address, he repeated the theme that the Vietnam War was part of the American tradition of opposing "aggression." He said that "we have defended against Communist aggression—in Korea under President Truman—in the Formosa Straits under President Eisenhower—in Cuba under President Kennedy—and again in Vietnam."[32]

But the Vietnam War was different, and public consensus over the Cold War eroded in 1966. A "credibility gap" opened between what U.S. officials in Washington and Saigon said about progress in the war and the popularity and legitimacy of the government of the Republic of (South) Vietnam. Some Americans now challenged the assurances given by earlier presidents that the United States had acted benevolently and in the interest of the rest of the world since 1947. Critics of LBJ's Vietnam policy looked back at the history of the past two decades and decried what Arkansas Democratic senator J. William Fulbright, the chairman of the Foreign Relations Committee, called the "arrogance of power."[33] Opponents of U.S. Vietnam policy pointed to American support for dictatorial anticommunist governments in South Korea, the Dominican Republic, Guatemala, Iran, Haiti, or Cuba before Castro as evidence that American assertions that it supported freedom throughout the world were false.

In response to these challenges, Johnson adjusted his tone to mollify critics who sought an end to the Cold War. When Johnson spoke about foreign affairs in his 1967 State of the Union address, he noted the "transition" in American relations with the Soviet Union and Eastern Europe. The Cold War itself now should be a thing of the past. He said, "We have avoided both the acts and the rhetoric of the cold war. When we have differed with the Soviet Union . . . I have tried to differ quietly and with courtesy, and without venom. Our objective is not to continue the cold war, but to end it."[34]

The war in Vietnam became less popular in 1967, and Johnson faced challenges to his foreign policies across the political spectrum. In his 1968 State of the Union address, he reverted to appeals to strength, patience, and steadfastness of will. After outlining the unsatisfactory situation in Vietnam and racial tensions at home, he said that "it is our will that is being tried, not our strength; our sense of purpose, not our ability to achieve a better America." He assured the public that "we have the strength to meet our every challenge; the physical strength to hold the course of decency and compassion at home; and the moral strength to support the cause of peace in the world."[35]

Johnson's standing with the public declined throughout 1967 as the war in Vietnam dragged on inconclusively. It revived briefly in early January 1968 to an approval rating of 48 percent, but it fell to 40 percent after North Vietnam and the National Liberation Front launched an offensive throughout South Vietnam at the end of the month.[36] On March 31 he announced his decision not to seek reelection and promised to open negotiations with the Democratic Republic of (North) Vietnam. In November voters selected Richard M. Nixon, the Republican presidential candidate, over Vice President Hubert H. Humphrey.

Johnson did not follow Truman's or Eisenhower's precedent of delivering a separate farewell address in January 1969. His State of the Union address of January 14 was a wistful and often sad valedictory. Johnson began by telling Congress that he had not wanted to address them in person, but was persuaded to do so because of his own long congressional career. The speech stood in sharp contrast to earlier messages, since it did not place all international affairs under the single umbrella of the Cold War. Johnson avoided unflattering characterizations of communist ideology. Instead, he noted a common theme running through "the continuing crisis in the Middle East, the conflict in Vietnam, the dangers of nuclear war, [and] the great difficulties of dealing with the Communist powers." He said, "They and their causes—the causes that gave rise to them—all of these have existed with us for many years." He expected these problems to continue, perhaps into the indefinite future. "Several Presidents have already sought to try to deal with them. One or more Presidents will try to resolve them or try to contain them in the years that are ahead of us." While Johnson omitted explicit contrasts between the United States and the Soviet Union, he referred, as his predecessor had, to American assets which included "our economy, the democratic system, . . . the good commonsense and sound judgment of the American people, and their essential love of justice."[37]

Less than a week later, Richard Nixon became president, and he proclaimed the beginning of a new era in the Cold War. He said that popular desires for peace had altered the terms of discussion of international affairs. "For the first time, because the people of the world want peace, and the leaders of the world are afraid of war, the times are on the side of peace." Simply put, people around the globe were tired of the Cold War and feared the consequences of fighting it more than they looked forward to winning it. He announced that "after a period of confrontation, we are entering an era of negotiation." It was a new phase in the Cold War, but not its end. Nixon continued the imagery of strength as a deterrent to war and the keeper of the peace. "To all those who would be tempted by weakness, let us leave no doubt," he said, "that we will be as strong as we need to be for as long as we need to be."[38]

Beyond the Rhetoric of Good and Evil

So ended more than two decades of presidential declarations of American intentions and policies toward the Soviet Union and communism. Five presidents tried to cement a wide political consensus about the virtues and justice of the American position in the Cold War. They applied the lessons of recent history. They cast the Soviets as having begun the Cold War in violation of the norms and expectations of the world community in the aftermath of World War II. They identified U.S. interests and values with those of the world at large. They contrasted the religious, political, economic, and social traditions and institutions of the United States with those of its communist adversaries.

This effort at consensus building succeeded, for the most part, in the first decade of the Cold War. But then cracks appeared. The danger of atomic war introduced new themes into presidential rhetoric. From Eisenhower's administration onward, presidents referred more often to the common interests of the nuclear powers in avoiding a catastrophic war. Kennedy presented both the bellicose and the conciliatory postures in his rhetoric. Johnson's presidency was eventually submerged by popular unhappiness with the Vietnam War. Opposition to the Vietnam War expanded to challenge the basic assumptions underlying U.S. policies in the Cold War. More and more Americans came to believe that the United States had betrayed its ideals with international interventions. Cold War critics believed that U.S. presidents had made the world more dangerous with their confrontational stance toward the Soviet Union and communism. Public anxiety over the dangers created by demonizing the Soviet Union eventually led Johnson to advocate the end of the Cold War. When Nixon stressed the need for peace in his Inaugural address, he acknowledged the desire to move beyond the Cold War.

Yet the conflict continued, with variations in its intensity, for the next twenty years. Presidents after 1969 employed many of the same rhetorical techniques developed during the Cold War. Ronald Reagan, one of the most militantly anticommunist presidents, often used the religious imagery, the metaphors of U.S. strength, and the predictions of eventual victory favored in the early Cold War. Once the Cold War ended, the American predictions that the conflict would end with the demise of the Soviet Union seemed to have been validated. But the dangers of leaders portraying their adversaries as the embodiment of evil returned in the early twenty-first century. During the war on terror following the al Qaeda attacks on the United States on September 11, 2001, President George W. Bush regularly referred to a global struggle between the forces of good and evil. He insisted that people everywhere must choose between siding with the United States or siding with terrorists. In the year after 9/11, this approach proved to be popular. But opinion turned sharply against the Bush administration during the war in Iraq that began in March 2003. As that war continued, a new consensus began to emerge about presidential rhetoric. People in the United States, traditional American allies, and countries hostile to the United States came to believe that an American president's references to evil in the world, his appeals to recent history to justify American military actions, and his invocations of divine providence made the world only more dangerous.

Notes

1. Robert Dallek, *Flawed Giant: Lyndon Johnson and His Times, 1961–1973* (New York: Oxford University Press, 1998), 302.

2. Harold Lasswell, *Propaganda Technique in the World War* (New York: Peter Smith, 1927, reprinted 1938), 77, 96–97.

3. Frank Costigliola, "Reading for Meaning: Theory, Language, Metaphor," in Michael J. Hogan and Thomas G. Paterson, eds., *Explaining the History of American Foreign Relations*, 2nd ed. (New York: Cambridge University Press, 2004), 294.

4. Martin J. Medhurst, Robert L. Ivie, Philip Wander, and Robert L. Scott, *Cold War Rhetoric: Strategy, Metaphor, and Ideology* (Westport, Conn.: Greenwood Press, 1990); Amos Kiewe, ed., *The Modern Presidency and Crisis Rhetoric* (Westport, Conn.: Greenwood Press, 1991).

5. Stephen J. Whitfield, *The Culture of the Cold War,* 2nd ed. (Baltimore: Johns Hopkins University Press, 1996), chapters 1–4.

6. Les K. Adler and Thomas G. Paterson, "Red Fascism: The Merger of Nazi Germany and Communism in the United States," *American Historical Review* 75, no. 4 (1970): 1046–64.

7. Harry S Truman, Special Message to the Congress on Greece and Turkey: The Truman Doctrine, March 12, 1947, in John T. Woolley and Gerhard Peters, *The American Presidency Project* [online], Santa Barbara: University of California (hosted), Gerhard Peters (database). Available at <http://www.presidency.ucsb.edu/ws/?pid=12846>. All excerpts from presidential addresses in this essay can be found at this website.

8. Truman, State of the Union address, January 7, 1948.

9. Truman, State of the Union address, January 4, 1950.

10. Truman, State of the Union address, January 8, 1951.

11. Gallup Poll, approval of President Truman, April 11, 1952.

12. Truman, Radio Report to the American People on Korea and on U.S. Policy in the Far East, April 11, 1951.

13. Truman, State of the Union address, January 7, 1953.

14. Truman, Farewell, January 15, 1953.

15. Eisenhower, State of the Union address, February 2, 1953.

16. Eisenhower, State of the Union address, January 7, 1954.

17. Eisenhower, State of the Union address, January 6, 1955.

18. Chris Tudda, *The Truth Is Our Weapon: The Rhetorical Diplomacy of Dwight D. Eisenhower and John Foster Dulles* (Baton Rouge: Louisiana State University Press, 2006), 127.

19. Eisenhower, State of the Union address, January 5, 1956.

20. Eisenhower, State of the Union address, January 9, 1958.

21. Eisenhower, State of the Union address, January 9, 1959.

22. Eisenhower, State of the Union address, January 7, 1960.

23. Eisenhower, State of the Union address, January 12, 1961.

24. Eisenhower, Farewell address, January 15, 1961.

25. Kennedy, Inaugural address, January 20, 1961.

26. Kennedy, State of the Union address, January 30, 1961.

27. Kennedy, State of the Union address, January 12, 1962.

28. Kennedy, State of the Union address, January 14, 1963.

29. Kennedy, "Commencement address at American University," June 10, 1963.

30. Fredrik Logevall, *Choosing War: The Lost Chance for Peace and the Escalation of the War in Vietnam* (Berkeley: University of California Press, 1999), 66–74; Robert Dallek, *An Unfinished Life: John F. Kennedy, 1917–1963* (Boston: Little, Brown, 2003), 763–65.

31. Johnson, State of the Union address, January 4, 1965.

32. Johnson, State of the Union address, January 12, 1966.

33. J. William Fulbright, *The Arrogance of Power* (New York: Random House, 1966).

34. Johnson, State of the Union address, January 10, 1967.

35. Johnson, State of the Union address, January 17, 1968.

36. Gallup Poll, approval of President Johnson, October 6, 1967, 37 percent; January 4, 1968, 48 percent; February 2, 1968, 40 percent.

37. Johnson, State of the Union address, January 14, 1969.

38. Nixon, Inaugural address, January 20, 1969.

5

HARD SELL

The Korean War

Marilyn B. Young

An old antiwar poster asked, "What if they gave a war and nobody came?" To paraphrase that poster, what if they tried to sell a war and nobody bought? Judging by the past, the answer is that they'd have it anyhow. It's not that people won't support wars, even shoddy ones, as the experience of the United States in the years 1975 to 1991 indicates, provided the wars are very short and there are few American casualties.[1] With enough time and rising casualty figures, people begin to ask more probing questions: Is this war really necessary? What have these deaths achieved?[2] The common assumption among many politicians, pundits, and historians is that if only the president could bring the people to understand the necessity of the war into which he has led them, the complaining would stop and everyone would support the government.

In the case of the war in Korea, Steven Casey has stressed the degree to which President Harry Truman was constrained in his marketing of that conflict, America's first post-1945 war. If Truman went too far, he risked inciting a public call for immediate preventive war against the Soviet Union or, later in the war, against China. Casey suggests that Truman's enforced moderation made it impossible for his administration to mobilize public opinion behind his policies.[3] The corollary would seem to be that, had Truman been free to mobilize opinion fully, the public might have supported the war, maybe even with enthusiasm. I have two possibly contrary propositions: first, that the lack of public enthusiasm for the Korean War may not have been due to poor presidential marketing; rather, that people had serious doubts about the value of the war they were being asked to fight or, indeed, about the value of fighting any war at all. The second proposition is that while any administration would prefer public enthusiasm and understanding, wars can be prosecuted without either. Public acquiescence in the deaths suffered and inflicted in Korea represented an achievement for the government and one that would serve future administrations.

Most of the other essays in this volume explore the ways various presidents have marketed wars, both hot and cold, to an often reluctant public. This essay takes up the other side of the marketing process and examines how the public responded to the selling of a war. Rather than focus on presidential salesmanship, it addresses issues of public acceptance and resistance, as reflected in the press, movies, literature, and opinion polls.[4] These sources reveal that the Korean War was a hard sell from the outset—even in the age of McCarthy, the public responded with ambivalence to "Mr. Truman's War" on the Korean peninsula.

A Confusing War

The Korean War was not only hard to sell during the three years in which it was fought; it has been a hard sell ever since. It is remembered as having been forgotten: a product that failed to move, a war that wasn't new and improved, a Pinto of a war. Sometimes those who write powerfully and movingly about other wars simply refuse to discuss this one. Thus in his book *The Soldiers' Tale: Bearing Witness to Modern War,* Samuel Hynes wrote, "I have nothing to say about the war in Korea, a war that came and went without glory, and left no mark on American imaginations—though nearly as many Americans died there as in Vietnam."[5] W. D. Ehrhart, a Vietnam veteran and poet, went in search of the poetry of the Korean War and discovered only a small body of work, most of it written a decade or more after the war was over. Indeed, it was the Vietnam War, Ehrhart wrote, that "seems to have been a catalyst for most of these poets, releasing pent-up feelings that had perhaps been held in check by the personal and cultural stoicism bequeathed to them by their generational older brothers." When he asked the authors why Korea had passed by so silently, several answered in terms of the war's "lack [of] nobility," of it having been a "non-war," "futile" with "few positive images." These are the very reasons generally adduced to explain the volubility of Vietnam veterans.[6]

Over 2 million Americans served in Korea; 33,686 Americans and between 2 and 3 million Koreans died in it; 103,284 Americans and uncounted Koreans were wounded—all in the space of three years. The war was reported daily in the press and weekly in national newsmagazines. It produced stark photographs that filled the pages of *Life* and disturbing reflections on the nature of modern warfare by frontline correspondents who observed it close up.[7] It was televised, featured on the radio, and dramatized on movie screens within months of its beginning. Major fighting—such as the retreat south before the onslaught of Chinese troops in the winter of 1950—produced giant headlines. Young men everywhere had reason to fear being drafted. Still, the Korean War seemed to be swallowed up even as it unfolded. The real sales job the government did was this: it managed to wage an immensely bloody war with a conscript army as if the war weren't quite happening. Or rather, it fought with the sullen acquiescence of a public whose one recourse to change, given the prevailing political atmosphere, was electoral—a recourse the public took with alacrity in 1952.

Although in the first few months of the conflict in Korea, every poll indicated initial public support for Truman's intervention, there were many signs that the public was less than enthused and more than a little confused about the war. Members of Congress grumbled that it would never have been necessary if Truman had done right by Chiang Kai-shek, and when ground troops were ordered to the peninsula on 30 June, some voices were raised about the constitutionality of it all. No one greeted news of the war with pleasure. Veterans of WWII were bitter about being recalled to the military after so brief a respite. William Styron, a reserve officer in the Marine Corps, recalled that for veterans like himself, "who had shed their uniforms only five years before—in the blissful notion that the unspeakable orgy of war was only a memory and safely behind—the experience of putting on that uniform again and facing anew the ritualistic death dance had an effect that can only be described as traumatic."[8] Styron was not alone. Hanson Baldwin, military analyst for the *New York Times,* reported on a growing "mutiny" among reserve Air Force officers who refused flight duty in Korea in protest against what they felt to be the disruption of their settled lives so soon after their demobilization.[9]

At first, the Korean War fit more or less comfortably into a WWII template. Even the way the war began was reminiscent—or at least the way the beginning was reported. North Korean tanks did not drive or rumble but surged and swept across the 38th parallel to fall upon an unsuspecting South Korea in images that melded Nazi Blitzkrieg with Japanese perfidy in Pearl Harbor. To be sure, it was all happening in a country most people could neither visualize nor locate. But thick arrows moving relentlessly across clearly defined borders were familiar markers on the geography of the American imagination.

One difficult issue in the first month of war was how to name what was occurring. It could not be a war—no congressional declaration had been given or requested. Newspapers described what U.S. troops were doing as a "police action." But, Richard Rovere observed, "this describes their role, not the country's." Or, as a character in the 1951 film *Fixed Bayonets* put it, "If this is a police action, where are the cops?"[10]

Without a name to identify it, congressmen feared it would be impossible to tell when whatever it was ended. There was "no word or phrase in the vocabulary of foreign relations to describe our present role in Korea." But it could not be called a war. Second only to speedy mobilization to meet the Korean commitment was the necessity to "avoid giving the world, in particular the Soviet Union, the impression that we consider general war inevitable."[11] Whatever the Russians thought, according to a Gallup poll in late June, fully 57 percent of the public believed World War III had begun.[12]

There was considerable confusion, too, about who the enemy was.[13] The country was given to understand that the Russians were behind the North Korean move, which led some impatient people to demand a nuclear attack on Moscow. Others prepared for a long drawn-out war of resistance. Buster Campbell, president of the Northwest Ski Association and ski coach at the University of Washington, announced the organization of 5,000 skiers as "a potential mountain guerrilla force in case of invasion by an enemy." The unit was trained to guard mountain passes, hydroelectric projects, domestic water supplies, power lines, and communications as well as "to carry on guerrilla warfare." Campbell and his fellow veterans of the 10th Mountain Division were determined, he told the *New York Times*, to have "something concrete to do in the event of war."[14]

There were a few public protests against the war, and they were put down by the police. "Red 'Peace' Rally Defies Court; Routed by Police; 14 Held, 3 Hurt," read the *New York Times* headline on August 3, 1950. In late July 1950, the New York Labor Conference for Peace was refused permission to hold a peace rally in Union Square Park. The police ban was upheld by the State Supreme Court, which declared that a rally would "interrupt traffic, making control impossible, and seriously inconvenience many thousands of homegoers." Moreover, Judge Eugene L. Brisach observed, "This meeting is one which would provoke incidents. . . . The right of public assembly is a paramount one, but its application does not require the destruction of the balance of the public." On the day of the rally, a crowd, estimated by the sponsors as 15,000 strong, gathered in defiance of the ban, and 1,000 policemen were on hand to meet them. (The police counted 2,000 demonstrators and 8,000 "spectators and bystanders.") "On the whole," the *Times* reported, the police "used restraint," although demonstrators who refused to disperse were "severely beaten," and mounted police "rode onto crowded sidewalks." Fourteen people were arrested on various charges, including calling a policeman a "Cossack" and trying to bite him.[15]

The merchants, businessmen, lawyers, farmers, and housewives of Webster City, Iowa, did not organize peace rallies and were certainly not "Reds." Still, "[d]own at the grass roots," *U.S. News & World Report* reported on December 15, 1950, "what people want is peace, if they can get it." Many people "are quite willing to give up in Korea, permanently." There was not much objection to Chinese admission into the United Nations. "If we mean to shut out all representatives who don't agree with us," a group of farmers agreed, "there's no reason to have a world organization." Indeed, the people of Webster City were all for a negotiated peace, the sooner the better. They thought there was no "real quarrel" between the United States and China, that the Chinese had been "engineered" into the Korean War by the Russians. Few of the citizens of Webster wanted to drop atom bombs on anyone. While most had supported Truman's initial intervention, the overwhelming majority now saw it as a mistake. Those interviewed denied they were isolationist: "I can't conceive of the United States as operating on a purely national or Hemisphere basis. The world is not that simple any longer," a spokesman for a group of farmers told the reporter. Nor were they pacifists: "It's foolish to fight little fires until Russia is ready to launch an all-out attack. We should classify areas. Where they are minor, as Korea is, let them go." They were all for increasing the pace of mobilization and arms production. The reporter's conclusion was that people wanted peace; if they couldn't get it, "they will accept war, preferably a decisive war."[16]

The note consistently struck in newspaper interviews with random citizens echoed the voice of Webster, Iowa: a longing for peace, an assumption that peace was the normal state of things. On occasion, that longing for peace was translated into a desire for the sort of war people had imagined WWII to have been: a total war to be followed, *this* time, by total peace. Sometimes both views were expressed simultaneously, as in an emphatic letter to Truman from Mrs. Steve Evans of Forbus, Texas. "I am pleading with you *not to drop the A Bomb*," she wrote. "I have five sons in the service. Three are in Korea. And at the moment I don't know if the other two have been sent there or not. One is missing since July. . . . Deep down in my heart something tells me he is a prisoner in China. If you order the A Bomb dropped, that will cause a civil war here because mothers and fathers won't sit back and let their sons be killed when it could have been prevented. Order the Chinese to give our prisoners up and tell them you will draw our troops out, and then let the A Bomb drop. But first it should be dropped on Russia. Please help our boys first and dear God, send my darlings back to me. And *give us peace once more*." Mrs. Jane Culbertson of St. Louis, Missouri, whose husband was a prisoner of war, urged Truman to sign a cease-fire as soon as possible: "We, the little people, did not send our boys to Korea—it is time the men responsible bring them back."[17]

There were also protests from soldiers on active service. A young lieutenant accosted the reporter Margueritte Higgins: "As his lips trembled with exhaustion and anger, he said, 'Are you correspondents telling the people back home the truth? Are you telling them that out of one platoon of twenty men, we have three left? Are you telling them that we have nothing to fight with, and that it is an utterly useless war?'" The journalist Mike Royko remembers thinking: "What is this? I didn't know anyone who was in Korea who understood what the hell we were doing there. . . . We were over there fighting the Chinese, you know? Christ, I'd been raised to think the Chinese were among the world's most heroic people and our great friends. . . . I was still mad at the Japs."[18]

In the spring of 1951, a Marine lieutenant, worried his letter might not reach the president, took the precaution of sending a copy to his local newspaper, the Fort Wayne *News-Sentinel*. Lieutenant Gale C. Buuck wanted the following questions answered: "How many YEARS are you going to let American manpower, materials, and money drain into this Korean sewer? How many more of my men must die on account of your stubborn refusal to pull out of Korea? . . . None of us know why we are here and none of us can understand why we stay. Never have American men fought in a more useless war. . . . Surely, someone back home ought to wake up Congress or somebody and get us out of here." Buuck's plea received a great deal of local publicity. The *News-Sentinel* ran the letter and endorsed its views in an editorial. "You have asked the same questions, Lieutenant, which we and many of our readers have been asking. . . . 'Shall we pull out of Korea?' If the Commander-in-Chief had been able to justify sending you to Korea in the first place, he might find answering this one much easier. But having no clearly defined purpose, Mr. Truman has no clearly defined answer." Of course, Truman had defined the purpose of the war: to repel aggression. The problem was that the war continued, requiring renewed and slightly different statements of purpose: to liberate the north; to give prisoners of war freedom of choice. By the spring of 1951, none were satisfied nor satisfying.

The Chinese reproduced Buuck's letter as a propaganda leaflet, with a safe-conduct pass on the reverse side.[19]

Individual congressmen occasionally called for peace and were red-baited. In May 1951, Edwin Johnson, Democratic senator from Colorado, introduced a cease-fire resolution in the Senate. After a series of rhetorical "whereas's," which condemned the "hopeless conflict of attrition and indecisiveness," the immorality of "slaughtering additional millions of human beings" so as to force an "uneasy peace upon the vanquished," Johnson called for "an immediate cease-fire, a return to the *status quo ante*, a full exchange of prisoners, and the withdrawal of all non-Korean forces from the peninsula." A week after this speech, Johnson was interviewed on the popular radio program *Pro and Con*. Most of the press, he pointed out, had "shied away" from any discussion of his resolution, and some had accused him of being a "defeatist, an isolationist, an appeaser," but the response from his constituents had been overwhelmingly positive.

The *New York Times* reported Johnson's resolution in a single paragraph; it featured the Soviet reaction to Johnson's resolution far more prominently.[20] When asked if he was troubled that *Pravda* had praised his resolution, Johnson responded that it was "good news. Peace is not a one-way street. There can be no peace in the world unless Russia agrees to it." Wasn't this appeasement? Johnson, unimpressed, said that all his resolution did was "turn Korea back to the Koreans. . . . Korea is a testing ground for negotiating peace. . . . If we wait for an unconditional surrender before we start developing peace terms, we better start preparing for a hundred years' war."[21] Predictably, the right wing of the Republican Party attacked, Senator Knowland leading the charge, but Johnson's speech represented an eloquent version of an increasingly popular position.

Republican opposition to the war, on the other hand, was consistently incoherent. Having greeted news of the administration's intervention in Korea with approbation, it took awhile to gather grounds for partisan attack. Privately, Senator Robert A. Taft expressed concern that the United States was in danger of becoming an "imperialistic nation"; publicly he insisted the Korean War was entirely a consequence of Truman's failure to ensure victory for Chiang Kai-shek in China. As that failure had occurred several years earlier, it was unclear what to do now. Over the course of the next three years, Republicans veered between calls for total withdrawal and equally impassioned calls for policies that threatened a vast expansion of the war. The closest approach to a coherent policy was former president Herbert Hoover's call for the United States to transform America into a

Gibraltar for the defense of western civilization: "We can," Hoover declared in December 1950, "without any measure of doubt, with our own air and naval forces, hold the Atlantic and Pacific Oceans with one frontier on Britain (if she wishes to cooperate), and the other on Japan, Formosa and the Philippines."[22] Nothing in Hoover's speech indicated what to do, immediately, in Korea.

Nevertheless, the Republicans' awareness of the depth of public disaffection ran all through their 1952 presidential campaign. However opportunistic, Senator Everett Dirksen's speech putting Taft's name in nomination at the 1952 Republican Convention was at the same time a powerful call for peace in Korea: "Once it was deemed the primary duty of government to keep the nation at peace. In the last twenty years those in power have given us the biggest, costliest, bloodiest war in the history of Christendom. They have given us more. They have given us an undeclared, unconstitutional one-man war in Korea, now in its third year. As one Korean G.I. put it, 'We can't win, we can't lose, we can't quit.' He might have added, 'We can only die.'"[23]

An Ambivalent War in Hollywood

The film industry was ready from the first to help the government explain why it had to send the boys to Korea. The industry's reaction to the outbreak of war was a rush on the registration of possible titles. On June 28, the Title Registration Bureau of the Motion Picture Association announced it had received five titles hand-delivered by various producers: *Korea, South Korea, Crisis in Korea, Formosa,* and, rather ominously, *Indochina. Film Daily* boasted of the film industry's instant response to the call to battle: "For the third time in a generation, the awesome shadow of Mars shot full across the American industry . . . and, as twice before . . . the industry fell into line and asked for its marching orders from the government."[24]

Francis S. Harmon, who had chaired the coordinating committee between Hollywood and various government agencies during WWII, returned to act as liaison.[25] Any request for military assistance in the making of a movie had to come before the Motion Picture Production Office. If, in the view of the Motion Picture Section of the relevant service, the script did not make a contribution to the "national Defense and the Public good," no cooperation would be forthcoming. Scripts were rewritten to gain the military's approval and the free hardware that went with it.[26]

The war in Korea was the unspoken background to educational films on preparing for atomic warfare and military service. In the tradition of Frank Capra's *Why We Fight,* the Movietone News Division of 20th Century Fox released a thirty-minute war promotional called *Why Korea?* which won the 1950 Academy Award in the best short documentary category.[27] In a brief review, *Variety* explained that it was designed to "clear up possible doubts as to the wisdom or necessity of sending troops to such a remote and seemingly unimportant area," and thought it would be "enlightening to those who have been in the dark as to 'Why Korea?'"[28] The first task of the documentary was to remove any lingering sense that the Soviet Union had played a major role in WWII, and it did so initially by listing the casualties in WWII, starting with the British and ending with the Norwegians, without mentioning the Soviet Union.

This was followed by a capsule history of the background to the Korean War in the form of a recitation of pre–WWII aggression and appeasement, including the Soviet attack on Finland. When the Soviet Union itself was attacked, "we thought the Russians had learned a lesson and we came to their aid." Reversing the military history of WWII, the narrator continues: "Without our help, the Russians would surely have lost." That established, the rest of the film lists Soviet violations, from free elections in Korea and Eastern Europe, to disorder in France ("Frenchmen fighting Frenchmen under directions from Moscow"), Italy, Colombia, Greece, China, Iran, Great Britain, and even New York, where communist leaders, who would have been liquidated in Russia, were given a fair and open trial. In a declaration of globalization *avant la lettre,* the film concludes: "There are no longer any geographic boundaries. Blood shed in Korea today is the same as if blood were shed in Rome, Paris, London, New York, Washington, Chicago, or San Francisco. . . . What we are defending is not geographic borders, but a way of life."[29] Nevertheless, the secretary of the Independent Theater Owners of Ohio asked the membership to delay showing *Why Korea?* until the government agreed to sponsor a second feature, *Why We Should Get Out of Korea.*[30]

Film Daily and 20th Century Fox pledged themselves to the war effort (in the light of HUAC's ongoing attack on Hollywood, this was hardly surprising), yet the films actually produced during the war did not march to battle with any great clarity. On the whole, Hollywood preferred the certainties of the war recently and decisively won to a "police action," whose origins and ends were both uncertain. But WWII functioned, implicitly, to sanctify the new war. Reviewers spelled it out. In November 1950, *American Guerrilla in the Philippines,* starring Tyrone Power, opened in theaters across the country. "Now that Americans are again battling in another Far Eastern land," the *New York Times* reviewer observed, "where the nature of warfare is erratic in the face of a grim, deceptive foe, there is a fitful contemporary graphicness" about the film. The reviewer went on to characterize the similarities: "The many scenes . . . of tattered hordes of fleeing refugees, strung across strange and rugged landscapes; of marauding Oriental troops; of bearded, unkempt American fighters inhabiting alien hovels in alien lands and dauntlessly improvising devices and designs as they go—all have a timely appearance."[31] Movietone news showed scenes from the Korea battlefront, but as a main feature, the Korean films never performed well at the box office.[32]

Nevertheless, several movies about the war were produced while it was being fought. The first and only enduring film was made in October 1950 over the course of ten days of low-budget shooting on sound stages and, for the outdoor scenes, in Griffiths Park, Los Angeles.[33] *Steel Helmet* was directed by Samuel Fuller, a veteran of World War II and apparently as sick of war as he was certain the country would continue to fight them. On only one occasion is the reason for the war mentioned in the film and then in terms so abstract they would serve any country in any war at any time. "When your house is attacked," says a soldier who had been a conscientious objector during WWII, "you have got to defend it." The explanation can hardly be heard because it is spoken over the chatter of a machine gun. There was a larger problem: the audience first had to believe that America's house was located everywhere and anywhere in the world, or it would not be clear how the North Koreans could otherwise have attacked it.

Two other patriotic moments in the film were also problematic. A North Korean prisoner of war appeals to a black soldier on the basis of racial solidarity, pointing out that he can eat with whites only when there's a war on and must always ride in the back of the bus. The soldier staunchly replies that 100 years ago his people weren't allowed on the bus, in 50 years he expected to get to the middle, and in another 50 all the way to the front. He is clearly willing to wait, but his answer leaves something to be desired as a defense of the values for which it is presumed the war is being fought. The Japanese-American soldier in the unit similarly rejects the prisoner's reminder of wartime internment. Internment had been wrong, but he was an American and America solved its own problems. A critical reviewer for the army's Motion Picture Section worried that "the Red PW" had the better arguments.[34]

The movie ends with a straggling line of soldiers walking slowly away from the camera as the words "There is no end to this story" scroll onto the screen. The implication that Korea might be only one of a potentially endless series of American wars made *Steel Helmet* an unlikely vehicle for national mobilization.

I Want You, released on Christmas Eve in 1951, was meant to overcome what the *New York Times* movie critic Bosley Crowther called the average American's resistance to "the necessity of facing up to another war and then finally standing still for it because that is the patriotic thing to do." *I Want You* opens with an aerial shot of an average American town, "the way it would look," the narrator intones, "to a bird or to a bomber pilot straightening out for his run over the target" or, he hastens to add, "to a low-flying angel." The narrative connects three stories of reluctance to serve: the first about a businessman, played by Dana Andrews, a married man with two children; the second about his younger brother; the third about the son of a worker in the business Andrews owns whose father seeks to have him exempted from the draft.[35] Andrews volunteers for Korea, less out of a sense of patriotism than of obligation. How otherwise will he be able to face his children in the future when they ask, "What were you doing, Daddy, when the world was shaking?" His wife, played by the ideal housewife and mother, Dorothy McGuire, puts his decision in domestic terms. In the words of Crowther's acerbic review, she explains that he is going so as "to defend his kiddies and his home." "All in all the running crisis of the 'cold war,'" Crowther concluded, "has been absorbed in the cotton padding of sentiment. A straight recruiting poster would be more convincing and pack more dramatic appeal."[36]

However, the movie wasn't as straightforward as a poster; in fact, it was radically ambivalent. A picture-perfect family dinner party explodes when Dorothy McGuire, not known for raising her voice, denounces her young brother-in-law's professed preference for a nuclear war that would settle everything once and for all without his having to serve. She despises him, she says, for his readiness to incinerate the world, but she despises him equally for his selfish desire to avoid the military. The political message is clear: preemptive nuclear war is as unacceptable as pacifism, and that leaves "limited war" the only alternative. What McGuire insists upon is not belief in the specific war in Korea but rather acquiescence in whatever war is on hand.

This message is briefly questioned by McGuire's hitherto meek and submissive mother-in-law, who, having lost one son to World War II, is desperate to keep her remaining two sons safe at home. Standing in her living room, surrounded by her husband's World War I trophies, she suddenly turns on him. She raises her arm and, with one violent sweep, cleanses the mantelpiece of military paraphernalia, pulls sabers and helmets and unit citations off the walls, declaring that she has always hated this room. Turning to her astonished husband, she reminds him that he had not been a hero after all but only a general's orderly, who had nevertheless raised his sons on war stories. "You were *proud* when our son died," she charges, and for a moment the obscenity of taking pride in such a death is evident.

Yet, in the end, the worker's son is drafted, he dies, and the younger boy goes to war, spurred by his girlfriend's admiration and, if not persuaded, at least not protesting his draft board's claim that he would be fighting for his freedom to choose where he worked and not to be afraid of a "knock at the door in the middle of the night." In the closing frames of the film, Dorothy McGuire turns her back to the camera and shepherds her two children into their large white house. The house, the children, the town, have all been made safe by war.

Even those who claimed to have liked the film, like the editor of the *Los Angeles Daily News*, praised it in language that revealed the fragility of its argument. The editorial acknowledged that, of course, all "a poor little citizen's" instincts are to "seek a snug harbor for himself and his family" as a storm rages outside the door. His sense of duty may tell him that he has to help fight the storm, but his "intelligence tells him about the doubts that beset millions in the United States today." The greatness of *I Want You* lay in its demonstration that "the citizens must accept their responsibility for the war."[37] Thus it was obedience that the film championed, not intelligence.

A Different Sort of War

But blind obedience was a totalitarian demand. Americans, it was presumed, fought in the name of the reasoned morality of the cause. President Truman laid it out for reporters in an informal speech after lunch at the Muehlebach Hotel in Kansas City, Missouri. He called for a worldwide mobilization against the "menace" of the "inheritors of Genghis Khan and Tamerlane, who were the greatest murderers in the history of the world."[38] Yet in the early days of the war, there were warnings that murderousness was not confined to the other side. In August 1950, John Osborne wrote a long essay that ran in both *Life* and *Time*.[39] From the outset, Osborne confessed his distress at what he felt he had to report: "This is a story that no American should ever have to write," he began. "It is the ugly story of an ugly war." Before telling it, however, he gave the good news: U.S. troops were superb. They may have been raw when they arrived and even abandoned positions they should have held, but "in a land and among a people that most of them dislike, in a war that all too few of them understand and none of them want, they became strong men and good soldiers—fast." U.S. firepower and the ability to coordinate and use it had been "thrilling" to observe.

In Korea, these fine soldiers were having forced upon them "acts and attitudes of the utmost savagery." By this Osborne meant not the "inevitable savagery of combat in the field, but savagery in detail—the blotting out of villages where the enemy *may* be hiding; the shooting and shelling of refugees who *may* include [the enemy] or who *may* be screening an enemy march upon our positions." Even harder to witness was the "savagery by proxy, the savagery of [our ally]. . . . They murder to save themselves the trouble of escorting prisoners to the rear; they murder civilians simply to get them out of the way or to avoid the trouble of searching and cross-examining them. And they extort information . . . by means so brutal that they cannot be described."

Osborne was told that soldiers had seen North Korean soldiers change out of their uniforms into ordinary Korean peasant garb, and so, he suggested, their suspicion of refugees was not surprising: "Every time they see a column of peasants coming toward them they reach for their guns, and sometimes they use their guns."[40] He was present at a particularly tense moment when a call came through to the regimental command post that a column of 300 to 400 refugees were moving right into the lines of a company of U.S. soldiers. "Don't let them through," the major in command ordered the regimental commanders. And if they won't go back, a staff officer asked? Then fire over their heads, came the answer. And then? "Well, then, fire into them if you have to. *If you have to,* I said." "From the command post," Osborne wrote, "an urgent and remonstrating voice speaks over the wire into the hills. 'My God, John. It's gone too far when we are shooting at children.'" And then in response to the unheard voice from the outpost, the same officer said, "'Watch it, John, watch it! But don't take any chances.'"[41]

Osborne's point was that Korea was a different sort of war, one fought "amongst and to some extent by the population of the country." A purely military approach would not work; the problem had to be engaged at a political level. Otherwise, Osborne warned, the U.S. effort was doomed, and along with it, the American soldier, who had then to fight in ways Osborne could not bear to describe in too great detail.

Korea was not the first time the U.S. military had fought a war "amongst and to some extent by the population of the country." But few Americans remembered the suppression of insurgencies in the Philippines or Nicaragua. The image of war perfected and perpetuated by combat reporting in World War II had encouraged Americans to believe their wars were without ambiguity, against regular troops on the ground and clearly marked enemy territory from the air. Osborne did not name what he described as a guerrilla war, nor did he name his description of the appropriate response, counterinsurgency. His effort in this article was to warn readers about the peculiar nature of this new, "savage" war.

On October 9, 1950, over the caption "U.S. Fighting Man: Winner—and Still Champ," a *Newsweek* cover photo showed an exhausted soldier, helmet askew, holding at gunpoint a Korean soldier, whose arms are raised high in the air. The American looks dazed; the Korean terrified. Inside was the story of the capture of Seoul, which had been, General Douglas MacArthur assured the world, "conducted in such a manner as to cause the least possible damage to civil installations." The *Newsweek* correspondent's gloss was laconic: "He could tell that to the Marines." The city had been 60 percent "burned, wrecked or damaged. . . . American artillery and flame-throwers turned concrete buildings into hollow shells and slums into ashes." The accompanying pictures were stark: a small child, seated amidst the ruins of some building, another group of children searching the wreckage, a group of "Red POWs cowering in a ditch," and two Korean women, naked from the waist up, arms clutching at their pants while somehow also attempting to cover their breasts. They are surrounded by heavily equipped American soldiers and one man, an officer or perhaps an interpreter, with a notebook. The caption called their expression "sullen" and identified them as "Red 'nurses'" who had been captured while "firing guns."

There were two letters of protest, both by women. Joan Aida Waterson, "College Student," felt some comment from the "'home front'" was called for. She had been distressed by the picture of the women, who should not perhaps, as nurses or as women, have been engaged in combat, but who nevertheless deserved more dignity than they were given. The second letter, from a nurse in Middleboro, Massachusetts, was harsher. "We as Americans criticize the way the Reds treat the American prisoners of war," Helen McDonald wrote. But the picture of the nurses "partially disrobed at the mercy of four 'men'" made McDonald "thoroughly ashamed of our forces in their treatment of POWs." "It's no wonder the Reds treat our soldiers, nurses, etc., the way they do," she went on, "when they see pictures like this." As a nurse,

"I'm sure if I happened to be in their shoes I'd fire a gun to protect myself against such a predicament, too." Why, she asked, had they been made to strip? Because, the editors explained, "GIs have learned from bitter experience that North Koreans often conceal hand grenades in their clothing. Hence, all prisoners are stripped and searched."

Several readers wrote to denounce McDonald for her excessive concern for enemy captives, and in a later issue she clarified her position. *Newsweek* had edited the original letter without her permission. The full text made abundantly clear that her protest was against not the treatment of the nurses but the publication of the picture: "Won't you do your part in keeping such pictures out of your magazine," she asked the editors. "The UN and we Americans could emphasize the 'Golden Rule' just a little bit more by banning the publication of atrocity pictures. It only embitters the enemy and gives them ideas to do likewise."[42]

Stories of North Korean and Chinese atrocities against American troops were graphically reported, giving the reader a sense that the country was fighting an especially barbarous enemy. Yet a Manichean view of the war was difficult to sustain. In early July, a story detailing the treatment accorded suspected guerrillas caught behind South Korean lines led Telford Taylor, former chief counsel at Nuremberg, to warn against oversimplified judgments of the enemy: "We will make ourselves appear ridiculous and hypocritical if we condemn the conduct of the enemy, when at the same time troops allied with us are with impunity executing prisoners by means of rifle butts applied to backbones."[43] In late October 1950, Charles Grutzner reported on the state of things in Seoul following the recapture of the city by UN forces. Suspected political prisoners, including 1,200 women and 300 children, were being held in "severe conditions." About 200 had been found guilty at trials "in which they were not permitted to face their accusers." The warden of the prison confessed that he was unable to feed or properly care for such numbers; moreover, he believed "many prisoners, especially the women, are innocent of Communist charges." Despite the overflowing jail, large numbers of people continued to be arrested. "Among the less pleasant sights in this oriental metropolis," Grutzner wrote, "is a man with hands tied walking with a downcast head, while tied to the rope behind him is his wife, her hands also bound, and a baby in a cloth wrapping on her back."[44]

In November, Grutzner described in detail the killing of some of these prisoners, and in December the wholesale execution of political prisoners in Seoul by the Rhee government was widely reported. "The executions were not brought to public notice," the *New York Times* reported, "until United

States and British units happened to move into an area bordering the execution ground. . . . [They] were horrified upon seeing truckloads of old men, women, youths, and several children lined up before open graves and shot down by South Korean military policemen with rifles and machine guns." Although American military authorities refrained from interfering, British soldiers did physically block further executions.[45] A generally supportive *Time* condemned the shootings as a disgrace to the South Korean government.[46] Finally bowing to the bad publicity, Rhee ordered a review of all death sentences, decreed that henceforth executions would be individual rather than en masse, and released all prisoners sentenced to less than ten years in jail. An outraged letter to the *New York Times* demanded to know why American forces had not prevented the executions from the start. "Why did we hesitate to interfere? Are we not in Korea against precisely this sort of lawlessness and violence? . . . As an American, as a veteran, as a teacher, and as a simple human being, I demand that we act in this matter. If moral survival means anything—and it should mean everything—our hands must be clean."[47]

The impossibility of keeping one's hands clean, which Osborne had warned about almost a year earlier, was occasionally made clear by frontline reporters. Buried in a *New York Times* story on the interference of ham radio operators in the shelling of Seoul in March 1951, George Barrett described what it was like to be on the receiving end of American firepower. He wrote of a napalm raid on a village of about 200 people where the dead were left unburied "because there is nobody left" to do the job. He had come across a sole survivor, an old woman whom he found "dazedly hanging up some clothes in a blackened courtyard filled with the bodies of four members of her family." Elsewhere in the village, the dead had "kept the exact postures they had held when the napalm struck—a man about to get on his bicycle, fifty boys and girls playing in an orphanage, a housewife strangely unmarked, holding in her hand a page torn from a Sears-Roebuck catalogue crayoned at mail order number 3,811,294 for a $2.98 'bewitching bed jacket—coral.'"[48]

In a report published in April, Barrett warned that the immense firepower of U.S. forces was responsible for growing bitterness among Koreans of all political persuasions. UN forces withdrawing from Pyongyang had employed a scorched earth policy, "leaving blackened paths of their own whenever they have been forced to withdraw along their sectors." No one questioned the need to deny military equipment to the enemy, but "many of the ruins created by the United Nations troops do little or nothing" to hamper the Chinese or North Koreans. Korean civilians fled with the UN forces "not so much to get away from the Communists but to get out of the path of the shelling and bombing." Then, without naming names, Barrett went on: "There seems to be a growing feeling that if a general policy of 'preserve Korea' wherever militarily possible could be laid down more emphatically, the troops in the field and the pilots in the planes would be more selective and careful in their choice of targets." Barrett understood that a soldier, sensing a sudden movement, could not be blamed "if the figure darting behind a distant barn turns out later to be a woman carrying her child." "But," he continued, without further comment, "there are cases of infantry-men resting for a short break, putting matches to a straw hut to get warm."[49]

When he returned from his two-year stint as a war reporter, Barrett reflected on the behavior of American troops in a lengthy essay for the *New York Times Magazine* that focused on Sgt. William A. "Ned" Nedzweckas, grabbed from easy duty in Hokkaido, Japan, to fight in Korea. The hardest phase of the war, Barrett reported, was the fight back up the peninsula to drive Chinese troops north of the 38th parallel. Guerrillas behind the lines were a constant threat, and one of the "nastiest jobs" Ned had to do was "to take it out on the civilians" as, Barrett at once added, "the Communists were also taking it out on the civilians." When a village was suspected of sheltering "Red bands," Ned's unit was ordered to go in "and burn down all the houses to check the guerrillas." Ned would enter shouting "'Okay, Sayonara! Sayonara!'" Then, as flames consumed their houses, the "startled cries of the villagers as they dashed out of the huts would fade quickly into staring silence as they huddled together, frightened, in a paddy field."[50]

Ned had few questions about *how* he had to fight. "To veterans of the last two World Wars, who experienced deep personal feelings against the Germans and Japanese," Barrett wrote, "there is an eerie character about the professional, calm, and almost disinterested way men in Korea kill and get killed. . . . There is one phrase the G.I. in Korea has taken as his own: 'That's the way the ball bounces.' It spells out the fatalistic acceptance that characterizes the combat man in Korea." The combat man did, however, wonder *why* he was fighting. "'What are we doing over here?' is about the only question that gives real concern to Ned," Barrett wrote, "and it's a question that none of the high-sounding declarations put out by generals and morale groups . . . has been able to answer for most G.I.s." Not that it mattered: "Understand it or not," Ned was "prepared to finish the job." In spite of his "confusion," Barrett wrote, "he vaguely senses, when nailed down on the subject, that Communist aggression in Korea is aggression everywhere."

Vagueness was acceptable. What the administration could not afford was a specific sense that the United States should not be in Korea at all, and it could generally count on senior news executives to cooperate. In August 1950, Edward R. Murrow sent a disheartening report from Tokyo. "This is a most difficult broadcast to do," he began, in a tone reminiscent of John Osborne's dispatch. After talking extensively with troops and officers, he concluded that a recent offensive he had witnessed was "meaningless," although it had cost "hundreds of lives and drained vital supplies." The battle had been fought solely because, as one officer put it, "We decided we needed a victory." He went on: when he walked through "dead valleys, through villages to which we have put the torch by retreating, what then of the people who live there? . . . Will our occupation of that flea-bitten land lessen, or increase, the attraction of Communism?"[51] CBS did not broadcast the program.

An Invisible War

By the fall of 1952, as the cease-fire talks dragged on and the war settled into a deadly routine, as public support sank to 37 percent, the war became invisible to everyone except to those who continued to fight it—forgotten before it had ended. Charles Cole, on leave from the Navy, found no Korean War news in his hometown newspaper: "Korea just didn't seem to exist."[52] David Hackworth returned from Korea in 1952 to a "country without a cause." It was "as if Korea, that distant battlefield, did not exist at all, or that Killed, Missing, or Wounded in Action were words reserved for someone else's son. To date, more than 105,000 Someone Else's Sons."[53]

James Michener complained in a series of articles for the *Saturday Evening Post* that the men fighting the war had become "forgotten heroes."[54] Reflecting on his service as a public information officer during 1951, Lee Judge described his frustration "over a war the world seemed to have forgotten."[55] A week in which there had been 2,200 American casualties was reported by *U.S. News & World Report* under the headline "Korea: The 'Forgotten' War." Ground battles, the journal reminded its readers, were as intense as in any previous war; air battles had grown to WWII size; casualties had doubled. Yet the headlines were dominated by news of domestic shortages of beef and new cars, strikes, and government scandal. Korea was "half forgotten," receding in the public mind "to the status of an experimental war, one being fought back and forth for the purpose of testing men, weapons, materials, and methods, on a continuing basis." While men died at an ever-increasing rate, "the war [is] almost forgotten at home, with no end in sight."[56]

Max Ascoli, editor of *Reporter* magazine, observed in sorrow and anger that there has "never been a great fuss made about those who have fought and who still are ready to fight in Korea. Few entertainers have volunteered to go to the dismal peninsula. Blood donations have lagged pitiably." Korea, Ascoli wrote, was a "peripheral suburban war," which had lost its "news value" because of "repetitiousness."[57]

The people Samuel Lubell interviewed, as he traveled the country in the months before the 1952 presidential election, were entirely focused on the war; people cursed at the very mention of Truman's name. There was widespread agreement that the war had staved off a recession or worse, but the Democratic Party's campaign slogan, "You never had it better," left people feeling guilty. In Weatherford, Texas, an Adlai Stevenson supporter observed to a neighbor that if the Republicans won, they'd all be "selling apples again," to which his friend replied: "Maybe so, but at least it won't be a bloody apple." Voters in Iowa, Detroit, and Los Angeles used the term "blood money" to describe the current economic good times.

Public reaction to Korea, Lubell wrote, punctured the myth that "'the people only have to be told the facts to do what is expected of them.' The expression 'We don't know what the War is all about' was voiced most frequently by persons with sons or husbands in Korea. Clearly they did not lack information; but emotion had stopped their ears to all explanations of why we were fighting in Korea."[58]

Lubell predicted that the era of limited war was over; the 1952 election amounted to a public repudiation of such policies. "The same dread that the American people might not support a prolonged attrition," he wrote in 1956, "which would prompt our politicians to try to avoid involvement could be expected to spur them to get any war over with quickly once we're engaged."[59] His prediction held for barely five years.

The war did not so much end as stop. "It has been a strange war," an editorial in the *Wall Street Journal* observed. "It came with sudden stealth in an unsuspected place. Now it seems to end in a whimper. In the strange quiet that follows the silenced guns, none of us feel great transport; we have too often been brought to hope only to meet disillusion. Rather, we feel a numbness. Tomorrow we may have to pick up our arms again—if not in Korea, then elsewhere. But we know that even if this truce vanishes tomorrow, or if it should be followed by a greater trial, neither we nor our enemies can any longer doubt our resolution. That is the victory of the truce of Panmunjon."[60] *Life* was similarly low-key. "It was plain that the end of fighting in Korea . . . did not promise either surcease from anxiety or lasting peace. . . . Since there was no real victory, there was no occasion for celebration."[61]

Throughout the war, the Truman administration had labored against the immense reluctance of the country to go to war again, especially for reasons they found less than compelling. Equally, throughout the war, it could count on acquiescence, however sullen. William Styron, who had been called up in the summer of 1950, two years later published a novella based on his experience which captured the public mood. The narrator, Lieutenant Culver, speaks for all those men actually mobilized for Korea and symbolically for the nation as a whole: "It had all come much too soon and Culver had felt weirdly as if he had fallen asleep in some barracks in 1945 and had awakened in a half-dozen years or so to find that the intervening freedom, growth, and serenity had been only a glorious if somewhat prolonged dream. A flood of protest had welled up in him, for he had put the idea of war out of his mind entirely, and the brief years since Okinawa had been the richest of his life." But the protest only wells up—it has no issue.[62]

A passive public did not notice other aspects of this first of the limited wars. During World War II, American dead and wounded came to almost 1 million men, a significant number even when compared with countries that suffered greater losses. In Korea, the disparity of casualties between the United States and Korea was so enormous one might have expected considerable commentary.[63] Instead, the numbers seem to have been taken as more or less ordinary: 2 to 3 million Koreans to 33,000+ Americans. (Later, 3 to 4 million Vietnamese to 58,000+ Americans, 100,000 + Iraqis to 5 Americans; over 4,000 Americans—and counting as of September 2009— and to between 100,000 and 600,000 Iraqis—and counting.) Generally speaking, the press during the Korean War protected the public from a too concrete knowledge of what U.S. military power had wrought later. From the very beginning, bombing runs were described as precision targeting, and the targets identified were always military. There was acknowledgment that noncombatants did get hurt, but the issue was always cast in terms of intention. "The issue of intention," Sahr Conway-Lanz has written, "and not the question of whose weapons literally killed civilians or destroyed their homes, became the morally significant one for many Americans. If soldiers and officials did not intend the harm inflicted on noncombatants, Americans decided that their country's methods conformed to the humanitarian notions that undergirded the norm of noncombatant immunity."[64]

The war had been unpopular, although opinions varied on how to end it: as many, or more, Americans urged an all-out nuclear war against China or the Soviet Union as wanted a quick negotiated peace. In its aftermath, there was no investigation of how the war had been fought, but only of American prisoners of war who, by dying in unprecedented numbers, collaborating with the enemy, and choosing to remain among the communists, had failed to embrace the war sufficiently.[65] The main political expression of public dissatisfaction was the resounding defeat of the Democratic Party. Succeeding administrations would remember the political price and work to avoid it, but Korea seemed to hold few general lessons for the future.[66] The larger goals of U.S. foreign policy and its war-fighting practices remained largely unexamined. Perhaps for that reason, the country slipped easily, without undue protest, into another limited war in Asia, one which none of the presidents who fought it were ever able to sell for very long.

Notes

1. I am thinking here of the homeopathic post-Vietnam wars: Operation Urgent Fury (Grenada), Operation Just Cause (Panama), Operation Uphold Democracy (Haiti), Operations Desert Shield and Desert Storm (Iraq), Operation Restore Hope (Somalia), Operation Deliberate Force (Bosnia), and Operation Allied Force (Kosovo). Of these, only Restore Hope, during which eighteen American soldiers were killed and their bodies mutilated, drew sustained public ire.

2. As George C. Marshall remarked after World War II, maybe a king could indulge in a long war, "but you cannot have such a protracted struggle in a democracy in the face of mounting casualties." Quoted in Mark Stoler, this volume. Stoler makes it clear that selling an *unlimited* war, even after Pearl Harbor, even by a master politician like FDR, was no easy matter. See chapter 3, "Selling Different Kinds of War."

3. See Steven Casey, "White House Publicity Operations during the Korean War, June 1950–June 1951," *Presidential Studies Quarterly* 35, no. 4 (2005): 691–717. Casey argues the case at meticulously documented length in *Selling the Korean War: Propaganda, Politics, and Public Opinion in the United States, 1950–1953* (New York: Oxford University Press, 2008).

4. The single best source on the literature, film, and memorialization of the Korean War is James R. Kerin Jr., "The Korean War and American Memory" (PhD diss., University of Pennsylvania, 1994). See also W. D. Ehrhart and Philip K. Jason, eds., *Retrieving Bones: Stories and Poems of the Korean War* (New Brunswick, N.J.: Rutgers University Press, 1999). Paul M. Edwards has compiled a useful bibliography that

includes literature, *The Korean War: An Annotated Bibliography* (Westport, Conn.: Greenwood Press, 1998). An excellent collection of essays on the subject is Philip West and Suh Ji-moon, eds., *Remembering the "Forgotten War": The Korean War through Literature and Art* (Armonk, N.Y.: M. E. Sharpe, 2001).

5. Samuel Hynes, *The Soldiers' Tale: Bearing Witness to Modern War* (New York: Allen Lane/Penguin Press, 1997), xiii.

6. W. D. Ehrhart, "Soldier-Poets of the Korean War," *War, Literature & the Arts* 9, no. 2 (1997): 8. Much of the publication on Korea, as well as two TV documentaries about it, is explicitly the product of the Vietnam War. Callum McDonald's book title is a succinct expression of this: *Korea: The War before Vietnam* (New York: Free Press, 1986).

7. See Susan Moeller's book *Shooting War: Photography and the American Experience of Combat* (New York: Basic Books, 1989) for an interesting analysis of the changing nature of war photography from WWII through Vietnam. See also David Donald Duncan's *This Is War! A Photo-Narrative in Three Parts* (New York: Harper, 1951) and Charles and Eugene Jones, *The Face of War* (New York: Prentice-Hall, 1951) for a taste of just how disturbing the photographs got. Note that Duncan and the Jones brothers published while the war was still being fought. Correspondents like John Osborne (*Time, Life*) and George Barrett (*New York Times*) wrote some especially vivid dispatches, and Homer Bigart (*New York Times*) became the bane of MacArthur's existence in the early months of the war, as he reported, in the most unadorned prose, the flight/retreat of U.S. troops before the North Koreans' advance.

8. William Styron, *This Quiet Dust and Other Writings* (New York: Vintage Books, 1993), 334.

9. Hanson W. Baldwin, "A New Era in Air?" *New York Times*, 1 May 1952, 16. Part one of this two-part series was subtitled "'Mutiny' of Reservists Who Refuse to Fly Dramatizes a Menace to Aviation Power." Part II appeared the next day and was subtitled "Reasons for Decline of Interest in Flying Are Listed—Youth Is Seeking Security." Among the reasons for the decline, Baldwin listed the increasingly technological nature of flying, which reduced the glamour. On the other hand, he reported that the Marines were also having trouble recruiting. The Korean War, he concluded, left younger people "cold." *New York Times*, 2 May 1952, 9.

10. About the difficulty of naming, see Richard Rovere, "Letter from Washington," *New Yorker*, 5 August 1950, 48. A Marine Corps marching song took the metaphor a step further: "We're Harry's police force on call / So put your pack back on / The next stop is Saigon." Quoted in Kerin, "The Korean War and American Memory," 54.

11. Richard Rovere, "Letter from Washington," *New Yorker*, 5 August 1950.

12. Paul G. Pierpaoli Jr., *Truman and Korea: The Political Culture of the Early Cold War* (Columbia: University of Missouri Press, 1999), 29.

13. "Say, Joe, what does a North Korean *look* like?" a carnival game operator in a *New Yorker* cartoon asked his friend as he set up the target for a game. *New Yorker*, 15 July 1950, 18.

14. "Skiers in Northwest United as Defense 'Guerrillas,'" *New York Times*, 19 December 1950, 20.

15. Russell Porter, "Red 'Peace' Rally Defies Court," *New York Times*, 3 August 1950, 1. Later that evening, 500 demonstrators were dispersed when they tried to rally at Madison Square Park. Seven hundred policemen were on hand to monitor the behavior of "persons known to be Communist sympathizers" in the area of Times Square. The *Times* was gentler toward the newly organized American Women for Peace, 700 of whose members held a brief demonstration at the White House and then sent a delegation to lobby Congress and the State Department for peace in Korea. It reported the gathering in a straightforward manner, including the "shock" expressed by the acting president of AWP at a press conference in the face of "clever questions trying to prove us a Red delegation." Dr. Clementina J. Paolone described herself as an Italian American, "of Roman Catholic upbringing, and one of the 'good loyal American women that shout for peace.'" But the newspaper offered its readers, without comment, Dr. Paolone's office address. The headline was "700 Women Besiege Capital for Peace; Largely from New York City," 9 August 1950, 19. In December, about 1,000 women demonstrated at the UN. David Anderson, "Youthful 'Peace' Gathering Stages a Protest Sit Down at Lake Success," *New York Times*, 1 December 1950, 7. Note that the *Times* always put the word *peace* in quotation marks. On this occasion, 150 teenagers, led by Paul Robeson Jr., sat down in the morning, and twenty-one buses carrying 1,000 members of American Women for Peace arrived that afternoon, packing the Economic and Social Council room.

16. "Man on the Street Says: 'Try for Peace, Arm for War,' Reported from Webster City, Iowa," *U.S. News & World Report*, 15 December 1950, 24–25. The National Opinion Research Center reported in February 1951 that 57 percent of those polled would be in favor of seating the People's Republic of China in the UN if that would bring peace in Korea. Hugh Garland Wood, "American Reaction to Limited War in Asia: Korea and Vietnam, 1950–1968" (PhD diss., University of Colorado, 1974), 141.

17. Quoted in D. M. Giangreco and Kathryn Moore, *Dear Harry: Truman's Mailroom, 1945–1953: The Truman Administration through Correspondence with "Everyday Americans"* (Mechanicsburg, Pa.: Stackpole Books, 1999), 323. Mrs. Evans signed herself "A mother with a heart full and her hands full also . . ." Hers was among the few answered on this subject—a letter hoping she would be sustained by pride in her sons' service. See also the letter from Mrs. Culbertson, 346–47.

18. "The Good War," in Studs Terkel, *An Oral History of World War Two* (New York: Pantheon, 1984), 137.

19. "Bravo, Lieutenant," *News-Sentinel*, 29 March 1951, 6; Giangreco and Moore, *Dear Harry*, 349–50.

20. "For Halt in Korean War," *New York Times*, 18 May 1951, 3; 21 May 1951, 6. The full text of the resolution was published in the *Congressional Record*, but nowhere else. A few congressmen spoke for it, including Senator John Butler, R-Md, Senator Warren Magnuson, D-Wash, and Representative Thor C. Tollefson, D-Wash. The Senate never

acted on it. See Edwin Mantell, "Opposition to the Korean War: A Study in American Dissent" (PhD diss., New York University, 1973), 159.

21. *Congressional Record*, 15 May, June 17, 1951, 5424, 7192.

22. Ronald J. Caridi, *The Korean War and American Politics: The Republican Party as a Case Study* (Philadelphia: University of Pennsylvania Press, 1968), 133.

23. Ibid., 223.

24. David Detzer, *Thunder of the Captains: The Short Summer of 1950* (New York: Crowell, 1977), 153.

25. Thomas Doherty, *Projections of War: Hollywood, American Culture, and World War II* (New York: Columbia University Press, 1993), 276.

26. Though not always. Howard Hughes, director of the 1952 big budget *One Minute to Zero*, refused to remove a scene in which the hero, played by Robert Mitchum, orders his troops to fire point-blank at a mass of approaching refugees. The rest of the movie is dedicated to proving that he had no choice (there were North Korean soldiers hiding among the civilians) and that communist atrocities were far worse. See Suid, *Film and Propaganda*, vol. 5 (microfiche supplement), documents M-442 to M-450.

27. José Ferrer and Judy Holliday also won Oscars and, the following week, were reported by *Time* as near the top of HUAC's "Pink List." *Time*, 16 April 1951.

28. *Variety*, 24 January 1951, 6.

29. See May, "Reluctant Crusaders," 117. John Steelman, who was on Truman's White House staff, cooperated with Darryl F. Zanuck on the film.

30. Peter Gietschier, "Limited War and the Home Front: Ohio during the Korean War" (PhD diss., Ohio State University), 221.

31. Bosley Crowther review, *New York Times Film Reviews*, volume for 1950, 2466.

32. May, "Reluctant Crusaders," 127. May has calculated that no Korean War film "reached the top five moneymaking productions during the 1950s. Instead, thirty-two failed to reach the top fifty grossing films in any year." The majority of anticommunist/Korean War films were financial failures. May's conclusion is that the "effort to create a cold war consensus and voluntary support for the war failed on all fronts."

33. Portions of these reflections on the movies have appeared in my essay "The Korean War: Ambivalence on the Silver Screen," in *The Korean War at Fifty: International Perspectives*, ed. Mark F. Wilkinson (Lexington, Va.: John A. Adams '71 Center for Military History and Strategic Analysis, Virginia Military Institute, 2004).

34. Suid, *Film and Propaganda*, vol. 5 (microfiches supplement). See documents M-436 to M-441.

35. Andrews was the star of the 1946 Oscar-winning movie *Best Years of Our Lives*. In a sense, *I Want You* was the sequel.

36. *New York Times Film Reviews*, volume for 1951, 2574–75.

37. May, "Reluctant Crusaders," 121–22.

38. Paul P. Kennedy, "Truman Calls Reds Present-Day Heirs of Mongol Killers," *New York Times*, 24 December 1950, 1. "I have been trying to mobilize the moral force of the world," Truman went on. "Catholics, Protestants, Jews, the Eastern church, the Grand Lama of Tibet, the Indian Sanskrit code—I have been trying to organize all

these people to the understanding that their welfare and the existence of decency and honor in the world depends on our working together instead of trying to cut each other's throats." Truman kept an office in the hotel, which was close to Independence.

39. John Osborne, "The Ugly War," *Time*, 21 August 1950. Osborne was the senior correspondent in the Pacific for *Time* and *Life*.

40. Scenes of North Korean soldiers doing exactly that appeared in two Korean War films: *Steel Helmet* and *One Minute to Zero*. Both films also show, and justify, American soldiers committing war crimes. In *Steel Helmet*, an unarmed prisoner of war is executed; in *One Minute to Zero*, the hero orders a heavy artillery barrage against a column of refugees.

41. See Charles Hanley's book *The Bridge at No Gun Ri: A Midden Nightmare from the Korean War* (New York: Henry Holt, 2001) and Sahr Conway-Lanz's *Collateral Damage: Americans, Noncombatant Immunity, and Atrocity after World War II* (New York: Routledge, 2006) for details on U.S. policy toward refugees.

42. *Newsweek* cover photo, 9 October 1950. Inside, the editors explain this somber black-and-white photograph: a "U.S. Marine orders captured North Koreans to keep their hands up—and, in effect, tells the rest of the world that America not only will fight future aggression but will also win." Perhaps to balance this one, the full-color cover of the 23 October issue is of a very different sort of soldier: one hand is clenched into a fist, the other holds aloft his rifle; his eyes smile; his mouth is wide open in a yell of defiance. "New Army: Bullets and Guts," the caption reads. Inside we learn what may be responsible for this particular soldier's excellent spirits: he isn't in Korea but rather on his way to Virginia for further training as an engineer. The letters about the nurses appear in the November 6 issue on pp. 4–6. The letters attacking McDonald appeared first on November 20, p. 24; more letters, including McDonald's self-defense, are in the December 4 issue, pp. 4–6.

43. Letter to the Editor, "Atrocities in Korea," *New York Times*, 16 July 1950. Taylor acknowledged the difference between conventional and guerrilla warfare as well as the differences between the "traditions and practices of warfare in the Orient" and the West. "The laws of war and war crimes," he wrote, "are not weapons like bazookas and hand grenades to be used only against the enemy. The laws of war can be 'law' in the true sense only if they are of general application and applied to all sides."

44. Charles Grutzner, "Communist Suspects Jam Cells of War-Smashed Prison in Seoul," *New York Times*, 28 October 1950, 3.

45. Charles Grutzner, "27 Executed in Seoul Cemetery for Collaboration with Red Foe," *New York Times*, 3 November 1950, 1. The article began: "A Kiisang girl, the equivalent of Japanese geisha girl, died today with a love song on her lips." For the December reports, see "Seoul Executions Stir Westerners," 17 December 1950, 6; "9,330 Tried in Seoul as Red Supporters," 18 December 1950, 2; "British Troops Bar Executions," 19 December 1950, 4.

46. "A Matter of Convenience," *Time*, 25 December 1950, 19. The title was in response to a comment by General Lee Ho, vice chief of Martial Law Headquarters, reported by the *New York Times* in its December 17 account of the executions. The

general observed that civilians sentenced to death were usually hanged in prison, "but we have found that shooting by firing squad is more convenient."

47. "Rhee Terms News of Killings Untrue," 19 December 1950, 4; "Seoul Halts Execution of Political Prisoners," 21 December 1950, 5; Richard J. H. Johnston, "Seoul to Mitigate Prisoners' Terms," 22 December 1950, 2; "Korean Executions Protested," letter to the editor by Marius Livingston, Princeton, N.J., 28 December 1950, 22.

48. George Barrett, "Radio Hams in U.S. Discuss Girls, So Shelling of Seoul Is Held Up," *New York Times*, 9 February 1951, 1:3–3:2.

49. George Barrett, "UN Losing Favor by Korean Damage," 3 March 1951, 2.

50. George Barrett, "'That's the Way the Ball Bounces,'" 23 November 1951, 66–67. The quotes that follow are from this article.

51. *In Search of Light: The Broadcasts of Edward R. Murrow, 1938–1961*, ed. Edward R. Bliss (New York: Knopf, 1967), 167–69. Bliss's headnote states that it "was not used because, in the judgment of CBS, it might hurt the war effort" (166).

52. Charles F. Cole, *Korea Remembered: Enough of a War; The USS* Ozbourn's *First Korean Tour, 1950–1951* (Las Cruces, N.M.: Yucca Tree Press, 1995), 212, 273.

53. David Hackworth and Julie Sherman, *About Face: The Odyssey of an American Warrior* (New York: Simon and Schuster, 1989), 211.

54. James Michener, "The Forgotten Heroes of Korea," *Saturday Evening Post*, May 1952, 19–21, 124–28.

55. Lee Judge, *Reporter Magazine*, 14 June 1952, 22.

56. "Korea: The Forgotten War," *U.S. News & World Report*, 5 October 1951, 21.

57. Max Ascoli, *Reporter*, 22 January 1951, 1; 24 June 1952, 1. The polls in the spring of 1952 indicated immense impatience with the war. In the spring of 1952, Gallup showed 51 percent believed the war had been a mistake. But only 16 percent urged withdrawal, and 49 percent thought the United States should launch an all-out attack on China. See Wood, "American Reaction," 222, 154; and Benjamin C. Schwartz, *Casualties, Public Opinion, and U.S. Military Intervention: Implications for U.S. Regional Deterrence Strategies* (Santa Monica, Calif.: RAND, 1994).

58. Samuel Lubell, *Revolt of the Moderates* (New York: Harper and Bros., 1956), 41, 42, 265n5. He draws here on material first published in his report for the *Saturday Evening Post*, 7 June 1952: "Is America Going Isolationist Again?" 19–21, 48–54. What struck Lubell most forcibly was the uneven distribution of risk: the contrast between those who had relatives in the war or were themselves subject to the draft and those protected, largely by economic circumstances, from such dangers.

59. Lubell, *Revolt of the Moderates*, 45. It would take the Vietnam War to fulfill his prediction, the Gulf War to implement it, and Operation Iraqi Freedom to demonstrate that the American state has always found a way to sell a war.

60. "The Truce," *Wall Street Journal*, 27 July 1953, 6.

61. Quoted in Susan Moeller, *Shooting War: Photography and the American Experience of Combat* (New York: Basic Books, 1989), 321.

62. William Styron's novella *The Long March* appeared in the first issue of *discovery* [*sic*] magazine in 1952 and was then republished in a Modern American Library edi-

tion in 1956. Page numbers refer to that edition (but note a more recent edition: *The Long March and In the Clap Shack* (New York: Vintage, 1993), 7. The one character who rebels does so in a form that is at once self-defeating and the fulfillment of what the Marines have asked him to do.

63. It wasn't totally absent. See, for example, Freda Kirchwey, "Liberation by Death," *Nation*, 10 March 1951, 215–16.

64. Conway-Lanz, *Collateral Damage*, 184.

65. On prisoners of war, see Raymond B. Lech, *Broken Soldiers* (Urbana: University of Illinois Press, 2000), Susan Carruthers, *Cold War Captives: Imprisonment, Escape, and Brainwashing* (Berkeley: University of California Press, 2009); Charles S. Young, "Name, Rank, and Serial Number: Korean War POWs and the Politics of Limited War" (PhD diss., Rutgers University, 2003); Ron Theodore Robin, *Making of the Cold War Enemy* (Princeton: N.J.: Princeton University Press, 2001).

66. There were many specific lessons: a new Uniform Military Code of Conduct was issued, designed to stiffen the spine of future prisoners of war, and everyone agreed that China should never be provoked into participating in a new war in Asia.

6

EISENHOWER'S DILEMMA

Talking Peace and Waging Cold War

Kenneth Osgood

A few hours after the government of the Soviet Union announced the death of Joseph Stalin, two jet fighters screamed over a tiny town in western Washington state. The residents of Shelton panicked. Assuming that Stalin's death had touched off a Soviet attack on the United States, they jammed police phone lines with urgent requests for help and information.[1] Fortunately for Shelton, the pilots of the aircraft were not Russians. They were Americans participating in a training exercise from an Air Force base forty miles away. Undoubtedly Shelton residents had seen or heard Air Force planes flying overhead on many occasions before, but still they assumed the worst: World War III had come at last. Their hysterical reaction reflected the popular mood of the early Cold War—a mood shaped by the frightful conviction that World War III was virtually inevitable. Gallup polls in the early 1950s revealed that most Americans believed they would live to see a war between the United States and the Soviet Union. Indeed, most expected that their own towns and cities, even in remote locations like Shelton, would be attacked with atomic or hydrogen bombs in the event of such a war.[2]

The popular expectation that global war was likely, if not inevitable, provided a salient motivating factor for the American public's support for the national security policies of their government in the early Cold War. Even though government officials privately admitted that the Soviet Union wanted to avoid war, American presidents and their advisors rarely revealed this skepticism to the public. They perceived that an appropriate level of fear served a useful purpose: it stimulated the war mentality necessary for sustaining public support for high defense spending, economic aid to foreign countries, overseas propaganda programs, and other costly national security expenditures. Officials also realized that fear served U.S. foreign policy interests. They were keenly aware of the fact that what kept the North Atlantic alliance together was the possibility of a Soviet invasion of Western Europe. Successive presidential administrations from Harry Truman to Ronald Reagan capitalized on the fear of a possible Soviet invasion to sell their Cold War policies to domestic and international audiences alike.

Yet there were moments when that fear subsided, when the Cold War consensus—the widely shared conviction that the Cold War needed to be prosecuted until the end—was at risk. The death of the tyrannical leader of the Soviet Union in March 1953 was one such moment. Briefly the hope for peace eclipsed the fear of war. Indeed, the months following Stalin's death may have represented the best chance for peace. Within days of Stalin's passing, his successors signaled a new course in Soviet foreign policy. Georgy Malenkov, the new head of the Soviet government, announced that he was open to negotiations on a wide range of issues that divided East from West, thus inaugurating a peace blitz that continued in fits and starts for the remainder of the decade. As new research in the Kremlin's archives suggests, Malenkov and even his blustering successor, Nikita Khrushchev, searched earnestly—if imperfectly—for ways to deescalate the Cold War and the strategic arms race.[3] This policy—known as "peaceful coexistence"—remained the official policy of the Soviet government until the early 1960s.

By raising hopes for a thaw in the Cold War, peaceful coexistence exerted a powerful impact on public opinion around the world. Among American allies in Europe especially, fear of global war declined and hope for peace increased. Public opinion research conducted by the American government in the first five years following Stalin's death suggested a perceptible trend in European sentiment. Peaceful coexistence appeared to be fueling an upswing in popular support for East/West negotiations—a mood that translated into increased pressure on allied governments for progress on disarmament and nuclear arms control. That sentiment from abroad contrasted markedly with majority opinion in the United States. After all, the death of Stalin in Russia coincided with the apex of Senator Joseph McCarthy's hunt for communists in the United States. Despite some minor cracks in the Cold War consensus, most Americans remained doggedly anticommunist, deeply suspicious of Soviet motives, and generally supportive of rearmament measures. Thus if public opinion from abroad was pressuring the United States to negotiate disarmament agreements with its communist adversaries, public opinion at home was pushing in the other direction: to extend and preserve America's military superiority over the Soviet Union.

This posed an unexpected challenge to the newly elected president, Dwight D. Eisenhower. Having masterminded the defeat of Nazi Germany during World War II, Eisenhower assumed the presidency two months before Stalin's death, pledging to "win" the Cold War.[4] His top goal was implementing a new approach to the Cold War that he called the "New Look." He wanted to eliminate deficit spending and shore up the American economic position by spending less money on defense. He would do so by getting U.S. allies to shoulder more responsibility for their own defenses and by relying on nuclear weapons rather than on manpower (which was more expensive) to deter the USSR from embarking on general war. These goals required U.S. allies to increase their conventional forces while the United States enlarged its stockpile of nuclear weapons.

But selling these policies to American allies was a tricky matter after Stalin's death. As Eisenhower saw it, the promise of "peaceful coexistence" generated false hopes for peace that weakened European support for rearmament and fueled opposition to the U.S. nuclear weapons buildup. It threatened the foundation of the New Look. How could Eisenhower convince the world of the need for more armaments when Stalin's successors were proclaiming their earnest desire for disarmament and an overall relaxation of tensions? Or, more broadly, how could he convince the world that the Cold War—with its spiraling arms race and lingering threat of nuclear war—needed to continue when there appeared to be a chance for peace? Competing public opinion pressures at home and abroad further complicated matters. Domestic opinion in the United States generally supported the administration's policies of strength, while public opinion abroad generally favored a less confrontational, more cooperative approach. Eisenhower thus faced a dilemma: how to satisfy growing international sentiment for progress toward peace while at the same time pursuing policies of strength?

Eisenhower attempted to deal with these contradictory impulses through a psychological warfare strategy that used the language of peace to sell the Cold War. His strategy was to convince the world that Soviet peace protestations were nothing but propaganda. He would show the world that the United States earnestly sought peace, but that Soviet hostility and intransigence thwarted American peacemaking and compelled the United States to adopt policies of strength. And he would do so not just with words but with deeds. He would offer the Soviets dramatic proposals for negotiation and disarmament that he knew they were likely to reject, thus putting the onus on the USSR for the continuation of the Cold War and its arms race while lending moral legitimacy to the cause of Western rearmament.

Crusading for Peace

Although, strictly speaking, the Cold War was not a war, Americans often talked and acted as if it were. From the Truman Doctrine to the Reagan Doctrine, the United States conducted the Cold War as a war by other means—a war waged by propaganda, covert action, paramilitary operations, economic competition, political gamesmanship, and "limited" proxy wars around the globe. The Cold War produced or enflamed numerous hot wars around the world—most notably in Korea, Vietnam, and Afghanistan. Even in peacetime it had an unmistakable military component. The antagonists maintained massive standing armies, poised for immediate attack, and they developed thousands of weapons of mass destruction—all costing untold millions of dollars, sucking up tax revenues and generating colossal debt. As such, the Cold War required continuous selling. Lacking the immediacy of armed combat, and having no equivalent of a "Pearl Harbor" to provide moral justification for the conflict, the Cold War in fact required more selling than a hot war—something American officials were acutely aware of from the earliest days of the conflict. The nuclear arms race in particular demanded incessant salesmanship to convince the public that ever more destructive weapons and delivery systems were necessary and desirable.

Obviously the selling of the Cold War was deeply intertwined with domestic politics. Whenever presidents sell a bellicose national security policy, they must win support from various domestic constituencies comprising different political parties, ideological inclinations, classes, ethnicities, and backgrounds. Not infrequently, presidents bend or shape their foreign policies to accord with domestic political constraints. So obvious is the president's need for domestic support that it is often forgotten that presidents also rely on support from international audiences. Every president since Franklin Roosevelt has had to reconcile America's power with the need for international support for the projection of that power. Other countries have been valued because they could provide bases, staging grounds, armed forces, logistical aid, economic assistance, or political support. They could use their leverage to win support from other states and to isolate adversaries. Or they could deny such assets to the United States. The skill with which American leaders presented their policies, together with the seeming moral legitimacy and necessity of those policies, has had a lot to do with determining whether a particular conflict would enjoy broad international support, as was the case of the Korean and Persian Gulf wars, or whether the United States would be effectively isolated, as was the case with the Vietnam and Iraq wars. Americans recently saw this process play out most unsuccessfully in the run-up to the 2003 war in Iraq. President Bush's aggressive posturing—with starkly Manichean "good vs. evil" and "with us or against us" rhetoric—succeeded in garnering political support at home for the Iraq invasion but failed miserably at winning much more than token international support.

Eisenhower, like other modern presidents, confronted an intractable problem when it came to selling war and Cold War in the media age. He could not give different messages to domestic and international audiences. Anything he said at home could be picked up by media outlets overseas—and vice versa. He needed to court domestic opinion to secure support for his expanded program of nuclear armament and other national security initiatives, but at the same time he needed to ensure the continued cooperation and friendship of American allies.

The language of peace seemed to offer a solution to this problem. Although Eisenhower often seemed more awkward than articulate, few presidents spoke in more moving terms about the importance of peace. Eisenhower understood, perhaps better than any other president with the possible exception of Wilson, that waging war demanded the moral legitimacy of a pursuit for peace. For eight years, he labored to convince the world of his country's peaceful intentions. His presidency both began and ended with passionate warnings about the perils of a prolonged arms race and the dangers of a military industrial complex run amok. Peace was one of the most consistent themes in his rhetoric. He referred to peace in more than 1,000 separate public statements and in 92 percent of his formal addresses.[5] Believing that a positive crusade for peace was more likely to sustain support for U.S. Cold War policies than fear of communism alone, Eisenhower employed a rhetorical strategy that used appeals for peace to promote international and domestic support for a long-term struggle against the Soviet Union.

Eisenhower was especially attuned to the attitudes of the European allies. As commander of allied forces in Europe during the war and as head of NATO in the 1940s, Ike worked tirelessly to cement allied unity, and he continued these efforts as president. Before and during his time in the White House, Eisenhower was guided by his belief that U.S. allies would most willingly follow American leadership if they perceived the United States as committed to the causes of peace, freedom, and other positive goals. "I do think it extremely important," he told Winston Churchill, "that the great masses of the world understand that, on our side, we are deadly serious in our search for peace and are ready to prove this with acts and deeds and not merely assert it in glittering phraseology."[6] As he explained to a group of legislators, his goal was "to convince the world that we are working for peace and not trying to blow them to kingdom come with our atom and thermonuclear bombs."[7]

Eisenhower also had political motives for cultivating the peace theme. Although many historians—myself included—have written about Eisenhower as if he were somehow immune from domestic politics, in fact he was a shrewd political operator who cultivated a clearly defined image to garner political support at home.[8] He realized that presenting himself as a peacemaker contributed to his popularity—it softened the image of a man who had been a soldier his whole life and who had gained fame through war. As a candidate for the presidency in 1952, his political handlers advised him to play up the theme of peace, since it resonated with a public that was growing increasingly tired of the stalemated war in Korea, with its drawn-out and seemingly pointless negotiations.[9] Accordingly, he self-consciously promoted an image of himself as an experienced soldier who had turned to the task of peace. His stump speeches emphasized this point over and over again. In September 1952, for example, Eisenhower told a group of Republican women: "I have commanded your sons in war. . . . They and I know war's horrors, and they and I, therefore, hate war and all its evil works. That is a hatred every one of us shares, just as the desire for peace is the desire of all of us."[10] His major foreign policy speech as a candidate made the point even stronger. Speaking in Denver, Eisenhower exclaimed that "peace may be at stake" in the presidential election. "I know something about war: its strategy, its requirements, its tragic cost in blood and treasure; its criminal waste. Therefore I shall not rest as long as I believe I can contribute to the cause of peace. . . . No other cause could so completely enlist my energies."[11] Eisenhower, the lifelong soldier, was beating the swords into plowshares—or so he wanted the electorate to believe.

The other key theme Eisenhower developed during his campaign was "crusade." He had won the crusade in Europe in WWII, and now he argued that a crusade to "conquer communism" offered "the sure road to peace."[12] Eisenhower's repeated calls for a crusade against communism—with its implication of a morally righteous "holy war"—appeared on the surface to conflict with his calls for peace. After all, much of his campaign rhetoric blasted the Democrats for not being tough enough on the communists. His campaign attacked "containment"—the foreign policy of his predecessor—for being too passive. As a candidate Eisenhower exaggerated communist infiltration of the United States, attacked godless communism, and called for a coherent strategy for waging and winning the Cold War. Framed this way, Eisenhower's crusade hardly promised peace in his time.

But the two themes of "peace" and "crusade" look contradictory only if one assumes that peace signified a negotiated end to the Cold War. Eisenhower framed his peace rhetoric carefully and deliberately to make clear that his vision of peace required more, not less, struggle. Using a rhetorical sleight of hand that equated peace with victory in the Cold War, Eisenhower was careful not to suggest that peace meant coexistence or cooperation with the Soviet enemy. Peace had to be *won*. "I say to you tonight from my deepest conviction," he announced in Philadelphia, "peace can be won. We can win a peace that will be just and enduring."[13] In Eisenhower's formulation, peace was not something to be made or achieved through negotiations or compromise; it was the prize to be won, the end result of the enemy's surrender. In such a way Eisenhower employed a rhetorical twist that was a common feature of Cold War rhetoric: peace was evoked not as an alternative to international conflict, but as a euphemism for continued Cold War.

Eisenhower continued to develop these themes after winning the election. His first inaugural address did not use the word *crusade*, but it might as well have, for the speech painted the American people as driven by faith to win a colossal battle against evil.[14] Dripping with religious imagery, the speech was an ideological call to arms cloaked in righteousness. "The forces of good and evil are massed and armed and opposed as rarely before in history," Eisenhower began, sounding like a general addressing his troops in the dramatic final scene of a war movie. "This conflict strikes directly at the faith of our fathers and the lives of our sons." The task for Americans was to unite in a renewed offensive against an enemy ideology with which there could be no compromise. "We shall never try to placate an aggressor by the false and wicked bargain of trading honor for security. Americans, indeed all free men, remember that in the final choice a soldier's pack is not so heavy a burden as a prisoner's chains." Even in this bellicose call to arms, Eisenhower framed his call for a crusade against communism as a search for a "secure peace in the world." Nine times he evoked the hope of peace, while carefully holding it out as the lofty prize to be won when evil had been defeated. The winning of the Cold War and the pursuit of peace were rhetorically intertwined, linked symbiotically into a single overarching quest. Such themes represented a conscious effort to promote Eisenhower's personal image as a peacemaker. They also served as an appealing motivational ploy for the American public, addressing a deeply held belief in American goodness and casting the country's role in the world as a noble mission for a greater good.

Public Opinion and "Peaceful Coexistence"

If Eisenhower perceived early on the value of casting himself as peacemaker, changes in Soviet foreign policy led him to attach even greater significance to emotive, rhetorical calls for peace. Foremost among these was the "peace offensive" launched by Stalin's successors immediately following Stalin's death on 5 March 1953. Ten days after the tyrant's demise, the new head of the Soviet government, Georgy Malenkov, made an unexpected appeal for international cooperation. "There is no disputed or unresolved question that cannot be resolved by peaceful means, on the basis of mutual agreement," he declared in a widely publicized speech.[15] Over the next two weeks there followed a barrage of symbolic measures to demonstrate Soviet goodwill— "more Soviet gestures toward the West than at any other similar period," the State Department noted. Substantive signs of change emerged during the next five months, as the Soviet Union relinquished its territorial claims on Turkey, reestablished diplomatic relations with Israel, helped bring the Korean War to a close, worked to improve relations with Yugoslavia and Greece, and continued to declare its interest in "peaceful coexistence" with the West.[16]

Eisenhower and his advisors dismissed these measures as treacherous manifestations of a new political warfare strategy. The National Security Council summarized the consensus view in the administration when it concluded that the Soviet peace offensive was "designed to divide the West by raising false hopes and seeking to make the United States appear un-yielding."[17] The State Department added that the purpose of the Kremlin's peace campaign was "perfectly obvious: by this method the Communists hope to crack the wall of resistance which the West has been constructing, and to bring about an eventual slowing-down of the armaments program of the Free World."[18] Eisenhower insisted that "there had been no change since Stalin." The Soviets remained committed to "destroying the Capitalist free world by all means, by force, by deceit, or by lies."[19] Assuming that the totalitarian nature of the Soviet system made fundamental change impos-sible, neither Eisenhower nor his advisors considered seriously the possibility of reaching an accommodation with Stalin's successors.[20] "Russia was a woman of the streets," Eisenhower said bluntly in an unguarded moment, "and whether her dress was new, or just the old one patched, it was certainly the same whore underneath."[21]

By and large, the American public shared the Eisenhower administration's pessimistic assessment of Soviet intentions. Gallup polls throughout the 1950s revealed that Americans held an extremely negative view of the Soviet Union that was unaltered by the death of Stalin. In a series of polls, Gallup asked Americans to rate their feelings about Russia on a scale of minus five to plus five, with minus five signaling "something you dislike very much." In October 1953, seven months after Stalin's death, a whopping 90 percent of Americans expressed dislike for Russia (by choosing a negative number), and an overwhelming percentage indicated that they had the worst possible feelings toward Russia. Seventy-two percent said they disliked Russia "very much." Only 2 percent of Americans admitted to having positive feelings toward Russia. Subsequent polls in 1954 and late 1956 conveyed essentially the same response, indicating that American attitudes remained virtually unaffected by the Soviet peace campaign. In subsequent decades—from the early 1960s on—these attitudes would soften, but in the years after Stalin's death Americans remained decidedly hostile toward Russia, peace campaign or not.[22] By way of contrast, as late as December 1953 a majority of Americans registered favorable opinions of Joseph McCarthy, this despite the fact that many of them expressed disagreement with his methods.[23]

Most Americans saw sinister motives behind the USSR's peace campaign. In April 1953, the majority of Americans indicated that they thought Soviet peace protestations were some form of deception or that the new Soviet leadership was seeking a breathing spell during the struggle for Stalin's succession. Less than 4 percent said that the Soviets wanted peace. Others were confused: 29 percent said they did not know what to make of Soviet peace talk. A month later, only 22 percent said that there had been a "real change" in Soviet foreign policy since the death of Stalin, and 60 percent said there had been none.[24] Americans also registered little desire for negotiations with Stalin's successors. Three weeks after Stalin's death, Gallup asked Americans if they thought the United States should strengthen its efforts to try to settle differences with Russia. Half believed the United States "had gone far enough," and a quarter registered "no opinion."[25] Some Americans expressed optimism for a change in the Cold War climate, but a clear majority showed little inclination to trust the Soviets.

If the public remained skeptical about the chances for peace, it was remarkably resigned to the possibility of war. As the 1952 presidential election was getting under way, Gallup asked Americans to identify two or three things they would like to see the next president do. Only 14 percent chose "avoiding war with Russia." A year later, a quarter of Americans expressed the view that the United States should resolve the stalemated Korean conflict by bombing Manchuria and "go[ing] all out against Russia."[26] More ominous was the response to Gallup's question, "Do you think the time will come when we can live peacefully with Communist Russia, or do you think it is only a matter of time until we will have to fight it out?" In June 1954—as negotiations were taking place to end the conflicts in Korea and Indochina—a whopping 71 percent believed it was only a matter of time before the United States and the USSR went to war.[27]

Public opinion may have been taking its cue from the press. Most American journalists remained deeply suspicious of Soviet intentions. As Jeffrey Brooks has shown, press coverage in the six months after Stalin's death included three times more negative assessments of the Soviets' intentions as positive ones.[28] The influential New York Times was especially pessimistic; its editorial pages consistently argued against "wishful thinking" about chances for peace. The Times dismissed Soviet peace moves as mere tactical maneuvers, part of the Leninist pattern of making tactical retreats and reaching agreements and temporary compromises on the road to consolidating power. Echoing this analysis, C. L. Sulzberger editorialized in the Times that the "ruthless" Malenkov was merely seeking time to entrench his rule. "The Soviet menace continues regardless of which individual leader rides the juggernaut."[29]

Such pessimistic assessments were expressed widely in the American media. The Wall Street Journal concluded that there were two explanations for the changed attitudes of the Soviets: the new regime needed a breathing spell to establish its power, and it believed a policy of conciliation could undo the Western alliance. The New York Herald Tribune was one of a handful of papers that expressed hope that "the end of the Cold War may be in sight."[30] This was clearly a minority view. Very few American observers spoke of the possibility of ending the Cold War. Of a total of 1,116 articles discussing the Soviet Union in March and April 1953, only fifty suggested that the United States might or should accept a "truce" with Moscow.[31] "If we are wise we will continue to increase our power," the Syracuse Post-Standard advised. "There is little basis for hope that Stalin's successors will be any less ruthless than was the man who has imprisoned millions behind the Iron Curtain," the *San Diego Union* reported. The *Chicago Sun-Times* concluded that as long as communists remained in power, "the lasting peace the world longs for will be as far away as it was when Stalin lived."[32]

Europeans were much less likely than their American allies to write off Soviet intentions as meaningless tactical retreats or propaganda moves. Across the Atlantic there was far greater hope that Stalin's death would bring about a relaxation of tensions. Winston Churchill thought he perceived a "new breeze blowing on the tormented world." [33] Beginning in May 1953, the aging British prime minister—who had just a few years earlier coined the phrase "iron curtain"—began a tireless campaign to promote a summit conference between Western leaders and Stalin's successors. French leaders also hoped that a détente could be forged now that Stalin was dead. They were hopeful that East-West negotiations might lead to a face-saving settlement in Indochina as well as a relaxation of tensions that would obviate the need for German rearmament. Two successive French premiers, Pierre Mendès-France and Edgar Faure, soon echoed Churchill's call for a summit, as did Churchill's own successor, Anthony Eden.[34]

American policymakers and pundits believed these leaders were spinelessly following the pace of public opinion in their countries. C. L. Sulzberger summarized the European attitude for the *New York Times* with an article headlined "Europe Clings to Hope of Let-up in Cold War." "The requisite urgency seems to have gone out of the air," he observed. "An odd apathy seems to have gripped Europe's masses. . . . There is much wishful thought that the chances of peace are improved."[35] American intelligence estimates and public opinion analyses consistently reported that Europeans were prone to wishful thinking about the possibility of peace. Officials expressed particular concern about the "emotional neutralism" of European public opinion. U.S. policymakers routinely characterized European sentiment as apathetic, frightened, confused, and naively predisposed to neutralist ideas and wishful thinking.[36] The National Security Council concluded U.S. allies perceived "the actual danger of Soviet aggression as less imminent than the United States." They feared that the American hard line would "involve Europe in general war" or "indefinitely prolong Cold War tensions."[37]

Public opinion surveys conducted by the U.S. Information Agency revealed a wide gap between European and American perceptions of the Cold War and the arms race. Most Europeans were decidedly less convinced that another world war was on the horizon. In December 1953—when 70 percent of Americans expected to see another war in their lifetimes—only about 10 percent of Europeans expressed concern that there would be another war in the near future. Moreover, in contrast to Americans who assumed that such a war would involve nuclear weapons, large percentages of Europeans felt that it was unlikely that atomic weapons would be used. Only a third of West Germans, for example, considered it likely that another world war would involve the use of nuclear weapons. Simultaneously, the overwhelming majority of Europeans supported an all-embracing ban on atomic weapons—a view that troubled American officials because it coincided with the official Soviet position on disarmament. In February 1955, 80 percent of Italians, 85 percent of West Germans, and 87 percent of the French supported an atomic ban. By contrast, fewer than 40 percent of Americans agreed.[38]

The Eisenhower administration was especially concerned by signs of an upswing in neutralist sentiment in Europe. From October 1954 to February 1955, the percentage of West Germans who thought their country should favor neither side in the Cold War increased from 31 percent to 36 percent. Even greater percentages favored remaining neutral in the event of war: over half of the French, West Germans, and Italians wanted their countries to stay out of a U.S.-Soviet war.[39]

The trend toward "neutralism" in Great Britain was more pronounced and more worrisome to American officials. This was, after all, America's closest ally. British opinion, according to U.S. analyses, reflected "suspicion and uncertainty about the moral rightness and political astuteness of U.S. policies and leadership" and "growing fear about the vulnerability of the island to the destructive potential" of thermonuclear weapons. There also was an alarming increase in the percentage of those advocating neutrality. In October 1954, 29 percent favored a neutral course in the Cold War, but four months later, 40 percent did so. Equally alarming were signs that British public opinion agreed with the Soviet disarmament position. In public opinion surveys, three-fourths expressed support for an international agreement to ban the bomb.[40] In Eisenhower's view, Churchill's relentless pursuit of a summit conference merely reinforced these trends toward British neutralism. Although the prime minister may very well have been following rather than leading public opinion, Eisenhower thought Churchill was playing into the Kremlin's hands. A summit, Eisenhower wrote to Churchill in December 1954, "would merely give a false impression of accord which, in our free countries, would probably make it more difficult to get parliamentary support for needed defense appropriations."[41] Churchill's talk of summits merely encouraged the type of wishful thinking that made it difficult to sell rearmament, Eisenhower believed.

Eisenhower and his advisors saw Soviet peace propaganda as the root cause of neutralist and pacific trends in European public opinion. "Peaceful coexistence" nurtured "false hopes" that a negotiated settlement might be possible and fostered doubts about the entire Cold War enterprise. Because "the world-wide hope for peace is certain to far overshadow the fears of long-range communist designs," the State Department argued, public opinion in the West would not support the armaments programs necessary to keep the pressure on the Kremlin.[42] Fear had been the psychological glue that held free world coalitions together, but now that fear, along with allied unity and resolve, was dissipating. "During the Stalin regime," Eisenhower opined, "the Soviets seemed to prefer the use of force—or the threat of force—to gain their ends. . . . So long as they used force and the threat of force, we had the world's natural reaction of fear to aid us in building consolidations of power and strength in order to resist Soviet advances."[43] How could the United States continue to pursue policies of strength, through rearmament and alliance building, when fear of the Soviet Union was subsiding?

Selling the New Look

The divide between European and American perceptions of the Cold War suggested that Eisenhower needed to tread carefully when selling the New Look. Eisenhower found himself torn in two directions. On the one hand, he needed to stiffen the resolve of the American people by reminding them that meeting the Soviet threat required material sacrifices for national security. Despite signs that the American public seemed to share Eisenhower's view of the Soviet threat, Eisenhower and his advisors doubted they would long support high taxes for defense. "You could get the American people to make these sacrifices voluntarily for a year or for two or three years," Eisenhower told the NSC, "but no eloquence would sell this proposition to the American people for the indefinite future." Even moderate defense spending required an active campaign to mobilize public support. "If we are to obtain more money in taxes," the president told his advisors, "there must be a vigorous campaign to educate the people."[44]

On the other hand, scare tactics to mobilize Americans at home portended disastrous consequences abroad. While reminding the American people of the danger before them, Eisenhower could not in the process reinforce European fears of being embroiled in a nuclear war. "This presents a delicate problem," a top secret report on psychological warfare concluded in the summer of 1953, "but a balance can be struck between providing the American people with information that will permit them to grasp one of the basic realities of their world, and driving more vulnerable and therefore nervous allies into neutralism."[45] At a minimum Eisenhower would need to tone down his rhetoric—to include, as it were, less talk of crusades and more calls for peace.

More importantly, he would need to convince allied leaders and their publics that the Soviets were engaging in mere psychological warfare rather than sincere diplomacy. If the West was going to continue building its strength—through nuclear weapons development, German rearmament, and other measures—it needed to be convinced that no realistic chance for peace existed. Eisenhower explained to his secretary of state in September 1953 that the United States needed to prove to the world that "increased military preparation had been forced upon us because every honest peaceful gesture or offer of our own had been summarily rejected by the Communists."[46] Accordingly, during Eisenhower's first term in the White House, he devised three major campaigns to cast doubt on Moscow's peace campaigns and to prove to the world the peaceful intentions of the United States. Each was intended to expose the implacable hostility of the Soviets while bolstering the U.S. image as peacemaker. Each employed the language of peace to sell Eisenhower's approach to the Cold War.

A Chance for Peace?

The first of these peace initiatives occurred a month after Stalin's death. Speaking to the American Society of Newspaper Editors on 16 April 1953, Eisenhower delivered one of the most important speeches of his presidency.[47] Calling his address "A Chance for Peace," Eisenhower spoke to the world's hope that Stalin's death provided a new opportunity for international cooperation. With timeless rhetorical flourish, Eisenhower reminded his audiences of the costly consequences of a strategic arms race: "Every gun that is made, every warship launched, every rocket fired signifies, in the final sense, a theft from those who hunger and are not fed, those who are cold and are not clothed. . . . Under the cloud of threatening war, it is humanity hanging from a cross of iron." These words, among Eisenhower's most widely quoted, appeared to signal his willingness to end the arms race and work for an early end to the Cold War. Yet the overall tone and message of the speech elevated the cause of waging Cold War over that of making peace. Employing the same black-and-white rhetoric he had used during the campaign and in his inaugural address, Eisenhower described the Cold War as a moral struggle between good and evil, right and wrong. In such a contest, the free world "must, at any cost, remain armed, strong, and ready for the risk of war."

Stifling wishful thinking about détente, Eisenhower emphasized that peace required much more than a reduction of tensions. He warned his listeners not to accept Soviet peace overtures until they had proven their goodwill through deeds: "We welcome every honest act of peace. We care nothing for mere rhetoric." He cautioned against a status quo settlement merely to preserve the peace. At a minimum, Eisenhower suggested, the Soviet leadership needed to prove its good faith through an "honorable" armistice in Korea, an end to hostilities in Indochina and Malaya, and a peace treaty with Austria. These "deeds" of good faith also needed to include freedom for Eastern Europe and a united Germany that was free to rearm and participate in the western alliance. The speech was a psychological war-fare exercise designed to wrestle the peace initiative away from the Kremlin. While requesting proof of Soviet sincerity, Eisenhower offered neither con-cessions from the West nor proposals for negotiation. Rather than promote peace *from* the Cold War, Eisenhower promoted a vision of peace that could only be achieved *through* it. He told the world that it faced a simple choice between two bleak possibilities, a new world war or prolonged Cold War, thus rhetorically guiding his audiences to the conclusion that sustained ef-fort in the Cold War was the only real option before them. All the while, he framed his call for a Cold War crusade as a quest for peace.[48]

Lest Eisenhower's speech be misinterpreted to suggest that an actual chance for peace was at hand, Secretary of State John Foster Dulles clarified matters two days later. Speaking before the American Society for Newspa-per Editors—the same body Eisenhower had addressed—Dulles mocked Malenkov's conciliatory rhetoric as a "peace defensive," forced on the Soviet Union by Western policies of strength. He argued that Stalin's death meant that the West needed to continue its process of building strength to induce the Soviets to make real concessions. The president, he said, had offered a series of "tests" that the Soviet leadership needed to pass to demonstrate their good intentions: "[The] Soviet leadership is now confronted by the Eisenhower tests. Will it meet, one by one, the issues with which President Eisenhower has challenged it? . . . We await the deeds which will give an-swer to these questions." As Lloyd Gardner has noted, Dulles was playing "bad cop" to Eisenhower's "good cop."[49] His phrasing was less delicate than Eisenhower's, but his words were not out of sync with the president's. Both had made essentially the same point: there would be a chance for peace only if the Soviets capitulated to American demands.

Atoms for Peace

Eisenhower made his second "peace" initiative at the end of 1953. Addressing the United Nations in December, he offered his celebrated "Atoms for Peace" proposal. He suggested that the superpowers donate some of the nuclear materials from their stockpiles to an international agency that would use them for peaceful purposes in agriculture, medicine, and electric power production. Eisenhower explained that this would provide immediate benefits to the world community. He also claimed that it would pave the way for future disarmament agreements by enhancing superpower trust. The most important theme of the speech, however, revolved around freeing the world from the grip of atomic fear. Eisenhower spoke optimistically of a "day when fear of the atom will begin to disappear from the minds of the people." "My country wants to be constructive, not destructive," he announced, stressing that atomic materials should be used to serve the needs rather than the fears of humanity. "This greatest of destructive forces can be developed into a great boon, for the benefit of all mankind." Eisenhower pledged to strip the atom of its military casing and adapt it to the arts of peace. The dreaded atom would become a force for peace, a source of life.[50]

Although Eisenhower presented Atoms for Peace as a first step toward U.S.-Soviet cooperation, his main goals were to dramatize Soviet intransigence, highlight the American commitment to peace, and stimulate public acceptance of the New Look. On one level, the proposal was a political warfare tactic to discredit Soviet peace overtures by offering a seemingly realistic proposal that the Soviet leadership would likely refuse. Eisenhower's national security advisor, Robert Cutler, told the president: "The virtue of making proposals lies not so much in the likelihood of their acceptability by the other side, but in the opportunity provided by the United States— once the proposals have been made and not accepted—to put into effect a new and better (for the long run) basic policy than that we now have."[51] The proposal would not be accepted, Cutler implied, but that was not really the point. Public opinion would blame Soviet intransigence, rather the administration's national security policies, for the New Look's atomic buildup.

On another level, the initiative was part of a broader effort to mold public perceptions in the thermonuclear age. As the administration explored ways to sell the New Look, a particular concern centered on how to present the awesome destructive power of thermonuclear weapons to the American people and to the world. Several of Eisenhower's advisors argued that if the United States was to continue developing ever more destructive weapons, it needed to play up the peaceful applications of nuclear energy to ease public fears of the atom. Stephan Possony, a consultant to the Defense Department who had played an important role in devising Atoms for Peace, argued: "It must indeed be realized that the atom as a peace and prosperity maker will be more acceptable to the world than the atom as a war maker . . . even the atom bomb will be accepted far more readily if at the same time atomic energy is being used for constructive ends."[52] Ingeniously, then, Atoms for Peace actually promised to facilitate the buildup of nuclear weapons by distracting public attention from weapons testing and development. The initiative sought to manage fears of nuclear annihilation by cultivating the image of the "friendly" atom. As a secret government report explained, the Atoms for Peace campaign would cause people "to no longer think of mushroom clouds and mass destruction when hear[ing] the words *atom, atomic,* or *atomic energy,* but rather of the peaceful uses of atomic energy in the fields of industry, agriculture, and medicine."[53] By flooding the media with talk of the peaceful applications of atomic energy, the administration hoped to divert attention from the nuclear buildup taking place under the New Look.

In the aftermath of the Atoms for Peace speech, the Eisenhower administration sought to continually publicize the plan in order to contrast American willingness to negotiate with Soviet intransigence. The administration also orchestrated an extraordinary public relations campaign that saw every arm of the executive branch—from the Department of Labor to the Post Office—hyping the proposal in statements and press releases. The U.S. Information Agency made Atoms for Peace a top propaganda theme in its operations around the world. It churned out news story after news story hyping U.S. discoveries and accomplishments in peaceful atomic research; it sent traveling Atoms for Peace exhibits to dozens of countries; it produced scores of films highlighting peaceful atomic research; and its radio broadcasts included regular features on the subject. By generating widespread media coverage of American research in atomic energy, the USIA sought to show "all peoples" that the United States was "interested primarily in human aspirations rather than building up armaments."[54] Such efforts made Atoms for Peace one of the largest peacetime psychological warfare operations in U.S. history.

There is reason to doubt, however, that Atoms for Peace worked as well as Eisenhower and some of his advisors wanted to believe. A month after Eisenhower's speech, the USIA conducted a flash poll in six countries to ascertain international reactions to the president's proposal. In no country had a majority even heard of Atoms for Peace. Only about a third of Europeans were aware of it. Most people were also deeply skeptical it could work. In all countries surveyed, less than a third of the public thought Atoms for Peace would be implemented. On the crucial issue of whether foreign public opinion believed that the United States was trying to prevent war, the survey revealed that public attitudes remained essentially unchanged by the speech. In five of the six countries, pluralities felt that the United States was doing what it could to stop war, but, as the USIA noted, "This sentiment is not overwhelming, with anywhere between a quarter to a half of the people questioned having no opinions on the subject." In France, the percentage who thought the United States was not working hard enough to prevent war actually increased from two years before—from 32 percent to 40 percent. Foreign public opinion also registered confusion about Soviet intentions. Asked whether Russia was doing all it could to prevent war, from a third to more than half expressed no opinion. The proportion of those who believed Russia was not working for peace remained high, but it appears not to have been affected by Atoms for Peace. The government's admittedly imperfect polling data suggests Atoms for Peace did not quite meet its goal of increasing confidence in U.S. peace efforts relative to those of the USSR.[55]

Open Skies and the Geneva Summit

The third major peace initiative of Eisenhower's first term came in July 1955. By this time, Eisenhower had agreed to a summit meeting with the new Soviet premier, Nikita Khrushchev, in the city of Geneva, Switzerland. Even though this would be the first time that the heads of the U.S. and Soviet governments had met in person since WWII, Eisenhower had resisted calls for a summit for more than two years. He feared the meeting would enhance Soviet prestige while undermining public support for rearmament by stimulating naive hopes for peace. Yet despite his efforts to dramatize Soviet intransigence with such measures as Chance for Peace and Atoms for Peace, international pressure for a summit increased steadily. According to U.S. government analyses, half of all Europeans supported the summit conference, and the European press overwhelmingly advocated a "Big Four" meeting to test Soviet intentions.[56] More remarkably—considering the American public's unremitting hostility toward Russia—even larger percentages of Americans advocated the summit. Whenever Gallup asked Americans if they favored a meeting with the heads of the American, British, and Soviet governments, three-fourths of respondents answered yes.[57] Eisenhower reluctantly bowed to public opinion and agreed to the summit in May 1955. Eisenhower later recalled that he had acquiesced in the summit because he did not wish to "appear senselessly stubborn in my attitude toward a Summit meeting—so hopefully desired by so many." John Foster Dulles admitted that "we never wanted to go to Geneva, but the pressure of people of the world forced us to."[58]

Eisenhower saw the summit as an opportunity to put forth another dramatic appeal for progress in arms control. He proposed a system of aerial inspection, whereby the United States and the Soviet Union would permit overflights of their territory in order to verify compliance with any arms control agreements that might be reached. "Open Skies," as it became known, promised to overcome the most difficult hurdle in disarmament negotiations: inspection and verification of agreements. Quite reasonably, inspection was seen as a necessary condition for disarmament in order to prevent one side or the other from "cheating." He also promoted it as a means of preventing war by making surprise attacks more difficult. Yet Open Skies was effectively a one-sided proposition. The United States had little to risk and everything to gain by making the proposal. Open Skies would pry open the "iron curtain" by legalizing reconnaissance flights over Soviet territory, but offered no commensurate benefits for the USSR. For this reason, officials in the Eisenhower administration never really expected the Soviets to accept Open Skies. Few were surprised when Khrushchev denounced the scheme as an espionage plot.

Trends in European public opinion compelled Eisenhower to make the Open Skies proposal at Geneva. Eisenhower was especially influenced by advice he received from Nelson Rockefeller, his advisor on psychological warfare. The two met to discuss Geneva on 6 July. Calling the summit "the most important psychological-propaganda forum in the world," Rockefeller urged Eisenhower to take bold steps to assure the world of his commitment to peace. He warned that the Soviets would use the conference to drive a wedge between the United States and its allies by raising hopes for an early end to the Cold War and by making the United States appear intransigent and militaristic. Public opinion trends in Europe made it imperative that Eisenhower offer a new and striking proposal on disarmament, Rockefeller argued. He pointed out that recent public opinion surveys revealed that most people favored an all-out ban on the use of nuclear weapons, including both strategic and tactical weapons. "This trend in European public opinion may eventually reduce both the strength of our alliance and our freedom to use atomic weapons. Unless we do our utmost to work for disarmament— an aspiration widely cherished by the people of Western Europe—it is very likely that there may be a significant increase in neutralist sentiment both on the Continent and in Britain, together with a growth in pressure for abandoning the use of atomic weapons."[59]

Rockefeller hinted at a significant vulnerability in the administration's New Look security doctrine. The U.S. ability to rely overwhelmingly on nuclear weapons for its defense could be circumscribed by public anxiety about such weapons. To arrest public pressure for atomic disarmament, the United States needed to appear earnest in seeking arms limitation. Then it could lay the onus for failure to achieve atomic disarmament squarely on the backs of the Soviet Union. He argued that Open Skies was essential to reverse "the unfavorable image of the U.S. as a trigger-happy militaristic power, uninterested in resolving the cold war."[60] Eisenhower found this argument persuasive. Speaking to the NSC the day after his meeting with Rockefeller, the president pointedly referred to polls that showed a strong sentiment for reduction of East-West tensions among West Europeans. This was a convincing reason for doing something dramatic at the summit, he suggested.[61]

Eisenhower's performance at the Geneva summit earned him tremendous acclaim in Europe. The European press praised the U.S. role in creating the "spirit of Geneva." According to USIA analysis, "Newspapers of all political shades and opinions were virtually unanimous in considering the conference eminently successful in improving the international atmosphere and contributing to a new spirit in East-West relations." Polling data revealed that Eisenhower's reputation as peacemaker was greatly enhanced by Geneva and Open Skies. Among Europeans surveyed, 69 percent believed that he was "working sincerely towards 'world peace.'" Making these figures more remarkable, Europeans gave higher marks to Eisenhower than they did to their own leaders. Approval of Eisenhower jumped 24 percent in France and 14 percent in Italy after the conference. Part of this success clearly stemmed from Eisenhower's Open Skies proposal, as more than a third of Europeans could name the proposal without prompting, and over 60 percent approved of the plan. The same percentage believed that the United States did "all it should to make the conference a success," while only 37 percent believed that the USSR did.[62]

Yet the Eisenhower administration was curiously unsatisfied with the results of the conference. Even though Eisenhower scored a PR coup with Open Skies, officials believed that the summit produced dangerous trends in international opinion. The USIA reported that public opinion trends in the aftermath of Geneva included reduced fear of Soviet aggression and increased faith in Soviet peaceful intentions. The administration's research on European public opinion revealed a "rather sharp decline in popular feelings that the Soviets are 'insincere.'"[63] Nearly half of those surveyed said that the Soviet delegation was "working sincerely towards 'world peace.'" There was also a huge jump in public confidence that peace between the United States and the USSR could be achieved: 81 percent of British and about 65 percent of Austrians, Italians, and French said they were "more hopeful" that "some of the big problems of the world can be solved." Attitudes toward the Soviet Union also improved. The percentage of West Europeans indicating they had "bad" or "very bad" opinions about the USSR declined from 50 percent in October 1954 to 37 percent after the summit. The percentage of people indicating they had a "fair" opinion of the USSR almost doubled—from 16 percent to 28 percent. According to the USIA's opinion analysis, "The Russian leaders accomplished a 'public relations' success of no mean proportions by reducing substantially the unpopularity of the Soviet Union in Western European eyes and the fear of Soviet aggression."[64]

To the Eisenhower administration, such trends in international public opinion portended a dangerous relaxation of vigilance that could erode popular support for NATO, American cold war policies, and rearmament efforts. Concerned that excessive optimism for a Cold War thaw would relax defense preparations, the Eisenhower administration tried to offset these attitudes with propaganda stressing the continuing need for Western strength and unity. The USIA made a concerted effort to dampen international enthusiasm for the "spirit of Geneva." One official summarized the Information Agency's perspective:

> The information job in the post-Geneva period is much more difficult than before but it is more necessary. Disarmament and other plans which would weaken our defenses must be fought. The notion of banning the bomb has made much headway and must be countered. The let-down of our allies must be combated—we must hammer on collective security and oppose the resurgence of neutralism.

The USIA's propaganda reminded audiences that peaceful coexistence was only a tactical change designed to weaken the West. "We do not consider that relaxation of tension and a more peaceful atmosphere permit us either to scrap programs for individual and collective self-defense, or to tolerate covert aggression and to sanctify the injustices of the *status quo*." Above all, the USIA stressed vigilance. It credited Western policies of strength for bringing about Moscow's new conciliatory demeanor. If such policies continued, the agency's propaganda line emphasized, further concessions might be in the offing—but a relaxation of vigilance might lead to more international tension, since it would encourage the aggressive designs of the Kremlin.[65]

Ensuing events—and perhaps also the USIA's discouraging propaganda—dampened public enthusiasm for the spirit of Geneva. In November, Geneva hosted a follow-up conference of the "Big Four" foreign ministers. It was a decisive failure. Most Europeans blamed Soviet intransigence for the collapse of the foreign minister's conference, but the U.S. image also suffered as many doubted the United States was doing all it could to advance the cause of peace. According to the USIA's public opinion analysis, the July summit had helped assure many of Eisenhower's commitment to a policy of peace, but the lack of progress afterwards produced a "let down feeling": "Underlying this 'let down' feeling is a hard substratum of neutralist sentiment and the lurking suspicion that the foreign policies of the United States . . . might inadvertently precipitate a local war which would eventually engulf the whole world in thermonuclear destruction."[66]

Over time, the popular Open Skies idea also contributed to the relative decline in American prestige in Western Europe. The Eisenhower administration's insistence on the Open Skies plan to the exclusion of other conventional proposals, such as a promising offer made by the USSR in May 1955, suggested that the United States was being too rigid and uncompromising.[67] Moreover, within the United States, Open Skies was no smashing success. Public opinion surveys revealed that many Americans did not understand the technology Eisenhower was proposing—aerial photography—and only a third approved of Eisenhower's Open Skies proposal.[68] As a PR stunt, Open Skies was a dud. As a move toward détente, it was a dismal failure.

Whether Soviet or American intransigence was to blame, by the end of the Eisenhower presidency the superpowers had made only the slightest progress toward détente. Eisenhower wrote later that the failure to reach an agreement on disarmament was one of the "greatest disappointments" of his presidency. For eight years, he claimed in his memoirs, his administration had toiled to secure some sort of agreement that would mark a first, even if only a small, step toward a satisfactory disarmament plan.[69] Perhaps Eisenhower was swayed by his own propaganda. Or perhaps he was merely continuing to promote the same image he had toiled to craft for a decade. Regardless, for most of his presidency, Eisenhower was more concerned that he appear open to negotiation than he was eager to negotiate. The pursuit of peace had a special place in the rhetoric and policies of President Dwight

D. Eisenhower. But it had more to do with image creation than conflict resolution. Not until late in his presidency—when the pressure of public opinion on the nuclear testing issue became unbearable—did Eisenhower give priority to negotiations over political warfare.[70]

Eisenhower publicly presented his diplomatic efforts as measures to promote world peace, but he saw diplomacy more as a tool for waging the Cold War than as a means of achieving détente. Faced with a domestic public opinion that was skeptical of Soviet intentions and committed to maintaining military superiority over the USSR, on the one hand, and allied public opinion that was hopeful for a relaxation of tensions, on the other, Eisenhower maneuvered so that he met the allies' expectation for progress toward peace while simultaneously avoiding any conciliation in actual policy. Paradoxically, however, the very fact of these efforts put more pressure on Eisenhower to continue negotiating with the enemy.[71] Thus he faced another dilemma: by selling the Cold War with the language of peace, Eisenhower put more pressure on himself to end it.

Peace and War Propaganda

Eisenhower's rhetorical quest for peace is a reminder of an important, but often forgotten, dimension of modern war propaganda. War—whether hot or cold—is not sold by fear alone. Positive, hopeful ideas—especially the hope for a better and more peaceful world to come—have been central elements in themes in presidential rhetoric ever since Woodrow Wilson led the charge for a "war to end all wars." Indeed, throughout the twentieth century, world leaders used appeals for peace to create the psychological conditions and moral space for war. As Harold Lasswell argued in his landmark study of World War I propaganda, selling war in the modern age virtually requires a parallel effort at promoting peace. In an age where peace is regarded as the normal state of society, populations must be convinced that every avenue toward peace has been exhausted and that war has been thrust upon them by a treacherous foe. As Lasswell put it: "So great are the psychological resistances to war in modern nations that every war must appear to be a war of defence against a menacing, murderous aggressor."[72]

If Lasswell is correct, then it should not be surprising to discover that "peace" was one of the most enduring themes of presidential rhetoric during the Cold War. American presidents used the word *peace* in every State of the Union address and all but one inaugural address between 1946 and 1991. Every address to the United Nations or to foreign legislative bodies referred to "peace," as did nearly all budget messages and addresses to joint sessions of Congress or state legislatures. Indeed, presidents evoked the theme of peace in 81 percent of their speeches and 69 percent of their press conferences during the Cold War. All told, Cold War presidents used the word *peace* in their public messages on 9,888 separate occasions—more often than such words as *liberty, evil, God, economy, prosperity, jobs, threat, Cold War, Soviet,* and *communism* or *communist.* The words *free* or *freedom* were used only slightly more often: on 11,054 discrete occasions and in 89 percent of all addresses. Although a whopping 96 percent of presidential addresses used the word *war,* only 15 percent did so without also referring to peace. Presidential rhetoric during the Cold War consistently portrayed Americans as peace-loving individuals who had been thrust into perilous conflict by evil and aggressive communist opponents. It also stressed the American commitment to working for peaceful solutions even as conflict continued.[73]

For whatever reason, American leaders have evinced a special interest in presenting their involvement in international conflicts as noble quests for higher purposes. Whether the senseless carnage of WWI, the global destruction of WWII, or the ongoing conflict in Iraq, Americans have been told that they were fighting not for their own prosperity or self-interest but to preserve peace, to end all wars, and to protect basic human freedoms. For many Americans, it often seemed, there was little or no contradiction between selling war and talking peace.

Notes

1. "Mock Raid Causes Panic; Linked to Stalin's Death," *New York Times,* 7 March 1953, 5.

2. Gallup asked respondents if they thought there was "much danger of world war" or if there would be "another world war in your lifetime." Those who answered "yes" reached a high point of 72 percent in March 1955. Most affirmative answers rested in the 60–70 percent range. See Gallup Poll 575 (20 November 1956), 566 (13 June 1956), 558 (4 January 1956), 548 (3 June 1955), 544 (1 March 1955), and 533 (30 June 1954). Gallup also asked Americans on a recurring basis from 1950 to 1958 whether they expected atomic or hydrogen bombs to be used in the event of another world war. Those who answered "yes" ranged from a low of 59 percent in 1956 to a high of 75 percent in 1958. See Gallup Poll 598 (14 April 1958), 582 (25 April 1957), 575 (20 November 1956), 529 (8 April 1954), and 455 (2 May 1950). Other polls asked Americans whether they felt it was likely their communities would be attacked with nuclear weapons in the event of WWIII. More than 50 percent replied consistently that they thought there was a "good chance" or a "fair chance" that their communities would be attacked. See Gal-

lup Polls 529 (4 April 1954), 517 (2 July 1953), and 463 (6 October 1950). Gallup Polls cited are from <http://brain.gallup.com>, a database of historical polling data available through most research libraries.

3. See especially James Richter, *Khrushchev's Double Bind: International Pressures and Domestic Coalition Politics* (Baltimore: Johns Hopkins University Press, 1994); Aleksandr Fursenko and Timothy Naftali, *Khrushchev's Cold War: The Inside Story of an American Adversary* (New York: W. W. Norton, 2006); and Klaus Larres and Kenneth Osgood, eds., *The Cold War after Stalin's Death: A Missed Opportunity for Peace?* (Lanham, Md.: Rowman & Littlefield, 2006).

4. State of the Union address, 2 February 1953, *Public Papers of the Presidents: Dwight D. Eisenhower, 1953* (Washington, D.C.: Government Printing Office, 1961): 12–34 (hereafter *Public Papers*).

5. Data is drawn from keyword searches of the digitized versions of the *Public Papers of the Presidents*, as provided by John Woolley and Gerhard Peters, *The American Presidency Project* [online] <http://www.americanpresidency.org>.

6. Quoted in Jeffrey Brooks, "Stalin's Ghost: Cold War Culture and U.S.-Soviet Relations," in Larres and Osgood, *The Cold War after Stalin's Death*, 125.

7. Hagerty Diary, 22 March 1955, U.S. Department of State, *Foreign Relations of the United States, 1952–1954* (Washington, D.C.: Government Printing Office, 1988), 9: 521 (hereafter *FRUS* followed by years and volume number).

8. To date, scholarship on the Eisenhower presidency (and indeed, on many other aspects of American foreign relations) has paid insufficient attention to the impact of domestic politics on U.S. foreign policy. On this point, see Fredrik Logevall, "Politics and Foreign Relations," *Journal of American History* 95 (March 2009). Although my previous work stressed the ways in which Eisenhower simultaneously reached both international and domestic audiences with his propaganda campaigns, it did not systematically address the ways in which the president may have been motivated by domestic political concerns. See Kenneth Osgood, *Total Cold War: Eisenhower's Secret Propaganda Battle at Home and Abroad* (Lawrence: University Press of Kansas, 2006).

9. David Halberstam, *The Fifties* (New York: Fawcett Columbine, 1993).

10. "Text of General Eisenhower's Address to G.O.P. Clubwomen," *New York Times*, 21 September 1952, 76.

11. James Reston, "Eisenhower Views Peace as at Stake in Election Fight," *New York Times*, 24 June 1952, 1; "Text of Eisenhower's Speech Outlining His Foreign Policy Views," *New York Times*, 24 June 1952, 20; Vincent P. DeSantis, "The Presidential Election of 1952," *Review of Politics* 15, no. 2 (April 1953): 131–50. If "peace" was one of the most salient themes in Eisenhower's presidential campaign, it also was a theme used by the Republican Party during the elections of 1954 and 1956. See George Gallup, "'Peace and Prosperity' Best Campaign Argument for GOP," *Gallup Political Series* no. 6, "What's the Best 'Talking Point' for Each Party?" *Public Opinion News Service*, 5 November 1955; George Gallup, "GOP Has Edge over Democrats in Handling Major U.S. Issues," *Public Opinion News Service*, 21 November 1955.

12. "Text of Eisenhower's Address on the Boston Common," *New York Times*, 22 October 1952, 16.

13. "Text of Eisenhower's Address in Philadelphia Outlining His Peace Program," *New York Times*, 5 September 1952, 12.

14. Dwight D. Eisenhower, First Inaugural Address, 20 January 1953, in Woolley and Peters, *The American Presidency Project* [online] <http://www.presidency.ucsb.edu/ws/index.php?pid=9600&st=&st1=>.

15. *Pravda*, 16 March 1953.

16. Carlton Savage to Paul Nitze, 1 April 1953, *FRUS 1952–1954*, 8: 1138; Jacob Beam to Department of State, 4 April 1953, *FRUS 1952–1954*, 8: 1140–43.

17. NSC 162/2, 30 October 1953, *FRUS 1952–1954*, 2: 577–97.

18. Department of State memorandum, n.d., *Declassified Documents Reference System*, 95/2722.

19. Quoted in Klaus Larres, "The Road to Geneva 1955: Churchill's Summit Diplomacy and Anglo-American Tension after Stalin's Death," in Larres and Osgood, *The Cold War after Stalin's Death*, 146.

20. Brooks, "Stalin's Ghost," 118–20.

21. John Colville, *The Fringes of Power: 10 Downing Street Diaries, 1939–1955* (New York: W. W. Norton, 1986), 683.

22. Gallup Poll 537 (21 September 1954). Less than 2 percent of respondents recorded positive feelings toward Russia. Nearly all indicated that they disliked Russia, with 73 percent indicating that they had the worst possible feelings toward Russia (-5 or "strong dislike"). The same question generated a nearly identical response a month earlier. See Gallup Poll 535 (3 August 1954). A 1956 poll asking the same question saw a nearly imperceptible shift, with just over 5 percent reporting positive feelings, 87 percent registering dislike at some level, and 69 percent indicating "strong dislike." See Gallup Poll 576 (19 December 1956). The first sign of change appeared in the 1960 poll. Those indicating they had "strong dislike" for Russia decreased to 57 percent in 1960, 39 percent in 1966, 25 percent in 1972, and 17 percent in 1973. In 1978, the last time the question was asked, 27 percent reported "strong dislike." See Gallup Polls 998 (28 March 1978), 874 (3 July 1973), 852 (23 May 1972), 738 (13 December 1966), and 637 (23 October 1960).

23. Gallup Poll 524 (9 December 1953). The positive view of McCarthy declined steadily over 1954 as the Army-McCarthy hearings got under way.

24. Gallup Poll 514 (17 April 1953), Gallup Poll 515 (14 May 1953).

25. Gallup Poll 513 (2 April 1953).

26. Gallup Poll 488 (19 March 1952), Gallup Poll 513 (2 April 1953). A near majority of 49 percent favored reducing the American military presence by training and equipping Koreans to do the fighting.

27. Gallup Poll 533 (30 June 1954).

28. Brooks, "Stalin's Ghost," 123–26.

29. "New Peace Drive," *New York Times*, 22 March 1953, E1; C. L. Sulzberger, "Malenkov Believed Seeking Time to Entrench His Rule," *New York Times*, 10 March

1953, 16; C. L. Sulzberger, "Europe Clings to Hope of Let-up in Cold War," *New York Times*, 15 March 1953, E3.

30. Joseph E. Evans, "The New Soviet Moves," *Wall Street Journal*, 18 June 1953, 6; *New York Herald Tribune*, 6 April 1953, quoted in Brooks, "Stalin's Ghost," 125.

31. Brooks, "Stalin's Ghost," 124.

32. "Excerpts from U.S. Editorials Commenting on the Death of Stalin," *New York Times*, 7 March 1953, 7.

33. Churchill quoted in John W. Young, *Winston Churchill's Last Campaign: Britain and the Cold War, 1951–5* (Oxford: Clarendon Press, 1996), 153.

34. Kathryn C. Statler, "Alliance Politics after Stalin's Death: Franco-American Conflict in Europe and in Asia," in Larres and Osgood, *The Cold War after Stalin's Death*, 157–76.

35. C. L. Sulzberger, "Europe Clings to Hope of Let-Up in Cold War," *New York Times*, 15 March 1953, E3.

36. Frank Schumacher, "Cold War Propaganda and Alliance Management: The United States and West Germany in the 1950s," paper presented to the Society for Historians of American Foreign Relations, June 2000; and Schumacher, "Democratization and Hegemonic Control: American Propaganda and the West German Public's Foreign Policy Orientation, 1949–1955," in Knud Krakau, ed., *The American Nation, National Identity, Nationalism* (Münster: Lit, 1997), 285–316.

37. NSC 162/2, 30 October 1953, *FRUS 1952–1954*, 2: 577–97.

38. The USIA surveys examined public opinion in West Germany, France, Italy, and Great Britain. Where I refer to "Europeans" above, I am referring to general trends across geographical lines. U.S. Information Agency, Research and Reference Service, "SR-1, Some Psychological Factors Relating to the Projected Big Four Meeting," 25 May 1955, Record Group [RG] 306, Special Studies 1955–59; and Media Briefs, 1961–62, of the Office of Research, box 1, National Archives, College Park, Md. (hereafter NA); "Additional Data on American Opinion Factors Relating to Four-Power Conference," Nelson A. Rockefeller Papers, RG 4, Washington, D.C., Files, subseries 7, box 4, "Four-Power Conference—Pre-Conference (1)," Rockefeller Archive Center, Sleepy Hollow, N.Y. (hereafter RAC).

39. U.S. Information Agency, Research and Reference Service, "SR-1, Some Psychological Factors Relating to the Projected Big Four Meeting," 25 May 1955, RG 306, Special Studies 1955–59; and Media Briefs, 1961–62, of the Office of Research, box 1, NA.

40. Intelligence Report no. 6979, "Neutralism in the United Kingdom on the Eve of Four-Power Talks," 30 June 1955, Rockefeller Papers, RG 4, Washington, D.C., Files, subseries 7, box 4, "Four-Power Conference—Pre-Conference (1)," RAC; Office of Research and Intelligence Report, "British Views about Nuclear Weapons: An Interpretation," 18 December 1957, RG 306, Production Division Research Reports, 1956–1959, box 4, NA.

41. Eisenhower to Churchill, 1 December 1954, in *The Papers of Dwight D. Eisenhower*, ed. Alfred D. Chandler and Louis Galambos (Baltimore: Johns Hopkins

University Press, 1970–96), 15: 1444–47 (hereafter *Eisenhower Papers* followed by volume number).

42. Department of State memorandum, n.d., *Declassified Documents Reference System,* microfiche 95/2722.

43. Eisenhower to Dulles, 5 December 1955, *Eisenhower Papers,* 16: 1921–23.

44. Lambie to Adams, 9 July 1953, White House Central Files, Subject Series, box 12, Candor and UN Speech (1), Dwight D. Eisenhower Library, Abilene, Kans. (hereafter DDEL); 134th NSC meeting, 25 February 1953, 165th NSC meeting, 7 October 1953, and Memorandum of Discussion, 16 July 1953, all in *FRUS 1952–1954,* 2: 514–34, 1110–14, 397.

45. Jackson Committee Report, *FRUS 1952–1954,* 2: 1965–66.

46. Eisenhower to Dulles, 8 September 1953, Eisenhower Diary, box 3, August/September 1953 (2), DDEL.

47. Eisenhower address before the American Society of Newspaper Editors, 16 April 1953, *Public Papers, 1953,* 179–88.

48. Robert L. Ivie, "Eisenhower as Cold Warrior," in *Eisenhower's War of Words: Rhetoric and Leadership,* ed. Martin J. Medhurst (East Lansing: Michigan State University Press, 1994), 14.

49. Lloyd Gardner, "Poisoned Apples: John Foster Dulles and the 'Peace Offensive,'" in Larres and Osgood, eds., *The Cold War after Stalin's Death,* 85.

50. Eisenhower address, 8 December 1953, *Public Papers, 1953,* 813–22.

51. Cutler comments on State Department draft, 19 October 1953, C. D. Jackson Papers, box 30, Atoms for Peace, Evolution (5), DDEL.

52. Stefan Possony, An Outline of American Atomic Strategy in the Non-Military Fields, 6 October 1952, WHO, NSC Staff Papers, OCB Secretariat series, box 3, Ideological Documents (4), DDEL.

53. Current Information Report, USIS Bonn to USIA, 2 November 1954 and 10 February 1955, both in USIA Historical Collection, Washington, D.C.

54. Top Secret Extract from OCB Minutes, 6 January 1954, and A Program to Exploit the A-Bank Proposals, 10 March 1954, both in OCB Central Files, box 121, OCB 388.3 (file #1) (2), DDEL. For details of U.S. actions to exploit Atoms for Peace, see OCB Central Files, boxes 121 and 122, OCB 388.3, DDEL.

55. Six Country Reactions to the President's December 8 Speech, White House Office, NSC Staff Series, OCB Central Files, box 121, OCB 388.3 (file #1) (2), DDEL; USIA Office of Research and Evaluation, Six Country Reactions to "Atoms for Peace" Speech, 8 January 1954, RG 306, Special "S" Reports of the Office of Research, 1953–1963, box 5, NA.

56. Department of State Office of Intelligence and Research, Attitudes toward the Four Power Conference, 15 June 1955, Nelson Rockefeller Papers, RG 4, Washington, D.C., Files, subseries 7, box 4, "Four-Power Conference—Pre-Conference (1)," RAC; Select Western European Public Reaction of United States Efforts for Peace in 1955, 20 February 1956, USIA Files, box 216, Legislation—1956 Disarmament Hearings, National Records Center, Suitland, Md.

57. Gallup Poll 512; Gallup Poll 513; Gallup Poll 518 (23 July 1953); Gallup Poll 521 (9 October 1953); Gallup Poll 544 (22 March 1955); Gallup Poll 549 (22 June 1955). Support for a summit declined in the aftermath of Sputnik. In March 1958, only 52 percent favored a summit between Eisenhower and Khrushchev. See Gallup Poll 597 (25 March 1958).

58. Dwight D. Eisenhower, *Mandate for Change: The White House Years, 1953–1956* (Garden City, N.Y.: Doubleday, 1963), 506; Dulles quoted in Walter L. Hixson, *Parting the Curtain: Propaganda, Culture, and the Cold War, 1945–1961* (New York: St. Martin's, 1996), 100.

59. Psychological Aspects of U.S. Position at Conference, Rockefeller to Eisenhower, 6 July 1955, Rockefeller Papers, box 4, Four-Power Conference—Pre-Conference (3), RAC.

60. Ibid.; Chronology of Mutual Inspection Proposal; Report of the Quantico Vulnerabilities Panel; and Annex B to the Report of the Quantico Vulnerabilities Panel, all in Rockefeller Papers, box 4, Four-Power Conference—Pre-Conference (3), RAC.

61. Cary Reich, *The Life of Nelson A. Rockefeller: Worlds to Conquer, 1908–1958* (New York: Doubleday, 1996), 590.

62. "Opinion Trends in the Aftermath of Geneva," 23 September 1955, RG 306, Special "S" Reports of the Office of Research, 1953–1963, box 10, NA; U.S. Information Agency, Research and Reference Service, "SR-2, Opinion Reactions in Western Europe to the Four-Power Conference," 3 August 1955, RG 306, Special Studies 1955–59; and Media Briefs, 1961–62, of the Office of Research, box 1, NA; Intelligence Report no. 6954, "Attitudes toward the Four Power Conference," 15 June 1955, Rockefeller Papers, RG 4, Washington, D.C., Files, subseries 7, box 4, "Four-Power Conference—Pre-Conference (1)," RAC.

63. Nelson Rockefeller to Harold Stassen, 30 November 1955, RG 59, lot 58 D133, box 214, Public Relations, part 2 of 2, NA.

64. Opinion Trends in the Aftermath of Geneva, 23 September 1955, RG 306, Special "S" Reports of the Office of Research, 1953–63, box 10, NA; Opinion Reactions in Western Europe to the Four-Power Conference, RG 306, Special Studies, 1955–1959; and Media Briefs, 1961–1962, of the Office of Research, box 1, NA.

65. Summary of discussion at Quantico II meeting, 26 August 1955, NAR Papers, RG 4, Washington DC Files, subseries 7, box 8, Quantico II: Establishment, Membership, Meetings, and Correspondence, RAC; Policy Information Statement for USIA, 5 August 1955; United States Post-Geneva Policy, 15 August 1955; Irwin to Rockefeller, 1 August 1955; and Irwin to Livermore, 18 October 1955, all in Rockefeller Papers, box 6, Four-Power—Post Geneva, RAC.

66. USIA, Select Western European Public Reaction to United States Efforts for Peace in 1955, RG 306, Intelligence Bulletins, Memoranda and Summaries of the Office of Research, 1954–1956, box 7, NA.

67. USIA, Select Western European Public Reaction to United States Efforts for Peace in 1955, RG 306, Intelligence Bulletins, Memoranda, and Summaries of the Office of Research, 1954–1956, box 7, NA.

68. Gallup Poll 551, 2 August 1955.

69. Dwight D. Eisenhower, *The White House Years: Waging Peace, 1956–1961* (Garden City, N.Y.: Doubleday, 1965), 467–68, 653.

70. Osgood, *Total Cold War*, 195–210.

71. Ira Chernus, "The Meanings of Peace: The Rhetorical Cold War after Stalin," in Larres and Osgood, *The Cold War after Stalin's Death*, 108.

72. Harold Lasswell, *Propaganda Technique in the World War* (New York: Alfred A. Knopf, 1927), 47, 60, 102, 105.

73. Data on presidential speeches is drawn from keyword searches of the digitized versions of the *Public Papers of the Presidents* from 1 January 1946 to 1 January 1991, <http://www.americanpresidency.org>. During this period, presidents used the word *peace* in 38 of 43 budget messages, 14 of 17 addresses to joint sessions of Congress, and 10 of 13 addresses to state legislatures. The numbers of public messages using other words mentioned in the text above are as follows: *liberty* (2,359), *evil* (900), *God* (4,191), *economy* (5,397), *prosperity* (3,001), *jobs* (3,831), *threat* (4,476), *Cold War* (273), *Soviet* (4,260), and *communism* or *communist* (2,264). Lyndon Johnson was the only Cold War president who did not speak of peace in his inaugural address (1965).

7

"WE NEED TO GET A BETTER STORY TO THE AMERICAN PEOPLE"

LBJ, the Progress Campaign, and the Vietnam War on Television

Chester Pach

On the evening of 11 August 1967, President Lyndon B. Johnson and six journalists sipped drinks and nibbled hors d'oeuvres while sitting on the Truman Balcony of the White House and talking about politics and war. The conversation was off the record, so Johnson was indiscreet, even vulgar. He said that French president Charles de Gaulle had made a "horse's ass of himself" on a recent trip to Canada. He predicted that German chancellor Kurt Kiesinger, who would soon visit Washington to talk about economic issues, would "try to trade me out of my drawers." As the president spoke, the sun turned "fiery orange," reminding CBS's Dan Rather of a Monet painting. "Sure is a beautiful day," the president declared. "Talk about anything you want."[1]

The war in Vietnam was the main topic of Johnson's casual conversation with reporters that day. Progress, patience, and persistence were the president's principal themes. Johnson read from classified messages about his efforts to ensure the fairness of the upcoming September presidential election in South Vietnam, but he cautioned against expecting "so much, . . . so soon." At least the South Vietnamese were trying to create a representative government. "Ho Chi Minh isn't holding any elections, . . . but nobody talks about that," the president complained. The South Vietnamese armed forces were also making progress, and Johnson quoted secret reports from U.S. commander William Westmoreland and Ambassador Ellsworth Bunker to back his claim. Although the president said he had done everything he could to let the enemy know that he wanted to end the war, there was no indication that the North Vietnamese desired serious negotiations. If they showed that they did, he would stop the bombing of North Vietnam "in a minute." Johnson confided that he was also hesitant to expand the air campaign, since U.S. planes had already struck "within half a mile of Ho Chi Minh's house." "That's as close as the people down there," he said while pointing toward the Washington Monument. "Reluctantly, prayerfully," he was nonetheless approving raids on a few more targets, but only with blunt warnings to the generals that if anything went wrong, "it's going to be your ass." The North Vietnamese, he said, were testing U.S. resolve and taking comfort in the growing popular discontent with the administration's war policies. The president, however, rejected quitting "in dishonor," as he had many times before, and reaffirmed his commitment to "helping South Vietnam to freedom."

Yet Johnson's uneasy manner undercut his message of hope and commitment in Vietnam. "This is a man who talks much with his hands," wrote Rather, a fellow Texan who covered the White House for CBS. "But in the talk about Vietnam, his hands remained clasphed [sic] between his legs. As he talked about the bombing, the muscles in his forearms tightened. The interwoven fingers pressed harder and harder against each other. From the second knuckle out, they went white, except for tiny red tips at the end of each finger." The strain of the Vietnam War showed even in that relaxed gathering on the Truman Balcony.

This meeting with reporters occurred as the administration began a new effort to rally support for a war that had become divisive and unpopular. More than 450,000 American troops were stationed in Southeast Asia; more than 100 died in combat most weeks. Yet two and a half years after U.S. forces had gone to war in Vietnam, there was no end in sight to the fighting. Johnson faced criticism from many directions; liberals and conservatives, hawks and doves, Democrats and Republicans all assailed his failures. The president's standing in the polls sank to a new low in early August, as only 39 percent of the public approved of his performance in office and just 33 percent supported his handling of the war. The president and his aides thought that this swelling public discontent showed not that they needed to revise their military or diplomatic strategies but that the American people were "skeptical, cynical, and—more often than not—uninformed." They decided to make more effective use of information from Vietnam "to put out our position over here at home." The result was the Progress Campaign, a public relations offensive aimed at showing that the United States was actually achieving its goals in Vietnam. The conversation on the Truman Balcony between Johnson and the journalists was part of this new attempt to sell the Vietnam War.[2]

The Johnson administration made a special effort during the Progress Campaign to sell the war in American living rooms. Vietnam was America's first television war—the first time that TV coverage had a critical effect on public understanding of a war effort and on a president's ability to sell war. There had been TV cameras in Korea, but even in 1953, the last year of fighting, less than half of American homes had televisions.[3] The network evening newscasts were then only fifteen minutes long and consisted of a frothy mix of headlines, amusing features, and even the afternoon baseball scores. But by the time the Johnson administration sent U.S. troops to war in Vietnam, network newscasts had expanded and matured. CBS and NBC switched to thirty-minute programs in September 1963; ABC followed suit in January 1967.[4] TV news experienced a golden age, when millions of Americans tuned in each evening to watch Walter Cronkite on CBS, Chet Huntley and David Brinkley on NBC, or ABC's "boy anchor," Peter Jennings, who was just beginning a long and distinguished career on U.S. television. A majority of Americans relied on television as their main source of news, and viewers considered TV "more believable" than newspapers by a margin of almost 2 to 1.[5] As one network producer explained, TV news had such power and appeal because of its ability, unlike print media, to transmit experience. Instead of just explaining the causes of famine, it showed hungry people. Rather than simply recounting the results of battle, it showed frightened peasants or wounded soldiers.[6] Americans turned to TV news to try to understand a strange, complicated, and frustrating war. TV news had become so influential that by late 1967 Johnson believed that the Vietnam War would be won or lost in American living rooms.

But the president thought he was fighting an uphill battle at a critical time in the war. Administration officials maintained that much of the TV reporting of the war was inaccurate, one-sided, or distorted, partly because reporters and editors opposed the president or his policies, partly because TV journalists, like the American public, were cynical or uninformed. Johnson was the first president to make what has become a familiar allegation in our electronic world—that hostile, ignorant, or sensational TV reporting might have a bigger effect than troops on the battlefield in determining the outcome of war. Johnson, however, failed to understand that firsthand knowledge of the difficulties with U.S. strategy rather than bias or sensationalism explained why prominent TV reporters had become skeptical of his war policies. "We need to get a better story to the American people," Johnson told his Vietnam advisors. Their need was urgent, since essential public support for the president's Vietnam policies was draining away as an election year approached. For a while, their upbeat statements and speeches on the network newscasts reclaimed some support for LBJ's war policies.[7] Yet they paid an enormous price when the Tet Offensive of early 1968 belied their claims of progress and delivered a devastating blow to the president's credibility. Ultimately, the president lost the war in American living rooms because his optimistic rhetoric simply did not explain the harsh realities of the war in Vietnam.

The War on Television

When Johnson sent American forces to war in 1965, the principle that was supposed to guide official U.S. relations with the news media in South Vietnam was "maximum candor consistent with security considerations." The chief U.S. information officer, Barry Zorthian, believed that such openness would produce accurate reporting, which could only help build support for the American war effort. There was no censorship during the Vietnam War, unlike during World War II or the Korean War. U.S. officials worried about practical problems of enforcement, but they were even more concerned about undermining favorable public attitudes back in the United States if "any significant number of our people believe . . . they were being misled." Instead, to maintain their accreditation, journalists had to refrain from reporting some types of information that might jeopardize air strikes or search-and-destroy missions that were in progress or that might otherwise endanger the lives of Americans in uniform. In return, they could count on transportation to battle areas, interviews with commanders, and official briefings about each day's military operations.[8]

While Zorthian was committed to "maximum candor," other U.S. officials, including the president, had different priorities. Arthur Sylvester, the assistant secretary of defense for public affairs, believed favorable coverage of the U.S. war effort was essential, and he had little compunction about securing it. Sylvester traveled to Saigon in July 1965 and told U.S. correspondents, "Look, if you think that any American official is going to tell you the truth, you're stupid."[9] Johnson sacrificed candor to political expediency as he took the United States deeper into the war by stealth and indirection. When he made critical decisions at the beginning of December 1964 that led first to intensified U.S. bombing of Laos and then to a sustained air campaign against North Vietnam, he told his advisors that he would "shoot at sunrise" anybody who leaked information about his actions.[10] When he authorized the dispatch of the first U.S. combat troops to South Vietnam in

March 1965 to protect air bases, he tried to persuade Secretary of Defense Robert McNamara to call them "security battalions." McNamara refused because he did not want to be accused of "falsifying the story."[11] When the president approved Westmoreland's request for a major increase in U.S. ground troops in July 1965, he revealed his decision at an afternoon news conference, when the viewing audience was small, and he tried to deflect attention with a surprise announcement that he was nominating Abe Fortas to the Supreme Court. Johnson also stated that U.S. troop strength would rise immediately to 125,000, with additional forces to follow, even though he had authorized an increase to 175,000 by the end of 1965. Although he had given Westmoreland the forces and the authority to take over the principal combat role from the South Vietnamese, he insisted that he had made no "change in policy whatever."[12]

Johnson may have wanted to avoid creating a war fever that would have complicated his efforts to control a limited war. He also may have hoped to deprive opponents of his Great Society of the argument that a nation mobilized for war could not afford costly social programs. Yet his compromises of candor produced charges of a "credibility gap"—a gulf between his words and actions—that became a staple in the criticism of his leadership. Johnson's strategy of fighting "a hot war in cold blood" also meant that the American people, while backing the commitment of troops, never rallied around the flag in the overwhelming numbers of earlier—and later—wars. Johnson himself predicted that public support, while "generally satisfactory" in the summer of 1965, "would become more doubtful" if U.S. forces were still at war in another year.[13]

Administration officials also quickly learned about the difficulties of fighting a war in the television age when CBS ran a sensational story by correspondent Morley Safer. A routine search-and-destroy mission in the village of Cam Ne on 3 August 1965 became a controversial event because Safer and his crew filmed U.S. marines using a cigarette lighter and a flame thrower to burn thatched huts. "A hundred and fifty homes were leveled in retaliation for a burst of gunfire," Safer asserted. "It will take more than presidential promises" to persuade a South Vietnamese peasant "that we are on his side."[14]

The story enraged Johnson. LBJ took the criticism personally, as he often did, and charged that CBS was "out to get us," even though the network's president, Frank Stanton, was a good friend. Johnson was so upset that he awakened Stanton with an early morning telephone call and started the conversation by asking, "Are you trying to fuck me?" The president alleged that Safer was a communist, but aides told him they could prove only that the correspondent was a Canadian. White House officials then pressured the network to replace Safer with an American correspondent who could provide a "balanced account of controversial situations." But CBS would not yield.[15]

Problems continued to plague U.S. efforts to secure favorable coverage. Reporters often questioned the credibility of information they received in the daily briefings in Saigon that they ridiculed as the Five O'Clock Follies. Some journalists even found that mixed in with the exaggerations and half-truths were "outright lies." Safer, for example, checked one briefing about a battle in 1966 that supposedly produced 240 enemy deaths and found that the geographic coordinates that the U.S. information officer had provided located the engagement in the South China Sea. After Safer's persistent questioning, the official closed his office door and admitted that the battle never happened: he had made up the incident on what had been a "slow" news day.[16]

Despite the strained relations between government officials and journalists, much of the TV news coverage of the war in 1965–66 reinforced themes that the Johnson administration used to build public support for its Vietnam policies. Many stories emphasized the courage and compassion of Americans in uniform, the sophistication of their military technology, and their staunchness in meeting aggression.[17] Like most Americans, TV correspondents had their own opinions about the war. Some supported U.S. policies; some were skeptical; others were indifferent or uncertain. Network policies, which emphasized objective reporting, left little room for the expression of personal views. Yet Johnson usually reacted only to what was wrong, critical, or unfavorable as he watched the TV reports on banks of televisions in his office and bedroom while using a remote control to turn the volume up on whatever network caught his attention. He complained in December 1965 after watching an NBC newscast that "Viet Cong atrocities never get publicized." Yet that very same evening both ABC and CBS had reported an enemy "terrorist" attack on U.S. troops in Saigon.[18]

Johnson worried about even occasional critical stories because he thought they complicated his efforts to sell the war. He believed that dramatic images in film reports and the simplification that inevitably occurred in three-minute stories could profoundly affect public support for his Vietnam policies. He also knew that the American people considered TV to be the most reliable of the news media. Because of the power that Johnson attributed to television, he tried hard to influence editors and reporters. He was renowned for his "treatment," a distinctive mixture of sweet talk and strong-arming that had made him such a formidable figure in the Senate. But the treatment usually failed to make journalists "get on the team," as it had uncommitted senators. Johnson's own difficulties in using television to establish a rapport with the American people may also have contributed to his sensitivity about critical reporting. Finally, and probably most important, television made it harder for the Johnson administration to fight the war in Vietnam by minimizing the costs and sacrifices and by failing to explain the risks and dangers. Television reports—even those suggesting that U.S. forces were winning—showed that the war was difficult and deadly. As public support eroded while U.S. troop strength and combat casualties climbed, it was easy for the president to blame the networks.[19]

During the first half of 1967, Johnson expressed his discontent about television coverage of the war with new vehemence. He charged that the networks were "infiltrated" and said that he was "ready to move on them if they move on us." At a dinner in March 1967 that network correspondents attended, he even alleged that CBS and NBC were "controlled by the Vietcong." In June, he complained about disproportionate coverage of antiwar protesters. "A student carrying a sign or a protester wearing a beard or an attention-seeker burning a draft card in front of a camera" was news, the president declared. But the volunteers for the armed forces were not.[20]

Behind the president's criticisms was concern about the growing political difficulties that the war was causing. A Gallup poll released in mid-June revealed that half the American people said that they lacked a "clear idea of what the war is about." Comparable figures for World War II showed that 78 percent believed they knew the purpose of the war, with only 18 percent uncertain. Gallup found declining hope that it would be possible to win the Vietnam War or achieve a lasting peace. Most Americans thought that some sort of political compromise would bring an end to the conflict, but only one-fourth of those surveyed believed that South Vietnam would be strong enough to survive after a U.S. withdrawal. Summarizing these results for Johnson, White House assistant Fred Panzer wrote, "Vietnam is the president's number one obstacle to higher popularity [and] re-election."[21]

As the war became more controversial, Johnson became more incensed about critical television reporting. Television's war was a mix of brief glimpses of frantic firefights and patrols that failed to find an elusive enemy; GIs building schools and hospitals in some hamlets and destroying others; soldiers and marines enjoying the urban pleasures of Saigon and Danang and enduring the hardships of combat in jungles or swamps. The reports about problems and failures angered the president. Increasingly, he made a simple equation between those critical stories and the declining support for the war that he saw in the polls. By mid-1967, the war had reached a critical stage. That summer's television reports from Vietnam provided more bad news, as some correspondents found new reasons to doubt the effectiveness of the U.S. war effort.

Summer of Discontent

Many network newscasts in June and July 1967 contained discouraging stories about the war. Searing criticism came from CBS's Murray Fromson, who believed that U.S. military advisors, after more than a decade of trying, could not get their South Vietnamese allies to fight aggressively. Fromson had been covering Vietnam on and off for more than a decade, and he stated bluntly, "On the basis of a record going back to 1956, it must be said that the advisory effort has largely been a failure."[22] There was also bad news about pacification—the effort to provide security and an improved quality of life for South Vietnamese peasants—from Cam Ne, the village that two years earlier had produced Morley Safer's sensational story. In July 1967, correspondent Howard Tuckner told viewers of NBC's *Huntley-Brinkley Report* that the South Vietnamese government had decided to destroy the village rather than save it. Government officials moved the residents of Cam Ne to one of the new "peace hamlets," which Tuckner described as "a monument to the failure of pacification." The NBC film showed desolate rows of tin-roofed huts surrounded by barricades and barbed wire, and an American volunteer who worked in the peace hamlets told Tuckner that they were really "concentration camps." The peace hamlets seemed just as harmful to Tuckner as the Marine cigarette lighters and flamethrowers had seemed to Safer.[23] CBS commentator Eric Sevareid, TV's most respected news analyst, also expressed his growing skepticism about U.S. strategy. Sevareid declared at the end of June that the fighting in Vietnam "appears to be accomplishing nothing measurable except casualties." A few days later, he told viewers that the Fourth of July holiday was a time not only to remember the marines who had fallen in the recent heavy fighting near the Demilitarized Zone (DMZ), but also to wonder whether their sacrifice was necessary. "Exactly what their deaths accomplished," he asserted, "we do not know."[24]

These reports occurred as the president made an important decision about how many more Americans in uniform to send to South Vietnam. Officials had been debating this issue since March, when Westmoreland asked for a minimum increase of 100,000 troops and an optimum expansion of 200,000 GIs. "To escalate or not to escalate," that was the question, according to ABC News anchor Peter Jennings. The answer would emerge after McNamara completed a trip to South Vietnam in early July. As NBC anchor David Brinkley explained, the president would assess whatever recommendation McNamara submitted for additional U.S. forces not only on the basis of how they might affect the fighting in Vietnam but also according to "the war's heavy pressure on the American economy, on the American attitude, and on the American political scene."[25] Brinkley's analysis was remarkably accurate. As the authors of the *Pentagon Papers* later concluded, "domestic resource constraints with all of their political and social repercussions, not strategic or tactical military considerations in Vietnam, were to dictate American war policy from that time on."[26]

After McNamara got back to Washington, the president settled the troop issue. While in Saigon, McNamara worked out a deal with Westmoreland to raise the troop ceiling to 525,000, a figure that no one announced, supposedly because of military security, until almost a month later. The new force level amounted to an increase of 47,000 GIs, the maximum number of troops that McNamara's civilian advisors believed they could provide Westmoreland without calling up the reserves. Avoiding the mobilization of the reserves was, for Johnson, "a major consideration," since the president worried that such a controversial step might push public discontent with the war to intolerable levels. During a press conference in the White House living quarters, the president chose his words carefully when he stated, "The troops that General Westmoreland needs and requests, *as we feel it necessary*, will be supplied."[27] Johnson, Westmoreland, McNamara, and General Earle Wheeler, the chairman of the Joint Chiefs of Staff, all professed that they had "a meeting of the minds," even though both generals were disappointed—even distressed—that the troop increase was only half their "minimum essential" request. In front of the TV cameras, however, they seemed to be "a very friendly group," according to ABC White House correspondent Frank Reynolds.[28]

As they made decisions about how many more troops to send into combat, administration officials complained that the reporters covering the war were more cynical and antagonistic than ever before. McNamara insisted that correspondents in Vietnam were in a "very bad mood." They thought the South Vietnamese government was hopelessly corrupt and unstable, pacification was "at a standstill," and the war wasn't "worth the price we are incurring." Leonard Marks, the director of the U.S. Information Agency, also visited South Vietnam in early July and concluded that journalists were more pessimistic and critical "about the course of the war . . . than at any time in the past two years." Rather than providing fair and balanced reporting, they had "a tendency to search for a critical story that might lead to a Pulitzer Prize."[29]

While these complaints were similar, the explanations for the journalists' alleged hostility and sensationalism were contradictory. Marks maintained that the main problems were inexperience and immaturity. He said that transfers and summer vacations had brought the replacement of "mature correspondents" with reporters who had never before had a "big assignment," knew little about "the complexities of any war and this war in particular," and carried with them "built-in doubts and reservations." Under Secretary of State Nicholas Katzenbach, who had traveled with McNamara, believed that the main problem was not lack of experience but that many reporters in Vietnam had "been out there too long." McNamara, Westmoreland, and Wheeler each acknowledged that there were times when they wished they could impose new restrictions on reporters, but they concluded, as they had earlier, that censorship would not work and they "would pay a terrible price for it."[30]

These simple and sweeping criticisms of the Saigon journalists hardly explained why some TV correspondents who were covering the war in mid-1967 became skeptical of U.S. policies and official sources of information. A good example is David Schoumacher, who went to South Vietnam in the spring of 1967 to report for CBS. Schoumacher had earned a degree in journalism from Northwestern University and gained considerable experience at several midwestern radio and television stations before joining CBS in 1963 and working in the Washington bureau. He also had graduated from the Reserve Officer Training Corps program at Northwestern and served for four years in the Air Force as a pilot in the Strategic Air Command. On the day that he arrived in Vietnam, he had dinner with two public information officers, one from the Air Force, the other from the Navy, on the roof of the Caravelle Hotel, the location of the CBS bureau in Saigon. "A hell of an argument" occurred, he recalled, and the dispute was so unexpected that he thought it was like a scene from *Alice in Wonderland*. To Schoumacher's astonishment, the two officers criticized U.S. policy in Vietnam, while he defended it. "I was this conservative SAC pilot . . . from the heartland of America," Schoumacher later explained. He worried about communist aggression in Vietnam and told the officers that "if we didn't draw the line here, we'd be fighting them in Honolulu."[31]

During the next few months, Schoumacher went through a "wrenching experience," as he questioned his most basic views about the war and the credibility of official information. He started with a conviction that "I could trust what I was being told by American officials and by American military officers. And it took not very long for me to discover that I was being lied to and that the system was built on rewarding lies. . . . You realize that the whole . . . military reporting system did not encourage truth telling, but the reverse." Schoumacher found that the optimistic accounts of battles that official briefers provided at the Five O'Clock Follies were at odds with his own firsthand experiences and those of other reporters. He also reached troubling conclusions about the effects of the U.S. war effort on Vietnamese civilians, as he spent most of his time near Danang, learned some Vietnamese, and became "more politically aware." His experiences persuaded him that the pacification program was "an unmitigated disaster" that was "creating enemies," not "winning hearts and minds." His criticisms were hardly unusual. Even McNamara thought that there were problems with the "other war," that progress in pacification was at best "slow," and that dramatic improvements were unlikely during the remainder of 1967.[32]

As Schoumacher's views changed, so did his reporting. One of Schoumacher's first stories from Vietnam on the evening news was about marines in Danang racing go-carts. Though far from home on Memorial Day 1967, the marines enjoyed their own version of the Indianapolis 500. "All the killing and the heat and the dirt of Vietnam really hasn't changed American boys very much," Schoumacher declared, "and that at least is reassuring." Thirty-five years later, he thought that assertion "stupid" and "simplistic," since Vietnam "changed them mightily." His subsequent reports probed more deeply. At the beginning of August, the CBS evening newscast carried his story about a marine mission into the DMZ that ran into a North Vietnamese ambush. Schoumacher noted that the marines who survived the ferocious enemy attack were not as quick as their commanders to proclaim the mission a success. He also pointed out that there was "no reliable word on casualties," since the marines claimed that there were only six fatalities, even though he counted eighteen bodies once the troops had returned to their base. Schoumacher also raised doubts about pacification in a report in mid-September on the relocation of Vietnamese civilians from an area near Chu Lai that the enemy controlled. Their new destination was Son Tra, a deserted village that itself had been previously evacuated. "No one seems to know where those villagers are now," Schoumacher declared in closing. "It's become a sort of a game of musical chairs—but with people." As Schoumacher later explained, he had great sympathy for the Americans in uniform who endured the hardships of war, but growing doubts about whether U.S. commanders really understood the effects of their decisions.[33]

He expressed that skepticism in an argument with General Lewis Walt, the commander of the Third Marine Amphibious Force.[34] At a cookout at the general's headquarters in Danang, Schoumacher drank "martinis that really loosened your lips." Eventually he said that he thought Walt was insulated from what was actually happening in the war, "and it got to be a very, very heated argument." Schoumacher recalled, "At some point I said to him that you really should read some Shakespeare." Making a reference to a scene in the play *Henry V*, he told Walt to "take a cloak and disguise yourself and go among the campfires and listen to what your troops are saying." Indeed, he continued, "You don't even have to go to the camp fires, you can just go right out . . . here at the foot of the wall. There's a French cemetery there and it has the whole American experience on those tombstones." The argument ended what was supposed to be a pleasant evening. It also showed that Schoumacher, the "straight arrow" devoted to "duty, honor, and country," had his beliefs shaken by the "intense experience" of Vietnam.[35]

For NBC correspondent David Burrington, the change in his views about the war was much more gradual. An army veteran who earned a degree in journalism from the University of Minnesota, Burrington was neither opposed to U.S. intervention in Vietnam nor cynical about U.S. policies. He started reporting from Vietnam in early 1966, and during the next year he reached the "depressing" conclusion that "our stated goal was not being met." "When I first went in," Burrington said, "I wonder[ed] how long it's going to take to win." But instead he began to see "a pattern" of abandoning pacified areas, which allowed the enemy to return. "They weren't making any progress," Burrington said about U.S. military forces, "and I think after a while this became very clear." Burrington and other journalists would sometimes hear from public information officers who thought their reporting wasn't sufficiently optimistic. "You guys aren't telling it the way it is," the information officers would complain. But this criticism didn't shake Burrington's conviction that the U.S. war effort was foundering. As he later explained, "We were going out [into the battle areas] and these guys in Saigon weren't."[36]

In mid-July 1967, Burrington filed a gloomy report about the U.S. marines near the DMZ who for months had endured relentless pounding from enemy guns. Heavy casualties left the marines short-handed, a problem that Westmoreland acknowledged as he pressed McNamara for more troops.

Burrington's report on NBC revealed that the companies he checked were anywhere from one-fifth to one-third understrength. As the film showed replacement troops arriving, Burrington predicted that they could antici-pate a bleak future. "More than half of these new men will be either killed or wounded during their tour here," he explained, "if the fighting continues as hot as it has during the past four months." The new troops got a brief orien-tation in rear areas before being moved into combat zones. But during this orientation, several of their M16 rifles jammed, which hardly helped their morale. "Drastic measures," Burrington concluded, might be necessary to deal with these difficulties, including sending some marines for a second tour of duty in Vietnam less than a year after they completed their first.[37]

White House counsel Harry McPherson watched Burrington's report and considered it "devastating" because it was so relentlessly grim. Yet the NBC film didn't surprise him, "since the Marines have been catching so much hell" near the DMZ and there had been other stories about "bewildered, depressed men." McPherson had some recent, firsthand experience, as he had made his first trip to Vietnam just two months earlier and returned "neither optimistic nor pessimistic, neither more hawk nor more dove." In a detailed report to the president, he praised "the quality of our people" in Vietnam but also urged LBJ to insist on honest assessments of the war from them. "There is a natural tendency in the military to feel that things are go-ing pretty well, and will go much better if we only have a few more bodies and bombs," McPherson declared. He thought that the president ought to be "wary" of "this hungry optimism." Perhaps because of his concerns about the candor of official reporting, McPherson didn't complain that Burrington's story was distorted, inaccurate, or unduly pessimistic. Even so, he lamented in a memo to press secretary George Christian, "it was really bad news on TV tonight."[38]

There was more bad news on 8 August when the CBS Evening News car-ried a film report in which correspondent Bert Quint asserted that the war was a stalemate. Quint was no stranger to controversy. He had covered the U.S. military intervention in the Dominican Republic in April 1965, and his stories contradicted administration claims that local communists might seize power and create "another Cuba." Johnson was so upset that he asked CBS to recall Quint, but network officials refused. After Quint arrived in Vietnam in June 1967, it did not take him long to conclude that U.S. strategy was "leading to nothing." In early August, he accompanied a U.S. infantry unit in the Mekong Delta on what turned out to be "a walk in the sun," a pa-trol that failed to make contact with the enemy. Even though he had no film of any fighting, Quint was determined to file a story, as he later explained, "after sweating my balls off for ten hours." His report aired on the evening newscast that Walter Cronkite then anchored, even though producers at CBS, like those at the other two networks, wanted combat reports to include scenes of battle or "bang, bang." In his narrative, Quint maintained that the lack of action confirmed that the enemy had the initiative. While the film showed troops trudging through marshes and mud, Quint explained, "It's a painful, foot-by-foot, paddy-by-paddy, stream-by-stream pursuit of an enemy that rarely stands and fights, that prefers to hit and then run, make for sanctuary in Cambodia when the going gets too tough, regroup, infiltrate back into Vietnam, and then hit again." These U.S. missions, he said, had several purposes, "but even the generals do not pretend that winning the war is one of them." Americans were on the defensive against an enemy that could replace battle losses and then strike without warning. The "statements by American officials that there is no stalemate, that real progress is being made, ring hollow down here," he declared."[39]

Once again, Quint's reporting angered Johnson. The president learned about Quint's stalemate story from a staff assistant who compiled information about the network newscasts. Several years later, when he published the blockbuster novel *Jaws*, Peter Benchley would become well known to millions of Americans. But in the summer of 1967, Benchley was a junior White House aide who had just begun to keep his "eye on the tube." Benchley described Quint's story as "a very fatalistic film about the slow war of attrition." Even though Benchley himself criticized the president's Vietnam policies in conversations with other White House officials, he thought that Cronkite's evening newscast contained "a good deal of anti-administration material," especially about the war. The problem, he believed, was "lazy journalism," a failure to make the necessary effort to balance one-sided coverage. But the president put the blame elsewhere. He told Benchley, "If there's one man who is more against me on Viet Nam than Bill Fulbright, it's Walter Cronkite. . . . He's out to get me."[40] As usual, Johnson took criticism about Vietnam personally.

Quint's story about stalemate touched a nerve because it occurred only a day after the *New York Times* had published a front-page article that reached the same conclusion. Written by R. W. Apple Jr., the newspaper's Saigon bureau chief, the article maintained that "millions of artillery shells," "billions of rifle bullets," and almost 500,000 U.S. troops had become measures of "the most frustrating conflict in American history." "Victory is not close at hand," Apple asserted. "It may be beyond reach."[41] These two reports on consecutive days in two of the most prominent national news outlets helped make "stalemate" the most important theme in the reporting about the war.

The president and his advisors decided to take strong action quickly to challenge the view that the war was deadlocked. The idea that the war was a stalemate was at odds with the reports from top U.S. officials in Saigon, even those that acknowledged that a shortage of troops or the difficulties of winning the confidence of South Vietnamese peasants were real problems. Stalemate was also at odds with the president's political needs. Johnson could not afford a further decline in public support for the war, especially as stories about the approaching election began to appear on newscasts and in newspapers. The president and his advisors had to do better at selling the war. In August 1967, they began the Progress Campaign.

Progress or Stalemate?

"Stalemate," as Apple wrote, was "a fighting word in Washington," and administration officials came out swinging. The president called Barry Zorthian in Saigon, accused Apple of being "a Communist," and demanded that Zorthian do something to stop the critical stories. Wheeler cabled Westmoreland that he was concerned that the news reports about stalemate were responsible for criticism from "prominent members" of Congress who had previously supported the war effort. Westmoreland, too, was upset, since "every indicator" contradicted the idea of stalemate. He told Wheeler that he would hold news conferences and briefings to "clarify the situation in the mind of the public." He would do so carefully, however, "to avoid charges that the military establishment is conducting an organized propaganda campaign." While he worked "on the nerve ends" in Saigon, Westmoreland thought political and military officials should deal with "the roots" in Washington—"the confused or unknowledgeable pundits who serve as sources for each other."[42] Help soon came from the Vietnam Information Group, a new White House committee whose main task was to coordinate the administration's efforts to "get its story out on Vietnam." Among other activities, the group wrote speeches for members of Congress and prepared reports that the president or his aides could leak to sympathetic reporters.[43] The president thought that the time had come "to do something dramatic" to prove that the idea of stalemate was "pure Communist propaganda." National Security Advisor Walt Rostow informed Westmoreland, Bunker, and other important U.S. officials in Saigon that the president believed that providing the American people with "sound evidence of progress in Vietnam" had become "a critically important dimension of fighting the war."[44]

During this Progress Campaign, Johnson took the offensive. He was upbeat, insistent, and at times combative in asserting that U.S. forces were achieving their goals. He claimed that he had tried "a lengthy and imaginative list of . . . peace initiatives" and that his efforts had "met nothing but arrogant rebukes from Hanoi." He made these points to journalists, as he had that August evening on the Truman Balcony, as well as to union leaders, members of Congress, and other White House visitors. He also dismissed the idea of stalemate and charged that TV coverage of the U.S. war effort was one-sided and even vindictive. When he met a visiting group of Australian broadcasters, he expressed the latter criticism in bitter, personal terms. "I can prove that Ho [Chi Minh] is a son-of-a-bitch if you let me put it on the screen," LBJ declared. "But they [the networks] want me to be the son-of-a-bitch." Sometimes he challenged visitors to tell him what he should do differently to halt the fighting or negotiate a settlement. Inevitably they rejected the alternatives he posed, such as unilateral U.S. withdrawal or a halt to the bombing that would endanger Americans in uniform. While he claimed that antiwar protesters and congressional doves encouraged enemy persistence, he conceded that the war's unpopularity meant that he was in "deep trouble." Yet as he told a delegation from Harvard University and Wellesley College, "there has never been a major war when there hasn't been major trouble at home."[45]

In private meetings with advisors, however, he was more pessimistic, even resigned. He confided to his top Vietnam advisors in early October that if he had to decide that day, he would not seek another term in 1968. "We don't have the press, the newspapers or the polls with us," he explained. "I don't know if I want four more years of this." Neither did McNamara, who had grown so weary of his double life of public proponent of progress and private skeptic of the policies he helped formulate that he decided in November to leave the administration after the president found a replacement. Whatever Johnson decided about his own political future, he knew that he had to "do something about Vietnam quick" to quiet Democratic fears that "we will lose the election." So Johnson reminded his advisors that "the clock is ticking" and "we have got to sell our product to the American people."[46]

Johnson provided his most effective sales pitch at a news conference in mid-November. He wore a lapel microphone that allowed him to move around and use his full repertoire of persuasive skills to give the television audience a taste of his "treatment." He traced an upward slope with his hands to illustrate his assertion that, in Vietnam, "we are making progress." He clasped his hands together as he lauded the South Vietnamese government for holding elections "in the midst of all the horrors of war." He removed his glasses as he reflected on his achievements in office. "If I have done a good job of anything since I have been President, it is to insure that there are plenty of dissenters," Johnson quipped. Yet while he professed to welcome responsible criticism, he denounced the "storm trooper" tactics of protesters who endangered free speech expressing his amazement that the news media, "who insist on the right to live by the First Amendment," did not demand that these methods of dissent "be wiped out." NBC's Washington bureau chief, Bill Monroe, contributed to a chorus of praise when he declared that he had "never seen the President so effective on television."[47]

More favorable TV coverage occurred when Westmoreland visited Washington a few days later and announced that he could see light at the end of the tunnel. The general spoke at the National Press Club and declared, "We have reached an important point when the end begins to come into view." Westmoreland's "message of optimism," in the words of NBC's Brinkley, was that within two years the South Vietnamese would have made sufficient progress so that it would be possible to start withdrawing U.S. troops.[48]

The media blitz continued at the end of November, when CBS aired a special program with the country's two living five-star generals, Dwight D. Eisenhower and Omar N. Bradley. Both talked hopefully about victory in Vietnam. Bradley was cochair of the supposedly independent Committee for Peace with Freedom in Vietnam, a group that presidential assistant John P. Roche and members of the Vietnam Information Group had quietly helped organize. Neither of these superannuated military commanders was as mobile or imposing as Johnson had been at his recent press conference; they remained seated in an office on Eisenhower's Gettysburg farm while Harry Reasoner interviewed them. Both, however, still knew how to take the offensive. Bradley chided the news media for sensational reporting, while Eisenhower castigated the "kooks and hippies" who favored surrender. Both insisted that the critics didn't understand the war but that Westmoreland did and so the American people should support him.[49]

Yet some TV reports from Vietnam challenged that view. No reporter explained the human cost of the war better than John Laurence. In the summer of 1967, Laurence persuaded CBS to send him back to Vietnam. He had covered the war in 1965–66 and had become worried about the quality of much of the reporting, a concern that the *New Yorker's* television critic, Michael Arlen, shared. After reading one of Arlen's essays, Laurence said he felt compelled to act. CBS news executives also had reached the conclusion that television could provide better understanding of the war. Just before Laurence left for his second tour in Vietnam, Ralph Paskman, the manager of CBS News, showed him a memo from Richard Salant, the president of the network's news division, asking that correspondents provide more analysis. Salant wrote that he was tired of stories about battles won and battles lost, body counts and bomb tonnage, that failed to explain their significance. Laurence was ready to tell viewers what he thought these glimpses of the war meant. "I wanted to show Americans how costly the war had become, how brutal and wasteful it was, what it was doing to the individual young men who were trapped in it." Laurence found a partner in Keith Kay, a camera operator who had just finished a two-year stint in the army that he served mainly in a New York photo lab. Like Laurence, Kay had covered the war earlier; he was eager to get out of the army and get back to Vietnam. They formed a strong friendship and a professional partnership that produced some of the most memorable reporting about the war.[50]

In late October 1967, Laurence and Kay filmed an extraordinary story for the *CBS Evening News* that showed what the war was doing to the young men who fought it. A unit of the First Cavalry encountered sniper and machine-gun fire as it patrolled near the coastal town of Hoi An. No important territory was at stake; neither side suffered heavy losses; no one clearly won or lost the battle. The film showed the frantic action of soldiers in battle. Kay then pointed his camera at a soldier whose helmet bore the words "Haight Ashbury," the neighborhood in San Francisco that had become the center of the counterculture and that had drawn young people by the thousands during 1967's "Summer of Love." "It is a long way from San Francisco to South Vietnam," Laurence declared. "It was longer across that last rice paddy." The platoon commander, Lieutenant Jimmie Bass, concentrated on retrieving the body of a private whose name most of the soldiers couldn't remember, since he had joined the unit only a month earlier. He was a young man with red hair and freckles whose life ended when a sniper's bullet crashed into his head. As Kay's film showed Bass dragging the corpse, Laurence explained the significance of this routine skirmish. "There are a hundred platoons fighting a hundred small battles in nameless hamlets like this every week of the war. They are called firefights. And in the grand strategy of things, this firefight had little meaning for anyone but the red-headed kid who was killed here."[51]

Laurence's summary was as unusual as it was striking. Television correspondents rarely offered such direct, personal criticism of the war, even though their reports often contained interpretive comments, efforts to explain the larger significance of the fragment of the war they had covered that day. At all three networks, analysis was not supposed to become editorializing. How to draw that line, though, was always a judgment call, one that reflected a journalist's own style and conception of professional responsibilities or an editor's assessment of what was proper or fair. As he wrote his closing remarks about the red-haired soldier, Laurence thought that he had "a mandate from Salant" to draw that line a little differently, "to do more . . . to explain all these battles, all these firefights, all these civilians in distress." His explanation also grew out of his resentment over the "dishonesty" of Westmoreland and other U.S. officials who used "lies" and "propaganda" to "keep American public opinion stoked up for the war." For Laurence, honesty was "a fundamental value" that guided his reporting. The result was his exceptional story, which found in the life and death of an ordinary soldier the futility of the war.[52]

In late 1967, there were other TV news reports that raised questions about U.S. accomplishments or objectives in Vietnam, whether there was real progress in the war, and whether that progress really mattered. Yet despite these critical stories, the Progress Campaign achieved some success. By year's end, half of the American people thought that U.S. forces were making progress in Vietnam, an increase of 50 percent since the summer. The president once again enjoyed a favorable approval rating. Polls also showed that popular discontent with Johnson's Vietnam policies had diminished, even though by a margin of 38–49 percent Americans remained dissatisfied with his handling of the war. These improvements occurred because administration officials had encouraged many Americans to believe that in Vietnam "progress is our most important product."[53]

Chaos overwhelmed progress in public perception of the war when the Tet Offensive began at the end of January 1968. The enemy's biggest and most brazen offensive of the war surprised Westmoreland, worried the president, and stunned millions of Americans who watched the sensational violence on the evening newscasts. The fighting surged into remote villages, urban neighborhoods, and even the grounds of the U.S. embassy. All three networks carried unsettling stories about journalists who suffered wounds while covering a war that suddenly seemed more dangerous and deadly than ever before. Surely the most spectacular—and controversial—report aired on NBC, which showed film of South Vietnam's national police chief executing a prisoner with his handgun after a street battle in a Saigon suburb. Even though enemy forces suffered staggering losses and retreated from the territory they had attacked or seized, the breadth, fury, and surprise of their offensive enlarged the president's credibility gap. "All those comfortable, official assumptions about steady progress in the war turned out to be wrong," declared CBS correspondent Robert Schakne. U.S. officials made only a few, ineffective efforts to reply to such criticism. "What the hell is going on?" Cronkite asked in bewilderment after hearing the first news of the Tet Offensive. "I thought we were winning the war!" To answer that question for himself and millions of Americans, Cronkite visited the battlefields and refugee camps and then summarized his findings in a special, primetime program at the end of February. "To say that we are mired in stalemate seems the only realistic, yet unsatisfactory conclusion," he declared.[54]

"Stalemate" was no longer a fighting word in February. Instead it produced despair, even resignation in the Oval Office. "If I've lost Cronkite, I've lost the country," Johnson said glumly as he took the CBS anchor's opinion as a measure of the popular mood. But there was ample evidence of unprecedented discontent, as public support for the president's Vietnam policies sank to a new low of just 26 percent. Secretary of State Dean Rusk thought that the Tet Offensive had destroyed "the element of hope" that the administration had bolstered during the Progress Campaign. "People don't think there is likely to be an end," he stated in one of many White House meetings in February and March about the war. Criticism from Congress and commentators intensified when news leaked in mid-March that Westmoreland and Wheeler had requested 206,000 more troops to regain the initiative in the war. After McNamara departed at the end of February, the new secretary of defense, Clark Clifford, an erstwhile hawk, helped build a consensus in favor of a diplomatic initiative instead of military escalation. In his famous televised address of 31 March, LBJ announced limits on the bombing of North Vietnam in the hope of getting Hanoi to agree to negotiations. As Johnson biographer Randall Woods has explained, the president realized that he had become so controversial, that his credibility was so diminished, that he would have a better chance of gaining essential support for this peace initiative if he were "politically dead" rather than "alive." "Accordingly," Johnson told disbelieving viewers, "I shall not seek, and I will not accept, the nomination of my party for another term as your President."[55]

Johnson was angry about television coverage of Tet in particular and the war in general. He expressed his dissatisfaction when he spoke to the National Association of Broadcasters the next morning—on April Fool's Day, no less. "As I sat in my office last evening, waiting to speak, I thought of the many times each week when television brings the war into the American home," he said. No one, he continued, could know "exactly what effect those vivid scenes have on American opinion." Historians could "only guess" at what might have happened had there been the same sort of TV coverage in earlier wars during times of peril for U.S. forces. Despite these qualifications, Johnson clearly implied that his war policies had become so unpopular because Vietnam was the nation's first television war.[56]

Other critics of TV's Vietnam coverage echoed LBJ's complaints. Johnson's White House successor, Richard Nixon, insisted that he faced greater hostility from the news media than any previous president. Nixon's vice president, Spiro T. Agnew, denounced TV journalists for their alleged liberal, antiwar bias, in an effort to persuade Americans who were discontent with the war and the protests it produced to blame the networks rather than the White House or the Pentagon. A few journalists made similar arguments. Robert Elegant, who covered Vietnam for the *Los Angeles Times,* asserted that hostile television coverage ultimately led to U.S. withdrawal and Saigon's defeat and even to a "Vietnam syndrome" that hobbled U.S. foreign policy as it faced international challenges during the 1970s.[57] More recently, Bernard Goldberg, a former CBS correspondent, wrote a national best seller about a pervasive, liberal bias in network journalism.[58] Former secretary of defense Donald Rumsfeld also questioned the accuracy of television reporting of the Iraq war, even if he stopped short of alleging liberal bias. "What we are seeing is not the war in Iraq," Rumsfeld insisted as he discussed TV coverage at the beginning of the fighting in 2003, but "slices" of it. Each story provided the "particularized perspective" of the reporter but missed the big picture.[59]

No doubt TV newscasts contributed to the confusion and consternation that so many Americans experienced as they watched bleak reports about the Tet Offensive. But liberal bias, sensationalism, and distortion do not explain why the Progress Campaign ran into difficulties. The president and his aides had put their policies and their credibility at risk by selling progress and encouraging Americans to expect good news from Vietnam. The Progress Campaign was a last desperate effort—a hope against hope—to reclaim support for war policies that most Americans doubted or disliked. For a time, LBJ won back some of the skeptics, using television to sell his story of progress, even as he rebuked network journalists for myopic, misguided, or malicious criticism. By the end of 1967, Johnson believed that "the main front of the war is here in the United States" and that news reports, especially those on TV, would determine the outcome of that struggle.[60] LBJ lost that living room war, but the main reason was not because of the way TV journalists covered Vietnam. Instead, the president's problem was a war that, after three years of enormous effort and increasing cost, he could not win, end, or—ultimately—sell.

Notes

1. The account of this meeting in this and the next two paragraphs comes from two sets of notes by Rather, off-record session with the president at the White House, 11 August 1967, folder 1, box 4; and untitled notes, 11 August 1967, folder 5, box 6, all in Papers of Dan Rather, Howard Gotlieb Archival Research Center, Boston University (hereafter Rather Papers); and notes by Fleming on the president's conversation with six commentators, 11 August 1967, folder July/August 1967, meetings with correspondents, box 3, Meeting Notes File, Lyndon B. Johnson Library, Austin, Texas (hereafter LBJL).

2. *The Gallup Poll: Public Opinion, 1935–97*, CD-ROM ed. (Wilmington, Del.: Scholarly Resources, 2000), 1967: 2074–75; memorandum, George Christian to president, 22 August 1967, folder August 1967 [4 of 5], box 24, Handwriting File, LBJL.

3. Cobbett Steinberg, *TV Facts* (New York: Facts on File, 1985), 86.

4. On the development of TV News, see Chester Pach, "Television," in *Encyclopedia of American Foreign Policy*, 2nd ed., 3 vols., ed. Alexander DeConde, Richard Dean Burns, and Fredrik Logevall (New York: Charles Scribner's Sons, 2002), 3: 547–49.

5. Burns W. Roper, "Emerging Profiles of Television and Other Mass Media: Public Attitudes, 1959–1967," copy in folder Television, box 421, Office Files of Fred Panzer, LBJL (hereafter Panzer Files); Chester Pach, "From Vietnam to Iraq: The First Television War and Its Legacies," in *America, War, and Power*, ed. Lawrence Sondhaus and A. James Fuller (New York: Routledge, 2007), 126.

6. Memorandum by Reuven Frank, n.d. [1963], box 8, Papers of Elie Abel, Howard Gotlieb Archival Research Center, Boston University.

7. Notes of meeting, 15 November 1967, *Foreign Relations of the United States, 1964–1968* (Washington, D.C.: Government Printing Office, 2002), 5: 1032 (hereafter *FRUS* followed by years and volume number).

8. Transcript, oral history interview with Barry Zorthian, 1: 7, 24, LBJL; William M. Hammond, *Public Affairs: The Military and the Media, 1962–1968* (Washington, D.C.: U.S. Army Center of Military History, 1988), 144–45; Chester J. Pach Jr., "And That's the Way It Was: The Vietnam War on the Network Nightly News," in *The Sixties: From Memory to History*, ed. David Farber (Chapel Hill: University of North Carolina Press, 1994), 92.

9. Transcript, Zorthian oral history interview, 2: 3–8, LBJL; Martin Gershen, "The 'Right to Lie,'" *Columbia Journalism Review* 5 (1966/67): 14–16; Morley Safer, "Television Covers the War," reprinted in U.S. Congress, Senate, Committee on Foreign Relations, *News Policies in Vietnam*, Hearings, 17 and 31 August 1966, 89th Cong, 2d sess., 92.

10. George C. Herring, *America's Longest War: The United States and Vietnam, 1950–1975*, 4th ed. (New York: McGraw-Hill, 2002), 158; notes of a meeting, 1 December 1964, *FRUS, 1964–68*, 1: 965–69; Fredrik Logevall, *Choosing War: The Lost Chance for Peace and the Escalation of the War in Vietnam* (Berkeley: University of California Press, 1999), 269–71.

11. Transcript, telephone conversation between Johnson and McNamara, 6 March 1965, in *Reaching for Glory: Lyndon Johnson's Secret White House Tapes, 1964–65*, ed. Michael Beschloss (New York: Simon and Schuster, 2001), 215.

12. Transcript, President's News Conference, 28 July 1965, *Public Papers of the President: Lyndon B. Johnson, 1965*, 2 vols. (Washington, D.C.: Government Printing Office, 1966), 2: 801 (hereafter *Johnson Public Papers*); Chester Pach, *The Johnson Years* (New York: Facts on File, 2006), xviii–xix; Robert Dallek, *Flawed Giant: Lyndon Johnson and His Times, 1961–1973* (New York: Oxford University Press, 1998), 235–36, 275–77; Daniel Ellsberg, *Secrets: A Memoir of Vietnam and the Pentagon Papers* (New York: Viking, 2002), 94–97; Herring, *America's Longest War*, 164–66.

13. Randall B. Woods, *LBJ: Architect of American Ambition* (New York: Free Press, 2006), 617; Kathleen J. Turner, *Lyndon Johnson's Dual War: Vietnam and the Press* (Chicago: University of Chicago Press, 1985), 141, 176–77, 200–203; Burns W. Roper, "What Public Opinion Polls Said," in *Big Story: How the American Press and Television Reported and Interpreted the Crisis of Tet 1968 in Vietnam and Washington*, 2 vols., ed. Peter Braestrup (Boulder: Westview Press, 1977), 1: 700; memorandum of meeting, 19 August 1965, *FRUS, 1964–68*, 3: 338.

14. Report by Safer, CBS, TV-6412.2, Museum of Broadcast Communications, Chicago.

15. The account of the Safer incident is based on Pach, "And That's the Way It Was," 101–3; and Chester J. Pach Jr., "The War on Television: TV News, the Johnson Administration, and Vietnam," in *A Companion to the Vietnam War*, ed. Marilyn B. Young and Robert Buzzanco (Malden, Mass.: Blackwell, 2002), 451–52. For the Johnson profanity, see David Halberstam, *The Powers That Be* (New York: Laurel, 1979), 683.

16. Author interview with Morley Safer, 23 July 2001, Chester, Conn. See also Pach, "From Vietnam to Iraq," 130.

17. For detailed discussions of these news reports, see Pach, "And That's the Way It Was," 94–105, and Pach, "The War on Television," 453–55.

18. Notes of meeting, 17 December 1965, *FRUS, 1964–1968*, 3: 644–45; comments by Jennings, ABC, and Cronkite, CBS, both 17 December 1965, A20, Weekly News Summary, Assistant Secretary of Defense for Public Affairs, Record Group 330, National Archives at College Park, Md. (hereafter DODWNS).

19. Roper, "Emerging Profiles of Television and Other Mass Media," folder Televi-

sion, box 421, Panzer Files; Doris Kearns, *Lyndon Johnson and the American Dream* (New York: Harper and Row, 1976), 7, 246–47; David Culbert, "Johnson and the Media," in *Exploring the Johnson Years,* ed. Robert A. Divine (Austin: University of Texas Press, 1981), 214, 219, 222; author interview with Robert Pierpoint, 1 October 1999, Bodega Bay, Calif.; author interview with David Brinkley, 22 February 2000, Bal Harbour, Fla. For an elaboration of the themes in this paragraph, see Pach, "The War on Television," 455–56.

20. Dallek, *Flawed Giant,* 452–53; memorandum, "Dinner at Home of Sen. Henry Jackson," 10 March 1967, folder 1, box 4, Rather Papers; Remarks in Baltimore to Delegates to the National Convention of the United States Jaycees, 27 June 1967, *Johnson Public Papers, 1967,* 2: 656.

21. Memorandum, Fred Panzer to president, 16 June 1967, folder June 1967, and table, "Public Approval of LBJ's Handling of the War," 5 October 1967, folder October 1967, both in box 398, Panzer Files; *The Gallup Poll,* 1967: 2068–69; Roper, "What Public Opinion Polls Said," 1: 700.

22. Report by Murray Fromson, CBS, 12 July 1967, A103, DODWNS.

23. Report by Howard Tuckner, NBC, 13 July 1967, A103, DODWNS.

24. "Radio-TV Defense Dialog," 28 June and 3–4 July 1967, folder 4, box 12, Papers of Robert Goralski, State Historical Society of Wisconsin, Madison; Gary Paul Gates, *Air Time: The Inside Story of CBS News* (New York: Harper and Row, 1978), 42.

25. Comments by David Brinkley, NBC, 7 and 10 July 1967; and comments by Peter Jennings, ABC, 10 July 1967, both in A103, DODWNS.

26. *The Pentagon Papers: The Defense Department History of United States Decision-making on Vietnam,* Senator Gravel edition, 4 vols. (Boston: Beacon Press, 1971), 4: 528.

27. The President's News Conference, 13 July 1967, *Johnson Public Papers, 1967,* 2: 695 [emphasis added].

28. William C. Westmoreland, *A Soldier Reports* (Garden City, N.Y.: Doubleday, 1976), 230; Robert Buzzanco, *Masters of War: Military Dissent and Politics in the Vietnam Era* (New York: Cambridge University Press, 1996), 290–96; *Pentagon Papers,* 4: 514–28; reports by Frank Reynolds, ABC, 13 July 1967, and comments by David Brinkley, NBC, 12 July, both in A103, DODWNS.

29. Notes of meeting, 12 July 1967, *FRUS, 1964–68,* 5: 602; memorandum, Marks to president, 13 July 1967, vol. 34 [1 of 2], box 17, Memos to President, National Security File (hereafter NSF—Memos to President), LBJL; notes, General Westmoreland's History Notes, 6–18 August 1967, folder 20 History File I, box 13, Papers of William C. Westmoreland, LBJL.

30. Memorandum, Marks to president, 13 July 1967, vol. 34 [1 of 2], box 17, NSF—Memos to President; author interview with Katzenbach 26 June 2001, Princeton, N.J.; transcript, Zorthian oral history interview, 1: 24, LBJL; Westmoreland, *A Soldier Reports,* 419–22; notes of meeting, 12 July 1967; notes of meeting, 13 July 1967; and telegram 1954, Bunker to president, 26 July 1967, *FRUS, 1964–68,* 5: 602, 613, 640.

31. Author interview with David Schoumacher, 26 June 2002, Hume, Va.

32. Ibid.; draft memorandum, McNamara to president, 19 May 1967; and notes of meeting, 12 July 1967, both in *FRUS, 1964–68*, 5: 425, 601.

33. Report by Schoumacher, CBS, 31 May 1967, A97; and report by Schoumacher, CBS, 15 September 1967, A113, both in DODWNS; author interview with Schoumacher.

34. Schoumacher remembered that the argument was with Walt. But it may have been with Robert Cushman, Walt's successor, who became commander of the III MAF on 1 June, not long after Schoumacher arrived in South Vietnam.

35. Author interview with Schoumacher.

36. Author interview with David Burrington, 19 October 2001, Hillsborough, Calif.

37. Report by Burrington, NBC, 18 July 1967, A104, DODWNS.

38. Ibid.; memorandum, Harry McPherson to George Christian, 18 July 1967, folder Vietnam 1967 (Part 2) [3 of 3], box 29, Office Files of Harry C. McPherson, LBJL; memorandum, McPherson to president, 13 June 1967, *FRUS: 1964–68*, 5: 499–500.

39. Author interview with Bert Quint, 6 July 2001, Langley, Va.; report by Quint, CBS, 8 August 1967, A107, DODWNS.

40. Memorandum, Benchley to Christian, 12 August 1967, folder Television Comments, box 3, Office Files of Peter B. Benchley, WHCF, LBJL; transcript, Benchley oral history interview, 1, 38–44, LBJL; memorandum, Christian to President, 14 August 1967, folder Chronological August 1967, box 6, Office Files of George Christian (hereafter Christian Files), LBJL.

41. *New York Times*, 7 August 1967.

42. Ibid.; author interview with Zorthian, 5 December 2001, Washington, D.C.; transcript, Zorthian oral history interview, 2: 17–18, 4: 10, LBJL; Dallek, *Flawed Giant*, 475–76; cables, Wheeler to Westmoreland, 11 August 1967, and Westmoreland to Wheeler, 12 August 1967, vol. 37 [2 of 2], box 20, NSF—Memos to President, LBJL.

43. Memorandum, Johnson to Christian, 15 August 1967, PR 18, Confidential File, box 83, LBJL; memorandum, Christian to President, 22 August 1967, folder August 1967 [4 of 5], box 23, Handwriting File, LBJL.

44. Memorandum, Jones to president, 19 August 1967, Meeting Notes File, box 1, LBJL; telegram, Rostow to Bunker, 27 September 1967, vol. 43 [1 of 2], box 23, NSF—Memos to President, LBJL; Larry Berman, *Lyndon Johnson's War: The Road to Stalemate in Vietnam* (New York: Oxford University Press, 1989), 84–85; Pach, "The War on Television," 458–59.

45. Notes of meeting with Australian broadcast group, 20 September 1967, folder Sept. 1967—Meetings with Correspondents, box 3, Meeting Notes File, LBJL; notes of the president's meeting with Harry Reasoner, CBS, 14 August 1967; and notes of the president's meeting with educators from Cambridge, Mass., Colleges and Universities, 26 September 1967, both in box 1, Tom Johnson's Notes of Meetings, LBJL.

46. Notes of president's meeting with McNamara, Rusk, Rostow, and Christian, 4 October 1967, and notes of meeting with Saigon advisors, 21 November 1967, both in *FRUS, 1964–68*, 5: 856–60, 1150–59.

47. LBJ News Conference, 17 November 1967, WHCA tape no. 79, LBJL; letter, Sidey to president, 17 November 1967, folder November 1967 [4 of 4], box 26, Handwriting File, LBJL; memo, Fleming to president, 17 November 1967, folder Network Pool II, box 4, Christian files; *Johnson Public Papers, 1967*, 2:1048–49; Turner, *Lyndon Johnson's Dual War*, 204–5.

48. Remarks by Brinkley, NBC, 21 November 1967, A122, DODWNS.

49. "Who, What, When, Where, Why: Eisenhower and Bradley on Vietnam," CBS, 28 November 1967, tape 86, WHCA One-Inch Series, 1966–69, LBJL.

50. John Laurence, *The Cat from Hué: A Vietnam War Story* (New York: Public Affairs, 2002), 433–45; author interview with Laurence, 28 June 2002, Washington, D.C.; Michael J. Arlen, *Living-Room War* (New York: Penguin Books, 1982), 80–85.

51. Report by Laurence, CBS, 26 October 1967, A118, DODWNS; Laurence, *Cat from Hué*, 468–69.

52. Author interview with Laurence.

53. Roper, "What Public Opinion Polls Said," 1: 695, 700; Gallup, *The Gallup Poll*, 3: 2074, 2075, 2078, 2091, 2096; Dallek, *Flawed Giant*, 499; Chester J. Pach Jr., "Tet on TV: U.S. Nightly News Reporting and Presidential Policy Making," in *1968: The World Transformed*, ed. Carole Fink, Philipp Gassert, and Detlef Junker (New York: Cambridge University Press, 1998), 61–62. "Progress is our most important product" was General Electric's corporate slogan.

54. Report by Robert Schakne, CBS, 5 February 1968, A133, DODWNS; Don Oberdorfer, *Tet! The Turning Point in the Vietnam War* (Garden City, N.Y.: Doubleday, 1971; New York: Da Capo, 1984), 158; "Who, What, When, Where, Why: Report from Vietnam by Walter Cronkite," CBS, 27 February 1968, A596, Museum of Television and Radio, New York. For a detailed discussion of the news coverage of Tet, see Pach, "Tet on TV," 55–81.

55. Author interview with Christian, 25 August 1999, Austin, Texas; Ronald H. Spector, *After Tet: The Bloodiest Year in Vietnam* (New York: Vintage Books, 1993), 19; Woods, *LBJ*, 832; President's Address to the Nation, 31 March 1968, *Johnson Public Papers, 1968–69*, 1: 469–76.

56. Remarks in Chicago before the National Association of Broadcasters, 1 April 1968, *Johnson Public Papers, 1968–69*, 1: 482–86; Pach, "The War on Television," 463.

57. Pach, "Television," 3: 552–53.

58. Bernard Goldberg, *Bias: A CBS Insider Exposes How the Media Distort the News* (Washington, D.C.: Regnery, 2002).

59. Pach, "From Vietnam to Iraq," 125–26.

60. Notes of meeting, 21 November 1967, *FRUS, 1964–68*, 5: 1052; agenda, written by Rostow, breakfast meeting with the president, Tuesday, 21 November 1967, vol. 51 [1 of 2], box 25, NSF—Memos to the President, LBJL.

8

SELLING STAR WARS

Ronald Reagan's Strategic Defense Initiative

Paul S. Boyer

March 23, 1983, was a big evening at the White House. The dinner guests included the Joint Chiefs of Staff, Secretary of State George Shultz, the physicist Edward Teller, and other scientists. After greeting the assembled notables, President Ronald Reagan excused himself and went to the Oval Office to deliver a national address on his military budget. The guests, along with the rest of the nation, watched him on television.

Near the end of a speech calling for massive increases in military spending, Reagan, to the surprise of almost everyone, made a startling proposal. The United States, he said, should launch "a comprehensive and intensive" program to develop an antimissile system to defend the nation against nuclear attack. Moving beyond the familiar civil defense approach of saving lives once the missiles fell, Reagan advocated a far bolder strategy: to destroy incoming missiles in flight. With such a system in place, he suggested, nuclear weapons would become "impotent and obsolete."[1]

Rejoining his guests, Reagan basked in their enthusiastic praise of his proposal. The public response proved equally positive. "The reports are in on last night's speech," Reagan wrote happily in his diary the next day. "The biggest return—phone calls, wires, etc., on any speech so far and running heavily in my favor."[2]

The Strategic Defense Initiative and the Selling of a Renewed Cold War

Reagan's proposal, officially called the Strategic Defense Initiative (SDI), dramatically illustrates the power of a president to shape the public discourse on issues of war and peace. It grabbed the attention of not only the military establishment, arms control advocates, nuclear strategists, and members of Congress but also the media and the general public. At one stroke, observed the Union of Concerned Scientists, Reagan had "changed the entire landscape of space weapons debate. . . . [S]eldom has an arms issue moved as quickly from the periphery to the center of the policy arena." In a 1985 opinion poll, 84 percent of Americans said they had heard of Reagan's proposal.[3]

SDI had roots in Reagan's own background and in more than thirty years of strategic debate. This essay will examine this background as well as the debate the proposal triggered and its profound long-term effects. But the speech also helped build public support for the policies of an administration bent on a massive military buildup—including nuclear weapons—and on escalating the Cold War after years of détente. Further, Reagan's proposal directly targeted the Nuclear Weapons Freeze Campaign, a powerful grassroots challenge to his agenda. It is to this context that we turn first.

Ronald Reagan's election in 1980 put a veteran Cold Warrior in the White House and brought to power a group of intensely anticommunist Cold War hawks and neoconservatives (ex-Democrats who had become hard-line Cold Warriors). Reagan and his administration were deeply skeptical of key elements of U.S. foreign policy that had occurred since the 1960s: détente with the Soviet Union; arms control negotiations with Moscow; and the deterrence principle embodied in the 1972 Antiballistic Missile (ABM) Treaty. With the Soviets intent on world domination, they believed, America must build up its supposedly deteriorating military arsenal. The 1980 Republican platform promised to return America to "the position of military superiority that the American people demand." To achieve this, Reagan proposed spending $1.6 trillion in a five-year program of military buildup.[4] This included supremacy in nuclear weapons and a willingness to use them. Administration strategists spoke of "prevailing" in a "protracted" nuclear war. Reagan's first secretary of state, General Alexander Haig, refused to endorse a "no first use" pledge and spoke of a nuclear response "for demonstrative purposes" if Russia threatened Western Europe. This included supremacy in nuclear weapons and a willingness to use them.[5]

The heads of the Arms Control and Disarmament Agency under Reagan, Eugene Rostow and Kenneth Adelman, were hard-liners wholly unsympathetic to arms control. Pentagon hawks included Secretary of Defense Caspar Weinberger and top officials Richard Armitage, Richard Perle, Fred Iklé, and Paul Wolfowitz. Weinberger presided over the military buildup, including more nuclear warheads, strategic bombers, ICBMs, and nuclear-armed submarines. The piñata of new weaponry included 100 MX missiles (seventy-ton ICBMs each with ten independently targeted nuclear warheads) and 3,000 low-flying, air-launched cruise missiles. In congressional testimony, Weinberger called for expanding the nation's arsenal "across the full range of plausible nuclear war–fighting scenarios with the Soviet Union." This buildup, in turn, reflected the administration's larger strategic objective, formalized in National Security Council documents, of pursuing the Cold War more aggressively, rolling back Soviet power, and destabilizing the Moscow regime itself. Not merely *containing* Soviet power, but *prevailing* over it, by a full panoply of military, economic, diplomatic, and propaganda means, became the new mantra. These goals, in turn, precisely matched those of the Committee on the Present Danger, a shadowy but influential private group of Cold War hawks, several of whose leaders held high positions in the Reagan administration.[6]

Given its goal of military and nuclear supremacy, the Reagan administration was intensely hostile to the theory of nuclear deterrence, the cornerstone of the relative stability that characterized U.S.-Soviet relations from the mid-1960s to the late 1970s. According to this doctrine, known as Mutual Assured Destruction, often shortened to MAD (especially by its critics), the surest way to prevent a nuclear World War III was for the nuclear superpowers, the United States and the Soviet Union, to refrain from developing a full-scale defense of their civilian populations against nuclear attack. The knowledge that one's own society was vulnerable to counterattack, so went the logic of MAD, would deter either side from launching a nuclear first strike. This doctrine rested not only on the premise that no nation would start a war that could end in its own destruction but also on the assumption, articulated as early as 1945–46 by the strategist Bernard Brodie and many atomic scientists, that no defense against atomic attack was possible. J. Robert Oppenheimer summed up this belief in 1953 when he compared the United States and the Soviet Union to "two scorpions in a bottle, each capable of killing the other, but only at the risk of his own life."[7]

As a nuclear strategy, MAD never became wholly dominant. Some strategists and military figures continued to view nuclear war as winnable, to argue for research on defensive weaponry, and (as some still do) to promote "tactical" nuclear weapons for combat use. The civil defense programs of the 1950s and 1960s, featuring fallout shelters and school drills, violated the logic of Mutual Assured Destruction. Nevertheless, by the 1960s most U.S. policymakers accepted the MAD deterrence theory.[8]

Moscow also grasped the logic of MAD, and this principle underlay the 1972 ABM Treaty limiting both sides to two missile defense systems each, one defending the capital and the other protecting one Intercontinental Ballistic Missile (ICBM) launch site. Beyond that, each nation pledged "not to develop, test, or deploy" missile defense systems of any kind.[9] Each side, in short, left most of its population vulnerable, as a tacit pledge never to launch a nuclear first strike.

For Reagan and his top policymakers, the whole concept underlying the ABM Treaty was anathema. They believed that it unnecessarily tied the hands of the United States militarily and accepted stalemate, rather than U.S. victory, as the Cold War's ultimate outcome. And with their profound distrust of the Soviets, they were convinced that Moscow could not be trusted to abide by any agreement, including the ABM Treaty. In memos and media interviews in 1981–82, Secretary of Defense Weinberger called for a full-scale antiballistic missile system—a clear violation of the ABM Treaty and the deterrence doctrine underlying it. In 1982 congressional testimony, Richard Perle, assistant secretary of defense for international security policy, argued that the ABM Treaty should be "reinterpreted" or, if the Soviets objected, abrogated entirely.[10]

The overall tone of the early Reagan administration suggested a readiness to contemplate nuclear war in pursuit of U.S. national interests. Pentagon official Thomas K. Jones claimed that "with enough shovels" to dig shelters, Americans could survive a nuclear war relatively easily. Reporting this comment in his 1982 book, *With Enough Shovels: Reagan, Bush, and Nuclear War*, journalist Robert Scheer commented: "What is truly astounding about my conversation with T. K. is not simply that one highly placed official in the Reagan Administration is so horribly innocent of the effects of nuclear war. More frightening is that T. K. Jones's views are all too typical of the thinking of those at the core of the Reagan Administration."[11]

Much evidence confirms Scheer's conclusion. In a 1982 interview, Caspar Weinberger cited Bible prophecy to support his view that the world could end at any time. Said Weinberger: "I have read the Book of Revelation and, yes, I believe the world is going to end—by an act of God, I hope—but every day I think that time is running out." Reagan himself, in interviews with Robert Scheer during the 1980 campaign, saw nuclear war with the Soviets as a possibility and refused to rule out a preemptive U.S. nuclear strike.[12]

With nuclear war on the table, nuclear defense became crucial. Missile defense research became U.S. policy in a National Security Council document signed by Reagan in May 1982. This document, in turn, was based on a high-level interagency report, "U.S. National Security Strategy," which declared: "The United States should pursue the development of effective

BMD [ballistic missile defense] technology, evaluate its role in our overall strategic posture, and preserve the options to modify or withdraw from international agreements [i.e., the ABM Treaty] that would limit the deployment of a BMD system."[13]

Given the administration's preoccupation with nuclear war, traditional civil defense drew attention as well. Publicizing civil defense plans served two purposes: to reassure Americans that they could survive a nuclear attack and to convince the Soviets that U.S. nuclear threats were serious. After years on the back burner, civil defense received high priority in the early Reagan years. Rather than fallout shelters, the focus now was on crisis relocation planning (CRP): moving entire urban populations to nearby towns in a nuclear emergency. Tucson's designated relocation center was the small border town of Nogales, Arizona, whose hardware store, with two bathrooms, was assigned to shelter 542 evacuees. Far from reassuring the public, the CRP program heightened anxieties. Writes historian Dee Garrison: "[S]even states and 120 localities—home to about 90 million people—formally refused to participate in CRP. . . . In community after community . . . the anti–civil-defense protest grew louder and more visible."[14]

The talk of civil defense, coupled with the administration's bellicose tone, including talk of nuclear war–fighting strategies, stirred fear and protests. In the later 1970s, concern about the safety of nuclear power plants, deepened by the 1979 Jane Fonda film *China Syndrome* and the accident at the Three Mile Island plant in Pennsylvania, had stimulated antinuclear activism. By 1981, in response to the administration's saber rattling, the focus shifted from nuclear power to nuclear war. Amid mounting alarm over the military buildup and heightened Cold War tensions, Jonathan Schell's *The Fate of the Earth* (1982), a meditation on the implications of global thermonuclear war, published in the *New Yorker* and then in book form, became a best seller.[15]

The activism coalesced in the Nuclear Weapons Freeze Campaign, which was originated by Randall Forsberg, a doctoral student in political science at the Massachusetts Institute of Technology who had studied disarmament issues at the Stockholm International Peace Research Institute. While arms control talks proceeded, Forsberg proposed, the nuclear powers should adopt a verifiable moratorium on nuclear weapons research, testing, and deployment. Beginning with resolutions passed by New England town meetings in 1981, the movement quickly spread. A June 1982 rally in New York's Central Park drew an estimated 750,000 people. That August, a Freeze resolution introduced by Massachusetts Democrat Edward Markey failed in the House of Representatives by only one vote. In November, fifteen state legislatures, including Massachusetts, New York, California, Michigan, and Wisconsin, passed Freeze resolutions. Perturbed by this grassroots uprising, Reagan criticized the Freeze in several speeches, and National Security Advisor Robert McFarlane coordinated an administration campaign to blunt its impact.[16]

Problems in devising a secure basing system for the MX missiles caused the administration further headaches. As a series of implausible basing schemes, including a circular railroad track, roused public ridicule, congressional skepticism mounted. In December 1982, the House of Representatives voted to terminate the MX program. With a recession and with unemployment worsening the public mood, Reagan's approval rating fell to an anemic 35 percent by early 1983.[17]

These accumulating problems as Reagan tried to sell his costly military buildup to an uneasy public constitute the immediate political context of the SDI speech. In a December 1982 meeting with the Joint Chiefs of Staff (JCS), Reagan asked: "What if we begin to move away from our total reliance on offense to deter a nuclear attack and moved toward a relatively greater reliance on defense?" Knowing Reagan's indirect management style, the Joint Chiefs accurately took this to be an order. Prodded by National Security Advisor William Clark and his then deputy, Robert McFarlane, Admiral James Watkins, the Chief of Naval Operations (having independently concluded that MAD was "immoral" and "a political loser"), drafted a proposal for missile defense research. The JCS approved Watkins's draft and incorporated it in a February 11, 1983, report to Reagan. Meanwhile, Admiral John Poindexter of the NSC organized a study by military scientists. It concluded (Poindexter later recalled) that despite "lots of problems," missile defense was within "the realm of possibility" and "worth looking into." Seizing on these reports initiated by himself, Reagan told McFarlane to draft a proposal for a missile defense program for his upcoming speech on the military budget.[18]

Shockwaves erupted as the hastily prepared draft circulated. McFarlane urged a delay until the Allies could be consulted. White House science advisor George Keyworth was dismayed, since a recent study group on missile defense had expressed great doubts. General John W. Vessey Jr., chairman of the JCS, later recalled: "We were surprised that it went that fast. . . . [M]ore study had to be done. But it wasn't in the cards to stop the speech. The White House was full speed ahead." Even supporters of the idea favored more consultation before a public announcement, and they opposed describing missile defense as a step toward nuclear disarmament. Secretary of State George Shultz (having replaced Alexander Haig in July 1982) protested the implications for deterrence strategy and warned of Moscow's reaction. Caspar Weinberger, in Europe for a NATO meeting, did not see the draft, but Richard Perle, alarmed over the probable reaction of NATO allies, spent a frantic night on the phone trying to derail Reagan's announcement. Even Admiral Watkins, a key figure in the process, considered the speech premature and "unfortunate." Recalled George Keyworth: "I have never seen such opposition to anything, as that which I saw . . . during those few days at the White House."[19]

Ignoring the protests and continuing to stage-manage the process, Reagan ordered McFarlane to keep SDI "tightly under wraps" to avoid premature public or congressional criticism. On March 23, Reagan faced the cameras and delivered his blockbuster announcement. The sudden interjection of missile defense with all its promise into the public discourse bears witness to Reagan's shrewd political sense. Recalled McFarlane: "Reagan's view of the political payoff was sufficient rationale as far as he was concerned. By that I mean providing the American people with an appealing answer to their fears [by telling them] . . . 'For the first time in the nuclear age, I'm doing something to save your lives. I am telling you that we can get rid of nuclear weapons.'"[20]

The Roots of the Strategic Defense Initiative

While Reagan's proposal clearly served his immediate political purposes, it did not come out of the blue. The Pentagon's missile defense research program, dating to 1946, had gained urgency when the Soviets developed ICBMs and launched the Sputnik satellite in 1957. The Advance Research Projects Agency (ARPA), established in 1957, investigated laser weaponry and other antimissile defenses. One early plan, called Ballistic Missile Boost Intercepts, bore the appealing acronym BAMBI. In the early 1960s, Air Force Chief of Staff Curtis LeMay predicted that "directed energy weapons" would soon be able to destroy incoming missiles. Research continued despite the ABM Treaty, and by the early 1980s both technical journals and the popular media were discussing missile defense.[21]

High-visibility advocates included the émigré Hungarian physicist Edward Teller, Wyoming senator Malcolm Wallop, and retired army general Daniel Graham. Teller, Manhattan Project veteran, "father of the H-bomb," and a key figure in the Atomic Energy Commission's 1953 removal of J. Robert Oppenheimer's security clearance, was long prominent in nuclear affairs. Deeply distrustful of the Russians, Teller had successfully maneuvered to exclude underground tests from the 1963 Nuclear Test Ban Treaty and had later sought ways to circumvent it.[22] He was also a longtime nuclear defense enthusiast. In *The Legacy of Hiroshima* (1962) Teller had argued for the utility of nuclear weapons to repel Soviet aggression and for deploying antimissile defenses against a possible Soviet attack. In 1967, when then-governor Reagan toured the University of California's Lawrence Radiation Laboratory (later the Lawrence Livermore National Laboratory), Teller arranged for his benefit a seminar on nuclear defense. Predictably he opposed the ABM Treaty and the balance-of-power premises underlying deterrence theory. In the late 1970s, when Lawrence Livermore scientists concluded that powerful X-ray lasers could be created as a by-product of nuclear explosions, Teller believed he had found the ideal antimissile technology. Meeting with Reagan at the White House in September 1982, Teller urged funding for X-ray laser research.[23]

Government scientists and policy advisors proved skeptical, however. In 1982, White House science advisor George Keyworth (a Teller protégé) set up a panel headed by physicist Edward Frieman to investigate Teller's proposals. On the grounds of both expense and technical feasibility, the panel concluded that lasers held little promise as a military technology. Others warned that a missile defense involving nuclear explosions was a political nonstarter. Undeterred, Teller insisted that, with a Manhattan Project–like commitment, weaponized X-ray lasers could be deployed in space within five years. William F. Buckley, host of TV's *Firing Line,* gave Teller a public forum for his ideas.[24]

Senator Wallop, a conservative Republican and another missile defense enthusiast, was, in turn, influenced by Angelo Codevilla, a young Senate staffer whose interest in missile defense arose from his conviction that nuclear war with Russia was not only winnable but justifiable to end the communist threat. Under Codevilla's tutelage, Wallop published a 1979 article arguing that twenty-four orbiting battle stations armed with chemical lasers could destroy most ICBMs in a Soviet attack. Wallop organized briefings for senators where military contractors presented missile defense ideas. Again, however, most strategists proved skeptical. A Pentagon study concluded that 1,444 orbiting battle stations costing $1.5 trillion would be required to provide a secure defense system. "From the point of view of the defense community," writes Frances FitzGerald, "the project had a lunatic tinge to it." Nevertheless, Wallop besieged the White House with proposals and late in 1982 met directly with Reagan and Secretary Weinberger.[25]

Daniel Graham had served as deputy director of the CIA and military advisor to Reagan's 1976 and 1980 presidential campaigns. In 1981, funded by the conservative Heritage Foundation, Graham founded High Frontier, Inc., an advocacy group promoting space-based missile defense. In *High Frontier: A New National Strategy* (1982), Graham insisted that "a global ballistic missile defense system is well within our present technological capabilities and can be deployed in space in this decade." In 1981–82, High Frontier representatives met with top White House advisors and on several occasions with Reagan himself. In a now familiar pattern, however, an Air Force review panel dismissed Graham's scheme. (The introduction for his book by science fiction writer Robert Heinlein may have increased the skepticism.) In November 1982, Weinberger bluntly wrote Graham: "[W]e are unwilling to commit this nation to a course which calls for . . . a capability that does not currently exist." Nevertheless, Graham and his group, along with Teller and Wallop, continued to push their ideas.[26]

While these high-visibility advocates stimulated interest in missile defense among the public and in Washington's corridors of power, historians Frances FitzGerald and Paul Lettow have downplayed their influence and focused instead on how Reagan's rhetorical style, movie background, and vague but real antinuclear beliefs came into play as he faced the challenge of persuading Congress and the nation to support massive increases in military spending and a more confrontational approach to the Soviet Union.

A seasoned public speaker, Reagan welcomed ideas that had dramatic appeal, and he intuitively grasped that the image of a nation secure under a protective nuclear defense umbrella was such an idea. But the promise that SDI could render nuclear weapons "impotent and obsolete" was no mere rhetorical trope for Reagan. His view of nuclear weapons was deeply ambivalent. On one hand, he could discuss quite coolly the prospect of nuclear war with the Soviets; he never challenged those in his inner circle who argued that a U.S. first use of nuclear weapons would be acceptable in certain circumstances; and, as we have seen, his military buildup contemplated a major expansion of the U.S. nuclear arsenal. Nevertheless, as Paul Lettow has argued, hatred of nuclear weapons was also a part of Reagan's worldview from 1945 onward, even surviving his evolution from New Deal Democrat to conservative Republican. As he wrote in his memoirs, not entirely disingenuously, "For the eight years I was president, I never let my dream of a nuclear-free world fade from my mind." Reagan's public statements, diaries, and private letters, as well as the testimony of advisors, reinforce the point. Recalled John Poindexter of the National Security Council: "[Reagan] saw nuclear weapons as very evil and MAD as an evil policy." ACDA director Kenneth Adelman agreed: "He *hated* nuclear weapons."[27] Implausible as it may seem, Reagan's deep-seated hatred of nuclear weapons, along with the obvious political utility of the SDI speech, is relevant to understanding his SDI proposal.

Reagan's nuclear abolitionism, while sincere, also involved wishful thinking, reflecting his tendency to blur reality and Hollywood fantasy. Along with its general cinematic appeal, SDI also resonated with a specific movie. In 1940, Reagan had starred as FBI agent Brass Bancroft in a Warner Brothers B movie, *Murder in the Air,* whose plot uncannily anticipated SDI: U.S. scientists have developed a secret weapon, the "inertia projector," that can vaporize enemy aircraft. In words echoed in Reagan's SDI speech, a scientist excitedly describes the new weapon: "It not only makes the United States invincible in war, but in so doing promises to become the greatest force for world peace ever discovered." As the actor-turned-president encountered proposals for missile defense, the "inertia projector" may well have stirred in his memory.[28]

Building the Case for SDI: Discrediting the Nuclear Weapons Freeze Campaign

Reagan's SDI proposal, although only a brief coda to a speech defending his military budget and stoking Cold War fears, nevertheless offered an ingeniously crafted set of arguments. In building his case for missile defense, the president exploited deep ethical ambiguities in the prevailing doctrine of nuclear deterrence, Mutual Assured Destruction, or MAD. The critics of deterrence theory included not only Cold War hawks who believed that nuclear war was winnable but also religious leaders and others troubled by a strategy based on the fear—and the threat—of retaliation. The U.S. Catholic bishops expressed this ethical queasiness in a 1983 pastoral letter, *The Challenge of Peace.* Urging "a moral about-face" on nuclear issues, the bishops called on the world to "summon the moral courage and technical means to say no to nuclear conflict, no to weapons of mass destruction." Even a nuclear arsenal maintained for deterrent purposes, they went on, offered no "long-term basis for peace" and should be viewed with "profound skepticism." To be even minimally acceptable, they concluded, the MAD doctrine must be combined with serious efforts toward nuclear disarmament.[29]

Reagan echoed this theme. A strategic doctrine based on "the specter of retaliation," he said, offered "a sad commentary on the human condition." Surely "the human spirit must be capable of rising above dealing with other nations and human beings by threatening their existence." Ignoring MAD's goal of *deterrence*, Reagan dwelt on the scenario in which deterrence failed and the United States, having suffered a nuclear attack, would devastate the Soviet Union in a retaliatory spasm. "Would it not be better to save lives than to avenge them?" he said. "Are we not capable of demonstrating our peaceful intentions by applying . . . our ingenuity to achieving a truly lasting stability?" A missile defense program that could render all nuclear weapons "impotent and obsolete," he insisted, would "offer new hope for our children in the twenty-first century."[30]

Reagan also evoked powerful and deep-running themes in many citizens' perception of the United States: as a nation historically protected from foreign dangers, as a global leader in technological know-how, and as a peace-loving country playing a benign role in world affairs. Each of these themes merits attention.

SDI, Reagan suggested, could restore the nation's historic sense of security. Protected by oceans on the east and west, the United States had faced little threat from its northern or southern neighbors. Not since the War of 1812 had foreign troops menaced the U.S. mainland. The atomic bomb changed all that. The same fate that befell Hiroshima, Americans quickly realized in 1945, could now strike any U.S. city. Magazines published scenarios of terrorists secretly assembling an atomic bomb in a major city and then holding the nation hostage by threatening to detonate it. As the Soviets deployed ICBMs that could reach U.S. targets in minutes, the terror intensified.

In proposing SDI, Reagan exploited this sense of vulnerability. His military advisors, he said, had described "the bleakness of the future before us." But in a characteristic move, he transmuted fear into hope. A nuclear shield "to intercept and destroy strategic ballistic missiles before they reached our own soil," he reassuringly suggested, could restore the nation's sense of security and provide "a vision of the future which offers hope."[31]

Reagan appealed also to another core component of America's self-image: the pride in technological mastery. Earlier generations had built railroads and skyscrapers, led the world in steel production, and pioneered mass production. President Truman had hailed the Manhattan Project as "the greatest achievement of organized science in history." Reagan implicitly evoked this history. "The very strengths in technology that spawned our great industrial base and that have given us the quality of life we enjoy today," he insisted, could surely now master the new technical challenge of deploying a national missile-defense system.[32]

Reagan invoked as well a still deeper theme in the national ideology: American innocence. Other nations might harbor sinister designs or initiate war for selfish aims, but America's purposes were pure. The point was crucial because it spoke directly to a central problem with SDI. In the "Alice in Wonderland" realm of nuclear strategy, "defensive" measures could readily be perceived as offensive. If the United States repudiated the ABM Treaty and pursued a full-scale nuclear defense while maintaining an increasingly lethal offensive nuclear capacity, this could be seen as laying the groundwork for a nuclear first strike. Indeed, Reagan acknowledged the dilemma: "I clearly recognize that defensive systems . . . raise certain problems and ambiguities," he said. "If paired with offensive systems, they can be viewed as fostering an aggressive policy, and no one wants that." Still, he left no doubt that while pursuing nuclear defense, he intended to preserve and even expand the offensive triad of nuclear bombers, ICBMs, and nuclear-armed submarines. While Reagan the visionary described a world free of nuclear weapons, Reagan the Cold Warrior made it clear that "modernizing [U.S.] strategic forces" remained a high priority.[33] Indeed, as we have seen, he devoted most of the speech to justifying his massive defense budget and denouncing proposed cuts by "liberals" in Congress. Describing the Soviet Union's alleged military superiority and expanding influence worldwide, he offered a long shopping list of new U.S. weapons systems, nuclear and conventional, after years of supposed neglect.

In part, this emphasis on maintaining the nation's offensive nuclear capacity was designed to reassure America's NATO allies, likely to be unnerved by a strategy that focused on defending America. Directly addressing this issue, Reagan declared: "As we pursue our goal of defensive technologies, we recognize that our allies rely upon our strategic offensive power to deter attacks against them. Their vital interests and ours are inextricably linked— their safety and ours are one. And no change in technology can or will alter that reality. We must and shall continue to honor our commitments."[34]

In seeking to dispel the suspicions aroused by developing a defensive shield while maintaining a first-strike capability, Reagan offered no answer other than to endorse arms control talks and assert the claim of national innocence, despite the fact that America had first used atomic bombs in 1945. "The United States . . . will never be an aggressor. . . . We seek neither military superiority nor political advantage. Our only purpose . . . is to search for ways to reduce the danger of nuclear war." In short: trust us;

SDI is simply another way "of demonstrating our peaceful intentions" and fulfilling the nation's mission of "changing the course of human history" for the better.[35]

Most nations proclaim their purity of purpose, but Reagan here invoked an especially potent theme in America's self-perception. He often quoted John Winthrop's image of America as a "city on a hill" (subtly enhancing it to "a *shining* city on a hill") and Pope Pius XII's post–World War II comment: "Into the hands of America, God has placed an afflicted mankind." Addressing the National Association of Evangelicals (NAE) two weeks before the SDI speech, he declared: "There is sin and evil in the world, and we're enjoined by Scripture and the Lord Jesus to oppose it with all our might." Only through a "great spiritual awakening," he assured the conservative Protestant leaders, "can we hope to survive this perilous century." As for the Soviets, he said, "Let us pray . . . that they will discover the joy of knowing God. But until they do, let us be aware that while they preach the supremacy of the state . . . over individual man . . . , they are the focus of evil in the modern world." Nuclear freeze advocates, he warned, failed to grasp the Cold War's moral dimension as a "struggle between right and wrong and good and evil."[36] The NAE and SDI speeches really share a single message: in the global Manichean conflict between good and evil, America's purposes are pure, as are any means that further those purposes—including the Strategic Defense Initiative.

Reagan's attack on the Freeze campaign in his NAE speech continued in the SDI address. Insisting that he shared the Freeze advocates' commitment to halting the nuclear arms race, he declared, "I know that all of you want peace, and so do I." But, he went on, "a freeze now would make us less, not more, secure and would raise, not reduce, the risks of war." Having dismissed the Freeze proposal, he pivoted abruptly and introduced his own vision for peace: the Strategic Defense Initiative. The tactic echoed Woodrow Wilson's response to pacifist critics as he led America into World War I: "What I am opposed to is not [their] feeling . . . , but their stupidity. My heart is with them, but my mind has contempt for them. I want peace, but I know how to get it, and they do not."[37]

Reagan's goal of derailing the Freeze campaign succeeded brilliantly. As debate shifted to the merits of SDI, the Freeze initiative faded. The far-right *Manchester* [N.H.] *Union Leader,* praising Reagan's blow against "the peacenik movement," quoted conservative activist Phyllis Schlafly: "[Reagan's proposal] can't kill a single human being, Russian or American; so there's nothing for the pacifists to be agitated about." A watered-down

Freeze resolution passed the House of Representatives in May 1983, but by then the campaign was fading. As the movement's historian commented in 1990: "Star Wars enabled the president and all sorts of freeze opponents to sound like antinuclear activists, and this marked the beginning of the end for the movement. . . . Ronald Reagan's landslide reelection in 1984 dealt the . . . movement a crippling blow."[38] Using the bully pulpit, Reagan had done what presidents do better than anyone else: redirected the public discourse on his own terms, leaving the Freeze campaign in the dust.

The Opposition Mobilizes: Strategists, Scientists, Editorialists, Cartoonists

In his diary the night of the SDI speech, Reagan basked in the praise of his White House guests, but also noted that several had predicted that SDI "would be a source of debate for some time to come."[39] They got that right! With Reagan's speech, missile defense, long the domain of think-tank theorists, burst into the public arena. Teller, Wallop, and Daniel Graham praised it, as did the physicist Robert Jastrow, an advisor to the U.S. space program. Within the administration, no one openly challenged SDI, despite the pre-speech uproar. Defense Secretary Weinberger and science advisor Keyworth endorsed the idea. A few expressed doubts. General Vessey of the Joint Chiefs, asked by ABC's Sam Donaldson if the Soviets would not simply build more ICBMs to circumvent SDI, replied cautiously: "Well, time alone will tell." A commission headed by diplomat Brent Scowcroft looking into the MX basing problem stated in an April 6 report to Reagan: "Current technology offer[s] no real promise of being able to defend the United States against massive nuclear attack in this century." But even hawkish military leaders and officials like Richard Perle with little enthusiasm for rendering nuclear weapons "impotent" got on board or remained discreetly silent, viewing SDI as a useful counter to the Freeze campaign and a potential bargaining chip in arms control talks with Moscow.[40]

Beyond the administration, however, the response in political, media, scientific, and diplomatic circles was deeply skeptical. The only thing Reagan had left out, said Congressman Tom Downey, a New York Democrat, "was that the Evil Empire was about to launch a Death Star against the United States." Congressman Edward Markey of Massachusetts blamed Edward Teller, who, he said, was promoting "a pinball outer-space war between the Force of Evil and the Force of Good." A *St. Louis Post-Dispatch* editorial voiced criticisms that would circulate widely in the months ahead. Behind

Reagan's "noble rhetoric," it said, SDI threatened "a major escalation of the arms race in [space,] the only environment that is now relatively free of military activity." If the United States actually deplored a missile defense system, the editorial went on, it "would certainly lead the Soviets to fear that, under the cover of such a system, the U.S. might launch a first-strike, a concern that would wreck the stability of the strategic balance." Reagan's real aim, the *Post-Dispatch* charged, was "to sell to the American people his extravagant military buildup."[41]

As for SDI's technical aspects, Reagan's address dealt only in generalities. As he wrote to a supporter: "Frankly I have no idea what the nature of such a defense might be. I simply asked our scientists to explore the possibility of developing such a defense." The JCS report to Reagan included "no program definition," recalled General Vessey, and simply proposed "that defenses might enter into the equation more than in the past."[42]

However, the missile defense ideas already being promoted by Teller, Graham, and others involved space-based lasers, and these became the focus of debate. Many scientists placed the odds of destroying an incoming missile by such means at close to zero—comparable to hitting a bullet with a bullet. Computer scientists emphasized the mind-boggling complexity of the necessary programming and the impossibility of testing it in real-world conditions. Even were the practical hurdles surmountable, argued MIT computer science professor Joseph Weizenbaum, SDI would still be a bad idea because it was "a step toward the militarization of space and society" and an example of politicians' tendency to seek "technological fixes" for "underlying human problems." MIT political scientist George Rathjens, on a CBS News special, called SDI "cruel and irresponsible," like giving cancer patients the quack medicine laetrile. In the *Washington Post*, former undersecretary of defense William J. Perry called weaponizing lasers "immensely complex" and astronomically costly. Repelling a full-scale missile attack, he asserted, would require hundreds of orbiting satellites programmed with pinpoint accuracy and armed with lasers ten times more powerful than any existing ones.[43]

The Union of Concerned Scientists (UCS), a Cambridge, Massachusetts, advocacy group, marshaled the technical case against SDI in *The Fallacy of Star Wars* (1984) and other publications. Through UCS efforts, over 700 members of the prestigious National Academy of Sciences signed a 1985 petition urging a ban on all weapons in space. (Daniel Graham's High Frontier struck back, calling UCS "a miniscule clutch of leftists with a hyperactive Xerox machine.") Nuclear strategists and diplomats, including six former secretaries of defense, joined in the attack, criticizing SDI as a threat to deterrence doctrine and to the ABM Treaty. Zbigniew Brzezinski, national security advisor to President Jimmy Carter, assembled their arguments in a 1986 book.[44]

Beyond technical and strategic analyses, the debate also unfolded in the media and the mass culture. As historian Edward Linenthal argues, policy debates involve "the effective use of public symbols," and the SDI controversy illustrates the point. Reagan deployed symbolic imagery, but so did the critics. Editorial writers, magazine editors, and political cartoonists joined the fray—most to oppose Reagan's initiative. The *Washington Post* cartoonist Herblock pictured SDI as a fairy tale in which missiles bounce harmlessly off a rainbowlike shield while carefree Americans cavort beneath.[45]

Media critics gleefully portrayed Reagan embracing sci-fi fantasies of laser weaponry and orbiting battle stations. A *Philadelphia Inquirer* cartoon pictured Reagan as a boy playing with his space toys while two adults, labeled "Arms Control" and "Science," look on in dismay. Like Congressmen Downey and Markey, they drew their imagery from the movies, TV, video games, and comic book superheroes. A *Time* cover portrayed Reagan with an array of futuristic weaponry and referred to his "video game" vision. A *Chicago Tribune* editorial invoked both an early video game and TV's *Star Trek*: "What . . . more *American* way out of the nuclear dilemma than to build Pac-Man weapons? . . . Warp speed, Mr. Spock!" In a *San Diego Union* cartoon, Reagan studies a *Space-Age Defense* manual with his "Crack Team of Experts": the homesick alien from the movie *ET* and the *Star Wars* droids R2D2 and C3PO. Another cartoonist pictured Reagan floating in space surrounded by Superman, Tinker Bell, Dumbo the Disney elephant, and a cow jumping over the moon. Humorist Art Buchwald imagined the chimpanzee from Reagan's 1951 movie *Bedtime for Bonzo* offering strategic advice.[46]

The critics' most effective mass-culture appropriation was to label SDI "Star Wars," from George Lucas's 1977 movie featuring apocalyptic combat in space. The nickname stuck, reducing Reagan's proposal to the level of Hollywood myth. Historian Paul Lettow, a Reagan admirer, calls this move "probably one of history's most successful instances of semantic subversion." While most SDI backers rejected the label, Phyllis Schlafly welcomed it, since Lucas's movie involved "the triumph of good over evil through adventure, courage, and confrontation." When William Safire of the *New York Times* sought to undermine the "Star Wars" label by inviting suggestions for a sexier acronym than "SDI," he received 600 entries, including WACKO (Wistful Attempt to Circumvent Killing Ourselves).[47]

Defenders of SDI Mobilize

SDI backers entered the fray as well. An umbrella organization launched by Daniel Graham, the Coalition for the Strategic Defense Initiative, claimed nearly 200 member groups. Right-wing organizations such as Joseph Coors's Heritage Foundation and Beverly LaHaye's Concerned Women for America warned of a worsening Soviet threat. These proponents echoed Reagan's themes, including the argument that SDI posed the kind of technological challenge Americans welcomed. "Research into exotic weapons is much further advanced than is generally realized," asserted William Buckley's *National Review.* "To imagine that technology can somehow be made to stand still goes against all historical experience." General James Abrahamson, named head of the Pentagon's SDI research program, declared: "I don't think anything in this country is technically impossible. We have a nation which indeed can produce miracles." Georgia congressman Newt Gingrich insisted that "a free people's ingenuity, daring, and courage" were equal to the SDI challenge. Reagan himself returned to this theme in promoting SDI in his 1985 State of the Union address. The only "barriers to our progress," he declared, were "those we ourselves erect."[48]

Those who argued that U.S. ingenuity could surely devise a workable missile defense cited specific precedents. Representative Ken Kramer, a Colorado Republican, called SDI "a Manhattan Project for peace." Caspar Weinberger argued on TV's *Meet the Press* that America's success in sending a man to the moon should quiet all doubts about SDI. General Abrahamson pointed to NASA's space shuttle program as proof of the "miracles" that Americans could achieve. When the space shuttle *Challenger* blew up on launch in 1986, President Reagan even wove this disaster into an argument for SDI, hailing the lost astronauts for their willingness to take risks—an inevitable part of technology's onward march. (To critics, the disaster underscored the danger of technological hubris.)[49]

SDI defenders, including Reagan, reiterated the theme of recovering America's sense of invulnerability. Addressing Maryland schoolchildren, Reagan called SDI "our modern-day Fort McHenry, [which] shielded Baltimore from cannon attack." Colorado's Ken Kramer called his SDI bill the "People Protection Act." Supporters cited the biblical exhortation: "If a strong man shall keep his house well guarded, he shall live in peace."[50]

Proponents also echoed Reagan's theme of American innocence. Weinberger on *Meet the Press* dismissed the idea that Moscow might interpret SDI as a U.S. move toward gaining a first-strike capability: "The Soviets have no need to worry," he said. "They know perfectly well that we will never launch a first strike." Weinberger's assistant, Richard Sybert, asked the same question by Robert Scheer, retorted: "Offense and aggression are not the American way."[51]

While warring cultural symbols influenced the debate, so did federal dollars distributed to military contractors, think tanks, and universities. A *Philadelphia Inquirer* cartoon portrayed Reagan as a fairy hovering over a university researcher and asking: "Do you believe in 'Star Wars'?" When the scientist says, "Er, not really," Reagan responds, "Some 'pixie dust' will cure that," and showers him with dollars. Another cartoonist pictured SDI researchers as "Star Whores."[52]

Reagan Wins the Battle for Public Opinion

Despite the barrage of criticism and ridicule, Reagan's invocation of resonant themes in America's self-image, and his confident assurances that missile defense could make America secure again with one dramatic technological breakthrough, succeeded where it counted: in the arena of public opinion. The president's panacea proved more appealing than the plan of the nuclear freeze advocates. As for the approach favored by the proponents of deterrence theory—patient negotiations, incremental arms control efforts, modest confidence-building measures—described by Edward Linenthal as "managerial stoicism,"[53] it lacked the drama of Reagan's soaring vision.

Reagan's approval ratings surged after his SDI speech (economic recovery helped as well), and in 1984 he won a crushing reelection victory over Walter Mondale. As for SDI specifically, numerous polls suggest overwhelming public support. In a September 1984 poll, 80 percent of Americans backed Reagan's proposal. Despite "considerable political and scientific controversy," wrote the pollster and statistician Ronald H. Hinckley in 1992, SDI "was popular with the American public from its inception." In a 1986 poll that asked which was "the better way to deter or avoid a nuclear war," 68 percent chose missile defense and only 29 percent chose deterrence theory as embodied in the ABM Treaty. Polling data also reveals that few Americans understood the details of arms control negotiations, deterrence theory, or the technical issues in the missile defense debate. In these circumstances, the amorphousness of Reagan's "vision" worked in its favor. As Hinckley writes, "Whether something is technologically feasible is not fertile ground for public discussion. . . . The public decided [about SDI] on the basis of broad perspectives on American know-how and not on the specific capabilities of the scientific community." In a 1985 *New York Times*/CBS News poll, 62 percent of the respondents expressed the view that a missile defense system would work.[54] As in so many other areas, Reagan's upbeat, broad-brush approach carried the day. His folksy speaking style, the product of his training as an actor, certainly helped as well. The day before the speech, he wrote in his diary: "On my desk was a draft of the speech to be delivered tomorrow night on TV . . . , hassled over by NSC, State and Defense. Finally I had a crack at it. I did a lot of rewriting . . . to change bureaucratese into people talk."[55] Not for nothing was he called "the Great Communicator."

In a perceptive rhetorical analysis of the SDI speech, Gordon R. Mitchell has noted the series of rhetorical questions by which Reagan led his audience to his intended conclusion: "Wouldn't it be better to save lives than to avenge them?" "Isn't it worth every investment necessary to free the world from the threat of nuclear war?" "Are we not capable of demonstrating our peaceful intentions by applying all our abilities and our ingenuity to [the task]?" By this means, Mitchell suggests, Reagan created a "participatory moment," giving ordinary citizens the sense that they themselves were working out a solution to nuclear dangers that had stumped the experts. "By appearing to draw the solution to the Cold War's ominous nuclear dangers from the audience itself, Reagan opened up a space for citizens to see themselves as relevant and potentially efficacious actors in the drama of superpower politics and diplomacy."[56] In a brilliant move, Reagan appropriated the grassroots energy of the Nuclear Weapons Freeze Campaign and turned it to his own very different purposes.

SDI Evolves from Political Ploy to Multi-Billion Project and Diplomatic Football

With Republicans in control of the White House and the Senate (through 1987), the Democratic majority in the House had no hope of halting SDI. Soon after his speech, Reagan signed an NSC directive ordering a major missile-defense research effort. In March 1984, Weinberger established the Strategic Defense Initiative Organization (SDIO) as a freestanding division within the Defense Department, with an initial appropriation of $1.4 billion.[57]

SDI also took on a life of its own in the diplomatic arena. When Strategic Arms Reduction Talks (START) resumed in Geneva in January 1985, the Soviet negotiators focused on halting "the militarization of space," meaning SDI. The technological wizardry touted by SDI supporters may have left U.S. scientists unpersuaded, but it seemingly awed the Soviets. Their obsession with SDI, concluded Assistant Defense Secretary Fred Iklé, arose from their "exaggerated imagination of a very successful second Manhattan Project." While Reagan, Weinberger, and Perle opposed any concessions on SDI, National Security Advisor McFarlane, Secretary of State Shultz, and Paul Nitze, the chief U.S. negotiator, viewed it mainly as a bargaining chip. McFarlane pushed Congress to fund SDI and organized a renewed public relations drive not because he considered it technically feasible but to preserve its value for negotiating purposes and to pressure the Soviets economically as they pondered countermeasures.[58]

But if SDI helped keep Moscow at the negotiating table, it also blocked a successful outcome. Reagan resisted any restraints on SDI research, even when Shultz assured him that concessions on SDI could win major reductions in strategic arms. If the U.S. program succeeded, Reagan argued somewhat implausibly, the technology could be shared with Moscow.[59]

The Soviets did agree to decouple intermediate-range missiles from SDI, and the 1988 INF Treaty removed all missiles from Eastern and Western Europe. But without U.S. concessions on SDI, the Soviets refused all cuts in long-range strategic weapons. When Reagan and Soviet premier Mikhail Gorbachev met at Reykjavík, Iceland, in October 1986, SDI was the deal breaker. The U.S. rigidity on this point, suggested Gorbachev, "contained many emotional elements . . . which were part of one man's dream." Not until 1991, after the Cold War's end and with Reagan out of office, did the two sides sign the START I Treaty, slashing their strategic arsenals by 25 percent.[60]

Theodore Roosevelt once boasted: "I took the [Panama] Canal Zone, and let Congress debate, and while the debate goes on, the canal does also." Ronald Reagan might have said the same of SDI. The whole process vividly illustrates how programs, once launched, take on lives of their own, outliving both the presidents who propose them and their original rationale. As missile defense became entrenched in the military budget, the annual appropriation reached $3.7 billion by 1989, when Reagan left office. The Cold War ended, the Soviet Union collapsed, and in 1993 President Bill Clinton's defense secretary, Les Aspin, even declared "an end to the Star Wars era"—but the funding flowed on. Through the 1990s, annual appropriations averaged $3.5 billion.[61]

Under President George W. Bush, missile defense spending burgeoned. The appropriation in FY2002, the first Bush budget, hit $7.8 billion. Now focused on threats from "rogue nations" such as North Korea, the renamed Missile Defense Agency (MDA) deployed six interceptor missiles in silos at

Fort Greely, Alaska, in 2004—twenty-one years after Reagan's SDI speech. From 1985 to 2006, total appropriations for missile defense totaled nearly $100 billion. Despite a test-failure rate nearing 40 percent, including the failure of a major test in December 2004, the administration requested a staggering $9.3 billion for the MDA for FY2007, the highest in the program's history and more than the *total* 2006 budgets for the National Park Service, the Food and Drug Administration, the Smithsonian Institution, the National Archives, the National Endowments for the Arts and the Humanities, and the administration's highly touted "Millennium Challenge" program to combat poverty and disease in Africa. In its final budget, released in January 2008, the Bush administration upped the ante still higher, requesting a staggering $10.4 billion for the Missile Defense Agency, plus nearly $2 billion more for missile defense–related projects buried elsewhere in the budget.[62]

The Bush administration's plans for antimissile installations in Poland and the Czech Republic, to protect Europe from Iranian missiles, stirred angry protests in Moscow and even raised questions in NATO. A March 2007 report by the U.S. Government Accountability Office, a congressional watchdog agency, expressed grave reservations about the entire missile defense concept. Retorted Lieutenant General Henry A. Obering III, the head of the Missile Defense Agency: "I do believe we are on the right track." Reagan's rhetorical appeals to America's self-image as he made the case for SDI in 1983 survived the decades as well. "Technology will once again make this country the leader of the world," President Bush told a California audience in 2006, "and that's what we're here to celebrate."[63] To anyone familiar with the quarter-century history of the U.S. antimissile program, the mélange of controversy, skeptical assessments, upbeat claims, and rhetorical flights could only induce a weary sense of déjà vu.

Conclusion

Ronald Reagan's Strategic Defense Initiative offers a classic example of a president shoring up support for his military policies by stressing the reassuring themes of peace and security. This strategy was hardly unique. As this volume makes only too clear, presidents from the 1890s to the present have employed many rhetorical strategies to build support for war—or, in Reagan's case, for a military buildup and renewed Cold War confrontation. Further, beginning in 1945, successive administrations employed a variety of diversionary tactics to mask the reality of their nuclear weapons programs and strategies. In the early postwar years, with the nation's atomic resources and industrial capacity overwhelmingly directed into bomb production, the Atomic Energy Commission under David E. Lilienthal endlessly touted the exciting civilian promise of atomic energy. During the presidency of Dwight D. Eisenhower, as the buildup of nuclear weapons and delivery systems continued, the administration's rhetoric, articulated by Eisenhower in a 1953 United Nations speech, celebrated "Atoms for Peace"—the sharing of U.S. nuclear materials and knowledge with other nations for benign purposes.[64]

President Reagan's missile defense proposal, with its gauzy vision of rendering nuclear weapons "impotent" through the miracle of futuristic technology, perpetuated this pattern of lulling the public through reassuring rhetoric. As in so many other instances throughout America's history, the reality behind the manipulative propaganda was quite different.

Notes

1. Ronald Reagan, "Peace and National Security" address, March 23, 1983, reprinted in the *New York Times,* March 24, 1983, and widely available on the Web. The Strategic Defense Initiative section may be found in *Reagan as President: Contemporary Views of the Man, His Politics, and His Policies,* ed. Paul Boyer (Chicago: Ivan R. Dee, 1990), 207–9. Except as otherwise cited, all quotes from the speech are from this source. For more about the White House dinner, see Frances FitzGerald, *Way Out There in the Blue: Reagan, Star Wars, and the End of the Cold War* (New York: Simon & Schuster, 2000), 207–8.

2. FitzGerald, *Way Out There,* 208 (Reagan diary entry); Paul Lettow, *Ronald Reagan and His Quest to Abolish Nuclear Weapons* (New York: Random House, 2005), 102.

3. John Tirman, ed., *The Fallacy of Star Wars: Based on Studies Conducted by the Union of Concerned Scientists* (New York: Vintage Books, 1984), vi, vii; Keith B. Payne, *Strategic Defense: "Star Wars" in Perspective* (Lanham, Md.: Hamilton Press, 1986), 240 (1985 poll).

4. Walter LaFeber, *America, Russia, and the Cold War, 1945–1992,* 7th ed. (New York: McGraw-Hill, 1993), 305.

5. Ibid.; Walter Isaacson, "Fighting the Backbiting," *Time,* Nov. 16, 1981, 22–23; "Bomb Alert," *Time,* November 23, 1981, 19.

6. Robert Scheer, *With Enough Shovels: Reagan, Bush, and Nuclear War* (New York: Random House, 1982), 29–30, 36–52; FitzGerald, *Way Out There,* 86, 119, 148–51 (Weinberger quote, 150), 156–58, 186; Lettow, *Ronald Reagan,* 48, 57, 64–65, 83–86. While the United States had a preponderance of nuclear bombers and submarine-launched ballistic missiles (SLBMs), the Soviets had more ICBMs. The MX was designed to rectify this imbalance, but many Americans saw it as simply piling more nuclear bombs

on an already massive and terrifying accumulation. See Robert A. Hoover, *The MX Controversy: A Guide to Issues and References* (Claremont, Calif.: Regina Books, 1982); Lauren H. Holland and Robert A. Hoover, *The MX Decision: A New Direction in U.S. Weapons Procurement Policy?* (Boulder: Westview Press, 1985); Isaacson, "Fighting the Backbiting."

7. Bernard Brodie, *The Absolute Weapon: Atomic Power and World Order* (New York: Harcourt, Brace, 1946), 28: "[N]o adequate defense against the bomb exists, and the possibilities of its existence in the future are exceedingly remote"; Paul S. Boyer, *By the Bomb's Early Light: American Thought and Culture at the Dawn of the Atomic Age* (New York: Pantheon Books, 1985; 2nd ed., Chapel Hill: University of North Carolina Press, 1994), 33–81, passim; Edward Tabor Linenthal, *Symbolic Defense: The Cultural Significance of the Strategic Defense Initiative* (Urbana: University of Illinois Press, 1989), 71 (Oppenheimer quote).

8. Lawrence Freedman, *The Evolution of Nuclear Strategy*, 3rd ed. (New York: Palgrave Macmillan, 2003); Keith B. Payne, *Nuclear Deterrence in U.S.-Soviet Relations* (Boulder: Westview, 1982); Michael Charlton, *From Deterrence to Defence: The Inside Story of Strategic Policy* (Cambridge: Harvard University Press, 1987), based on a BBC radio series. For works that continued to treat nuclear war as a real option, see Herman Kahn, *On Thermonuclear War* (Princeton: Princeton University Press, 1960) and *Thinking about the Unthinkable* (New York: Horizon Press, 1962).

9. Crockett L. Grabbe, *Space Weapons and the Strategic Defense Initiative* (Ames: Iowa State University Press, 1991), appendix 16, "The 1972 Anti-Ballistic Missile Treaty," 193–98, quoted passage, 195.

10. Ibid., 197–98, 203. Article XV of the ABM Treaty stated that either nation could withdraw from the treaty, after giving notice, "if it decides that extraordinary events related to the subject matter of this Treaty have jeopardized its supreme interests."

11. Scheer, *With Enough Shovels*, 18–26 (quoted passages, 18). T. K. Jones's full title was deputy undersecretary of defense for research and engineering, strategic and theater nuclear forces.

12. Scheer, *With Enough Shovels*, frontispiece (Weinberger), 240–41, 252–53 (Reagan).

13. Quoted in Lettow, *Ronald Reagan*, 67.

14. Dee Garrison, *Bracing for Armageddon: Why Civil Defense Never Worked* (New York: Oxford University Press, 2006), 156–67 (quoted passages, 163, 165).

15. J. Samuel Walker, *Three Mile Island in Historical Perspective* (Berkeley: University of California Press, 2004); Boyer, *By the Bomb's Early Light*, 360; Jonathan Schell, *The Fate of the Earth* (New York: Alfred A. Knopf, 1982).

16. David S. Meyer, *A Winter of Discontent: The Nuclear Freeze and American Politics* (New York: Praeger, 1990); Garrison, *Bracing for Armageddon*, 172–73; FitzGerald, *Way Out There*, 178–82, 190–91, 199–200 (McFarlane's anti-Freeze campaign), 203. Although the Freeze campaign was clearly an important factor in Reagan's SDI speech, Paul Lettow mentions it only in passing (85) in his otherwise exhaustive *Ronald Reagan and His Quest to Abolish Nuclear Weapons*.

17. Holland and Hoover, *The MX Decision;* Paul S. Boyer et al., *The Enduring Vision: A History of the American People,* 5th ed. (Boston: Houghton Mifflin, 2004), 954 (recession); FitzGerald, *Way Out There,* 187–91.

18. Lettow, *Ronald Reagan,* 86–96 (Reagan quote, 86, as reported by Reagan's aide Martin Anderson; Watkins quote, 96; Poindexter quotes, 92 and 270 n. 63); FitzGerald, *Way Out There,* 195–98.

19. Lettow, *Ronald Reagan,* 101–8 (Watkins and Lettow quotes, 106); 274n150 (Keyworth quote); FitzGerald, *Way Out There,* 204–6. Although Keyworth publicly defended SDI, his aide for national security and space, Victor Reis, strongly opposed it and eventually resigned over the issue.

20. FitzGerald, *Way Out There,* chap. 5, "To the Star Wars Speech," 147–209, makes a convincing case for the political motivations behind the SDI proposal (McFarlane quote, 203–4); journalist Hedrick Smith made this point as well in his contemporary analysis of the speech, "The President Out Front," *New York Times,* April 1, 1983, A1, A9; Lettow, *Ronald Reagan,* 102 ("tightly under wraps"). Lettow stresses the degree to which SDI was Reagan's personal project (82–83, 244–48, and elsewhere).

21. Erik K. Pratt, *Selling Strategic Defense: Interests, Ideologies, and the Arms Race* (Boulder: Lynne Rienner, 1990), 9–52, 97 (growing attention to BMD in early 1980s); Paul Boyer, *Fallout: A Historian Reflects on America's Half-Century Encounter with Nuclear Weapons* (Columbus: Ohio State University Press, 1998), 177 (LeMay); Donald R. Baucom, *The Origins of SDI, 1944–1983* (Lawrence: University Press of Kansas, 1992).

22. William J. Broad, *Teller's War: The Top-Secret Story behind the Star Wars Deception* (New York: Simon & Schuster, 1992); FitzGerald, *Way Out There,* 127–41; Peter Goodchild, *Edward Teller: The Real Dr. Strangelove* (Cambridge: Harvard University Press, 2004); Dan O'Neill, *The Firecracker Boys* (New York: St. Martin's Press, 1994).

23. Edward Teller, *The Legacy of Hiroshima* (Garden City, N.Y.: Doubleday, 1962), 128–29; Lettow, *Ronald Reagan,* 18–19, 81–82; FitzGerald, *Way Out There,* 127–29, 134–35.

24. FitzGerald, *Way Out There,* 139–41, 144–45; Lettow, *Ronald Reagan,* 96.

25. Malcolm Wallop, "Opportunities and Imperatives of Ballistic Missile Defense," *Strategic Review* (Fall 1979): 13–21; FitzGerald, *Way Out There,* 121–24, 129–31, 143–44 (quoted phrase, 130). While Teller's X-ray lasers involved directed energy from a nuclear blast, Wallop and Graham favored chemical lasers produced by the reaction of gases such as hydrogen and fluorine. For brief explanations of the two systems, see Tirman, ed., *The Fallacy of Star Wars,* 90–93, and his figures 14 and 15.

26. Lieutenant General Daniel O. Graham, *High Frontier: A New National Strategy* (Washington, D.C.: High Frontier, Inc., 1982); *New York Times,* Jan. 3, 1996 (Graham obituary); Linenthal, *Symbolic Defense,* 7 (Graham quote), 123n17; FitzGerald, *Way Out There,* 131–43 (Weinberger quote, 143).

27. Lettow, *Ronald Reagan,* 6 (Reagan quote), 132 (Poindexter and Adelman quotes). For similar comments about Reagan by Weinberger, Shultz, Perle, and others see 60,

61, 100, 133, 235. This is, indeed, Lettow's central theme. See, e.g., 4, 113, 118–21, 191–94, 226, 243.

28. Michael Paul Rogin, *Ronald Reagan, The Movie and Other Episodes in Political Demonology* (Berkeley: University of California Press, 1987), 1–3; Leslie Gelb, "The Mind of the President," *New York Times Magazine,* Oct. 6, 1985, 21–24ff.; Linenthal, *Symbolic Defense,* 6–7 (quote from "Murder in the Air" script). Both Garry Wills, *Reagan's America: Innocents at Home* (New York: Doubleday, 1987) and Lou Cannon, *President Reagan: The Role of a Lifetime* (New York: Simon & Schuster, 1991) discuss the centrality of movie imagery for Reagan.

29. National Conference of Catholic Bishops, *The Challenge of Peace: God's Promise and Our Response* (Washington, D.C.: U.S. Catholic Conference, 1983), vii, 51–62, quoted passages vii, 58, 61. This document was published on May 3, 1983, after Reagan's SDI speech, but drafts circulated widely beforehand. See also Douglas P. Lackey, ed., *Ethics and Strategic Defense: American Philosophers Debate Star Wars and the Future of Nuclear Deterrence* (Belmont, Calif.: Wadsworth, 1989) and Douglas P. Lackey, *Moral Principles and Nuclear Weapons* (Totowa, N.J.: Roman and Allanheld, 1984).

30. Boyer, ed., *Reagan as President,* 207, 208; *New York Times,* Nov. 24, 1983, A20 (Reagan speech).

31. Boyer, *By the Bomb's Early Light,* 9, 13–26; Boyer, ed., *Reagan as President,* 207, 208. Earlier in the speech, foreshadowing the missile-defense proposal, Reagan described it as offering "new hope for our children in the twenty-first century." *New York Times,* March 24, 1983.

32. Truman quoted in Boyer, *By the Bomb's Early Light,* 266; Reagan SDI speech, quoted in Boyer, ed., *Reagan as President,* 208.

33. Reagan SDI speech, quoted in Boyer, ed., *Reagan as President,* 208.

34. Ibid. For Western European concerns about SDI, see Robert M. Soofer, *Missile Defenses and Western European Security: NATO Strategy, Arms Control, and Deterrence* (New York: Greenwood, 1988); Regina Cowen et al., *SDI and European Security* (Boulder: Westview Press, 1987); Hans Günter Brauch, ed., *Star Wars and European Defence: Implications for Europe: Perceptions and Assessments* (New York: St. Martin's Press, 1987); Ivo H. Daalder, *The SDI: Challenge to Europe* (Cambridge, Mass.: Ballinger, 1987); and Sanford Lakoff and Randy Willoughby, eds., *Strategic Defense and the Western Alliance* (Lexington, Mass.: Lexington Books, 1987).

35. Boyer, ed., *Reagan as President,* 207, 209; *New York Times,* March 24, 1983 ("The United States . . . will never be an aggressor").

36. Ronald Reagan, "Address to the National Association of Evangelicals," March 8, 1983, in Boyer, ed., *Reagan as President,* 165–69, quoted passages, 166, 167, 168, 169; Scheer, *With Enough Shovels,* 260 (Reagan interview, quoting Pope Pius XII). Reagan often used this quote in public settings as well.

37. *New York Times,* March 24, 1983, A20 (Reagan speech); Boyer et al., *The Enduring Vision,* 696 (Wilson quote).

38. Meyer, *A Winter of Discontent,* 222, 254; *New York Times,* May 5, 1983, 1ff.; *Manchester Union Leader,* "Why Not Try Survival?" March 25, 1983 (including the

Schlafly quote), in Boyer, ed., *Reagan as President*, 209–10. Writing in the *New York Times* two days after the SDI speech, Leslie Gelb speculated that the main aim of this portion of the speech was to undercut the Freeze movement. *New York Times*, March 15, 1983, 1.

39. Lettow, *Ronald Reagan*, 112.

40. Edward Teller, *Better a Shield than a Sword* (New York: Free Press, 1987); Daniel O. Graham, *The Non-Nuclear Defense of Cities: The High-Frontier Space-Based Defense against ICBM Attack* (Cambridge, Mass.: Abt Books, 1983); Robert Jastrow, *How to Make Nuclear Weapons Obsolete* (Boston: Little, Brown, 1985); Lettow, *Ronald Reagan*, 130; FitzGerald, *Way Out There*, 210 (Scowcroft Commission), 247, 254; James Carroll, *House of War: The Pentagon and the Disastrous Rise of American Power* (Boston: Houghton Mifflin, 2006), 407; "Onward and Upward with Space Defense," *Bulletin of the Atomic Scientists*, June/July 1983 (Vessey), in Boyer, ed., *Reagan as President*, 215.

41. FitzGerald, *Way Out There*, 210, 211; "A Star Wars Defense," *St. Louis Post-Dispatch*, March 25, 1983, A14, in Boyer, ed., *Reagan as President*, 210–11.

42. FitzGerald, *Way Out There*, 202; Lettow, *Ronald Reagan*, 113 (Reagan letter).

43. *Washington Post*, March 27, 1983 (Perry), in Boyer, ed., *Reagan as President*, 216; Linenthal, *Symbolic Defense*, 13 (Rathjens); Joseph Weizenbaum, "The Strategic Defense Initiative," *Risks Digest* 1, no. 5 (September 4, 1985), online at <http://catless.ncl.ac.uk/Risks/1.5.html>.

44. Tirman, ed., *The Fallacy of Star Wars*, esp. "Political and Strategic Implications," 153–76; Union of Concerned Scientists, *Empty Promise: The Growing Case against Star Wars* (Boston: Beacon Press, 1986); Linenthal, *Symbolic Defense*, 30, 32 (National Academy of Sciences petition and High Frontier statement); Zbigniew Brzezinski et al., *Promise or Peril: The Strategic Defense Initiative. Thirty-five Essays by Statesmen, Scholars, and Strategic Analysts* (Washington, D.C.: Ethics and Public Policy Center, 1986). See also FitzGerald, *Way Out There*, 247–48, and Grabbe, *Space Weapons and the Strategic Defense Initiative*, chap. 8, "Offensive Uses of Defensive Weapons," 86–99, and chap. 20, "Strategic Defense and Arms Control Treaties," 205–16 (letter by former secretaries of defense, 110).

45. Linenthal, *Symbolic Defense*, xiii (quoted phrase), 109 (Herblock cartoon). A useful compendium is Philip M. Boffey, *Claiming the Heavens: The* New York Times *Complete Guide to the Star Wars Debate* (New York: Times Books, 1988). For the congressional reaction, see FitzGerald, *Way Out There*, 210–11, 241–55.

46. FitzGerald, *Way Out There*, 211 (*Time* cover); Linenthal, *Symbolic Defense*, 14 (*Chicago Tribune* editorial), 23, 26, and 27 for reproductions of the cartoons mentioned.

47. Linenthal, *Symbolic Defense*, 15; Lettow, *Ronald Reagan*, 113.

48. "'Star Wars,'" *National Review*, April 13, 1983, in Boyer, ed., *Reagan as President*, 211–12 (quoted passage, 212); Linenthal, *Symbolic Defense*, 9 (Reagan quote), 33, 43 (Gingrich quote), 66; FitzGerald, *Way Out There*, 248 (Abrahamson quote), 380.

49. Linenthal, *Symbolic Defense*, 52, 62, 78.

50. Gerald M. Boyd, "President Is Critical of 'Liberals' Who May 'Chop Up' Star

Wars," *New York Times,* Oct. 19, 1986, A10; Linenthal, *Symbolic Defense,* 66–67 (biblical citation), 69 (Fort McHenry); Tirman, ed., *The Fallacy of Star Wars,* ix (Kramer bill). Reagan himself cited the "strong man" biblical passage (Luke 11:21) in a July 13, 1985, radio address defending SDI: <http://www.reagan.utexas.edu/archives/speeches/1985/71385a.htm>. SDI opponents went on to quote the next verse: "But when a stronger man than he shall come upon him, and overcome him, he taketh from him all his armour wherein he trusted, and divideth his spoils."

51. Boyer, ed., *Reagan as President,* 214 (Weinberger); Linenthal, *Symbolic Defense,* 48 (Sybert).

52. Linenthal, *Symbolic Defense,* 36, 37; Pratt, *Selling Strategic Defense,* 23–25, 42, and 98–100, esp. Table 52 (99) listing the top twenty-five BMD contractors in 1983; William J. Broad, *Star Warriors: A Penetrating Look into the Lives of the Young Scientists behind Our Space Age Weaponry* (New York: Simon & Schuster, 1985); Mark Patiky, *Beyond Star Wars: Profiting from Breakthrough Technology* (Alexandria, Va.: KCI Communications, 1988); Richard W. Bryant, *The Strategic Defense Initiative, Business Opportunities, and Technological Potential* (Norwalk, Conn.: Business Communications Co., 1986); *The Star Wars Program and the Role of Contractors,* hearings before the Committee on Governmental Affairs, U.S. Senate, 102nd Cong. 2nd sess., July 24, 1992 (Washington, D.C.: Government Printing Office, 1992).

53. Linenthal, *Symbolic Defense,* 116.

54. Hinckley, *People, Polls, and Policymakers,* 72, 73, 77. The 1986 poll was conducted by the National Strategy Information Center, a nonpartisan Washington-based polling organization (xiv). Keith B. Payne, *Strategic Defense: "Star Wars" in Perspective* (Lanham, Md.: Hamilton Press, 1986), 239 (1984 poll). The 1984 poll was worded: "Would you support a U.S. attempt to build a defensive system against nuclear missiles and bombers?"

55. Quoted in Gordon R. Mitchell, *Strategic Deception: Rhetoric, Science, and Politics in Missile Defense Advocacy* (East Lansing: Michigan State University Press, 2000), 52.

56. Ibid., 52–56, quoted passages, 53. See also Thomas P. Goodnight, "Ronald Reagan's Reformulation of the Rhetoric of War: Analysis of the 'Zero Option,' 'Evil Empire,' and 'Star Wars' Addresses," *Quarterly Journal of Speech* 72, no. 4 (November 1986): 390–414, esp. 403–8.

57. FitzGerald, *Way Out There,* 243–44; CBS News, "A Look Back at the Polls," <http://www.cbsnews.com/stories/2004/06/07/opinion/polls/main621632.shtml>; *The World Almanac and Book of Facts* (New York: World Almanac Books, 2006), 64 (party alignments in Congress, 1983–87); Missile Defense Agency, "Historical Funding for MDA, FY85–07," at <http://www.google.com/search?hl=en&q=historical+funding +for+mda+fy85–07&btnG=Google+Search>.

58. Lettow, *Ronald Reagan,* 90, 130, 135, 138–57, 167, 175, 215 (Iklé quote).

59. Ibid., 208–9, 226, 246.

60. Ibid., 184 (Gorbachev quote), 217–26, 233.

61. Missile Defense Agency, "Historical Funding for MDA, FY85–07; Department of Defense, News Briefing, May 13, 1993, "The End of the Star Wars Era," <http://www.fas.org/spp/starwars/offdocs/d930513.htm>.

62. Missile Defense Agency, "Historical Funding for MDA, FY85–07; "U.S. Missile Defense Set to Get Early Start," *Washington Post*, 2 February 2004, A10; "U.S. Missile Defense Test Fails," *Washington Post*, 16 December 2004, A5; "Missile Defense Test Is Halted after the Target Rocket Fails," *New York Times*, 26 May 2007, A9; *The World Almanac and Book of Facts, 2006* (New York: World Almanac Books, 2006), 90–91 (Federal Budget statistics); Center for Defense Information, February 8, 2008, "An Initial Look at MDA's FY09 Budget Request: A Morass Becomes Murkier," <http://www.cdi.org/friendlyversion/printversion.cfm?documentID=4204>. Antimissile deployments were also planned at Vandenberg Air Force Base in California.

63. "U.S. Tries to Ease Concerns in Russia on Antimissile Plan," *New York Times*, February 22, 2007, A6; "House Panel Considering Cuts in Budget for Missile Defense," *New York Times*, May 10, 2007, A5; "Untransformed," *New Yorker*, September 25, 2006, 62 (Bush quoted).

64. Boyer, *By the Bomb's Early Light*, part 4, "Anodyne to Terror: Fantasies of a Techno-Atomic Utopia," 107–30; Paul Boyer, *Fallout: A Historian Reflects on America's Half-Century Encounter with Nuclear Weapons* (Columbus: Ohio State University Press, 1998), 30, 89, 116 ("Atoms for Peace" program).

9

THE MINISTRY OF FEAR

Selling the Gulf Wars

Lloyd Gardner

A big story broke in the *New York Times* on February 19, 2002. Shortly after the 9/11 attacks, the Pentagon had created an Office of Strategic Influence with the mission of influencing public opinion abroad, especially in Islamic countries. The idea was to plant stories with foreign media organizations through outside concerns that might not have obvious connections with the Department of Defense. Its commander, Brigadier General Simon Worden, envisioned a broad campaign that would use disinformation and covert activities. "It goes from the blackest of the black programs to the whitest of white," a senior Pentagon official said.[1]

But that was not the most interesting part of the story. The reporters revealed that the Pentagon had hired an international consulting firm based in Washington, the Rendon Group, "to help the new office." Headed by John Rendon Jr., who liked to describe himself as an "information warrior," the firm was most famous for its work with the Kuwaiti royal family to publicize supposed Iraqi atrocities to influence Congress before Gulf War I. But the Rendon Group had also worked with the Central Intelligence Agency to create the Iraqi National Congress, an exile group dedicated to the overthrow of Saddam Hussein. The *Times* story caused a furor in the White House, according to a reporter for the *Washington Post*. There would be no change in the administration's "strict policy of providing reporters with the facts," promised Karen Hughes, a close advisor to President George W. Bush. "The president is a plain-spoken, truthful man," protested another White House aide, "and he expects that same high standard from every public affairs spokesperson in the government." Whoever leaked the story about the OSI, said a third official, did the president "a tremendous disservice."

That left the door ajar to a question: Was it the existence of the OSI that did the president a disservice, or the leak?[2]

Secretary of Defense Donald Rumsfeld hinted that it had been the revelation that the OSI existed rather than what it did that caused the trouble. Answering questions at a news briefing, Rumsfeld complained that some of the negative editorial comment and political cartoons had been off the mark. "But that's life. We get up in the morning, and we live with the world like we find it. Therefore, the office is done. It's over. What do you want, blood?! (Laughter)."[3]

Of course, it was not done and it was not over. Over the next two years, stories continued to surface about a "bitter, high level debate" in the Pentagon over how far it could go to manipulate opinion abroad. No one was alarmed about the traditional use of deception to mislead an enemy. But what the stories touched on was the very serious matter of how the war was being sold to the American public through the manipulations of companies like the Rendon Group and the influence of powerful individuals gathered in Washington think tanks, whose agendas included such matters as the quest for Persian Gulf oil as well as the elimination of potential threats to Israel.[4]

From Friend to Enemy

In the 1980s, Washington had regarded Saddam Hussein as a "friend," on the principle that the enemy of my enemy is at least worthy of some consideration. On the day after the German invasion of the Soviet Union, Winston Churchill famously said that if Hitler invaded Hell, he would make a passing favorable reference to Satan in Parliament. Saddam Hussein's eight-year war with Iran qualified under the same criteria. But when he threatened to move into Kuwait in the summer of 1990, Washington was concerned—if not quite sure what to do. The American ambassador in Baghdad, April Glaspie, told the Iraqi dictator that the United States disapproved of the use of military force to settle such disputes. She assured Hussein, however, that President George H. W. Bush desired better relations with Baghdad. Then she asked—in a perfectly friendly way, she said—for an explanation of the troop movements near the border. She gave no indication what Washington's response would be to an invasion. After the invasion, Baghdad distributed a transcript of the conversation that suggested Washington had given

Iraq a green light. In the transcript, Glaspie relates that the long-standing American attitude is to take no position on intra-Arab border questions. "We have no opinion on the Arab-Arab conflicts," it quotes the ambassador, "like your border disagreement with Kuwait." Glaspie's own cable is much less detailed on this key point: "The Ambassador," it reads, "said that she had served in Kuwait 20 years before; then, as now, we took no position on these Arab affairs."[5]

To make matters more confused, Joseph Wilson, Glaspie's number two at the time, wrote in his memoirs, *The Politics of Truth*, that while the ambassador's meaning was clear—the United States desired a peaceful settlement—President Bush himself reasserted Washington's desire for better relations in a manner that may have helped to persuade Saddam Hussein that he would not face anything more than moral censure and certainly not military intervention. In truth, Wilson wrote, no one threatened "U.S. military action should he fail to heed our entreaties not to invade Kuwait."[6]

Bush's ultimate decision to "liberate" Kuwait did seem to emerge in fits and starts. There is something of an urban myth about the whole affair, centered on the role of British prime minister Margaret Thatcher. The "Iron Lady," a sobriquet she obviously enjoyed, supposedly told Bush, "Remember, George, this is no time to go wobbly." Actually, what Thatcher thought about the crisis worried him least, especially as compared with the problem of overcoming the threat of an "Arab solution" leaving Iraq in control of Kuwait in exchange for promises not to attack elsewhere. With his position enhanced by adding Kuwait's 10 percent of the world's proven oil reserves to Iraq's resources, Saddam Hussein would then become the arbiter of OPEC's policies and a challenger to American suzerainty. "I worried from day one about the talk of an 'Arab Solution,'" Bush explained later.[7]

The real worry, then, had to do with the possibility that after having made peace with Iran, Saddam Hussein would seek to establish himself as the overlord of the world's oil supply. As far back as the so-called Carter Doctrine, announced in the wake of the Iranian Revolution and Russian intervention in Afghanistan, American leaders had warned the Soviet Union (and the world) that the United States would not tolerate unfriendly forces interfering with access to the Persian Gulf oil fields. "Let our position be absolutely clear," intoned Jimmy Carter in his 1980 State of the Union speech. "An attempt by any outside force to gain control of the Persian Gulf region will be regarded as an assault on the vital interests of the United States of America, and such an assault will be repelled by any means necessary, including military force." If that was not enough, Carter underlined what those interests were: "It contains more than two-thirds of the world's exportable oil."[8]

Carter created the Rapid Deployment Force (RDF) that later became Central Command (Centcom) and initiated the policy of creating a circle of military bases around the Gulf. In 1982, the commanding officer of the new command, General Robert Kingston, described his mission succinctly: "to assure the unimpeded flow of oil from the Arabian Gulf."[9] When Iraq attacked Kuwait in 1990, the mission had not changed, but it was not so easy to sell the idea of war without an opponent as powerful and apparently menacing as the Soviet Union. Choosing among Middle East regimes on a moral basis was also more difficult when there appeared to be so many "mini-evil empires."

Washington had supported Iraq at a time when Saddam Hussein's most heinous crimes—some real, some asserted—were taking place, such as the use of poison gas. If he had been, as he claimed, a barrier against Iranian radicalism, sceptics argued, what did it matter if he settled affairs with Kuwait, an oligarchy whose ruling family deserved little sympathy? A war for the vaguer goal of a Bush-proclaimed "New World Order" was a hard sell.

Congress, controlled by Democrats, had doubts, some relating to the so-called Vietnam Syndrome, and worried about what a war would do to the economy facing a deepening economic recession. Yet if Saddam got away with it, he might force a rise in the price of oil or, even worse, go after Saudi Arabia next, America's close ally and the number one supplier of Persian Gulf crude. The worldwide implications seemed tremendous. Bush writes in his joint memoir with Brent Scowcroft that he realized full well the perils of a military solution. "We had a big job ahead of shaping opinion at home and abroad and could little afford bellicose mistakes at the start."[10]

Bush had several audiences to satisfy. The first was the American public and, through that avenue, the Congress. Then there was the international community, including former Cold War rivals Russia and China. As it turned out, in Gulf War I it was easier to persuade the world than it was folks on the home front. The latter required the greatest effort and, ultimately, the sort of rhetoric that set the nation on a fateful course. At the first press conferences, however, the president did not commit himself to a specific course of action. He did not accuse Iraq of seeking to develop nuclear weapons or demonize Saddam Hussein as the reincarnation of Hitler. These would come later.

For the moment Bush was content to tease his questioners and let them describe in their queries possible alternative actions. His most quotable early statement came in a brief press conference on August 5, 1990: "This will not stand. This will not stand, this aggression against Kuwait."[11]

Bush's greatest achievement in these first weeks was to secure passage of resolutions in the United Nations condemning the invasion and demanding an Iraqi withdrawal. Iraq had long counted on the Soviet Union as a supporter, but now, with Mikhail Gorbachev as the head man in the Kremlin, Moscow allied itself with the West at least so far as imposing sanctions. Bush worked the international telephone as well as previous presidents had worked phone lines to Capitol Hill. He also sent Defense Secretary Dick Cheney and General Norman Schwarzkopf to Saudi Arabia to persuade a nervous King Fahd, worried about domestic opposition, to accept American military forces on Saudi soil.

Getting Fahd's approval for Operation Desert Shield was, as Cheney told interviewers later, the real breakthrough in establishing the conditions for driving Iraq out of Kuwait: "When King Fahd said that he was prepared to accept our proposition, I was pleased, obviously. That was something that was very important to achieve but, secondly, I also had a sense that this particular decision then triggered a whole sequence of pretty momentous events. Hundreds of thousands of troops going to the desert—U.S. deploying major force halfway round the world was obviously a significant event."[12]

Fahd's consent did trigger momentous events. For example, it pretty much ruled out what Bush feared most, a negotiated Arab solution that would leave Saddam Hussein in a powerful position in the world oil market. Saudi Arabia's agreement also sent a strong signal to the American Congress that it was reasonable to be worried about future Iraqi actions. Even after the first forces started arriving in Saudi Arabia, however, the president remained coy about the next steps. At an early meeting in the White House, the chairman of the Joint Chiefs, General Colin Powell, asked "if it was worth going to war to liberate Kuwait." Cheney immediately warned him not to ask questions outside his purview and to stick to military matters.[13]

Powell was convinced that Iraq did not intend to attack Saudi Arabia. He also feared that an effort to liberate Kuwait could cause huge disruptions in the Middle East, strengthening Iran and Syria, an outcome that would not improve long-term American prospects. Such views would get him in trouble later, of course, in the Bush II administration, with the same antagonist, Dick Cheney, and label him a Cassandra. But at the time his views were shared by many in Congress, and this continued to be a problem for the White House in selling the war.[14]

Making A Good War

By October 1990, it was clear that moral suasion and political pressure on Saddam would not be enough. Desert Shield had provoked the Iraqi dictator into making his own bellicose statements. He had reacted to Bush's statements about how the aggression would not stand by attempting to link Kuwait with the Palestinian cause, a ploy he hoped would rally Arab opinion to his side and embarrass the Saudi rulers and others. Instead, it only gave Bush the opportunity to point out that before the invasion Hussein had said he would "burn Israel to the ground."

The quotation appeared in several forms at the time. It was used later to justify Gulf War II, and it popped up again in obituaries of Saddam Hussein after he was hanged. Sometimes it was said he was planning only to burn half of Israel and other times to burn Israel to a crisp. Very seldom is the speech put in context as a response to Israel's warnings that it would launch a new attack if it suspected Iraq of reconstructing its nuclear facilities, which Israel had destroyed in a 1982 attack. "Iraq, for its part," writes Scott Ritter, "put Israel on notice that any such attack by Israel would result in an Iraqi counterattack, including the use of chemical weapons that would, according to Saddam Hussein, 'burn half of Israel.' . . . U.S. intelligence data, specifically satellite photographs of western Iraq, had been provided to Israel (via Israeli liaison officers dispatched to Washington, D.C.) to help detect any suspicious Iraqi activity in the deserts of western Iraq."[15]

By extending the crisis to the Israeli-Palestine question, Hussein actually helped to sell the war in the United States. Stories about his use of chemical weapons against Iranian forces and Iraqi Kurds became common items in the media, also making it easier to demonize him. Yet Bush still worried about congressional support, even though newspaper polls showed strong popular backing for his actions. On October 17, 1990, he candidly recorded in his diary a conversation with Brent Scowcroft:

A day of churning. Brent Scowcroft, my trusted friend, comes for dinner. We talk about how we get things moving, and what we do about the [question of] provocation [to justify the use of force]. The news is saying some members of Congress feel I might use a minor incident to go to war, and they may be right. We must get this over with. The longer it goes, the longer the erosion. I think we can draw the line in the sand—*draw it in the sand in American life.*[16]

The line had to be drawn in American life, he wrote in his diary, to win support for military action. Important Senate leaders, such as Georgia's much respected Sam Nunn, had not been convinced that military action was the best course. After the war, Secretary of State James Baker was reminded that some people had felt, "Hey, it was just a gas station, and the gas station had changed hands." No, Baker replied, the administration did not see it that way, absolutely not. It had always been American policy to preserve "free access to the oil of the Persian Gulf." Saudi Arabia was not only America's best friend in that regard; it was a guarantor that the price line would always be reasonable. It could not play that role if Iraq controlled Kuwait's reserves as well as its own. "My suggestion that it boiled down to jobs," Baker added, "got a lot of attention and flack, but the fact of the matter is it would have boiled down to jobs if Saddam Hussein had been able to control the flow of oil from the Persian Gulf or to, by controlling his own oil and Kuwait's oil, act in a way to influence prices."[17]

Still, as Baker said, the war could not be sold to the public as a struggle to maintain control of oil supplies without supplying a good reason to help people overcome their doubts. Bush's vision of a new world order was much more than a cover story. With the end of the Cold War, noted Scowcroft, a new world order was inevitable. "We certainly had no expectation that we were entering a period of peace and tranquility. Indeed, the outlines of a very messy world were already perceptible." The idea of a New World Order (always put in capital letters) inevitably took on a life of its own, he added, and suggested something much grander, if not quite utopian, in scope and depth. For Scowcroft and other realists, however, it meant only stopping people like Noriega in Central America and Saddam Hussein from causing too much trouble. That was task enough for the remaining superpower, without making foreign policy into a missionary voyage to the end of history.[18]

Realists inevitably fight a losing cause in the battle to limit objectives, nevertheless, because a decision to send men to their death for anything less than a struggle between good and evil cannot be tarnished with crude oil. In a recent history of Western civilization, Robert Osborne writes the Roman Empire was based on an "indefinable entity." "If Romans had simply been out to grasp whatever they could, then it is likely that Rome would have been either a small kingdom or a short-lived empire. The empire endured because most Romans believed that Rome was an expression of common humanity and was therefore a force for good." It fought never-ending wars, but "Romans believed that conflicts with other states were provoked by others, and that when Romans were forced to take over another territory, they brought with them the benefits of Roman civilization." Another way of putting it would be to say that all empires consider themselves gifted with an exceptional burden of responsibility for the "civilized" world.[19]

The elder Bush understood the point. The opposition in Congress to be overcome stemmed in part from Vietnam-era concerns about presidential power to wage war without legislative consent and a related Vietnam-era issue, the "Credibility Gap." As Bush prepared to send the first 150,000 troops to the Middle East in the buildup for Operation Desert Storm, Democrat Dante B. Fascell, chairman of the House Foreign Affairs Committee, warned about a repeat of the 1964 Gulf of Tonkin "incident" that Lyndon B. Johnson maneuvered into a grant of powers to wage war and send half a million soldiers to Southeast Asia. "If there is a provocation, it's got to be a real one," said Fascell. "If there's an additional provocation, it can't be two whales passing in the night. It has to be something that can stand the scrutiny of the media, and of the public, and of history." Fascell's comment referred to LBJ's sardonic admission that American sailors might have been firing at nothing more than whales, something that he misrepresented as an encounter with North Vietnamese torpedo boats to persuade Congress to vote for the Gulf of Tonkin resolution.[20]

Iraq had given no indication it would provide the necessary provocation by attacking Saudi Arabia. The war had to be sold on Kuwait alone. Encouraged by its American backers, the Kuwaiti government hired the famous public relations firm Hill and Knowlton, complete with its bipartisan stable of famous PR/Politicos such as Ron Brown and Frank Mankiewicz, whose liberal credentials stretched from Robert Kennedy to George S. McGovern, to promote the public demonization of Saddam Hussein and thus the need for a war to "liberate" the sheikdom. Hill and Knowlton masterminded "the largest foreign-funded campaign ever aimed at manipulating American public opinion."[21]

The campaign reached its high point on October 10, 1990, with "hearings" held by the Congressional Human Rights Caucus. The hearings had all the trappings of a regular congressional committee taking testimony for legislative purposes, but it was in reality only an association of politicians, headed by two representatives who also chaired the Congressional Human Rights Foundation, a separate legal entity that enjoyed free housing valued at $3,000 a year in H&K's Washington office. In other words, it was a front organization. The big advantage over regular hearings, of course, was that no testimony was taken under oath and therefore subject to perjury. The star witness that day was a 15-year-old girl, Nayirah, who said that she had been a volunteer in a hospital in Kuwait City when Iraqi troops burst in and seized babies in incubators. "They took the babies out of the incubators, took the incubators, and left the babies on the cold floor to die."[22]

Nayirah could not give her last name, it was said, out of fear of reprisals. If she had done so, it would have emerged that she was the daughter of the Kuwaiti ambassador to the United States and a member of the ruling Sabah family. Before it could be established that she had been lying not only about her name but about witnessing the incubator raid, the story had become a legend on the order of the undocumented German atrocities in Belgium that inflamed American opinion at the outset of World War I.

Five days after Nayirah's "testimony," President Bush told a fund-raiser for a Texas Republican gubernatorial candidate, "I met with the Emir of Kuwait. And I heard horrible tales: newborn babies thrown out of incubators and the incubators then shipped off to Baghdad." He used the story five more times in the next month, embellishing it as he went along. In a speech to troops at Dhahran, he said, "It turns your stomach to listen to the tales of those that have escaped the brutality of Saddam the invader. Mass hangings. Babies pulled from incubators and scattered like firewood across the floor." The story then gained immense credibility from a report by the highly respected organization Amnesty International. It stood unchallenged until Alexander Cockburn wrote the first article disputing the incubator raid in the *Los Angeles Times* on January 17, 1991. It came too late. The bombing of Baghdad had begun the night before.[23]

Meanwhile, Bush had talked about Saddam the invader, a phrase that recalled the legend of Vlad the Impaler, the murderous model for Bram Stoker's vampire, Count Dracula. But the incubator story was quickly supplemented and then enlarged out of all proportion to Saddam-as-Hitler. No person in history was more reviled than Hitler. At one point a reporter challenged Bush's frequent references to Saddam as the new Hitler, asking if the Iraqi dictator had done anything that could possibly be equated with the Holocaust. Bush's reply was a study in equivocation that seemed to suggest that—if anything—Saddam was *worse* than the Nazi leader. "I didn't say the Holocaust [compared]," he began, but "I was told—and we've got to check this carefully—that Hitler did not stake people out against potential military targets and that he did, indeed, respect—not much else, but he did, indeed, respect the legitimacy of the Embassies. . . . Go back and take a look at your history, and you'll see why I'm as concerned as I am."[24]

The reference was to Americans in Kuwait held hostage in the embassy or hiding somewhere in the city away from Hussein's troops. The hostage "crisis" served Bush's purposes in several ways both as a reminder to everyone of the Iranian hostage crisis and his stronger-than-Carter response and as a necessary "provocation" in itself if nothing else happened. The situation was actually more like a diplomatic standoff than an international crisis, as other embassies had shut down and their nationals had already left for home. Asked why the United States did not do the same, an administration official replied, "Because we don't want to acquiesce to the annexation of Kuwait." If Iraq refused to allow supplies into the embassy, Bush railed, "it would be directly contravening a mandate from the United Nations and we would view that very seriously."[25]

Saddam backed off, offering passage out of Kuwait to all the Americans in early December, coupled with various invitations to what Baghdad insisted would be serious negotiations—always, of course, to involve the Arab-Israeli question. The hostages were airlifted out, and Bush took up an invitation to have Secretary Baker meet with the Iraqi foreign minister, but only for the purpose of sending a letter to Saddam reiterating the demand contained in UN resolutions that Iraq withdraw from Kuwait by January 15, 1991. The administration's unqualified success in the UN and in building a coalition that included the Soviet Union stood in some contrast to continued concerns about erosion of support at home. So Bush upped the stakes again. Portraying Saddam Hussein as a villain among villains, an evildoer on the scale of Adolf Hitler, was supplemented by the introduction of Iraq's supposed nuclear weapons program as a reason for military action.[26]

Iraq's nuclear ambitions had been the subject of a recent National Intelligence Estimate that concluded Saddam Hussein was closer to obtaining a bomb than had previously been thought. Nevertheless, the existence of the program had not been considered an urgent matter until it was introduced by President Bush as part of his campaign to shore up support for his policies. CIA director William Webster asserted that one could have no real confidence the area would ever be secure, unless Saddam were "disassociated from his weapons of mass destruction."[27]

What made this assertion problematic was the prewar decision that whatever action was taken to drive Iraq out of Kuwait did not include a march on Baghdad, thus leaving in limbo the matter of disassociation. The UN resolution that mandated military action did not call for such a *denouement*, and the administration had no intention of asking for one. Indeed, quite the opposite, as Bush feared being dragged into a civil war.

Bush delayed any votes in Congress until after Baker met with the Iraqi foreign minister, Tariq Aziz, on January 3, 1991, in Geneva. As he expected, the Iraqi hard line at the meeting produced the necessary votes against an antiwar resolution and in favor of a war resolution. He had vowed to go ahead regardless of the outcome of the debate, but he would have been hard pressed to keep that pledge.[28]

The campaign to make Gulf War I a "good war" ended on a somewhat comical note when the *New York Times* reported an echo of World War II in the current crisis. Apparently there had appeared on Iraqi radio a "Baghdad Betty" who warned the American troops poised to attack that bad things were happening back home: "G.I. you should go home. . . . While you're away, movie stars are taking your women. Robert Redford is dating your girlfriend. Tom Selleck is kissing your lady. . . . Bart Simpson is making love to your wife." President Bush promptly called Iraqi radio ridiculous and stupid. But the story had not originated with Iraqi radio or with Hill and Knowlton; rather, it was a joke Johnny Carson had told on *The Tonight Show* months earlier.[29]

An Unfinished War

In later years, Bush offered several answers to questions about why, once the war started in January 1991, coalition forces did not go to Baghdad to "disassociate" Saddam Hussein from his weapons of mass destruction. Talking to veterans of the 100-hour war in 1999, the former president said about all the implied criticism, "It burns me up." He was not in the business of second-guessing his military commanders, who, he said, told him the mission was accomplished when the Iraqi army surrendered. "I don't believe in mission creep," he added. He could have been in Baghdad in another 48 hours, but what then? "Which sergeant, which private, whose life would be at stake in perhaps a fruitless hunt in an urban guerilla war to find the most-secure dictator in the world?" America would be an occupying power in an Arab land with no allies. "It would have been disastrous."[30]

Bush hoped that the Iraqis would do the job for him by removing Saddam Hussein, without the consequences of leaving Iraq in a chaotic situation. After all, there was still Iran to worry about. Hussein's longevity was kind of a sore spot with him, to be "out of work while Saddam Hussein still has a job.

It's not fair." Steven Hurst, a commentator on Gulf War I rhetoric, concludes that the shift from oil and jobs to nuclear weapons did not increase support for the war, but may have stabilized the level of support. What most certainly happened, on the other hand, was a sense of disillusionment because of Hussein's survival.[31]

Bush's successors used that disillusionment for purposes of organizing a new campaign to remove Saddam Hussein from power as part of a general effort to accomplish permanent American hegemony in the Middle East. The leaders of this movement were the so-called neo-cons associated with the Project for the New American Century (PNAC). It could also be argued that the elder Bush was a victim of his own rhetoric, at least to the extent that his political enemies could capitalize on the failure to remove Saddam as evidence that he had, at a critical moment, indeed gone "wobbly" just as the Iron Lady, Margaret Thatcher, had feared all along.[32]

Colin Powell, whose role in both Gulf Wars remains the subject of great interest as a tragic figure exploited by the second President Bush, told a PBS interviewer five years after Gulf War I that demonizing Saddam Hussein had already had consequences. "When you demonize an enemy such as the President tended to do with Saddam Hussein and others did—and frankly I did it from time to time because it was useful putting a face on this crisis—but, in so demonizing him, by the President and the rest of us, you raised expectations that you would do something about him at the end of the day."[33]

Bush celebrated the first Gulf War by asserting that the United States had kicked the Vietnam syndrome for evermore and by telling Americans on January 29, 1991, that they were truly exceptional: "Among the nations of the world, only the United States of America has had both the moral standing and the means to back it up. We are the only nation on this earth that could assemble the forces of peace." The postwar regime imposed on Saddam Hussein included no-fly zones where his forces were prohibited and demands that he allow continual inspection of suspected facilities for producing weapons of mass destruction. As arguments arose over compliance, criticism of the elder Bush grew stronger. Groups loosely associated with what was called the neoconservative movement demanded stronger action. Foremost among these was the PNAC, whose organizers pelted Bill Clinton with letters demanding a positive effort to overthrow the Iraqi government and secure American interests in the Middle East.

The signers of these letters included key members of the elder Bush's administration who were just as happy that Clinton was in the White House in the 1990s because it gave them an opportunity to attack the Democrats, even though their real target was the supposedly "realist" agenda followed in Gulf War I. Thus Paul Wolfowitz, perhaps the most frequent witness before Congress, who recycled his testimony into *Wall Street Journal* articles, asserted that the 1991 coalition could be resurrected by a new Republican president committed to bold action. It was only because other world leaders feared Clinton's inconstancy that they professed not to be ready for a new battle to liberate Iraq from the tyrant.[34]

The PNAC campaign bore early fruit in the Clinton administration. Congress passed the Iraq Liberation Act on October 31, 1998. At the signing ceremony, Clinton said:

> Today I am signing into law H.R. 4655, the "Iraq Liberation Act of 1998." This Act makes clear that it is the sense of the Congress that the United States should support those elements of the Iraqi opposition that advocate a very different future for Iraq than the bitter reality of internal repression and external aggression that the current regime in Baghdad now offers.
>
> Let me be clear on what the U.S. objectives are: The United States wants Iraq to rejoin the family of nations as a freedom-loving and law-abiding member. This is in our interest and that of our allies within the region.

In mid-December, the United States launched Operation Desert Fox, the heaviest bombing campaign after Gulf War I until the new hostilities in 2003. Secretary of State Madeline Albright spoke of "degrading" Iraq's capacity to develop weapons of mass destruction (WMD). "I don't think we're pretending that we can get everything, so this is—I think—we are being very honest about what our ability is." Almost every time she spoke about Iraq, Albright's comments practically repeated the neoconservative critique, whether it was a paraphrase of Margaret Thatcher's "no time to go wobbly" or addenda to the elder Bush's rhetoric about Saddam being worse than Hitler. At Tennessee State University on February 19, 1998, she told the crowd that the world had not seen, "except maybe since Hitler, somebody who is quite as evil as Saddam Hussein." She feared a worst-case scenario should Saddam "break out of the box that we kept him in." He could also become, she said, the salesman for weapons of mass destruction—"he could be the place that people come and get more weapons."[35]

These were all arguments used for going to war again in the Gulf when George W. Bush became president in 2001. Albright's rhetoric contrasted sharply with James Baker's assessment of where matters stood in the years after Gulf War I. Reviewing the accomplishments of the war, Baker told an interviewer flatly that the war had eliminated Iraq's WMD program. "It eliminated him really as a significant threat to the West's economic lifeline; it knocked this dictator who was sitting astride the West's economic lifeline off of it. So the war accomplished a whole host of things that are very beneficial to this day."[36]

9/11 as Catalyst

When George W. Bush was elected president by an act of the Supreme Court, the stage for a new rhetorical campaign had already been set. The 9/11 attacks provided the opportunity to renew the fight to overthrow Saddam Hussein, but more than that, it allowed the White House to reshape the world and fit it into the American dream. Some observers referred to the Bush administration's policies as "muscular" Wilsonianism, after Woodrow Wilson's famous quest to make the world safe for democracy. Under the younger Bush, moreover, it became truly a faith-based dream. It was more compelling in its power than party politics, and it rejected "realist" thinking in favor of character assessment. An early clue to what was in store came in Bush's description of an encounter with Russian leader Vladimir Putin in June 2001: "I very much enjoyed our time together. He's an honest, straightforward man who loves his country. He loves his family. We share a lot of values. I view him as a remarkable leader." Putin responded in kind. "I found [Mr. Bush] a rather sincere person, pleasant to talk to. I don't know if I should say this, but he also appeared to me to be a little bit sentimental." And back again to Bush, "I looked the man in the eye. I was able to get a sense of his soul."[37]

The real clue to Bush's praise of Putin, however (and however much they would come into sharp disagreement later), was the sorting out of nations according to Bush's soul evaluations. The lineup of villains in what would be called the "Axis of Evil" in Bush's 2002 State of the Union message began with Saddam Hussein and included the mullahs of Iran and North Korea's Kim Jong-il, all of whom, it was argued, sought to terrorize the world with their weapons of mass destruction (WMD).

Despite the younger Bush's "faith-based" approach to his perceived enemies, the *modus operandi* for justifying a war against Saddam had been established years earlier, in the aftermath of Gulf War I, with the organization of the CIA-sponsored Iraqi National Congress (INC), and its front man, Ahmed Chalabi. It took $23 million in start-up fees to get it going, and the CIA relied upon the Rendon Group, headed by a former McGovernite liberal, John Rendon, to do most of the PR work to keep the INC afloat. Eventually, the Rendon Group netted close to $100 million. The stated goal of the INC was the removal of Saddam Hussein from power. To that end it promoted the idea, through testimonials from exiled anti-Saddam figures, that the Iraqi WMD programs had been reconstituted bigger and more menacing than ever. As intelligence specialist James Bamford writes, "The key element of Rendon's INC operation was a worldwide media blitz designed to turn Hussein, a once dangerous but now contained regional leader, into the greatest threat to world peace. Each month, $326,000 was passed from the CIA to the Rendon Group and the INC via various front organizations."[38]

Eventually, after some failed lie detector tests and other disillusioning experiences, the CIA grew wary of Chalabi's operation. But there were others who more than filled in for the agency in the new administration of George W. Bush, especially Vice President Dick Cheney and Secretary of Defense Donald Rumsfeld. Under their aegis, the Office of Strategic Information came into being, and large contracts were let to the Rendon Group. Cheney tried to make the OSI seem like just another military operation: "It's sometimes valuable from a military standpoint to be able to engage in deception with respect to future anticipated plans." But the OSI was part of the bailiwick assigned to Under Secretary Douglas Feith, who became the essential funnel for INC "intelligence" on WMD to other strategic places in the administration, especially the office of the vice president. From there it would make its way into the media, via interviews on *Meet the Press* or CNN or Fox News.[39]

Perhaps the most famous description of the mind-set inside the Bush White House as it received INC "bulletins" came in an exchange that reporter Ron Suskind had with an anonymous presidential confidant. People like yourself, he told Suskind, were stuck "in what we call the reality-based community," those individuals who believed that "solutions emerged from your judicious study of discernible reality." When Suskind allowed that to be the case, murmuring something about enlightenment principles and empiricism, the aide cut him off. "That's not the way the world really works anymore. We're an empire now, and when we act, we create our own reality. And while you're studying that reality—judiciously, as you will—we'll act again, creating other new realities, which you can study too, and that's how things will sort out. We're history's actors . . . and you, all of you, will be left to just study what we do."[40]

With the publication of *The Price of Loyalty*, Suskind and his co-author, former treasury secretary Paul O'Neill, revealed that at the very first cabinet meeting of the new administration, CIA director George Tenet, a holdover eager to establish a sound relationship with Bush, distributed pictures of Iraqi buildings suspected of hiding WMDs or work on WMDs. O'Neill found nothing unusual about the buildings as the conversation drifted off onto other subjects. In the immediate aftermath of 9/11 at another meeting, O'Neill discovered that the attack had pushed the concern about Saddam Hussein into the realm of obsession. "Imagine what the region would look like without Saddam and with a regime that's aligned with U.S. interests," Rumsfeld averred. "It would change everything in the region and beyond it. It would demonstrate what U.S. policy is all about."[41]

Immediately after 9/11, however, there was no sustained public effort to link Osama bin Laden and al Qaeda to Saddam Hussein and the attacks on the Twin Towers and the Pentagon. Tenet tried very hard to avoid coming down hard on the subject of Saddam and al Qaeda, writing what one observer called a "curious" letter to the chairman of the Senate Intelligence Committee, Bob Graham, which began with the statement that "Baghdad for now appears to be drawing a line short of conducting terrorist attacks with conventional or CBW [chemical and biological weapons] against the United States," but he was also providing training for "al Qaeda members in the areas of poisons and gases and making conventional bombs."[42]

Tenet's anguish was no doubt increased by several visits to the agency by Vice President Cheney, bringing him news of what his office and, especially, what Douglas Feith's office in the Pentagon had uncovered about the connections. Feith had established his own laboratory for second-guessing raw intelligence files. One day in August 2002, Feith drove over from the Pentagon to CIA headquarters in Langley, Virginia. He brought with him his own analysts for a showdown meeting with top CIA people. Their mission was to suggest that the CIA had gone about the Iraq business from the wrong end. Instead of building a hypothesis from scattered pieces of information, the proper way to do it was to "build a hypothesis, and then see if the data supported the hypothesis." It was indeed a critical moment. Feith and the Gulf War hawks accurately represented the administration's approach to all problems: the rejection of inductive logic in favor of deductive logic. As Feith defended the practice to a sympathetic reporter, "If you take thirty movie reviewers and show them the same movie, they will understand its meaning in thirty different ways, and they will even understand the plot in different ways, and I'm not talking about watching *Rashomon*."[43]

Another way of putting this point was in the famous (or infamous) "Downing Street memo." At a meeting with Prime Minister Tony Blair and other high British officials on July 23, 2002, the head of British intelligence, identified only in James Bond style as "C," reported on his recent trip to the United States. The subject of the meeting was what C found out in Washington: "Bush wanted to remove Saddam, through military action, justified by the conjunction of terrorism and WMD. But the intelligence and facts were being fixed around the policy. The NSC [National Security Council] had no patience with the UN route and no enthusiasm for publishing material on the Iraqi regime's record. There was little discussion in Washington of the aftermath after military action." The foreign secretary promised to take up these points with his opposite, Colin Powell, even though it appeared the decision had been made. "The case was thin," he told his colleagues. "Saddam was not threatening his neighbors, and his WMD capability was less than that of Libya, North Korea, or Iran."[44]

In the immediate aftermath of the 9/11 attacks, when Americans were asked who had been behind the attacks, only 3 percent mentioned Iraq or Saddam Hussein. By January 2003, 44 percent of Americans believed that "most" or "some" of the hijackers were Iraqi citizens. Actually, none were Iraqis, while most were from Saudi Arabia, America's supposed closest ally in the Middle East outside of Israel. A senior policy analyst for the RAND Corporation, Eric Larson, suggested that Saddam's past history, invasion of two countries, and his "interest" in developing nuclear weapons—if not actual nuclear capacity—had turned the tide. "There's a jumble of attitudes in many American minds, which fit together," said Larson, "as a mosaic that [creates] a basic predisposition for military action against Saddam."[45]

Perhaps the most important piece in the mosaic is hardly ever mentioned: the anthrax attacks. The attacks on the Twin Towers and the Pentagon were carried out by hijackers carrying box cutters. They managed to hold passengers and flight crews hostage while they turned the huge jets into lethal weapons that elevated the terrorist suicide bomber into a menace previously unimagined. Even so, the hijackers were not anonymous figures. They could be, and were, quickly identified. But what if a secret menace existed, a conspiracy that had no central mass but only individuals operating at great distances and down dark streets? The anthrax letters took the fear of terrorism into science-fiction territory. The anthrax attacks sent by means of a white powder in letters killed only five people. One of the victims was an elderly lady, another a photo editor, and the others were postal workers. The letters were mailed to media figures and to the offices of two United States senators, Tom Daschle and Patrick Leahy—both of whom had voiced reservations about the Bush administration's Patriot Act, submitted to Congress after the 9/11 attacks. Almost immediately, spokespersons for the administration went into action to make a three-way link between Osama Bin Laden, the putative author of the 9/11 attacks, the anthrax letters that were sent just a week afterwards, and Mohammed Atta, the key planner of the attacks and Iraq. The nexus of the whole plot was a supposed April 2001 meeting between Atta and an Iraqi intelligence agent in Prague. It all fit together, except that it didn't when it was discovered that Atta was actually in the United States at the time of the supposed meeting.

No one was more ingenious or persistent in spreading the rumor than Dick Cheney. He avoided a direct accusation that Saddam was behind the anthrax letters. But in a series of television appearances he expressed the idea that the hijackers were part of a terrorist group that distributed the letters and were linked to Atta, leaving viewers to draw their own conclusions. Within a few weeks of the attacks, it was discovered that the two strains of anthrax found in the letters had originated in the United States and could in no way be traced to Iraq. The timing of the anthrax letters—whose author(s) is/are still unknown—made it appear that there was a connection with the hijackers, but suspicion soon fell on an American scientist working at a Defense Department laboratory. For Cheney, nevertheless, that did not exonerate Saddam Hussein. In an interview with Tim Russert near the first anniversary of the attacks on the Twin Towers, this exchange took place:

MR. RUSSERT: But if he ever did that, would we not wipe him off the face of the Earth?
VICE PRES. CHENEY: Who did the anthrax attack last fall, Tim? We don't know.
MR. RUSSERT: Could it have been Saddam?
VICE PRES. CHENEY: I don't know. I don't know who did it. I'm not here today to speculate on or to suggest that he did. My point is that it's the nature of terrorist attacks of these unconventional warfare methods, that it's very hard sometimes to identify who's responsible.[46]

The anthrax question became a complicated issue—with overtones of conspiracy arising as the FBI failed to find the culprit(s)—but it served the administration's purposes very well indeed. Other anonymous aides used a related metaphor from health scares to talk about Saddam Hussein as a virus infecting the world that had to be eliminated like the source of a global epidemic. But the success of the campaign was perhaps best caught in the words of a Selma, Alabama, firefighter who expressed his firm belief that no one knew for sure who was already in the United States waiting to attack. What did that have to do with Iraq, he was asked. "They're all in it together—all of them hate this country." The reason? America's "prosperity."[47]

Equally effective was the so-called case of the yellowcake uranium the CIA had held to be unsubstantiated but that gained currency from Cheney's repetitions. For some time a report had been circulating that supposedly originated with Italian intelligence that Saddam had sought to purchase high-grade yellowcake uranium suitable for nuclear weapons from Niger in Africa. President Bush put the claim into his 2003 State of the Union speech, saying that the British government had learned about the deal. When challenged, Cheney left the impression that the yellowcake story could not be decided one way or other, but that it could not be denied that Saddam Hussein had a "robust" WMD program.

About the same time Cheney wondered who was responsible for the anthrax letters, President Bush addressed an audience in Cincinnati, Ohio. The speech has always been regarded as the key rhetorical effort to shape and direct public opinion in the months before the war. Like Cheney, Bush insisted that the threat was a multiform one that encompassed the danger of biological weapons. But he focused on Iraq's supposed nuclear capability. Hussein had held numerous meetings, he said, with Iraqi nuclear scientists, a group he called his "nuclear mujahideen"—his nuclear holy warriors. Casting himself in the role of John Kennedy at the time of the Cuban missile crisis, Bush intoned, "Facing clear evidence of peril, we cannot wait for the final proof—the smoking gun—that could come in the form of a mushroom cloud."[48]

The Cincinnati speech was timed for delivery shortly before Congress voted on giving Bush the authority to go to war. In the first Gulf War, the elder Bush skillfully used votes in the United Nations to win over Congress; now the younger Bush was hoping for a positive vote on Capitol Hill to impress the United Nations, where efforts to reconstruct the old coalition were faltering—more than just faltering, actually collapsing. Bush aides had quipped that the delay in moving forward was because no one should introduce a new product in August. But by September he was raring to go. His father had used the Hitler comparison. Fitting with his more right-wing base, the younger Bush painted Saddam as a Stalin clone. He warned Congress that voters would not look kindly on those who shirked their duty on the vote. Asked if he had heard what the Iraqi representative to the United Nations had said, Bush replied:

> THE PRESIDENT: I didn't hear it, but let me guess: the United States is guilty, the world doesn't understand, we don't have any weapons of mass destruction. It's the same old song and dance that we've heard for eleven long years. And the United Nations Security Council must show backbone, must step up and hold this regime to account. Otherwise, the United States and some of our friends will do so.
>
> For the sake of peace, for the sake of world security, for the sake of a viable United Nations, they must act. And if they don't have it in their will to do so, if they're not willing to fashion a resolution which is new and different and strong, and holds Iraq to account, holds them to the agreements they have made, the United States will be willing to do so.
>
> QUESTION: Should the American people prepare themselves for war with Iraq, Mr. President?
>
> THE PRESIDENT: The American people must understand the serious threat which Iraq places on America. We've learned after September the 11th that oceans no longer protect us from an enemy. We also know full well this is a man who has invaded two countries, this is a man who has poisoned his own people, this is [a] man who's poisoned his neighbors, this is a man who says that Stalin is his hero, this is a man who hates, this is a man who doesn't believe in freedom, this is a man who has weapons of mass destruction and says he doesn't. He poses a serious threat to the American people. And the first step is to get the United Nations to prove to the world whether it's going to be relevant or whether it's going to be a League of Nations, irrelevant.[49]

The threatening "or else" tone recalled the "dead or alive" language of Bush's initial speech to Congress about the 9/11 attacks. If the UN Security Council showed no backbone, the United States with some of its friends, the "coalition of the willing," would do so—presumably with military force, as all other options had run out. Further inspections were useless, said Bush and Rumsfeld, while Tenet called the evidence that Saddam Hussein had WMD a "slam dunk." For a long time, Tenet clung to that description, before finally admitting that those were the two dumbest words he had ever uttered.[50]

Bush's talk about backbone was not directed solely at the UN, however, as he was continuing to have some difficulty with Secretary of State Colin Powell. When Powell finally agreed to give a speech to the UN outlining the administration's case just before the 2003 invasion, he still balked at the effort by Cheney's team to put into the speech references to the yellowcake uranium ore Saddam Hussein had supposedly attempted to obtain from the African Republic of Niger. Tenet was involved in the designing of this third piece of the mosaic as well. The convoluted story of the caper takes one from a staged break-in at the Niger embassy in Rome, to London's MI-6 headquarters, to Langley, and up the ladder to collaboration between Prime Minister Tony Blair and George Bush to create an illusion that, as Blair put it, Saddam Hussein could strike the United Kingdom within 45 minutes.[51]

Having failed to convince the CIA in the first go-around that the documents purporting the sale from Niger were genuine, the Bush administration apparently turned the case back over to the British. Tony Blair accepted the challenge and in September 2002 released what later became known as the "dodgy dossier" on Iraqi WMD with a report he introduced in the following words: "Gathering intelligence inside Iraq is not easy. Saddam's is one of the most secretive and dictatorial regimes in the world. So I believe people will understand why the Agencies cannot be specific about the sources, which have formed the judgements in this document, and why we cannot publish everything we know."[52]

In his January 28, 2003, State of the Union message, President Bush recited a litany of Iraq's WMD and included the yellowcake instance as proven fact: "The British government has learned that Saddam Hussein recently sought significant quantities of uranium from Africa." With those sixteen words, the mosaic was complete. After the war started, and after Bush had announced, "Mission Accomplished," all that had actually been achieved was the selling of the war. The yellowcake story fell apart the quickest. By July 11, 2003, the president had to admit, "I gave a speech to the nation that was cleared by the intelligence services." That same day, National Security Advisor Condoleeza Rice said that the CIA had cleared the State of the Union speech "in its entirety." And George Tenet fell on his sword: "These 16 words should never have been included in the text written for the president."

For a time, with Saddam's statue being pulled down in Baghdad, although not quite as advertised by joyous Iraqis, it seemed not to matter. ABC reporter Diane Sawyer interviewed the president on December 16, 2003, three days after Saddam Hussein was flushed from his "spider hole" near his home in northern Iraq. Was this the best day of his presidency, she asked? No, not the best, but he had talked to his dad, the elder President Bush, and could tell that his father's voice was filled with pride. "It was a touching moment." Much later in the interview, Sawyer turned to the criticisms that were being heard, specifically that there was no hard evidence that Saddam Hussein had WMD when the war began. His answers suddenly became filled with vocalized pauses. "What—I, I—made my decision based upon enough intelligence to tell me that this country was threatened with Saddam Hussein in power." Sawyer followed with a question about what it would take to convince him that he didn't have weapons of mass destruction. Having already said that it didn't make any difference whether Saddam had them or only aspired to have them, Bush became testy. "Diane, you can keep asking the question. I'm telling you—I made the right decision."[53]

At the Radio and Television Correspondents' Association Dinner on March 24, 2004, a very appropriate occasion, George Bush showed slides depicting what a satirist might say about this performance—standard operating procedure for these dinners where presidents are expected to roast themselves. At one point, Bush showed a photo of himself looking out a window in the Oval Office, and he said, "Those weapons of mass destruction have got to be somewhere."

"The audience laughed," reported David Corn. "I grimaced. But that wasn't the end of it. After a few more slides, there was a shot of Bush looking under furniture in the Oval Office. 'Nope,' he said. 'No weapons over there.' More laughter. Then another picture of Bush searching in his office: 'Maybe under here.' Laughter again."[54]

It is hard to imagine another slideshow like that one.

Afterword

It is often argued that Gulf War II was simply a continuation of the struggle with Saddam Hussein that began a decade earlier. Well, it was and it wasn't. Gulf War I was clearly a "realist's" war, however much it was sold as a moral obligation to stop the madness of another Hitler spreading across the Middle East. As inevitably happens, however, selling a war without invoking such images proved impossible. The impassioned rhetoric that the elder Bush used to bring Congress around provided the dark background against which the case for another military intervention was made, this time to eliminate a source of trouble and to give the United States a new footing outside Saudi Arabia, where it was feared the American military might have outworn its welcome. Without 9/11, it is unlikely that the case for war could have been made successfully, although it is certainly within reason to suggest that the activities of the Rendon Group, acting at the behest of the Central Intelligence Agency, could have brought about a war in a similar manner to yellow journalism in starting things off with a bang in 1898, a war that launched the American empire. What strikes one most forcefully, in the end, is that it seems to be getting easier and easier to accomplish such missions, as "globalization" brings with it a struggle for power and natural resources even greater than during the high imperialist era.

Notes

1. James Dao and Eric Schmitt, "Pentagon Readies Efforts to Sway Sentiment Abroad," *New York Times*, February 19, 2002.

2. Mike Allen, "White House Angered at Plan for Pentagon Disinformation," *Washington Post*, February 25, 2002.

3. "Defense Department Briefing," February 26, 2002, http://www.fas.org/sgp/news/2002/02/dod022602.html>.

4. Thom Shanker and Eric Schmitt, "Pentagon Weighs Use of Deception in a Broad Arena," *New York Times*, December 13, 2004.

5. Easy cross-references to the transcripts can be found in the article "April Glaspie," <http://en.wikipedia.org/wiki/April_Glaspie>.

6. Joseph Wilson, *The Politics of Truth: Inside the Lies That Led to War and Betrayed My Wife's CIA Identity* (New York: Carroll & Graf, 2004), 102.

7. Herbert S. Parmet, *George Bush: The Life of a Lone Star Yankee* (New York: Scribner, 1997), 454. The Thatcher comment nevertheless haunted Bush's presidency. It was taken up by both conservative and liberal critics and may have influenced his son's determination to go to war with Iraq in 2003.

8. Jennifer Huang, "A Cold War Legacy of Persian Gulf Conflict," March 19, 2003, <http://www.artsand media.net/cgi-bin/dc/newsdesk/2003/03/18>.

9. Ibid.

10. George Bush and Brent Scowcroft, *A World Transformed* (New York: Alfred A. Knopf, 1998), 315.

11. "Remarks and an Exchange with Reporters on the Iraqi Invasion of Kuwait," August 5, 1990, <http://www.margaretthatcher.org/archive/displaydocument.asp?docid=110704>.

12. PBS, *Frontline: The Gulf War* (program originally broadcast January 6, 1996), oral histories, Dick Cheney, <http://www.pbs.org/wgbh/pages/frontline/gulf/oral/cheney/5.html>.

13. Colin Powell, with Joseph Persico, *My American Journey* (New York: Ballantine Books, 1996), 451.

14. Ibid., 457.

15. Scott Ritter, *Target Iran: The Truth about the White House's Plans for Regime Change* (New York: Nation Books, 2006), 5.

16. Bush and Scowcroft, *A World Transformed*, 382, emphasis added.

17. At <http://www.pbs.org/wgbh/pages/frontline/gulf/oral/baker/5.html>.

18. Bush and Scowcroft, *A World Transformed*, 355.

19. Roger Osborne, *Civilization: A New History of the Western World* (New York: Pegasus Books, 2006), 102–3.

20. Quoted in Maureen Dowd, "Mideast Tensions: Bush Intensifies a War of Words against the Iraqis," *New York Times*, November 1, 1990.

21. Center for Media and Democracy, "How PR Sold the War in the Persian Gulf," <http://www.prwatch.org/node/25/print>.

22. Ibid.

23. John R. MacArthur, *Second Front: Censorship and Propaganda in the Gulf War* (New York: Hill and Wang, 1992), 65–68.

24. Press Conference, November 1, 1990, text available at <http://bushlibrary.tamu.edu/research/papers/1990/90110102.html>.

25. Dowd, "Mideast Tensions."

26. See Steven Hurst, "The Rhetorical Strategy of George H. W. Bush during the Persian Gulf Crisis, 1990–91: How to Help Lose a War You Won," *Political Studies* 32 (2004): 376–92.

27. Lawrence Freedman and Efraim Karsh, *The Gulf Conflict, 1990–1991: Diplomacy and War in the New World Order* (Princeton: Princeton University Press, 1993), 220.

28. Ibid., 291–95.

29. "Gulf War Stories the Media Loved—Except They Aren't True," <http://www.fair.org/index.php?page=1515>.

30. S. H. Kelly, "Bush Tells Gulf Vets Why Hussein Left in Baghdad," *Army Link News*, March 3, 1999, <http://www.fas.org/news/iraq/1999/03/a19990303bush.htm>.

31. Hurst, "The Rhetorical Strategy of George H. W. Bush."

32. For a left critique, see Andrew and Patrick Cockburn, *Out of the Ashes: The Resurrection of Saddam Hussein* (New York: Harper Perennial, 2000).

33. See <http://www.pbs.org/wgbh/pages/frontline/gulf/oral/powell/5.html>.

34. James Mann, *The Rise of the Vulcans: The History of Bush's War Cabinet* (New York: Viking, 2004), 235–38.

35. Daniel McKivergan, "The Clinton Folks Go to the White House to Discuss Iraq," <http://www.weeklystandard.com/weblogs/TWSFP/2006/01/the_clinton_folks_go_to_the_white_house_to_discuss_Iraq>.

36. See <http://www.pbs.org/wgbh/pages/frontline/gulf/oral/baker/5.html>.

37. Colonel Stanislav Lunev, "Bush-Putin Meeting: Breakthrough or Window Dressing?" July 25, 2001, <www.newsmax.com/archives/articles/2001/7/25/103834.shtml>.

38. James Bamford, "The Man Who Sold the War," *Rolling Stone*, November 17, 2005.

39. Ibid.

40. Ron Suskind, "Without a Doubt," *New York Times Magazine*, October 17, 2004.

41. Ron Suskind, *The Price of Loyalty: George W. Bush, the White House, and the Education of Paul O'Neill* (New York: Simon & Schuster, 2004), 85.

42. Jeffrey Goldberg, "The Unknown: The CIA and the Pentagon Take Another Look at Al Qaeda and Iraq," *New Yorker*, February 10, 2003.

43. Ibid.

44. The Downing Street memo has been reprinted many times. It first appeared in the *London Times*, May 5, 2005, the result of a leak intended to embarrass Tony Blair.

45. Linda Feldmann, "The Impact of Bush Linking 9/11 and Iraq," *Christian Science Monitor*, March 14, 2003.

46. Transcript of interview with Vice President Dick Cheney on *Meet the Press*, 8 September 2002, <www.mtholyoke.edu/acad/intrel/bush/meet.htm>. The entire exchange indicates even more that Cheney was seeking to pinpoint Saddam Hussein as the likely author of the attacks:

VICE PRES. CHENEY: It's also important not to focus just on the nuclear threat. I mean, that sort of grabs everybody's attention, and that's what we're used to dealing with. But come back to 9/11 again, and one of the real concerns about Saddam Hussein, as well, is his biological weapons capability; the fact that he may, at some point, try to use smallpox, anthrax, plague, some other kind of biological agent against other nations, possibly including even the United States. So this is not just a one-dimensional threat. This just isn't a guy who's now back trying once again to build nuclear weapons. It's the fact that we've also seen him in these other areas, in chemicals, but also especially in biological weapons, increase his capacity to produce and deliver these weapons upon his enemies.

MR. RUSSERT: But if he ever did that, would we not wipe him off the face of the Earth?

VICE PRES. CHENEY: Who did the anthrax attack last fall, Tim? We don't know.

MR. RUSSERT: Could it have been Saddam?

VICE PRES. CHENEY: I don't know. I don't know who did it. I'm not here today to speculate on or to suggest that he did. My point is that it's the nature of terrorist attacks of these unconventional warfare methods, that it's very hard sometimes to identify who's responsible. Who's the source? We were able to come fairly quickly to the conclusion after 9/11 that Osama bin Laden was, in fact, the individual behind the 9/11 attacks. But, like I say, I point out the anthrax example just to remind everybody that it is very hard sometimes, especially when we're dealing with something like a biological weapon that could conceivably be misconstrued, at least for some period, as a naturally occurring event, that we may not know who launches the next attack.

47. Feldmann, "The Impact of Bush Linking 9/11 and Iraq." The fullest account of the anthrax scare and its momentous impact on the public and the case for war is Phillip Sarasin, *Anthrax: Bioterror as Fact and Fantasy*, trans. Giselle Weiss (Cambridge: Harvard University Press, 2006). Despite its occasional lapses into postmodern jargon, Sarasin's book provides an excellent account of the politics of anthrax.

48. "President Bush Outlines Iraqi Threat," October 7, 2002, <http://www.whitehouse.gov/news/releases/2002/10/print/20021007-8>. He quoted Kennedy's words in the speech: "We no longer live in a world where only the actual firing of weapons represents a sufficient challenge to a nation's security to constitute maximum peril."

49. "Remarks Following a Visit with Homeland Security Employees and an Exchange with Reporters," September 19, 2002, in John T. Woolley and Gerhard Peters, *The American Presidency Project* [online] <http://www.presidency.ucsb.edu/ws/index.php?pid=73119&st=&stl= >.

50. James Risen, *State of War: The Secret History of the CIA and the Bush Administration* (New York: Free Press, 2006), 122–23.

51. Untangling the yellowcake story requires much fuller treatment than can be offered here. For two good accounts, see Michael Isikoff and David Corn, *Hubris: The Inside Story of Spin, Scandal, and the Selling of the Iraq War* (New York: Crown, 2006) and James Bamford, *A Pretext for War: 9/11, Iraq, and the Abuse of America's Intelligence Agencies* (New York: Doubleday, 2004).

52. See Image.guardian.co.uk/sys-files/Politics/documents/2002/09/24/dossier.pdf.

53. See <http://www.yuricareport.com/PoliticalAnalysis/BushInterviewByDianeSawyer12_16_03.html>.

54. See <www.thenation.com/blogs/capitalgames?pid=1336>.

10

CONCLUSION

War, Democracy, and the State

Robert J. McMahon

On August 26, 2002, Vice President Dick Cheney delivered a major speech before the Veterans of Foreign Wars in Nashville, Tennessee, in which he essentially called for war against Iraq. Cheney labeled Iraq a clear and present danger, connecting it to the al Qaeda attacks against the United States of September 11, 2001, and the broader terrorist threat that Americans now faced. "The president and I never for a moment forget our number-one responsibility," Cheney declared: "To protect the American people against further attack and to win the war that began last September eleventh. . . . We realize that wars are never won on the defensive. We must take the battle to the enemy." Since there was "no doubt" that Iraq possessed large stocks of biological and chemical weapons, the vice president reasoned, and since "many of us are convinced that Saddam Hussein will acquire nuclear weapons fairly soon," the United States simply could not afford to ignore this growing threat any longer. "The risks of inaction are far greater than the risks of action," Cheney warned. That was so because the Iraqi dictator was "amassing" weapons of mass destruction "to use against our friends, against our allies, and against us."[1]

Cheney's bellicose address formed the opening act of what became a concerted campaign by the George W. Bush administration to gain public and congressional support for an action that the president, vice president, and their leading advisors had already decided upon: the toppling by military force of the regime of Saddam Hussein. Fear played a central role in that campaign. On September 8, National Security Advisor Condoleeza Rice reiterated Cheney's chief themes while using even more frightening imagery. "The problem here is that there will always be some uncertainty about how quickly he can acquire nuclear weapons," she remarked. "But we don't want the smoking gun to be a mushroom cloud."[2] The president added his voice to the chorus four days later, in a major address before the UN General Assembly. Iraq represented "a grave and gathering danger," Bush proclaimed. He, too, emphasized that time was running out: "With every step the Iraqi regime takes toward gaining and deploying the most terrible weapons, our own options to confront that regime will narrow."[3]

On October 7, the president delivered a speech in Cincinnati that described the threat posed by Iraq in the most dire and alarmist terms yet. Bush called attention to the "high-level contacts" between Iraq and al Qaeda that, he said, "go back a decade." He asserted that Saddam Hussein possessed biological and chemical weapons, was "increasing his capabilities to make more," and was at the same time "moving closer to developing a nuclear weapon." Time was of the essence, Bush insisted; the United States could not afford to wait for additional evidence to materialize about Iraq's capabilities. "America must not ignore the threat gathering against us," the president cautioned. "Facing clear evidence of peril, we cannot wait for the final proof, the smoking gun that could come in the form of a mushroom cloud."[4]

The asserted but unproven links between al Qaeda, the terrorist organization that actually attacked the United States on 9/11, and the Saddam Hussein regime, which did not, formed a crucial part of the Bush administration's campaign of persuasion and manipulation. That campaign culminated, on February 5, 2003, with the highly publicized report to the UN by Secretary of State Colin Powell. Buttressed with charts, exhibits, and recently declassified intelligence reports, Powell's impressive presentation treated as incontrovertible facts matters that remained quite uncertain, even within U.S. and other Western intelligence circles. "Our conservative estimate is that Iraq today has a stockpile of between 100 and 500 tons of chemical weapons agent," he declared with certitude. Saddam "remains determined to acquire nuclear weapons." The secretary of state also spoke directly of what he called "the potentially much more sinister nexus between Iraq and the al Qaeda terrorist network," again offering as fact something that was anything but.[5]

Bush gave one last press conference before he announced, on March 20, the inauguration of hostilities against Iraq. During that appearance, he interchanged the terrorist attacks of 9/11 with the threat posed by Saddam Hussein's regime no fewer than eight times. Not once did any of the assembled journalists question the linkage.[6] The palpable fears engendered within American society by the first attack on the continental United States since the War of 1812 provided the Bush administration with a highly emotive point of reference, one that it exploited repeatedly in its efforts to mobilize popular support for the planned invasion of Iraq. The absence of any un-ambiguous evidence tying Iraq to al Qaeda hardly seemed to matter, as key administration spokesmen continually stressed, without significant qualifi-cation, that such links existed. Both public opinion polls and a key congres-sional vote that winter testify to the effectiveness of the administration's campaign of persuasion—and the scare tactics at the heart of that campaign. Fear, to put it bluntly, helped sell the American people on the need for war with Iraq.

President McKinley, in striking contrast, saw no need to scare the public into supporting war with Spain. As the crisis in Cuba deepened in early 1898, the prevailing dynamic was, in fact, almost exactly the reverse of that facing Bush in 2002–2003. The public at large and key elements within the Congress, aroused by sensational newspaper reporting about Spanish atrocities, were clamoring for war well *before* McKinley reached the decision that military conflict with Spain would serve American interests. Not only did this pro-war sentiment arise quite independent of any White House effort to create or stoke it, but, as George C. Herring's chapter makes clear, McKinley initially tried to tamp down that enthusiasm for fear that it might prematurely force his hand. When the Republican chief executive finally decided that only a resort to force would produce the results he desired, he acted with the assurance that strong congressional backing for a declaration of war could easily be attained; no elaborate sales job on his part would be needed. The McKinley administration's task, consequently, proved far less difficult than that of the Bush administration: it simply needed to sustain the substantial degree of popular support that it already had. The overwhelming success of U.S. arms and the short duration of the war with Spain, moreover, precluded the emergence of the problems that often plague democracies during unsuccessful or protracted conflicts—as Lyndon B. Johnson learned during the Vietnam War and George W. Bush would discover during the Iraq conflict.

McKinley's far more serious challenge came when he sought to persuade the public to accept, as the fruits of American military success, formal an-nexation of the Philippines. Ultimately, of course, he prevailed, earning a hard-won treaty victory in the Senate. Yet McKinley only achieved that desired outcome after engaging in an up-to-then unprecedented series of regional speaking tours. Significantly, he appealed not to strategic or exis-tential fears in his public addresses, as Bush would so notoriously do more than a century later, but instead to honor, patriotism, religious duty, and the nation's higher calling. If Bush's public relations exertions in the run-up to the Iraq War were designed to stoke fears within the body politic of an evil adversary's presumed capacity to wreak untold damage on Americans with weapons of mass destruction, McKinley's equally emotional exhortations were designed to appeal to the nation's ideals rather than its apprehensions.

Despite those fundamental differences, a common theme runs through these two highly divergent cases—and through each of the other cases so ably examined in this book. Simply put, from the late nineteenth century to the present, U.S. presidents have evinced a keen and abiding appreciation for the importance of public opinion in a democratic polity, especially on matters of war or peace. Whether they saw it as stubborn or malleable, a barrier or an enabler, presidents from McKinley to the Bushes have recognized the power of popular sentiment. American heads of state have, consequently, sought through a dizzying array of increasingly sophisticated means to placate, accommodate, educate, mobilize, or manipulate the citizenry at large and its congressional representatives. They have done so in order to gain the freedom of action that authoritarian leaders often take for granted. They have also done so to prevent the emergence of widespread opposition that could at once complicate their position as commanders in chief, thwart the attainment of desired military goals, and damage their political fortunes and those of their political party.

During the first half of the period covered by this volume, the nexus between executive initiative and public opinion typically reached a climax with the required debate and vote in Congress about a formal, presidentially requested declaration of war. In April 1917, President Woodrow Wilson gained overwhelming congressional support for his proposed declaration of war against the Central Powers. In December 1941, Franklin D. Roosevelt achieved near-unanimous backing for his proposed declaration of war against Japan and Germany. That each chief executive waited until the prospective enemy struck first—Germany's U-boat assault on U.S. shipping in the Atlantic in the first case; Japan's strike on Pearl Harbor in the second—allowed those Democratic leaders to make much stronger appeals for war than would have been the case had either sought earlier action from Congress.

The lopsided votes on Capitol Hill in 1917 and 1941, accordingly, should not be read as indicators of a pliable public during those years. As late as October 1941, it bears emphasizing, leading polls revealed that only 25 percent of the public supported formal U.S. entry into World War II. As Mark

A. Stoler notes, FDR displayed a continuing apprehension, throughout 1941, of losing public backing and then being hamstrung by a resurgence of isolationism. Indeed, Roosevelt acted with indirection, deception, and subterfuge from the late 1930s onward largely because of his awareness of the deeply held antiwar sentiments of ordinary Americans and their congressional representatives. He moved with caution and wariness as he incrementally pushed the United States into the role of co-belligerent in the war against Germany. Wilson, for his part, deliberately exaggerated the dangers Germany posed to U.S. security, demonized the enemy "Hun" in outrageous fashion, clamped down severely on virtually all forms of public dissent, and utilized novel methods of propaganda to foster national unity during wartime. All of those actions, as Emily S. Rosenberg's contribution reminds us, derived from a felt need to limit the boundaries of acceptable, and legally permissible, discourse in a nation that was anything but unified in its views during the "Great War."

Since World War II, American presidents have deliberately eschewed formal declarations of war. They have authorized military action in Korea, Vietnam, Kuwait, Afghanistan, Iraq, and elsewhere without ever asking Congress to approve a war declaration, acting instead on a definition of executive authority so expansive that it likely would have stunned the framers of the constitution. Truman set the precedent with his decision to intervene in Korea following the North Korean invasion of June 25, 1950. Critics then, and since, have argued that he wrongly denied the legislative branch its constitutionally sanctioned responsibility for deciding upon a matter of war or peace. Truman's secretary of state, Dean Acheson, strenuously disagreed, insisting on the president's right to dispatch U.S. combat forces to Korea based on "legal theory and historical precedent." Even more salient to the decision, though, was Acheson's belief that a congressional debate likely would have provided a forum for partisan critics of the administration that would just have hurt the morale of U.S. troops while puncturing the unity that temporarily prevailed at home. "The harm it could do seemed to me far to outweigh the little good that might ultimately accrue," he wrote later.[7]

Intent on avoiding the opprobrium heaped on Truman for bypassing Congress, Johnson sought what was, in effect, congressional preauthorization for military action in Vietnam. He had prepared what became the Tonkin Gulf Resolution of August 1964 well in advance of the alleged North Vietnamese attacks that ostensibly justified it, believing that it would be politically foolhardy to move forward in Vietnam without first securing congressional support. "It was my impression," recalled his national security advisor, McGeorge Bundy, "that President Johnson had been looking for some time for the proper peg to hang this resolution on, and what he was looking for was something that was overt, some hostile attack on American forces which would give an excuse to the Congress to pass the resolution that he wanted."[8] He got precisely what he wanted when Congress authorized him, according to the Tonkin Gulf Resolution, "to take all necessary measures to repel any armed attack against the forces of the United States and to prevent further aggression." It constituted a virtual blank check for military action.

George H. W. Bush and George W. Bush chose to follow Johnson's precedent rather than Truman's. Each of the Bushes, before initiating hostilities against Saddam Hussein's Iraq, sought a nonbinding congressional resolution that would put the legislative branch on record in support of military action—if the president deemed it necessary at some future point. They favored such an approach because, unlike a declaration of war, the chief executive's freedom of action could not be constrained by a nonbinding resolution, even if the Congress delivered a negative vote. In each case, consequently, legislators were given the opportunity to debate and vote for or against an enabling resolution *before* the president had reached a final decision for war and yet with the knowledge that a negative vote could not by itself derail a march toward war. Politically, the tactic worked well. Each of the Bush presidencies could claim that the dispatch of U.S. combat forces to the Persian Gulf had been sanctioned by Congress; yet they could also assert that, on constitutional grounds, neither *needed* that sanction and hence neither risked being reined in by a recalcitrant Congress.

Both Johnson and George W. Bush found maintaining public support for what became America's two longest wars far more problematic. As each conflict dragged on inconclusively, public support eroded. Chester Pach demonstrates with arresting detail how LBJ grew obsessed with the need to regain the public's backing. In early August 1967, just one-third of those polled expressed support for the president's handling of the Vietnam War. Blaming a hostile press for his plight, especially television reporters, Johnson launched a media blitz dubbed the "Progress Campaign" in an effort to highlight steady U.S. military success in Vietnam. "We have to sell our product to the American people," he insisted to his advisors. Although the public relations campaign achieved some temporary success, it was soon overwhelmed by the enemy's Tet offensive of early 1968. Johnson found himself saddled with a war that he could neither win nor end. That made selling it to the American people a virtually impossible task, as Pach rightly stresses. No amount of optimistic rhetoric could alter the hard and stubborn facts on the ground.

The final chapter of the Iraq War remains to be written. It may be too early to predict its effect on Barack Obama's administration, but Bush, who appeared saddled with a conflict that he could neither win nor end, suffered near-record lows in terms of public approval ratings largely for that reason. The original rationale for the U.S. invasion of Iraq—that country's alleged possession of weapons of mass destruction and its alleged links with al Qaeda terrorists—collapsed when chemical and biological weapons caches were not found and ties to al Qaeda could not be proven. *New York Times* columnist Frank Rich, a virulent critic of the war, sarcastically titled his exposé of the Bush administration's exaggerations and lies about the Iraqi threat *The Greatest Story Ever Sold*. No matter how effectively presidents mobilize public support for the initiation of hostilities, however, they invariably encounter enormous difficulties in holding such support whenever a clear and decisive victory is not attained within a reasonable period of time. Clearly, even under the best of circumstances, democratic polities grow restive during drawn-out, inconclusive wars. The leaders responsible for such conflicts typically pay the price with plummeting levels of public support. Stoler's citation of George Marshall's famous quote about democracies and war seems particularly apt in this regard. "We could not indulge in a Seven Years' War," the general observed by way of explanation for why the United States moved "brutally fast" in Europe during World War II. "A king can perhaps do that, but you cannot have such a protracted struggle in a democracy in the face of mounting casualties."[9]

This volume usefully reminds us that the preoccupation of America's modern presidents with public attitudes toward the nation's overseas commitments has not been confined just to incidents of hot war. As the essays by Robert D. Schulzinger, Kenneth Osgood, and Paul S. Boyer show, the battle for the hearts and minds of the American populace was waged with comparable vigor throughout the Cold War as well. Cold War presidents from Truman to Reagan recognized the great value of having a public that was broadly supportive of major foreign policy commitments—and, conversely, they recognized the danger of *not* having that support. For all the policy differences that distinguished their particular approaches to the Cold War, each of those presidents appreciated the importance of mobilizing and maintaining public support for the nation's strategic commitments and massive defense spending. Some of Eisenhower's most significant public addresses, as Osgood demonstrates, were sophisticated forms of propaganda designed to gain the high ground for the United States in its struggle with the Soviet Union while winning favor both with domestic and international audiences. Reagan's Strategic Defense Initiative, and his subsequent public relations campaign on its behalf, likewise stemmed from a quite conscious effort to shape public discourse.

Reagan worried, as had Eisenhower, that the costs of full-scale defense mobilization during peacetime might trigger substantial public resistance if America's intentions were not convincingly portrayed as benign, peaceful, and innocent. That 80 percent of Americans backed SDI, according to a September 1984 poll, suggests that Reagan largely succeeded in shrouding the missile shield idea in the comfortable cloak of American innocence and exceptionalism. Cold War presidents, as Schulzinger's valuable contribution points out, consistently used such rhetorical tropes in mobilizing the support of ordinary Americans for the nation's vast foreign policy and defense commitments.

If an appreciation on the part of America's leaders for the importance of popular support and a determination to mobilize it form constants in the episodes examined in this volume, these essays also show that over time presidents have employed dramatically different means of persuasion. While presidential rhetoric has remained an indispensable instrument for reaching and molding mass opinion from the late nineteenth century to the present, first the advent of motion pictures and radio and then television have allowed U.S. chief executives to reach ever-larger audiences and in a much more immediate, and intimate, manner. McKinley's regional speaking tours on behalf of Philippine annexation seem primitive when compared to the technological sophistication, splashy imagery, dramatic staging, and emotional appeals utilized by George W. Bush in his selling of the Iraq War. The early use of Madison Avenue advertising techniques by the Wilson administration and all attempts, prior to the 1930s, to gauge public opinion simply by scouring newspaper editorials would strike denizens of today's poll-saturated society as equally primitive. Changes in technology and expansions of and innovations within the mass media have, over time, given presidents bigger, more varied, and more sophisticated tools for presenting their versions of the truth—as well as for combating alternative versions. By the same token, as some of the essays in this book suggest, critics of government policies have also benefited from those technological changes, many of which have enabled them to get their countermessages to wider audiences as well.

Whether the efforts of different presidents to build support for their wartime and Cold War policies can best be described as public education, persuasion, mobilization, or manipulation constitutes one of the most hotly contested of the broader issues raised by this book. Is truth always the "first casualty" of war, as the famous Winston S. Churchill quote would have it? Or is it possible for a national leader in a democratic society to mobilize and persuade the citizenry to support war without shading the truth, and without engaging in outright subterfuge, manipulation, or lying? Can a shading of the truth at times be justified, as Roosevelt doubtless believed when he presented the *Greer* episode to the public as an unprovoked act of German aggression? Or as Lyndon Johnson evidently thought during the Tonkin Gulf affair? If so, when is that the case? What criteria should be applied? And who should decide? If a president is convinced that genuine national security issues are at stake, does he then have the right, or responsibility, to nudge public opinion in the direction he considers essential if being less than truthful will expedite such movement? And does a president ever have the right to present as "fact" information that remains contested, even if by so doing he can help build a consensus behind the actions he believes necessary to ensure the nation's physical well-being?

Those rank as some of the most basic and most controversial questions raised by the provocative essays featured in this important collection. Grappling with them is not just of fundamental importance in any full and fair reconstruction of the critical episodes in the nation's past presented herein. It is also of fundamental importance to issues of public policy, responsible leadership, and constitutional obligations that resonate with equal force in today's world. In an even broader sense, such questions are critical to any examination, across time and space, of the complex and inherently contentious relationship between war, democracy, and the state.

Notes

1. *New York Times*, August 27, 2002.
2. Quoted in Thomas E. Ricks, *Fiasco: The American Military Adventure in Iraq* (New York: Penguin, 2006), 58.
3. *New York Times*, September 13, 2002.
4. *New York Times*, October 8, 2002.
5. *New York Times*, February 6, 2003.
6. *New York Times*, March 21, 2003; Frank Rich, *The Greatest Story Ever Sold: The Decline and Fall of Truth from 9/11 to Katrina* (New York: Penguin, 2006), 69–70.

7. Dean Acheson, *Present at the Creation: My Years in the State Department* (New York: Norton, 1969), 414–15.

8. Quoted in Ted Gittinger, ed., *The Johnson Years: A Vietnam Roundtable* (Austin: Lyndon B. Johnson Library, University of Texas, 1993), 23.

9. Quoted in Mark A. Stoler, "Selling Different Kinds of War," this volume.

AFTERWORD

Editorial Note

A distinguished journalist and prolific author, David Halberstam came to personify the new trend of a more critical form of war reporting that emerged during the Vietnam War. His experience, as recounted below, provides a personal view of what happens when a correspondent gets in the way of the government's efforts to sell a war.

Born in New York City in 1934, Halberstam graduated from Harvard, where he was editor of the student newspaper. He covered the civil rights movement for Mississippi and Tennessee newspapers and then took a position with the Washington bureau of the *New York Times*. Following a stint in the Congo, in 1962 he was assigned to Vietnam, where the war between the U.S.-backed South Vietnamese government and the National Liberation Front insurgency supported by North Vietnam was heating up. Along with Neil Sheehan of the United Press International, Halberstam quickly sensed that the war was not going as well as U.S. spokespersons claimed. His critical dispatches gained the attention of diplomatic and military officials in Saigon and even of President John F. Kennedy, who sought to silence him by getting him transferred. Halberstam's perceptive reporting on Vietnam won him a Pulitzer Prize.

Halberstam left the *Times* in the late 1960s and became a prolific and versatile writer on a variety of subjects. An early book, *The Making of a Quagmire* (1965), told of his experiences in Vietnam, but it was *The Best and the Brightest* (1972) that established him as an author of note. This critical analysis of the Kennedy and Johnson administrations' handling of the Vietnam War included richly colorful sketches of the leading personalities. The villain was Secretary of Defense Robert McNamara, the "can-do man in the can-do era," as Halberstam called him. But the focus of the book was the fundamental question of how the best and the brightest Americans could be so terribly wrong in Vietnam.

Over the next three decades, Halberstam authored more than twenty books on topics ranging from the Japanese automobile industry to the 1949

American League pennant race. At his untimely death in April 2007, an account of the Korean War was in press and he was working on another book about the NFL championship game of 1958, generally considered the best football game ever played.

He had also intended to write a selection for this book. Graciously, his family allowed us to publish instead his talk at Florida Atlantic University's Alan B. Larkin Symposium on the American Presidency. That lecture—one of his last—appears below. It has been edited for publication by Kenneth Osgood and George Herring.

A WORM'S-EYE VIEW

David Halberstam

I would like to talk about the war and the presidency and the presidency selling the war. Rather than provide a lofty historian's perspective, I wanted to give you a worm's-eye view of the president selling a war and what happens when you're the reporter that the White House wants to roll over.

I will begin with the early 1960s in Vietnam and with a tape of a conversation in the White House in October 1963.[1] President John F. Kennedy was meeting with his national security advisor, McGeorge Bundy, his assistant secretary of defense for international security affairs, William Bundy, and his secretary of defense, Robert McNamara—the guy with the slicked-back hair, or, as Lyndon Johnson described him, "the guy with all the Stacomb on his hair." In the recording, Kennedy asks his advisors about the media's treatment of the conflict in Vietnam:

> Kennedy: "What about the press out there?"
> McNamara: "Miserable. . . . Terribly difficult. There are two or three good ones. But Halberstam and [Neil] Sheehan are the ones that are . . ."
> Kennedy: "Causing you a lot of trouble."
> McNamara: "Just causing a lot of trouble. They're allowing an idealistic philosophy to color all their writing."

The discussion soon turned to me and my reporting on Vietnam, as President Kennedy asked, "How old is Halberstam?"

William Bundy: "About twenty-five."

McGeorge Bundy: "[Class of] '55."

Kennedy: "[Was] he at Harvard?"

William Bundy: "Mac [McGeorge Bundy] was his teacher. Listen to him." (By the way, that is not true. I never took a course with him.)

McGeorge Bundy: "I want you to know that he was a reporter even when he was in college, and I dealt with him at the *Harvard Crimson* for two years. So I know exactly what you've been up against. [Laughter] A very gifted boy . . . who gets all steamed up. No doubt about it. That was ten years ago."

Kennedy: "He's one of those liberal *Harvard Crimson* types?"

Bundy: "Yes sir!"

There is an interesting footnote to that history. In 1964, I came back from two years in Vietnam. I was in Washington one night at a cocktail party, and I ran into Professor Arthur Schlesinger Jr., my old history professor from college. He was then working as a kind of in-residence historian/biographer for the Kennedy administration. He was very generous, and he kept telling me that I did a wonderful job in Vietnam—which I was quite ready to agree with. The president, he said, "used to say that he would find out more from my dispatches than he could from all the reports being sent in by the ambassadors, the State Department, and all the generals."

"What?" I asked. "If that's true, then why did he ask the publisher of the *New York Times,* [Arthur Ochs] Punch Sulzberger, to pull me out of there and send me to another assignment?"

At that point, I had already spoken to the Washington Bureau chief of the *Times,* a man named James "Scotty" Reston, who told me in detail about this meeting with Kennedy where the president had asked about getting rid of me. The story was that it was the first meeting of the young publisher with the president in October 1963. Sulzberger was extremely nervous. He had never met a president of the United States before, and he was going over there. He turned to Reston and said, "You know what? I never dealt with a president. What do I say? What do I do?" And Scotty said, "Relax. He is going to ask you about your children, and then you ask him about his children. Nothing to it."

So they walked in, the president looked at them, and the first question was, "What do you think about your young man in Saigon?"

"We like him just fine," the startled young publisher replied.

"You don't think," said the president of the United States, "that he's getting a little too close to the story?"

You could translate that to mean that he's getting to be a pain in the ass to me.

"No, we think he is doing just fine," said Punch, who by the way was quite hawkish on Vietnam. An ex-Marine, he probably didn't like my reporting but understood that if you are the publisher of the *New York Times* you get out of the way of your reporters.

"You weren't thinking," Kennedy inquired, "of transferring him to Paris or London?"

"No, we like him just where he is."

So I stayed in Vietnam awhile.

I told this story to Arthur Schlesinger back in 1964. By then he was writing his fine book about the Kennedy years, *A Thousand Days.*[2] Since Scotty Reston was a friend of his, I suggested that he call Scotty and check it out. He never did, and the story never made the book.

I also had problems with Lyndon Johnson. There was a moment when Johnson had just taken over as president, and a distinguished World War II correspondent named Robert Sherrod was going back to Vietnam. Lyndon wanted to see him before he went. Sherrod went in, and the president said he did not want Sherrod to be like me or Neil Sheehan, because we were traitors to our country. So there it was. "*We're* patriotic," Johnson was suggesting, but the reporters were not. Johnson's tactics were clear. *Isolate* the dissidents—the people who, in LBJ's words, were not on the team. Make other reporters in Washington fear to be with them, fear to be like them.

When somebody gets in a bad war, when the policy is wrong, when they choose the wrong track, reporters get crunched. If you doubted the war, if your dispatches were pessimistic, you were unpatriotic. *They* were wrapped in the flag, and you were not. I mention these stories because I was both reporter and, in a way I did not want to be, a participant in Vietnam. And more than a little in harm's way—and by harm's way I mean more from my own government than from the Vietcong.[3] For a very long time, my very career was in the balance. There were people there that wanted to destroy me, some of them in the government, some of them working for *Time* magazine.[4]

In time I became a historian. I went back and tried to figure out what had happened and why it had happened. So I saw the story in Vietnam from two distinctly different views. Someone once asked President Kennedy when he was campaigning for the White House how he had become a war hero. "It was actually involuntary," Kennedy said. The Japanese had sunk his ship, the famous PT-109. The same could be said for me as a historian. I went out to cover a war for a newspaper, and the war I thought I was going to cover did not exist. The war that I covered was completely different, and it changed me, and it changed what I thought. And it turned me really more from journalism to history.

So I can envision modern presidential power and its growth in the years after World War II in the abstract. I can envision it also with the heels of many a White House bureaucrat on my chest. Although I did not think of myself this way, I was an enemy of the people under constant attack from the government of the United States for writing stories that turned out to be demonstrably true.

The Kennedy administration believed that I was in effect a leader of the opposition in the modern political arena. I was the principal source of the only information that the White House did not control out of Vietnam. In time, they wanted to crush alternative information because if you have alternative information you can have an alternative policy. If you stamp out dissenting information, you stamp out dissenting political possibilities. And so I was disproportionately influential because of the newspaper I represented.

To put it in context, consider the media of that period, in the early 1960s. The *Washington Post* is now a great paper, but was then still unsure of itself. It had one foreign correspondent and a few national correspondents and really almost no one overseas and certainly no one in Saigon. The *Wall Street Journal* was not the formidable paper it has become with such a great foreign staff. The *New York Herald Tribune*, which had been a great paper, was in its death throes. The television correspondents were about to be the new stars of our profession, but they weren't there yet. TV news was just going in that period from fifteen-minute to thirty-minute shows. They didn't have satellites, and they didn't have color, and they didn't have resident correspondents in Saigon. If they did a story on Vietnam, they took the film on tape and sent it from Saigon to Hong Kong and then from Hong Kong to San Francisco. It was sort of like the Pony Express. If you compare it to the instantaneous quality of network television today in the age of CNN, the constant news in the background, it was just like the Pony Express before the railroad arrived.

The one paper that had power and influence was the *New York Times*. It had fifty foreign correspondents and twenty Washington correspondents. It was the paper in Washington that you had to read every day. The *Times* sold maybe 40,000 copies in Washington, but they went to the 40,000 people who wanted it. You could not work in that city without knowing what the *Times* was saying. So what I was doing in Saigon benefited from the enormous energy and strength of this paper. That made me disproportionately powerful.

We should also note that presidential power was in a dramatic upswing in those years. This was seventeen years after the end of World War II. Part of the growth of presidential power came from sweeping changes in communication technology. First with radio with Franklin Delano Roosevelt, and then television, the new media became an instrument of presidential power. The weapons of the era also conferred more power in the presidency. The speed of the new weapons—jets, jet bombers, missiles, delivering atomic warheads—mattered a great deal. Who had time for a deliberative body any more? Who had time for a senate to consider a declaration of war? We had to vest the power in the presidency. The president became more and more powerful.

Add to that the particular nature of the leader of the Soviet Union, Joseph Stalin. He was so dark and difficult, a threatening figure. Although he actually turned out to be cautious and conservative in dealing with the West, by and large, he was a man whose aura was quite terrifying. As Milovan Djilas has written about him: "Every crime was possible to Stalin for there was not one he had not committed. Whatever standards we use to take his measure . . . to him will fall the glory of being the greatest criminal in history. For in him were joined the criminal senselessness of a Caligula with the refinement of a Borgia and the brutality of a Tsar Ivan the Terrible."[5] So you have Stalin, you have weapons of atomic horror, and you have ever greater speed. All of this confers power in the presidency. No wonder then that almost unconsciously power moved from deliberative bodies to the executive branch: one man trusted to act speedily in this new terrifying atomic age and to stand up to the dictatorships we now saw as our enemies.

Arnold J. Toynbee, the great historian, talks about a process where a nation often unconsciously takes on the color and values of its sworn principal adversary. Unconsciously we began to do that. Some of our decision makers, almost without realizing it, began to envy the decision makers on the other side because they did not have a free press or a senate that they had to deal with. Our enemies seemed more singularly powerful because there were fewer checks on them. And so we gradually cloaked our needs in greater secrecy. Our sworn adversary did everything in secrecy. Even the Moscow phonebook was a classified document.

So we had an era that conferred more and more power on the presidents. They said what were the national security issues and they said what were the rights to secrecy, even though much of what they made secret should not have been so. The rest of the country, the media, and Congress were given more and more areas where they did not challenge the authority of the presidency.

Let me give you an example from August 1964. It was called the Tonkin Gulf incident, a classic example of deeding over too much secrecy to the presidency. Johnson had begun, under the aegis of the Central Intelligence Agency, what were called 34A raids. They were little speedboat raids designed to trigger the radars of North Vietnam. They were done secretly. It was a CIA operation—secret to the American press, secret to the American Congress, but I assure you not secret to the North Vietnamese, who knew we were doing it, nor to the Russians and the Chinese, who also knew we were doing it. So when North Vietnam shot at one of these 34A boats, it looked like it had been aggression against us. It was like one of those moments in an NBA basketball game where someone takes a swing at another player and the referee misses the first punch but sees the other player swinging back. Secrecy is a great danger. We do our best as a society in the sunlight. We work best in the sunlight. But there was all this stuff going on because of the Cold War that allowed the president ever more rights and ever freer hands.

For a variety of reasons, the tension between the government and the media was growing greater all the time. There is always going to be tension. It's a normal thing. It's a healthy thing. The more tension there is between the media and the government, the better. But with the growth of television, the quantum increase of its power in our country over the last forty or so years, the tensions have risen dramatically. There is a constant struggle over who will find an issue, who will get to hold the camera—the president or the media—and who will get to set the agenda. The leaders in this country tend to see television as their instrument of power, not that of their opponents or the members of Congress. The great struggle every day is over who holds the camera and which footage is shown. Can the president successfully control or at least intimidate the press so that they won't show stuff that he doesn't want shown?

But print is important as well, a little less so these days because print is in decline in an age of satellites and cable TV and the Internet. But even so, print journalists have an influence because what the *New York Times*, the *Washington Post*, and the *Wall Street Journal* write often appears on television the next day. Print defines; broadcast amplifies. Both are part of a constant struggle that gets bigger every year between the president and the media.

When Lyndon Johnson was president, for instance, he was absolutely convinced not only that I was a communist, which he would say to Bill Moyers, his press secretary, but that I was in cahoots with Morley Safer, a CBS reporter who was working in Saigon. Johnson thought that I was telling Morley what to report. We had never been in Vietnam at the same time, and I had never met Morley Safer as the president was saying this, but LBJ was accusing us of being in some kind of partnership. He was so convinced that we were in cahoots against him that it hung over him.

So there is this constant struggle going on as to who gets to control the agenda. And because of that there is a great growth in our economy in the area that is called "spin"—getting your version of an event out, and stopping the other side from getting its side out. The government is more and more in the spin business. The game—in the beginning, at least—is not as fair. It pits the White House with all its aides and allies against one given reporter. I can assure you from having been through it that it was very ugly and very personal. Day after day, there were attacks on me saying that I was unpatriotic, that I was left wing, that I was trying to give birth to an Asian Fidel Castro, that I never went out on operations with the military, that I was just hanging around Saigon at the bars. (In truth, I went out on about fifteen missions. John Paul Vann, the legendary American advisor there, later told me that he thought I should have been given the Combat Infantry Badge, which is something very much prized by infantrymen. Mercifully, reporters don't get medals, and I think that's the way it should be. But it was a sign that I had gone out on plenty of missions.) If you're a reporter, you can't answer back when you are attacked. What do you say? That you *are* brave? That you *are* going on missions? The only thing you can do is keep reporting. Meanwhile, there is this enormous bulldozer coming at you.

One of the terrible things that happens in something like this, when the White House does something like Vietnam, is that the president sets a policy and makes that policy the baseline. Something that isn't going to work has for a time a sense of truth. Even if it is a policy that is not likely to succeed, the president's policy becomes the real given, the truth.

In Vietnam, for example, that nation's colonial past, the crucial French-Indochina War [1946–54], was simply subtracted by the policymakers from their discussions of whether we could win. The fact that the other side, the Vietminh, had driven the French out and had a political dynamic that we would never be able to penetrate got pushed aside. It was replaced with Washington's "given." A more skeptical view of what a Caucasian, Christian, capitalist society can do in Asia during a revolutionary war was pushed aside. The new baseline is that this can be done and it is being done. Anyone who challenges it becomes the controversial person. *You're* the controversial person; *you're* the one challenging the truth because this policy, which can't work, is anointed as the truth.

You who become the critic get the spotlight on you and the scrutiny. All your weaknesses are unveiled. And you the reporter become the outsider, the troublemaker. You're the controversial one. It's your view which is not legitimized, your view which is under scrutiny. You're not the patriot. They own the flag. You're the one who isn't really a good American.

It gets ugly. You are attacked for your reporting, your personal behavior, your lack of manhood. *Time* magazine, which was always attacking me and my colleagues, once said that I had witnessed a photo of VC bodies and had broken into tears. I wish I had broken into tears. *Time* was clearly writing a manhood story: Make this guy look weak. My sources were investigated, too. John Paul Vann told me in 1964 that they were thinking seriously of court-martialing him because his briefings were so similar to what I was writing for the *New York Times*.[6]

They also investigated my family. A friend in the CIA once told me that they were having a bad day at the American embassy because they had run a check on my family. It had come back showing that my father was a much-decorated medic in World War I and an even more highly decorated combat surgeon in World War II, rising to the rank of lieutenant colonel. They weren't happy at the embassy that day, my friend told me.

When a war doesn't work, you have to work harder and harder to sell it. If a war works, you really don't have to sell it that much. It sells itself, I suppose you can say. When Washington decided that the existing press corps in Vietnam was too skeptical and could not be molded properly, they began to send to Vietnam, at taxpayers' expense, reporters from small-town newspapers—carefully making sure they could find someone from their hometown to see there. The reporters, probably grateful for the trip, generally tended to write stories that the government was pleased with.

In early 1963, a Vietcong colonel turned himself in, which was quite unusual, and a big press conference was scheduled in Saigon: a major show-and-tell. By chance, I had spent a lot of time up in I Corps up north where the VC colonel had turned himself in.[7] The senior American advisor up there was a friend of mine named Colonel Bryce F. Denno. He called me to warn me that the press conference was going to be bogus. "Listen," he said, "he [the VC colonel] came over to us *not* for political reasons. He had woman problems, and he wasn't going to be promoted, but he was completely contemptuous of the South Vietnamese troops, the army. So watch yourself if you cover this." Thus warned, I didn't cover the press conference. A few days later, I was interviewing the American ambassador in his office, and as I mentioned, somewhat cautiously, some of John Vann's warnings about the war being lost in the Mekong Delta, the ambassador asked me if I covered the VC colonel. I said that I had not. He thereupon took me and somewhat physically ushered me out of his office, the first time I think I was thrown out of an ambassador's office.

News was invented. An American VIP—an assistant secretary of defense or state, a two-star general—would fly out to Saigon. A press conference would be scheduled. The plane would land in Tan Son Nhut airport. The VIP ceremony would begin. The VIP hadn't even been in Saigon or seen anything, and he would start talking about how we were winning the war. I mean, he would answer questions before he even arrived. My young colleague, Neil Sheehan, would nudge me and say, "Ah, another foolish westerner come to lose his reputation to Ho Chi Minh."

Given that there was a constant drum roll against us, it may come as a surprise to learn that when I first arrived in Vietnam I was welcomed. My colleague who preceded me, Homer Bigart, the greatest reporter of his time, who had won a Pulitzer Prize twice in World War II and Korea, was viewed as too old, too cynical, too bitter. They were glad to see me for about a month. I was viewed as too young, too inexperienced, too emotional. In fact, though, someone with my particular background, with five years covering the early days of the civil rights movement, was probably better trained for Vietnam than someone who had spent time fighting in World War II.

When I got to Vietnam, I was twenty-eight years old. It was 1962, and I was determined to work as I always had. I would find the story, define it, find some good people to work with, preferably braver than I, and I would work harder than anyone else. And that would eventually bring me some acclaim and admiration for my reporting. I didn't think about the politics of it very much. I would just do my job. That's what I thought. I would just go out there and work hard. I was wrong. It never occurred to me—I was really quite innocent about the game about to be played and the size of the stakes—the harder I worked and the more accurate my stories, the more the government of my own country turned on me.

In the beginning, American officials tried to control the venue by controlling access and controlling who got on the helicopters. Initially, they wouldn't let us on helicopters. Eventually, they would let us go once every six weeks. Finally, I mean involuntarily, they pushed me into going to the most dangerous part of the country. Right near Saigon, about forty miles away in the Mekong Delta, was the town of My Tho. The South Vietnamese Seventh Armored Division was there. The Vietcong were there. The American 514th battalion and Colonel John Vann were there.

So I settled on the Seventh Division area. It was where most of the fighting was taking place in the heavily populated Mekong Delta. The war wasn't working there, even where there was a battle. If we killed a hundred VC, they could recruit and replenish with local people within a few weeks. It was going to be a war in continuum. In addition, the South Vietnamese would not listen to the advice the Americans were giving, and the VC were getting stronger all the time.

So I learned that the war didn't work. And I learned another thing that was really important: if you go at the business of being a reporter, and you do it seriously enough and honestly enough, American soldiers are always going to tell you the truth. If you hang around and you spend a couple days, and you walk through a few operations, and you talk to them at night at dinner, and you share their hardships, and you come back a second time, and a third time, and a fourth time, they will tell you the truth. They come to trust you, especially as they learn that you will protect them and not put their names in your stories. Gradually everybody in that area and in the next division, the Ninth Division, told me the truth. They told me that it didn't work.

So why didn't they listen in Washington? If I could find out that it didn't work, surely they could have, too. It wasn't a great secret. When he finally came out with his wretched book on Vietnam thirty years later, Secretary of Defense Robert McNamara had a sentence in there which I consider a bald-faced lie. He said: "None of us—not me, not the president, not Mac [McGeorge Bundy], nor Dean [Rusk], nor Max [Maxwell Taylor]—was ever satisfied with the information we received from Vietnam."[8] That's a sentence written by the chief messenger-slayer of that administration. Of course they could get the information they wanted. They didn't want good information. The dice were loaded. If you told the truth that it didn't work, and it wasn't going to work, you weren't going to get promoted. None of my great sources, all the colonels who were division and corps advisors, none of them got a star because they were known to be unenthusiastic about the chances for success. If you said that you didn't think it was working, you weren't promoted. If you played the game, you were promoted. Nobody was tougher on dissenters than McNamara.

There was a reason for this. There was a huge political investment being made on the part of first the Kennedy administration and then the Johnson administration, which mandated that you had to say that we were winning. What Kennedy wanted in 1963 was to keep the war on the back burner to run against Barry Goldwater in 1964 and then, perhaps, in 1965, to make some kind of deal. I don't think he would have sent combat troops there, but he wanted it on the back burner. He wanted it as a minor issue. What he wanted more than the reality of winning the war was the appearance of winning the war. My great sin as a reporter and that of my colleagues was in taking something that he wanted to keep on the back burner and moving it up to the front burner. And out of that came a war within a war between us and the government of the United States.

There was, in addition, a constant attempt to intimidate us. I will tell you one story about it in the fall of 1963. There had been a major battle in the Mekong Delta earlier that day, and Neil and I had not been able to get on a helicopter to get there. We were being deliberately frozen out. Usually we had been able to get helicopter connections, so we spent the morning calling people we knew trying to get aboard a helicopter. We called, among others, the ambassador, Henry Cabot Lodge Jr., and the chief commanding general, General Paul Harkins. It was clear that we weren't going to get aboard. It was very deliberate, and we were being taught a lesson.

That evening, instead of the normal briefing being done in the normal briefing room, it was done in a VIP room. Instead of the usual captain or major doing it, it was given by Major General Richard Stilwell, said to be the brightest officer in Saigon. In the room, in addition to ten or twelve reporters, was everybody else above the rank of colonel, maybe thirty generals and twenty colonels. They turned out the brass for us, and it was a calculated attempt to intimidate. General Stillwell began by criticizing Neil and me for bothering Ambassador Lodge and General Harkins for trying to get on the helicopters. They were very busy men, he said, and they have a lot of other important things to do, and we were never to call them again. He was telling us what we could and could not do in our jobs.

I am not one of these people who likes to stand up at press conferences and get in quarrels with the speakers. I almost never asked a question at a press conference in my entire career. I always wanted the stories for myself, and if you asked a question at a press conference, another reporter could pick up your story.

But that time I thought it had gone too far. I stood up, and I can still see myself doing it, and I can hear my heart pounding, and it's probably the proudest moment in my journalistic career. I told General Stilwell that millions of dollars of American gear, in terms of all those helicopters, were going into battle that day, along with probably 150 American troops, pilots, copilots, and gunners. The American taxpayers had the right to know what happened. In addition, I said, we were not corporals or privates. We didn't work for him. We would keep on asking questions. We worked for the *Times*, AP [Associated Press], UP [United Press], and other organizations. If he didn't like what we were doing, he was free to write our editors to say that he thought we were being too aggressive and pushing too hard to go to combat, but other than that we would keep on pressing. I was shaking as I was saying this. I looked over at the back, and there was a wonderful two-star general there, a wonderful regimental commander from World War II named Robert H. York. He was the one guy at the top level that was always trying to tell the truth because he lost a nephew there. I looked over, and he winked at me, and I thought, "God bless Bobby York. Thank you. I have one friend in this room." It is something I am still proud of.

It's an old struggle. It's not just Vietnam. It goes on today. Truth, as they say, is the first casualty of war. So don't be surprised, as it gets uglier in Iraq, if there are more and more attacks on the media. It goes with the territory, and the stakes get bigger every year. But remember that in the long run you cannot sell a war that doesn't work. The truth goes out, despite those who attack it.

Notes

1. The Miller Center at the University of Virginia has transcribed this conversation. It is available online at: http://tapes.millercenter.virginia.edu/clips/1963_1002_jfk_on_ journalists/index.htm.

2. Arthur M. Schlesinger Jr., *A Thousand Days: John F. Kennedy in the White House* (Boston: Houghton Mifflin, 1965).

3. *Vietcong* is a pejorative term formulated by the Americans and South Vietnamese and applied to the National Liberation Front of South Vietnam (NLF).

4. During the early stages of the Vietnam War, *Time,* under the leadership of legendary founder Henry Luce, was vehemently hawkish on the war. Around 1967, under new leadership, it became more critical.

5. Milovan Djilas, *Conversations with Stalin,* trans. Michael B. Petrovich (New York: Harcourt, Brace and World, 1962), 187.

6. Vann was the subject of Neil Sheehan's *Bright Shining Lie: John Paul Vann and America in Vietnam* (New York: Random House, 1988).

7. I Corps was one of four corps areas for the Army of the Republic of Vietnam. It included the five northern provinces of South Vietnam.

8. Robert S. McNamara, *In Retrospect: The Tragedy and Lessons of Vietnam* (New York: Vintage Books, 1995), 43.

CONTRIBUTORS

Paul S. Boyer is Merle Curti Professor of History Emeritus at the University of Wisconsin Emeritus. Among his many publications are *Fallout: A Historian Reflects on America's Half-Century Encounter with Nuclear Weapons* (1998); *Promises to Keep: The United States since World War II* (2004); *When Time Shall Be No More: Prophecy Belief in Modern American Culture* (1992); and *By the Bomb's Early Light: American Thought and Culture at the Dawn of the Atomic Age* (1985).

Andrew K. Frank is an associate professor of history at Florida State University. In addition to numerous articles on the South, he is the author or editor of *Creeks and Southerners: Biculturalism on the Early American Frontier* (2005); *The Routledge Historical Atlas of the American South* (1999); *American Revolution: People and Perspectives* (2008); and *Early Republic: People and Perspectives* (2009).

Lloyd C. Gardner is professor emeritus of history at Rutgers University and a past president of the Society for Historians of American Foreign Relations. He is the author or editor of more than a dozen books on American foreign policy, including *Approaching Vietnam: From World War II through Dienbienphu, 1941–1954* (1989); *Spheres of Influence: The Great Powers Partition in Europe, from Munich to Yalta* (1994); *Pay Any Price: Lyndon Johnson and the Wars for Vietnam* (1997); and with Marilyn B. Young, *The New American Empire: A 21st-Century Teach-In on U.S. Foreign Policy* (2005); *Long Road to Baghdad: A History of U.S. Foreign Policy in the Middle East, from the Vietnam War to the Present* (2008); and *Three Kings: The Rise of an American Empire in the Middle East after World War II* (2009).

David Halberstam was a Pulitzer Prize–winning journalist, best-selling author, and historian. For many years a correspondent for the *New York*

Times, Halberstam published nearly two dozen books, including *The Best and the Brightest* (1972); *The Fifties* (1993); *The Reckoning* (1986); *The Children* (1999); *War in a Time of Peace: Bush, Clinton, and the Generals* (2001); and *The Teammates* (2003). Halberstam's last book, *The Coldest Winter: America and the Korean War,* was published posthumously in 2007.

George C. Herring is emeritus alumni professor of history at the University of Kentucky, a past president of the Society for Historians of American Foreign Relations, and former editor of *Diplomatic History.* His published works include *From Colony to Superpower: U.S. Foreign Relations since 1776* (2008), *Aid to Russia, 1941–1946: Strategy, Diplomacy, the Origins of the Cold War* (1973); *America's Longest War: The United States and Vietnam, 1950–1975* (4th ed., 2001); and *LBJ and Vietnam: A Different Kind of War* (1994).

Andrew L. Johns is an assistant professor of history at Brigham Young University and the David M. Kennedy Center for International Studies. He has written numerous articles on the Vietnam War and on the impact of U.S. domestic politics on foreign policy. His books include *Vietnam's Second Front: Domestic Politics, the Republican Party, and the War* (2010) and, with Kathryn C. Statler, *The Eisenhower Administration, the Third World, and the Globalization of the Cold War* (2006).

Robert J. McMahon is the Ralph D. Mershon Distinguished Professor at Ohio State University and past president of the Society for Historians of American Foreign Relations. He is the author of several books, including *Colonialism and Cold War: The United States and the Struggle for Indonesian Independence, 1945–49* (1981); *The Cold War on the Periphery: The United States, India, and Pakistan* (1994); *The Origins of the Cold War* (1999); *The Limits of Empire: The United States and Southeast Asia since World War II* (1999); and *The Cold War: A Very Short Introduction* (2005).

Kenneth Osgood is an associate professor of history at Florida Atlantic University and the director of the Alan B. Larkin Symposium on the American Presidency. He is the author of *Total Cold War: Eisenhower's Secret Propaganda Battle at Home and Abroad* (2006), which won the Herbert Hoover Book Award, and coeditor of *The Cold War after Stalin's Death: A Missed Opportunity for Peace?* with Klaus Larres (2006) and *The United States and Public Diplomacy: New Directions in Cultural and International History* with Brian C. Etheridge (2010).

Chester Pach is an associate professor of history at Ohio University. He has written *Presidential Profiles: The Johnson Years* (2005); *The Presidency of Dwight D. Eisenhower* (1991); *Arming the Free World: The Origins of the United States Military Assistance Program, 1945–1950* (1991); and many articles and book chapters.

Emily S. Rosenberg is a professor of history at the University of California at Irvine and past president of the Society for Historians of American Foreign Relations. She has coauthored several textbooks, numerous articles, and *A Date Which Will Live: Pearl Harbor in American Memory* (2003); *Spreading the American Dream: American Economic and Cultural Expansion, 1890–1945* (1982); and *Financial Missionaries to the World: The Politics and Culture of Dollar Diplomacy, 1900–1930 (1999)*, which won the Robert Ferrell Senior Book Award from the Society for Historians of American Foreign Relations.

Robert D. Schulzinger is a professor of history at the University of Colorado at Boulder, past president of the Society for Historians of American Foreign Relations, and editor in chief of *Diplomatic History*. He is the author or coauthor of twelve books, including *The Wise Men of Foreign Affairs: The History of the Council on Foreign Relations* (1984); *Henry Kissinger: Doctor of Diplomacy* (1989); *A Time for War: The United States and Vietnam, 1941–1975* (1997); *U.S. Diplomacy since 1900* (5th ed., 2004); and *A Time for Peace: The Legacy of the Vietnam War* (2006).

Mark A. Stoler is professor emeritus at the University of Vermont and past president of the Society for Historians of American Foreign Relations. His many publications include *The Politics of the Second Front: American Military Planning and Diplomacy in Coalition Warfare, 1941–1943* (1977); *George C. Marshall: Soldier-Statesman of the American Century* (1989); *Debating Franklin D. Roosevelt's Foreign Policies, 1933–1945*, with Justus Doenecke (2005); *Allies in War: Britain and America against the Axis Powers, 1940–1945* (2005); and *Allies and Adversaries: The Joint Chiefs of Staff, the Grand Alliance, and U.S. Strategy in World War II* (2000), which won the Distinguished Book Award of the Society for Military History

Marilyn B. Young is a professor of history at New York University. She has written and edited numerous books, including *Rhetoric of Empire: American China Policy, 1895–1901* (1969); *Transforming Russia and China:*

Revolutionary Struggle in the 20th Century with William Rosenberg (1980); *The Vietnam Wars, 1945–1990* (1991); *Vietnam and America: A Documented History* with Marvin Gettleman, Jane Franklin, and Bruce Franklin (1985); *Human Rights and Revolutions* with Jeffrey N. Wasserstrom and Lynn Hunt (2000); *The Vietnam War: A History in Documents* with John J. Fitzgerald and A. Tom Grunfeld (2002); and *The New American Empire: A 21st-Century Teach-In on U.S. Foreign Policy* with Lloyd C. Gardner (2004).